The Structure of
Recognizable
Diatonic Tunings

EASLEY BLACKWOOD

The Structure of Recognizable Diatonic Tunings

PRINCETON UNIVERSITY PRESS

Published by Princeton University Press, 41 William Street,
Princeton, New Jersey 08540
In the United Kingdom: Princeton University Press,
Guildford, Surrey

Library of Congress Cataloging in Publication Data will be
found on the last printed page of this book

ISBN 0-691-09129-3

Publication of this book has been aided by
a grant from the Whitney Darrow Fund of
Princeton University Press

This book has been composed in Times Roman

Clothbound editions of Princeton University Press books
are printed on acid-free paper, and binding materials are
chosen for strength and durability
Paperbacks, although satisfactory for personal collections,
are not usually suitable for library rebinding

Printed in the United States of America by
Princeton University Press
Princeton, New Jersey

Music

Contents

Chapter IV. Extended Pythagorean Tuning

Preface

The purpose of this book is to establish and demonstrate a rigorous mathematical basis for recognizable diatonic scales generated by combinations of octaves and perfect fifths, and to determine the appropriateness of certain individual tunings for various portions of the existing polyphonic repertoire. No attempt has been made to relate this volume to earlier works on the subject, nor does it address the question of how to compose in hitherto unused tunings.

It is assumed that the reader has at least a layman's knowledge of the musical notation and the standard repertoire, as well as a working familiarity with parts of the material taught in any college algebra course, particularly logarithms and exponents.

A summary of the work may be got by reading in succession the introductions to the twelve chapters; these also contain condensed versions of the principal conclusions drawn. More detailed conclusions regarding specific tunings will be found in Chapter III, Section 7, Chapter VII, Section 5; Chapter IX, Sections 6 and 7; Chapter XI, Sections 6 and 8, and Chapter XII, Section 6.

Parts of the final chapter are drawn from material collected by the author while working on a research project funded by the National Endowment for the Humanities in conjunction with Webster College, St. Louis.

The author is greatly indebted to Professors Jan Berkhout, Irving Kaplansky and Joel Mandelbaum, who read the manuscript carefully and offered invaluable advice and criticism.

Chicago
April 1983

The Structure of
Recognizable
Diatonic Tunings

I Fundamental Properties of Musical Intervals

Introduction. As we shall eventually see (Chs. III, IV, VIII, IX, and X), the structure of recognizable diatonic tunings is basically an array of intricate interconnections among acceptable approximations to intervals, certain of which may be tuned individually so as to be free of beats produced by interacting harmonics. These interconnections, which are the very foundation of what is perceived as tonal harmonic motion, are shaped by the short-term span of human memory, the tolerance range of the human ear (Ch. X), and the peculiar manner in which intervals are perceived. This chapter is concerned primarily with the latter subject. Section 1 deals with the ear's logarithmic perception of pitch increments; in Section 2 we investigate the elementary aspects of the most euphonious intervals—the pure intervals—with particular attention to the unique property possessed by the octave. In Section 3 we derive a method for computing the beat frequency associated with intervals that depart slightly from the pure tuning. In Section 4 it is revealed that pure intervals cannot necessarily be expressed simply in terms of each other, as might have been supposed, or hoped. In Section 5 we define a new class of intervals in terms of which the pure intervals may be expressed rationally, and we investigate and describe the fundamentally important *interval size convention*. Section 6 describes the conventional method of measuring intervals in terms of a fixed unit, the *cent*. Section 7 shows how to express certain commonly occurring intervals in terms of the first few *basic intervals*—a technique that has extensive application in the theory of just tuning (Chs. V, VI, and VII). And finally, Section 8 gives several methods for determining the size in cents of an interval from its ratio, and vice versa. Also included is a short logarithmic table to facilitate computation if electronic means are unavailable.

1. The unique determination of musical intervals by frequency ratios. Before we begin the systematic investigation of our elusive subject, it will be helpful to recall certain elementary facts concerning the human

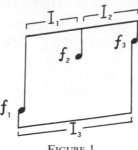

FIGURE 1

perception of musical sounds. We need not concern ourselves, however, with such questions as why a periodic disturbance in the atmosphere may be perceived as a tone, or why a higher frequency corresponds to a higher pitch. The purpose of our study is not to tackle problems of a metaphysical or biopsychological nature; rather it is to depict in mathematical terms, insofar as possible, the behavior of certain musical elements that we take as given.

The idea of a relation between two tones gives rise to the concept of an *interval*; this word may be defined as *the distance separating two pitches.* Thus an interval may be thought of as two pitches heard in succession, or simultaneously. *In order for two intervals to have the same sound other than a difference in register, it is both necessary and sufficient that the ratios of the frequencies forming them should be equal.* There is no known reason or proof for this statement; it is simply a fact which may be observed, and is to be regarded as an axiom. Now let there be two intervals, I_1 and I_2, the first composed of frequencies f_1 and f_2, and the second of frequencies f_3 and f_4. Let r_1 and r_2 be numbers such that $\dfrac{f_2}{f_1} = r_1$, and $\dfrac{f_4}{f_3} = r_2$. The axiom may now be stated as follows: intervals I_1 and I_2 are identical except for a difference in register if, and only if, $r_1 = r_2$.

Let us now consider the slightly different situation in which I_1 and I_2 are contiguous—that is, the higher pitch of I_1 coincides with the lower pitch of I_2—and call the three pitches involved f_1, f_2, and f_3, as in Figure 1. Clearly there exists another interval I_3 formed by pitches f_1 and f_3, and it is in accord with intuition to write $I_1 + I_2 = I_3$. In the present case, the frequency ratios are given by $\dfrac{f_2}{f_1} = r_1$, and $\dfrac{f_3}{f_2} = r_2$, or $f_2 = r_1 f_1$, and $f_3 = r_2 f_2$; and hence $f_3 = r_2(r_1 f_1) = r_1 r_2 f_1$. Let us now denote the

ratio of interval I_3 by r_3—that is, $\dfrac{f_3}{f_1} = r_3$, or $f_3 = r_3 f_1$. If in this equation
we now substitute $r_1 r_2 f_1$ for f_3, it follows at once that $r_1 r_2 f_1 = r_3 f_1$, and
also (since $f_1 \neq 0$) that $r_1 r_2 = r_3$. We may now state a fundamental principle proceeding directly from the axiom previously stated: *The
arithmetic process corresponding to the intuitive notion of adding two intervals is the multiplication of their frequency ratios.* Now if $r_1 r_2 = r_3$, then
$\log r_1 + \log r_2 = \log r_3$; thus $I_1 = \log r_1$, $I_2 = \log r_2$, and $I_3 = \log r_3$.
Hence I_1, I_2, and I_3 are numbers, and we may now state that *the number
corresponding to the intuitive notion of the size of an interval is the logarithm of its frequency ratio.*[1]

Obviously the frequency of any pitch is a positive number, hence the
case in which $r_1 < 0$ has no musical meaning. Now if $r_1 > 1$, then $0 <
f_1 < f_2$, and the interval is depicted as ascending. And if $0 < r_1 < 1$, then
$0 < f_2 < f_1$, and the interval is depicted as descending. Thus for an ascending interval, $\log r_1$ is positive, and for a descending interval, $\log r_1$ is
negative. Of course it is necessary to observe strictly this convention
regarding sign.

Example: Determine the ratio of the interval formed by adding the two
intervals whose ratios are $\frac{5}{4}$ and $\frac{6}{5}$. We have $(\frac{5}{4})(\frac{6}{5}) = \frac{3}{2}$, and so the sum is
the interval whose ratio is $\frac{3}{2}$.

Example: Find the ratio of the interval formed by subtracting the inter-
val whose ratio is $\frac{5}{4}$ from the one whose ratio is $\frac{5}{3}$. This difference may be
seen to be the sum of the two intervals if we construe the latter as ascending
and the former as descending. Hence we have $(\frac{5}{3})(\frac{4}{5}) = \frac{4}{3}$, and the resulting
difference has the ratio $\frac{4}{3}$.

2. Pure tuning, notes, and pitches. It has long been noted that the
common harmonious, consonant intervals are more or less accurately
represented by frequency ratios involving small integers. Thus the ratios
$\frac{2}{1}, \frac{3}{2}, \frac{4}{3}, \frac{5}{3}, \frac{5}{4}$, and $\frac{6}{5}$ correspond to those intervals known in musical terms
as an octave, perfect fifth, perfect fourth, major sixth, major third, and

[1] We assume a knowledge of the elementary properties of the logarithmic function, such
as can be found in any college algebra text. Specifically $\log_b x = a$ means the same as $b^a = x$;
also $\log x + \log y = \log xy$, $\log x - \log y = \log \dfrac{x}{y}$, and $x \log y = \log y^x$. From these relations, it also follows that $-\log x = \log \dfrac{1}{x}$, and $\log 1 = 0$. All this is true for any base b that
is greater than unity. For a concise and readable account, see L. M. Reagan, E. R. Ott, and
D. T. Sigley, *College Algebra*, (New York: Farrar and Rinehart, 1940), 135–141.

minor third, respectively. Here we should pause for a moment, however. It is not precise to use musical terms until exact definitions have been framed. For example, a "fifth" would seem to contain five units, but it is not yet apparent what these units are. So for the moment, instead of "perfect fifth," we shall use the more cumbersome phrase "the interval whose ratio is $\frac{3}{2}$," and similarly for the other terms above. We make an exception in the case of the octave, this word being universally understood to mean the interval whose ratio is $\frac{2}{1}$.

We now come to another phenomenon for which there is no known reason or explanation, and which must be simply observed and taken as self-evident—*the octave possesses unique musical characteristics*. Specifically, two *pitches* separated by an octave (or any number of octaves) are perceived as the same *note*, but in different *registers*. This gives rise to a distinction between *pitch* and *note* which we shall observe scrupulously. A *pitch* is a tone of a specific frequency, say f, but a *note* may be any of the several pitches whose frequencies are given by $f(2^n)$, where n is an integer or zero. It is important to observe that musical terminology generally names notes rather than pitches. When it is desired to specify a pitch, both the name of the note and the register must be given. Thus "middle C" is a pitch but "C" is a note—it may be any one of the eight or so pitches within the commonly used musical range of roughly 30–4300 Hz. That is, if we take middle C to be 264 Hz, we apply the name C also to the pitches of 33, 66, 132, 528, 1,056, 2,112, and 4,224 Hz.[2] All these numbers are obtained by multiplying or dividing the frequency of middle C by integral powers of 2.

When an interval whose ratio is composed of small integers deviates slightly from the exact value, it maintains its recognizable character, but takes on a rougher sound when the pitches forming it are played simultaneously. This is partly due to the presence of harmonics in the pitches themselves (it is assumed that the reader is familiar with this phenomenon), and partly to nonlinearities in the middle ear which produce both harmonic and intermodulation distortion. As an example, consider the interval formed by pitches of 200 Hz and 300 Hz. This interval has the sound of a smooth, exactly tuned "perfect fifth." The interval formed by pitches of 200 Hz and 302 Hz also sounds like a "perfect fifth," but trained musicians find it to be slightly out of tune. In particular, the third har-

---

[2] The recommended standard for middle C in theoretical work is 264 Hz. In just tuning, the A next above is 440 Hz, and in 12-note equal tuning it is 443.993 Hz.

monic of the lower pitch (600 Hz) interacts with the second harmonic of the higher pitch (604 Hz) to produce the subjective effect known as *beats*.[3] The beat frequency is the difference between the interacting frequencies, in this case 4 Hz. The response characteristics of the ear cause the beat frequency to be perceived as a faint wavering sound which seems to have no point of origin. The presence of beating intervals has generally been regarded as undesirable, especially in music in which major triads are treated as consonances. Intervals tunes so as to be free of beats are said to be tuned *purely*.

The prominence of beats produced by an impure interval varies greatly from situation to situation, and is much influenced by instrumental timbre. The beat frequency is important theoretically, for it provides an accurate indicator of how subjectively out of tune an impure interval is, even in situations where the beats themselves are virtually inaudible. For this purpose, it is necessary to fix the lower pitch in every case at an arbitrary reference point, and we shall use middle C as the standard.

The present writer is convinced that many earlier theorists have attached far too much importance to the desirability of tuning the most consonant intervals purely. Even so, it is almost certainly true that traditional tonal and pretonal polyphonic music is hardly enhanced by the presence of impure intervals. All in all, it is not unreasonable to proceed to the construction of scales and tuning systems for the existing polyphonic repertoire upon the assumption that impure intervals are undesirable. However, as will be seen (Ch. V, Sec. 4), it is impossible to construct scales that contain no impure intervals at all.

3. To determine the beat frequency of an impure interval. In the previous section, it was observed that the interval formed by frequencies of 200 Hz and 302 Hz produces beats at a rate that is the difference between the frequency of the third harmonic of the lower pitch (600 Hz) and the second harmonic of the higher pitch (604 Hz). More generally, an impure interval whose ratio is close to $\frac{3}{2}$ produces beats through an interaction of these same two harmonics, and the difference of their frequencies is the beat frequency. Let the frequency of the lower pitch be f; then the frequency of its third harmonic is $3f$. If the ratio of the interval

[3] A mathematical description of beats is outside the scope of the present work. See R. M. Courant, *Differential and Integral Calculus*, 2 vols. (New York: Interscience, 1952), vol. 1, 431–432.

is r, then the frequency of the higher pitch is rf, and the frequency of its second harmonic is $2rf$. The beat frequency is thus $2rf - 3f = f(2r - 3)$. Note that this quantity is positive if $r > \frac{3}{2}$, and negative if $r < \frac{3}{2}$. It will be convenient to adopt the convention that the beat frequency of an interval smaller than pure is given by a negative number.

Example: Determine the beat frequency of the interval whose ratio is $\frac{40}{27}$ and whose lower pitch is middle C (264 Hz). Since $\frac{40}{27}$ is only a little less than $\frac{3}{2}$ (the value of six decimals is 1.481481), the beat frequency is $264[(2)(1.481481) - 3] = (264)(-.037037) = -9.778$ per second.

Now let the ratio of any slightly impure interval be r where $r > 1$, and let r be nearly equal to $\dfrac{p}{q}$, the ratio of the pure version. The beat frequency of such an interval generally is the difference between the qth harmonic of the higher pitch and the pth harmonic of the lower pitch. If f is the frequency of the lower pitch, then rf is the frequency of the higher pitch. The qth harmonic of the higher pitch is then qrf, the pth harmonic of the lower pitch is pf, and the difference is $f(qr - p)$. This number is positive if $r > \dfrac{p}{q}$, and negative if $r < \dfrac{p}{q}$. To summarize, the beat frequency of a slightly impure interval whose ratio is r may be either $f(r - 2)$, $f(2r - 3)$, $f(3r - 4)$, $f(3r - 5)$, $f(4r - 5)$, or $f(5r - 6)$, depending on whether r is nearly 2, $\frac{3}{2}$, $\frac{4}{3}$, $\frac{5}{3}$, $\frac{5}{4}$, or $\frac{6}{5}$, respectively, and where f is the frequency of the lower pitch.

Example: Determine the beat frequency of the interval whose ratio is $\frac{81}{64}$ and whose lower pitch is an octave below middle C (132 Hz). We find that $\frac{81}{64} = 1.265625$, which is very near $\frac{5}{4}$. Hence the beat frequency is $132[(4)(1.265625) - 5] = (132)(5.0625 - 5) = 8.25$ per second.

Example: Determine the beat frequency of the interval whose ratio is $\sqrt[4]{8}$ and whose lower pitch is 132 Hz. In the next section, we shall prove that $\sqrt[4]{8}$ is not a fraction; but the beat frequency does not depend on whether or not r is a rational number. We find that $\sqrt[4]{8} = 1.681793$, only a little larger than $\frac{5}{3}$ ($= 1.666667$), and so the beat frequency is $132[(3)(1.681793) - 5] = (132)(5.045378 - 5) = (132)(.045378) = 5.990$ per second.

4. The unique prime factorization theorem. The most convenient mathematical approach to the common diatonic scale is to regard the intervals it contains as combinations of certain other intervals which we shall call *basic intervals*. But before proceeding to a definition, we should pause to observe that certain numerically simple intervals fail to combine as might be expected by an experienced musician. For example, if we start at some arbitrary pitch whose frequency is f ($f > 0$), and then proceed upward in such a manner that the frequency of each new pitch is $\frac{3}{2}$ of the one preceding, we may easily show that we will never again encounter the note with which we started. The frequency of each successive pitch will be $f\left(\frac{3}{2}\right)^m$, where $m = 1, 2, 3$, etc. If we are to encounter the initial note again, we must find a pitch higher than the initial pitch by some integral number of octaves, and the frequency of such a pitch is $f(2^n)$ where n is a positive integer. Thus we must have $f\left(\frac{3}{2}\right)^m = f(2^n)$, or $3^m = 2^{m+n}$, where m and n are positive integers. This last requires that there should be a number which is an integral power of both 2 and 3; but this is impossible since all the powers of 2 are even, and all the powers of 3 are odd.

The example just given is a special case of a more general principle known in elementary number theory as the Unique Prime Factorization Theorem. The musical consequences of this theorem are so sweeping that it will not be out of place to digress briefly and prove the theorem here, along with some of its immediate consequences.[4]

THEOREM 1. *A composite number can be resolved into prime factors in only one way.* The proof consists in showing that assuming the theorem to be false results in a logical contradiction. Hence we assume the existence of some numbers that have different sets of prime factors, and we call such numbers *abnormal numbers*. Now let n be the least abnormal number, with different sets of prime factors $p_1 p_2 p_3 \ldots$ and $q_1 q_2 q_3 \ldots$. It follows at once that no q can occur among the p's, for then $\frac{n}{q}$ would be an abnormal number less than n. We may assume with no loss of generality that p_1 is the least prime of the p-group, and q_1 is the least prime of the q-group. Under these conditions, we have $p_1^2 \leqslant n$ and also $q_1^2 \leqslant n$, hence $p_1^2 q_1^2 \leqslant n^2$ and $p_1 q_1 \leqslant n$. But rather more than this is true, for if $p_1 q_1 = n$, then $p_1 q_1 = p_1 p_2 p_3 \ldots$ and $q_1 = p_2 p_3 \ldots$. But this is impossible, for q_1 is a prime that is not equal to any of the p's, and hence we have $p_1 q_1 < n$. Now consider the number $n - p_1 q_1$; since $0 < n - p_1 q_1 < n$, $n - p_1 q_1$ is

---

[4] This proof is taken from G. H. Hardy and E. M. Wright, *Introduction to the Theory of Numbers*, (3rd ed.; Oxford: 1954), 21.

not abnormal. Since $p_1|n$ and $p_1|p_1q_1$,[5] we have $p_1|n - p_1q_1$, and similarly $q_1|n - p_1q_1$. Hence $p_1q_1|n - p_1q_1$ (since $n - p_1q_1$ is not abnormal), and therefore $p_1q_1|n$. But also $q_1\left|\dfrac{n}{p_1}\right.$; and since $\dfrac{n}{p_1} < n$, $\dfrac{n}{p_1}$ is not abnormal, and has the unique prime factorization $p_2p_3 \ldots$. Hence $q_1|p_2p_3 \ldots$; but this is impossible, as was demonstrated above. This shows that the assumption that there exists a least abnormal number is untenable, and consequently there are no abnormal numbers at all. Thus the unique prime factorization of an integer takes the form $p_1^{a_1}p_2^{a_2}p_3^{a_3} \ldots$ where all the a's are positive integers. If some of the a's are negative integers, the above expression represents the unique prime factorization of a fraction.

Two immediate consequences of Theorem 1 are of sufficient importance to be included in the category of theorems.

THEOREM 2.   *A fraction raised to an integral power cannot be an integer.*

Let the fraction be $\dfrac{a}{b}$ where a and b are integers, and let $\dfrac{a}{b}$ be in its lowest terms, so that $(a, b) = 1$.[6] Note that the imposition of this latter condition does not in any way limit the number of values that $\dfrac{a}{b}$ may assume. Next let $\left(\dfrac{a}{b}\right)^n = x$ where n and x are integers, or $a^n = xb^n$. Now a^n and xb^n are both integers, and by Theorem 1 the prime factorization of both must be the same, since they are equal. Hence all the prime factors of b^n are also factors of a^n, and consequently all the factors of b are also factors of a; but this contradicts the hypothesis that $(a, b) = 1$ except in the case where $b = 1$. But if $b = 1$, $\dfrac{a}{b}$ is an integer, not a fraction, and this proves Theorem 2.

THEOREM 3.   *An integral root of an integer cannot be a fraction.* Assume that $\sqrt[n]{x} = \dfrac{a}{b}$, where n, x, a, and b are integers, and let $(a, b) = 1$. We have at once $x = \left(\dfrac{a}{b}\right)^n$; and by Theorem 2, $b = 1$ under the conditions stated, and this proves Theorem 3.

---

[5] The symbol $a|b$ is read "a is a factor of b," or "b is divisible by a."

[6] The symbol (a, b) denotes the greatest common divisor of a and b. When $(a, b) = 1$, a and b have no factors in common other than unity, and we say that a and b are *coprime*.

Example: In the previous section, it was stated that $\sqrt[4]{8}$ is irrational. Since $1^4 < 8 < 2^4$, we have $1 < \sqrt[4]{8} < 2$, and it is plain that $\sqrt[4]{8}$ is not an integer. By Theorem 3, $\sqrt[4]{8}$ is not a fraction either, hence it must be an irrational number.

As we shall see, a great many of the numbers that arise naturally in music theory are irrational.

5. Basic intervals and the interval size convention.   In describing the interconnections that exist among intervals in a tuning, it will often facilitate matters to break the intervals down into their basic component parts. From a mathematical point of view, this is most readily accomplished by reducing the ratio to its lowest terms, and then factoring both the numerator and denominator into primes. Thus the "basic" intervals mathematically are those whose ratios are $\frac{p}{1}$ where p is a prime. However, musical considerations require a slightly different definition.

The following seemingly arbitrary preference springs from musical habit alone, and is a consequence of the unique properties of the octave and the fact that musical nomenclature generally names notes rather than pitches (Sec. 2 of this chapter). When it is required to determine an interval formed by two different notes, rather than two different pitches, a ratio will be chosen such that $1 < r < 2$. In musical terms, this means that the interval is construed as ascending from the first named note to the second, and as less than one octave. This preference, which we shall call the *interval size convention*, plays a vital role in the precise description of scales.

Now consider an interval whose ratio is $\frac{p}{1}$ where p is a prime greater than 2; such an interval is greater than one octave. If the interval is regarded as formed by two different notes, we may assign them registers in accordance with the interval size convention. To this end, we take the expression $\frac{p}{2^n}$, and select n so that $1 < \frac{p}{2^n} < 2$. If the higher pitch is fixed, this effectively transposes the lower pitch upward by n octaves so that it is still lower than the higher pitch, but by less than one octave. From $1 < \frac{p}{2^n} < 2$, it follows at once that $2^n < p < 2^{n+1}$, and we now frame our definition as follows: a *basic interval* is an interval whose ratio is $\dfrac{p}{2^n}$ where

p is prime and where n is chosen so that 2^n is the greatest power of 2 less than p. The first few basic intervals thus have ratios equal to $\frac{2}{1}$, $\frac{3}{2}$, $\frac{5}{4}$, $\frac{7}{4}$, $\frac{11}{8}$, $\frac{13}{8}$, $\frac{17}{16}$, $\frac{19}{16}$, etc. According to our musical habits, the first three basic intervals are consonant; but the situation is quite complicated regarding the next few, and will be dealt with at length in Chapter V, Sec. 5, and Chapter VI, Secs. 6 and 7.

The first three basic intervals play such a fundamental role in the evolution of scales and tunings that it is desirable to assign letters representing their respective sizes. Recalling that the size of an interval is the logarithm of its ratio (Sec. 1 of this chapter), we have

$$a = \log 2, \quad \bar{v} = \log \tfrac{3}{2}, \quad \bar{t} = \log \tfrac{5}{4}$$

In Chapter X, Sec. 2, it will be determined over what range these intervals may vary while still maintaining characteristics associated with the pure versions. The superior bars are to distinguish the pure intervals $\bar{v}$ and $\bar{t}$ from the more general versions, which will be written v and t. The symbol for the octave will always appear as a, it being generally agreed that this interval cannot be tuned any other way than in the ratio $\frac{2}{1}$.

We may now prove a theorem which makes possible the derivation of an interval's ratio from its expression in terms of the first three basic intervals.

THEOREM 4.   *If the size of an interval is $ma + n\bar{v} + q\bar{t}$, then its ratio is* $\left(\dfrac{2}{1}\right)^m \left(\dfrac{3}{2}\right)^n \left(\dfrac{5}{4}\right)^q$. From the definitions of a, $\bar{v}$, and $\bar{t}$, we have

$$ma + n\bar{v} + q\bar{t} = m \log 2 + n \log \tfrac{3}{2} + q \log \tfrac{5}{4}$$
$$= \log \left(\frac{2}{1}\right)^m + \log \left(\frac{3}{2}\right)^n + \log \left(\frac{5}{4}\right)^q$$
$$= \log \left(\frac{2}{1}\right)^m \left(\frac{3}{2}\right)^n \left(\frac{5}{4}\right)^q$$

and since the size of an interval is the logarithm of its ratio (Sec. 1 of this chapter), the result follows.

Example: Determine the ratio of the interval $\bar{v} + \bar{t}$. In this case, $m = 0$, $n = 1$, and $q = 1$, hence the ratio is $(\tfrac{3}{2})(\tfrac{5}{4}) = \tfrac{15}{8}$.

Example: Determine the ratio of the interval $4\bar{v} - 2a - \bar{t}$. Here we have $m = -2$, $n = 4$, and $q = -1$, so the ratio is

$$\left(\frac{2}{1}\right)^{-2}\left(\frac{3}{2}\right)^{4}\left(\frac{5}{4}\right)^{-1} = \left(\frac{1}{2}\right)^{2}\left(\frac{3}{2}\right)^{4}\left(\frac{4}{5}\right) = \frac{(1)(1)(3)(3)(3)(3)(2)(2)}{(2)(2)(2)(2)(2)(2)(5)}$$

$$= \frac{(3)(3)(3)(3)}{(2)(2)(2)(2)(5)} = \frac{81}{80}$$

To determine the composition of an interval from its ratio in terms of the basic intervals is a rather more complicated process, and will be described in Section 7 of this chapter.

6. Sizes of the basic intervals in terms of cents. In the expressions $a = \log 2$, $\bar{v} = \log \frac{3}{2}$, and $\bar{t} = \log \frac{5}{4}$, the logarithms may be taken to any base whatever, and so we may choose a base to suit our convenience. To this end, let the base be b, and then we may write $b^a = 2$, $b^{\bar{v}} = \frac{3}{2}$, and $b^{\bar{t}} = \frac{5}{4}$. Now let us regard $\frac{b}{1}$ as the frequency ratio of an interval. The above expressions may now be stated in musical terms as follows: the sum of a intervals each having the ratio $\frac{b}{1}$ is the interval whose ratio is 2 (one octave); the sum of $\bar{v}$ intervals each having the ratio $\frac{b}{1}$ is the interval whose ratio is $\frac{3}{2}$; and the sum of $\bar{t}$ intervals each having the ratio $\frac{b}{1}$ is the interval whose ratio is $\frac{5}{4}$. Thus the interval whose ratio is $\frac{b}{1}$ may be regarded as a unit of measure, and hence we select its size so that it will be smaller than any of the intervals that arise in the construction of scales in practical situations. Since musicians are familiar with the fact that modern keyboard instruments are tuned so that an octave is divided into twelve equal parts, and are familiar with the sound of all combinations formed by the interval $\frac{1}{12}a$, it is most convenient to divide this interval into one hundred equal parts and use the resulting interval of $\frac{1}{1200}a$ as our unit of measure. The interval $\frac{1}{1200}a$ is called a *cent*, and its frequency ratio is $2^{1/1200} = 1.000577789507$, an irrational number (Theorem 3; Sec. 4 of this chapter). From now on, the expression "log x", will be taken to mean $\log_{2^{1/1200}} x$.

TABLE 1

a	=	$\log \frac{2}{1}$ =	1200.000
$\bar{v}$	=	$\log \frac{3}{2}$ =	701.955
$\bar{t}$	=	$\log \frac{5}{4}$ =	386.314
		$\log \frac{7}{4}$ =	968.826
		$\log \frac{11}{8}$ =	551.318
		$\log \frac{13}{8}$ =	840.528
		$\log \frac{17}{16}$ =	104.955
		$\log \frac{19}{16}$ =	297.513

The pitch higher by one cent than A = 440 Hz is 440.254 Hz, and if the two are played together, a beat results which is their difference—approximately one beat in four seconds. But if the two pitches are played one after the other, it seems beyond the capability of the human ear to detect which is higher, at least in the author's experience.

In order to obtain numerical values for a, $\bar{v}$, and $\bar{t}$, it is necessary to compute log 2, log 3, and log 5. The means by which logarithms are calculated are beyond the scope of the present discussion, and so we simply give the results.[7] We shall, however, touch again upon this subject in Section 8 of this chapter. For the sake of reference, Table 1 includes the next five basic intervals as well as a, $\bar{v}$, and $\bar{t}$.

We may show that all the logarithms given above are irrational except log 2. Since $\log \frac{p}{2^n} = \log p - n \log 2 = \log p - 1200n$, we need only be concerned about log p. Now let $\log p = \frac{m}{n}$ where m and n are positive integers and p is a prime. Then $(2^{1/1200})^{m/n} = p$, and $2^m = p^{1200n}$. Since 2 and p are both prime, 2^m and p^{1200n} must be the identical prime factorization of the same integer (Theorem 1; Sec. 4 of this chapter), and therefore $p = 2$ and $1200n = m$. Hence integers m and n exist only when $p = 2$, and consequently all other values for $\log \frac{p}{2^n}$ are irrational numbers.

As the interval of one cent is practically at the limit of what can be perceived, it may seem somewhat academic to carry out the calculations to three decimal places. However, this is desirable, first to insure that

[7] See G. Chrystal, *Algebra*, 2 vols. (2nd ed.; London: A. and C. Black, 1926), vol. 2, 240–243.

accumulated rounding errors do not add to a significant amount, and second to reveal tiny differences between certain intervals that are arrived at by quite different means. In some cases, even more decimal places will be needed (Ch. VI, Sec. 6; Ch. VIII, Sec. 2; Ch. IX, Sec. 1; Ch. XII, Sec. 5).

7. To express an interval, given its ratio, as a combination of the first three basic intervals. We wish to determine how many and which of the first three basic intervals, ascending or descending, must be added together to produce the interval in question. Thus the problem is how to express the interval whose ratio is r as $ma + n\bar{v} + p\bar{t}$ where m, n, and p are positive or negative integers, or zero. We first observe that a solution can be obtained only under very special circumstances. We have $ma + n\bar{v} + p\bar{t} = \log r$, and upon substituting the values of a, $\bar{v}$, and $\bar{t}$ given in Section 5 of this chapter, we obtain

$$m \log 2 + n \log \tfrac{3}{2} + p \log \tfrac{5}{4} = \log r$$

$$(m - n - 2p) \log 2 + n \log 3 + p \log 5 = \log r$$

$$\log 2^{m-n-2p}3^n5^p = \log r$$

$$2^{m-n-2p}3^n5^p = r$$

If we write $m - n - 2p = q$, we now have $2^q3^n5^p = r$, and it is clear that q is also a positive or negative integer, or zero. By Theorem 1 (Sec. 4 of this chapter), $2^q3^n5^p$ is the unique prime factorization of r; hence the problem as stated can only be solved when r is a fraction whose numerator and denominator contain no prime factors other than 2, 3, or 5.

Now from the expressions defining a, $\bar{v}$, and $\bar{t}$, we may write $a = \log 2$, $\bar{v} = \log 3 - \log 2$, and $\bar{t} = \log 5 - 2 \log 2$. Hence $\bar{v} = \log 3 - a$, $\bar{t} = \log 5 - 2a$, and finally,

$$\log 2 = a$$

$$\log 3 = a + \bar{v}$$

$$\log 5 = 2a + \bar{t}$$

In order to solve the problem posed at the head of this section, we first resolve the given ratio into prime factors, next take the logarithm, then substitute the values given above for log 2, log 3, and log 5, and finally collect terms.

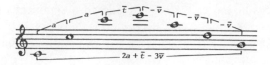

FIGURE 2

Example: Determine the composition of the interval whose ratio is $\frac{15}{8}$. We have $\dfrac{15}{8} = \dfrac{(3)(5)}{(2)(2)(2)}$, and $\log \dfrac{(3)(5)}{(2)(2)(2)} = \log 3 + \log 5 - 3 \log 2 = (a + \bar{v}) + (2a + \bar{t}) - 3a = \bar{v} + \bar{t}$. The reader should now review the first example in Section 5 of this chapter.

Example: Determine the composition of the interval whose ratio is $\frac{40}{27}$. We have $\dfrac{40}{27} = \dfrac{(2)(2)(2)(5)}{(3)(3)(3)}$, and $\log \dfrac{(2)(2)(2)(5)}{(3)(3)(3)} = 3 \log 2 + \log 5 - 3 \log 3 = 3a + (2a + \bar{t}) - 3(a + \bar{v}) = 2a + \bar{t} - 3\bar{v}$.

In musical terms—as yet not precisely defined—this means that if we start at some pitch and proceed up two octaves, up one pure major third, then down three pure perfect fifths, we arrive at a pitch whose frequency is that of the original pitch multiplied by $\frac{40}{27}$. In Figure 2 we illustrate the process in conventional musical notation as an aid to visualization.

It is most interesting to note that on the staff, interval $2a + \bar{t} - 3\bar{v}$ appears to be a perfect fifth, and yet its ratio is not $\frac{3}{2}$. This example serves to put us on our guard concerning two points: first, we cannot trust our musical habits when dealing with basic intervals; second, the notation fails to distinguish certain measurable differences. Thus the interval written as a perfect fifth may be either $\bar{v}$ or $2a + \bar{t} - 3\bar{v}$, but the notation does not tell which. This aspect of the notation will be discussed in Chapter V, Secs. 2 and 3, and Chapter XII, Sec. 2.

8. To find the size of an interval in cents, given its ratio, and vice versa.   In general, the solution to this problem requires the use of a printed logarithmic table, or electronic calculation. However, in the case where the interval may be expressed as a combination of the first three basic intervals, the problem involves only simple arithmetic. All that is necessary is to substitute the values given in Section 6 of this chapter for a, $\bar{v}$, and $\bar{t}$.

Example: Find the size in cents of the interval whose ratio is $\frac{40}{27}$. In the previous section, we found that this interval is equal to $2a + \bar{t} - 3\bar{v}$. Thus we have

$$2a + \bar{t} - 3\bar{v} = (2)(1200) + 386.314 - (3)(701.955) = 680.449 \text{ cents}$$

More generally, let r be the ratio of the interval in question, and let c be its size in cents. Now, since $c = \log_{2^{1/1200}} r$, we have

$$r = 2^{c/1200}$$

This relation is useful, for it furnishes a means for determining the decimal ratio of an interval whose size in cents is known. Now $\log_{10} r = \dfrac{c}{1200} \log_{10} 2$, $c = \dfrac{1200}{\log_{10} 2} \log_{10} r$, and $c = 3986.314 \log_{10} r$.

Using the previous example once again,

$$c = 3986.314 \log_{10} \frac{40}{27}$$

$$= (3986.314)(1.6020600 - 1.4313638)$$

$$= 680.449 \text{ cents}$$

Use of a seven-place table will give a result that is generally correct to six significant figures.

If electronic calculation is available, a better method—one that reduces rounding errors—is to use natural logarithms (to base $e = 2.718281828$), first expressing the ratio as a decimal, and we have

$$c = \frac{1200}{\ln 2} \ln r$$

Once again in the case of $\frac{40}{27}$, using a calculator that accurately displays ten digits,

$$c = \frac{1200}{\ln 2} \ln \frac{40}{27}$$

$$= (1731.234049)(.3930425881)$$

$$= 680.4487113 \text{ cents}$$

This is more decimal places than are usually needed.

For convenience and reference, we conclude this chapter with a brief table of logarithms to base $2^{\frac{1}{1200}}$, with which the answer may be quickly and easily calculated. The table gives logarithms of numbers from 1.01 to 10.09 correct to one decimal place, and may generally be relied upon to give to the nearest cent, the size of any interval whose ratio contains no more than three figures in the numerator or denominator.

Example: Find the size of the interval whose ratio is $\frac{7}{4}$. From the table, $\log 7 = 3368.8$ and $\log 4 = 2400.0$, and so $\log \frac{7}{4} = \log 7 - \log 4 = 3368.8 - 2400.0 = 968.8$ cents.

Example. Find the size of the interval whose ratio is $\frac{40}{27}$. The table does not include $\log 40$ or $\log 27$, but does give values for $\log 4.0$ and $\log 2.7$. Hence $\log \frac{40}{27} = \log \dfrac{4.0}{2.7} = \log 4.0 - \log 2.7 = 2400 - 1719.6 = 680.4$ cents.

Example: Find the size of the interval whose ratio is $\frac{13}{9}$. Again we must arrange the ratio so that both the numerator and denominator fall within the range of the table, and we have $\log \frac{13}{9} = \log \dfrac{2.6}{1.8} = \log 2.6 - \log 1.8 = 1654.2 - 1017.6 = 636.6$ cents.

Example: Find the size of the interval whose ratio is $\frac{256}{243}$. We have $\log \frac{256}{243} = \log \dfrac{2.56}{2.43} = \log 2.56 - \log 2.43 = 1627.4 - 1537.1 = 90.3$ cents. In this example, an accumulation of rounding errors causes the result to be wrong on the last place, the true value being 90.2 cents. However, the nearest whole value, 90 cents, is correct.

If numbers forming the ratio have more than three digits, use of the table is less practical. However, the table is adequate for all rough calculations the reader is likely to encounter in this and other works on the subject of tuning and temperaments.

If it is desired to round off numbers in the table to the nearest whole number, a 5 with a stroke through the tail (5̶) should be dropped, as the stroke indicates that the 5 in question was rounded from a smaller value. If there is no stroke through the 5, the last digit should be increased by 1. This convention is followed throughout this book.

TABLE 2

LOGARITHMS TO THE BASE $2^{1/1200}$

N	0	1	2	3	4	5	6	7	8	9
1.0	0.0	17.2	34.3	51.2	67.9	84.5	100.9	117.1	133.2	149.2
1.1	165.0	180.7	196.2	211.6	226.8	242.0	256.9	271.8	286.5	301.2
1.2	315.6	330.0	344.3	358.4	372.4	386.3	400.1	413.8	427.4	440.8
1.3	454.2	467.5	480.6	493.7	506.7	519.6	532.3	545.0	557.6	570.1
1.4	582.5	594.8	607.1	619.2	631.3	643.3	655.2	667.0	678.7	690.4
1.5	702.0	713.5	724.9	736.2	747.5	758.7	769.9	780.9	791.9	802.8
1.6	813.7	824.5	835.2	845.8	856.4	867.0	877.4	887.8	898.2	908.4
1.7	918.6	928.8	938.9	948.9	958.9	968.8	978.7	988.5	998.3	1008.0
1.8	1017.6	1027.2	1036.7	1046.2	1055.6	1065.0	1074.4	1083.6	1092.9	1102.1
1.9	1111.2	1120.3	1129.3	1138.3	1147.3	1156.2	1165.0	1173.8	1182.6	1191.3
2.0	1200.0	1208.6	1217.2	1225.8	1234.3	1242.7	1251.2	1259.6	1267.9	1276.2
2.1	1284.5	1292.7	1300.9	1309.0	1317.1	1325.2	1333.2	1341.2	1349.2	1357.1
2.2	1365.0	1372.9	1380.7	1388.5	1396.2	1403.9	1411.6	1419.2	1426.8	1434.4
2.3	1442.0	1449.5	1456.9	1464.4	1471.8	1479.2	1486.5	1493.9	1501.2	1508.4
2.4	1515.6	1522.8	1530.0	1537.1	1544.3	1551.3	1558.4	1565.4	1572.4	1579.4
2.5	1586.3	1593.2	1600.1	1607.0	1613.8	1620.6	1627.4	1634.1	1640.8	1647.5
2.6	1654.2	1660.9	1667.5	1674.1	1680.6	1687.2	1693.7	1700.2	1706.7	1713.1
2.7	1719.6	1726.0	1732.3	1738.7	1745.0	1751.3	1757.6	1763.9	1770.1	1776.3
2.8	1782.5	1788.7	1794.8	1801.0	1807.1	1813.2	1819.2	1825.3	1831.3	1837.3
2.9	1843.3	1849.2	1855.2	1861.1	1867.0	1872.9	1878.7	1884.6	1890.4	1896.2
3.0	1902.0	1907.7	1913.5	1919.2	1924.9	1930.6	1936.2	1941.9	1947.5	1953.1
3.1	1958.7	1964.3	1969.9	1975.4	1980.9	1986.4	1991.9	1997.4	2002.8	2008.3
3.2	2013.7	2019.1	2024.5	2029.8	2035.2	2040.5	2045.8	2051.1	2056.4	2061.7
3.3	2067.0	2072.2	2077.4	2082.6	2087.8	2093.0	2098.2	2103.3	2108.4	2113.5
3.4	2118.6	2123.7	2128.8	2133.9	2138.9	2143.9	2148.9	2153.9	2158.9	2163.9
3.5	2168.8	2173.8	2178.7	2183.6	2188.5	2193.4	2198.3	2203.1	2208.0	2212.8
3.6	2217.6	2222.4	2227.2	2232.0	2236.7	2241.5	2246.2	2250.9	2255.6	2260.3
3.7	2265.0	2269.7	2274.4	2279.0	2283.6	2288.3	2292.9	2297.5	2302.1	2306.6
3.8	2311.2	2315.7	2320.3	2324.8	2329.3	2333.8	2338.3	2342.8	2347.3	2351.7
3.9	2356.2	2360.6	2365.0	2369.4	2373.8	2378.2	2382.6	2387.0	2391.3	2395.7
4.0	2400.0	2404.3	2408.6	2412.9	2417.2	2421.5	2425.8	2430.0	2434.3	2438.5

TABLE 2   (*Continued*)

N	0	1	2	3	4	5	6	7	8	9
4.1	2442.7	2447.0	2451.2	2455.4	2459.6	2463.7	2467.9	2472.1	2476.2	2480.3
4.2	2484.5	2488.6	2492.7	2496.8	2500.9	2505.0	2509.0	2513.1	2517.1	2521.2
4.3	2525.2	2529.2	2533.2	2537.2	2541.2	2545.2	2549.2	2553.2	2557.1	2561.1
4.4	2565.0	2568.9	2572.9	2576.8	2580.7	2584.6	2588.5	2592.3	2596.2	2600.1
4.5	2603.9	2607.8	2611.6	2615.4	2619.2	2623.0	2626.8	2630.6	2634.4	2638.2
4.6	2642.0	2645.7	2649.5	2653.2	2656.9	2660.7	2664.4	2668.1	2671.8	2675.5
4.7	2679.2	2682.9	2686.5	2690.2	2693.9	2697.5	2701.2	2704.8	2708.4	2712.0
4.8	2715.6	2719.2	2722.8	2726.4	2730.0	2733.6	2737.1	2740.7	2744.3	2747.8
4.9	2751.3	2754.9	2758.4	2761.9	2765.4	2768.9	2772.4	2775.9	2779.4	2782.8
5.0	2786.3	2789.8	2793.2	2796.7	2800.1	2803.5	2807.0	2810.4	2813.8	2817.2
5.1	2820.6	2824.0	2827.4	2830.8	2834.1	2837.5	2840.8	2844.2	2847.5	2850.9
5.2	2854.2	2857.5	2860.9	2864.2	2867.5	2870.8	2874.1	2877.4	2880.6	2883.9
5.3	2887.2	2890.5	2893.7	2897.0	2900.2	2903.4	2906.7	2909.9	2913.1	2916.3
5.4	2919.6	2922.8	2926.0	2929.1	2932.3	2935.5	2938.7	2941.8	2945.0	2948.2
5.5	2951.3	2954.5	2957.6	2960.7	2963.9	2967.0	2970.1	2973.2	2976.3	2979.4
5.6	2982.5	2985.6	2988.7	2991.8	2994.8	2997.9	3001.0	3004.0	3007.1	3010.1
5.7	3013.2	3016.2	3019.2	3022.2	3025.3	3028.3	3031.3	3034.3	3037.3	3040.3
5.8	3043.3	3046.2	3049.2	3052.2	3055.2	3058.1	3061.1	3064.0	3067.0	3069.9
5.9	3072.9	3075.8	3078.7	3081.6	3084.6	3087.5	3090.4	3093.3	3096.2	3099.1
6.0	3102.0	3104.8	3107.7	3110.6	3113.5	3116.3	3119.2	3122.0	3124.9	3127.7
6.1	3130.6	3133.4	3136.2	3139.1	3141.9	3144.7	3147.5	3150.3	3153.1	3155.9
6.2	3158.7	3161.5	3164.3	3167.1	3169.9	3172.6	3175.4	3178.2	3180.9	3183.7
6.3	3186.4	3189.2	3191.9	3194.6	3197.4	3200.1	3202.8	3205.6	3208.3	3211.0
6.4	3213.7	3216.4	3219.1	3221.8	3224.5	3227.2	3229.8	3232.5	3235.2	3237.9
6.5	3240.5	3243.2	3245.8	3248.5	3251.1	3253.8	3256.4	3259.1	3261.7	3264.3
6.6	3267.0	3269.6	3272.2	3274.8	3277.4	3280.0	3282.6	3285.2	3287.8	3290.4
6.7	3293.0	3295.6	3298.2	3300.7	3303.3	3305.9	3308.4	3311.0	3313.5	3316.1
6.8	3318.6	3321.2	3323.7	3326.3	3328.8	3331.3	3333.9	3336.4	3338.9	3341.4
6.9	3343.9	3346.4	3348.9	3351.4	3353.9	3356.4	3358.9	3361.4	3363.9	3366.4
7.0	3368.8	3371.3	3373.8	3376.2	3378.7	3381.1	3383.6	3386.1	3388.5	3390.9

Table 2   (*Continued*)

N	0	1	2	3	4	5	6	7	8	9
7.1	3393.4	3395.8	3398.3	3400.7	3403.1	3405.5	3408.0	3410.4	3412.8	3415.2
7.2	3417.6	3420.0	3422.4	3424.8	3427.2	3429.6	3432.0	3434.3	3436.7	3439.1
7.3	3441.5	3443.8	3446.2	3448.6	3450.9	3453.3	3455.6	3458.0	3460.3	3462.7
7.4	3465.0	3467.4	3469.7	3472.0	3474.4	3476.7	3479.0	3481.3	3483.6	3486.0
7.5	3488.3	3490.6	3492.9	3495.2	3497.5	3499.8	3502.1	3504.4	3506.6	3508.9
7.6	3511.2	3513.5	3515.7	3518.0	3520.3	3522.6	3524.8	3527.1	3529.3	3531.6
7.7	3533.8	3536.1	3538.3	3540.6	3542.8	3545.0	3547.3	3549.5	3551.7	3553.9
7.8	3556.2	3558.4	3560.6	3562.8	3565.0	3567.2	3569.4	3571.6	3573.8	3576.0
7.9	3578.2	3580.4	3582.6	3584.8	3587.0	3589.1	3591.3	3593.5	3595.7	3597.8
8.0	3600.0	3602.2	3604.3	3606.5	3608.6	3610.8	3612.9	3615.1	3617.2	3619.4
8.1	3621.5	3623.6	3625.8	3627.9	3630.0	3632.2	3634.3	3636.4	3638.5	3640.6
8.2	3642.7	3644.9	3647.0	3649.1	3651.2	3653.3	3655.4	3657.5	3659.6	3661.6
8.3	3663.7	3665.8	3667.9	3670.0	3672.1	3674.1	3676.2	3678.3	3680.3	3682.4
8.4	3684.5	3686.5	3688.6	3690.6	3692.7	3694.7	3696.8	3698.8	3700.9	3702.9
8.5	3705.0	3707.0	3709.0	3711.1	3713.1	3715.1	3717.1	3719.2	3721.2	3723.2
8.6	3725.2	3727.2	3729.2	3731.2	3733.2	3735.2	3737.2	3739.2	3741.2	3743.2
8.7	3745.2	3747.2	3749.2	3751.2	3753.2	3755.1	3757.1	3759.1	3761.1	3763.0
8.8	3765.0	3767.0	3768.9	3770.9	3772.9	3774.8	3776.8	3778.7	3780.7	3782.6
8.9	3784.6	3786.5	3788.5	3790.4	3792.3	3794.3	3796.2	3798.1	3800.1	3802.0
9.0	3803.9	3805.8	3807.8	3809.7	3811.6	3813.5	3815.4	3817.3	3819.2	3821.1
9.1	3823.0	3824.9	3826.8	3828.7	3830.6	3832.5	3834.4	3836.3	3838.2	3840.1
9.2	3842.0	3843.8	3845.7	3847.6	3849.5	3851.3	3853.2	3855.1	3856.9	3858.8
9.3	3860.7	3862.5	3864.4	3866.3	3868.1	3870.0	3871.8	3873.7	3875.5	3877.4
9.4	3879.2	3881.0	3882.9	3884.7	3886.5	3888.4	3890.2	3892.0	3893.9	3895.7
9.5	3897.5	3899.3	3901.2	3903.0	3904.8	3906.6	3908.4	3910.2	3912.0	3913.8
9.6	3915.6	3917.4	3919.2	3921.0	3922.8	3924.6	3926.4	3928.2	3930.0	3931.8
9.7	3933.6	3935.4	3937.1	3938.9	3940.7	3942.5	3944.3	3946.0	3947.8	3949.6
9.8	3951.3	3953.1	3954.9	3956.6	3958.4	3960.1	3961.9	3963.7	3965.4	3967.2
9.9	3968.9	3970.7	3972.4	3974.2	3975.9	3977.6	3979.4	3981.1	3982.8	3984.6
10.0	3986.3	3988.0	3989.8	3991.5	3993.2	3994.9	3996.7	3998.4	4000.1	4001.8

II   The Diatonic Scale in Pythagorean Tuning

Introduction. The diatonic scale, with only slight variations in tuning, has served as the essential organizing element of the notes of multi-part music for over eight hundred years. There exists an infinite number of tunings for the diatonic scale in which conventional tonal and modal harmonic motion is recognizable (Ch. X), and we shall ultimately explore the properties of the entire family of recognizable diatonic tunings. But the nature of the organization is quite complex, and is best explored initially within the confines of one particular tuning. The tuning most readily comprehensible at the beginning, and presenting relatively few computational difficulties, is the one that is generated entirely by the first two basic intervals (Ch. I, Sec. 5), even though it will be shown that this tuning is unsuited to much of the existing repertoire (Ch. III, Sec. 7). The diatonic scale constructed from the first two basic intervals is said to be in *Pythagorean tuning*.

Our investigation of Pythagorean tuning departs from the traditional procedure, and is perhaps somewhat more difficult at the outset. However, it has two advantages: first, it corresponds accurately to conventional musical nomenclature and terminology, and serves to frame precise definitions; second, it remains unchanged in the generalization of the diatonic scale where the smaller interval generating the scale has a ratio other than $\frac{3}{2}$. Central to the whole approach is the interval size convention (Ch. I, Sec. 5), and the distinction between notes and pitches (Ch. I, Sec. 2), which the reader is advised to understand thoroughly before proceeding.

In Section 1 a definition of diatonic scale is framed that applies not only to Pythagorean tuning, but to the more general situation as well. Section 2 develops a method for computing the ratio and size in cents for all the Pythagorean intervals. In Section 3 we develop a basic algebra regarding the mathematical depiction of Pythagorean intervals—a system which also applies to the entire family of recognizable diatonic tunings. In Section 4 we give the ratio and size in cents of all the intervals formed by any two of the seven notes within a diatonic scale, when they are all ascending from one note to the next and within the compass of one octave. Section 5 shows in what order the notes of a diatonic scale occur, and in Section 6 we apply the technique of Section 3 to show that this order of notes produces only two different sizes of adjacent intervals.

1. Definition of diatonic scale. Let us begin with any pitch whatever, and find another pitch higher than the first by the second basic interval— the interval whose ratio is $\frac{3}{2}$ (Ch. I, Sec. 5). We now continue the process until we have a total of seven pitches, each higher than the one immediately preceding by the interval whose ratio is $\frac{3}{2}$. It will be recalled that this process yields seven different notes (Ch. I, Sec. 4). If these seven notes are now rearranged in ascending order within a compass of one octave, they form a *diatonic scale*. An exact description of how this may be done serves as a precise definition: Let there be seven pitches in ascending order, each higher than the one immediately preceding by the interval whose ratio is $\frac{3}{2}$. Now let these pitches be transposed up or down some number (not excluding zero) of octaves, this number being immaterial, in such a manner that the greatest interval formed by any two of the new pitches is less than one octave. When the pitches so obtained are rearranged in ascending order, the resulting array is called a seven-note diatonic scale, or more briefly, a *diatonic scale*. We call the interval whose ratio is $\frac{3}{2}$ the *generating interval* of the scale. It will be observed that the above definition of diatonic scale leaves open the question of which note is the starting point, and makes no stipulation in regard to register.

Clearly the seven notes of the diatonic scale form a variety of intervals when paired in different ways. We call these intervals *diatonic intervals*, and the characteristics of the scale are discovered by an investigation of the ratios, sizes in cents, and distributional patterns of the diatonic intervals.

It will frequently be convenient to add to the scale as defined an eighth pitch one octave higher than the initial pitch, whatever that is chosen to be.

2. Certain intervals as determined uniquely by the coefficient of $\bar{v}$. In order to determine the order of notes forming the diatonic scale as defined in the previous section, it will be most instructive to select one of the seven pitches of the generating array as an arbitrary point of reference, and then apply the interval size convention (Ch. I, Sec. 5) to the intervals formed by this note with each of the other six. Other properties of the scale are most readily discovered by applying the convention to all intervals formed by any pair of notes within the generating array. To these ends, we now develop a notation for such intervals which incorporates the concept of the interval size convention.

Since we have defined the diatonic scale in terms of the first two basic intervals a and $\bar{v}$, it follows that all diatonic intervals are of the form $i\bar{v} + na$, where i and n are positive or negative integers, or zero. The argument that follows applies not only to diatonic intervals, but to any interval which may be expressed in this form. We first observe that the ratio of such an interval is always $\left(\dfrac{3}{2}\right)^i 2^n = 3^i 2^{n-i}$ (Theorem 4; Ch. I, Sec. 5).

Now assume i to be a particular positive integer. We apply the interval size convention by specifying $1 < 3^i 2^{n-i} < 2$; i.e., n must be an integer such that $3^i 2^{n-i}$ is a positive improper fraction less than 2. Clearly $n - i$ must be negative, and if we write $n - i = -m$, the inequalities above may be written $1 < \dfrac{3^i}{2^m} < 2$. Thus the ratio has the form $\dfrac{3^i}{2^m}$, and since $2^m < 3^i < 2^{m+1}$, m is a unique positive integer chosen so that 2^m is the greatest power of 2 less than 3^i. Hence a given positive value for i determines interval $i\bar{v} + na$ completely and uniquely.

Now let i be negative, or let $i = -h$ where h is positive. The ratio of interval $-h\bar{v} + na$ is $\left(\dfrac{3}{2}\right)^{-h} 2^n = 3^{-h} 2^{n+h}$, and since $1 < 2^{n+h} 3^{-h} < 2$ upon applying the interval size convention, $n + h$ must be positive. Now let $n + h = p$, and then $1 < \dfrac{2^p}{3^h} < 2$. Next, taking reciprocals and reversing the inequality signs, we have $1 > \dfrac{3^h}{2^p} > \dfrac{1}{2}$, and finally $2^p > 3^h > 2^{p-1}$; i.e., the ratio has the form $\dfrac{2^p}{3^h}$ where p is a unique positive integer chosen so that 2^p is the least power of 2 greater than 3^h. Thus interval $i\bar{v} + na$ is uniquely determined by a negative i as well.

We may abbreviate interval $i\bar{v} + na$ by calling it simply interval i, or $\overline{\text{int}}\ (i)$, it being understood that this latter symbol applies the interval size convention, thereby determining the interval uniquely. In Chapter X, Sec. 2, it will be shown that certain essential properties associated with diatonic intervals (as well as some others) are retained when the generating interval has a ratio slightly different from $\frac{3}{2}$, and so we use the superior bar to distinguish $\overline{\text{int}}$ (i) where the generating interval is pure from the more general case, which will be written int (i) (Ch. VIII, Sec. 2, and Ch. X, Sec. 1). However, int (0) = na, and hence is independent of the size of the generating interval. For this reason, int (0) and $\overline{\text{int}}$ (0) would mean the same thing, and therefore we do not use the symbol $\overline{\text{int}}$ (0).

We sum up the above principles in the form of the following rule, distinguishing the two cases where $i > 0$ or $i < 0$:

When $i > 0$, the ratio of $\overline{\text{int}}$ (i) is a fraction whose numerator is $3^{|i|}$ and whose denominator is the greatest power of 2 less than $3^{|i|}$.

When $i < 0$, the ratio of $\overline{\text{int}}$ (i) is a fraction whose denominator is $3^{|i|}$ and whose numerator is the least power of 2 greater than $3^{|i|}$.[1]

Example: Find the ratio of $\overline{\text{int}}$ (4). By the above, the ratio is $\frac{3^4}{2^m}$, and the greatest power of 2 less than 81 is 64, so the ratio is $\frac{81}{64}$.

Example: Find the ratio of $\overline{\text{int}}$ (-5). The ratio is $\frac{2^p}{3^5}$, and the least power of 2 greater than 243 is 256, so the ratio is $\frac{256}{243}$.

It is important to bear in mind that the symbol int (0) has a special meaning. Since int (0) = na, it means *some number of octaves, not excluding zero, up or down.* Thus two pitches separated by int (0) are the same note, and have the same name.

In many situations, particularly those involving only the names of notes, n may be disregarded, as its value is immaterial. However, if we wish to find the size of $\overline{\text{int}}$ (i) in cents, we must know n as well as i. This may be done by first obtaining the ratio by the above rule, then using the method of Chapter I, Sec. 7 to find the interval's complete expression in terms of a and $\bar{v}$, and finally calculating the size in cents as shown in Chapter I, Sec. 8.

Example: Find the size in cents of $\overline{\text{int}}$ (4). We found above that the ratio of $\overline{\text{int}}$ (4) is $\frac{81}{64}$. Hence its complete expression in terms of the first two basic intervals is $\log \frac{81}{64} = 4 \log 3 - 6 \log 2 = 4(a + \bar{v}) - 6a = 4\bar{v} - 2a$. The size in cents is then $(4)(701.955) - (2)(1200) = 407.820$ cents.

Example: Find the size in cents of $\overline{\text{int}}$ (-5). The ratio was found to be $\frac{256}{243}$, and the complete expression in terms of a and $\bar{v}$ is $\log \frac{256}{243} = 8 \log 2 -$

---

[1] The symbol $|i|$ denotes the absolute value of i, and is the same as i when i is positive. When i is negative, $|i|$ changes the sign from negative to positive.

$5 \log 3 = 8a - 5(a + \bar{v}) = 3a - 5v$. The size in cents in thus $(3)(1200) - (5)(701.955) = 90.225$ cents.

A more direct method for obtaining the same results will be given in Chapter III, Sec. 1.

3. Combinations of intervals expressed as $\overline{\text{int}}$ (i). In the following discussion, x, y, i, i_1 and i_2 may be any positive or negative integers, or zero, so the relations we are about to derive are valid outside the range of the diatonic intervals. We consider the totality of notes to be named by the positive and negative integers, as well as zero, with the interval between note x and note $x + 1$ being $\overline{\text{int}}$ (1), ratio $\frac{3}{2}$, for all values of x. We recall that it was shown that all the notes are different (Ch. I, Sec. 4). Now the interval formed by any two of these notes may be represented as $\overline{\text{int}}$ (i), and we are naturally led to explore to what extent the symbol $\overline{\text{int}}$ (i) behaves algebraically, and how it conforms to the fundamental laws of arithmetic.

We consider first the sum $\overline{\text{int}}$ (i_1) $+ \overline{\text{int}}$ (i_2); by definition this is $(i_1 \bar{v} + n_1 a) + (i_2 \bar{v} + n_2 a) = (i_1 + i_2)\bar{v} + (n_1 + n_2)a = \overline{\text{int}}$ ($i_1 + i_2$) $+$ int (0), and so

$$\overline{\text{int}}\ (i_1) + \overline{\text{int}}\ (i_2) = \overline{\text{int}}\ (i_1 + i_2) + \text{int}\ (0)$$

In the general case, we must include int (0) on the right-hand side of this equation to provide for the possibility that $\overline{\text{int}}$ (i_1) $+ \overline{\text{int}}$ (i_2) $> a$, as the symbol $\overline{\text{int}}$ ($i_1 + i_2$) automatically imposes the interval size convention upon the sum. But if it can be shown that $\overline{\text{int}}$ (i_1) $+ \overline{\text{int}}$ (i_2) $< a$, then we may write $\overline{\text{int}}$ (i_1) $+ \overline{\text{int}}$ (i_2) $= \overline{\text{int}}$ ($i_1 + i_2$). In general, the validity of any equation involving intervals expressed as $\overline{\text{int}}$ (i) is not compromised by the addition of int (0) to either side.

By similar reasoning, we have also

$$x\ \overline{\text{int}}\ (i) = \overline{\text{int}}\ (xi) + \text{int}\ (0)$$

and again if it can be shown that $x\ \overline{\text{int}}$ (i) $< a$, we may drop the int (0) and write $x\ \overline{\text{int}}$ (i) $= \overline{\text{int}}$ (xi).

Clearly

$$\frac{\overline{\text{int}}\ (i) + \text{int}\ (0)}{x} = \overline{\text{int}}\left(\frac{i}{x}\right)$$

only when $x \mid i$; and if it can be shown that $0 < \overline{\text{int}}\left(\dfrac{i}{x}\right) < \overline{\text{int}}\ (i)$, we may

again drop the int (0) and write $\dfrac{\overline{\text{int}}\ (i)}{x} = \overline{\text{int}}\left(\dfrac{i}{x}\right)^2$.

If the sum of two intervals is one octave exactly, each is said to be the *inversion* of the other, and they exhibit the following property:

THEOREM 5.   *The inversion of* $\overline{\text{int}}\ (i)$ *is* $\overline{\text{int}}\ (-i)$. From the first equation of this section, we have at once $\overline{\text{int}}\ (i) + \overline{\text{int}}\ (-i) = \text{int}\ (0)$, and since $0 < \overline{\text{int}}\ (i) < a$ and $0 < \overline{\text{int}}\ (-i) < a$,   it   follows   that $0 < \overline{\text{int}}\ (i) + \overline{\text{int}}\ (-i) < 2a$, or $0 < \text{int}\ (0) < 2a$, i.e., in this particular case, the value of int (0) is always one octave, irrespective of the value of i.

As an immediate consequence of Theorem 5, we have

$$-\overline{\text{int}}\ (i) = \overline{\text{int}}\ (-i) + \text{int}\ (0)$$

and when this is combined with the first equation of this section, we obtain

$$\overline{\text{int}}\ (i_1) - \overline{\text{int}}\ (i_2) = \overline{\text{int}}\ (i_1) + \overline{\text{int}}\ (-i_2) + \text{int}\ (0)$$
$$= \overline{\text{int}}\ (i_1 - i_2) + \text{int}\ (0)$$

and if it can be shown that $\overline{\text{int}}\ (i_1) > \overline{\text{int}}\ (i_2)$, then $\overline{\text{int}}\ (i_1) - \overline{\text{int}}\ (i_2) = \overline{\text{int}}\ (i_1 - i_2)$.

From the definition of int (0), it follows that

$$x\ \text{int}\ (0) = \text{int}\ (0)$$

for all values of x, and so there is no use for the expression $-\text{int}\ (0)$.

We next prove a simple but fundamental theorem that relates intervals to the names of notes.

THEOREM 6.   *The interval between note x and note y is* $\overline{\text{int}}\ (y - x)$. Since the interval is formed by two notes, the interval size convention applies, and we may call the interval $\overline{\text{int}}\ (i)$. In Figure 3 the interval formed by note 0 and note x is $x\ \overline{\text{int}}\ (1) = \overline{\text{int}}\ (x) + \text{int}\ (0)$, and upon applying the interval size convention this becomes simply $\overline{\text{int}}\ (x)$. But in certain cases (for example, if $\overline{\text{int}}\ (x) > \frac{1}{2}a$ and $\overline{\text{int}}\ (i) > \frac{1}{2}a$), note y may be higher than note 0 by more than one octave, and to provide for this possibility, the

---

[2] See Ch. I, note 5.

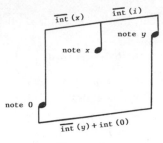

FIGURE 3

interval between note 0 and note y must be written $\overline{\text{int}}\,(y) + \text{int}\,(0)$. In Figure 3 it is clear that

$$\overline{\text{int}}\,(x) + \overline{\text{int}}\,(i) = \overline{\text{int}}\,(y) + \text{int}\,(0)$$
$$\overline{\text{int}}\,(i) = \overline{\text{int}}\,(y) - \overline{\text{int}}\,(x) + \text{int}\,(0)$$
$$= \overline{\text{int}}\,(y - x) + \text{int}\,(0)$$

But it is always true that $0 < \overline{\text{int}}\,(i) < a$, hence the value of $\text{int}\,(0)$ in this particular case is zero, and therefore $\overline{\text{int}}\,(i) = \overline{\text{int}}\,(y - x)$, and this proves the theorem.

An important consequence is the following:

THEOREM 7.   *The note higher than note x by* $\overline{\text{int}}\,(i)$ *is note $x + i$.* This follows at once, for the interval between note x and note is $x + i$ is $\overline{\text{int}}$ $(x + i - x)$, or $\overline{\text{int}}\,(i)$.

4. The family of Pythagorean diatonic intervals.   Let us call the notes of the diatonic scale 0, 1, 2, 3, 4, 5, and 6, this being the order in which they occur in the generating array, as described in Section 1 of this chapter. By Theorem 6 the diatonic intervals are all of the form $\overline{\text{int}}\,(y - x)$, where $0 \leqslant x \leqslant 6$ and $0 \leqslant y \leqslant 6$. Thus the total family of diatonic intervals is given by $\overline{\text{int}}\,(i)$ where $-6 \leqslant i \leqslant 6$, a total of thirteen intervals. In this case, it will be most convenient to regard $\text{int}\,(0)$ as one octave. For reference, we give the ratio and size in cents of all the Pythagorean diatonic intervals below in Table 3. The reader will find it a useful exercise to verify the results by using the methods of Section 2 of this chapter.

It should be observed that if the ratio of $\overline{\text{int}}\,(i)$ is multiplied by the ratio of $\overline{\text{int}}\,(-i)$, the product in every case is 2, illustrating Theorem 5.

It is important to bear in mind that $\overline{\text{int}}\,(x) > \overline{\text{int}}\,(y)$ does not necessarily imply that $x > y$. For example, $\overline{\text{int}}\,(3) > \overline{\text{int}}\,(2)$; but $\overline{\text{int}}\,(2) < \overline{\text{int}}\,(1)$.

TABLE 3

THE FAMILY OF PYTHAGOREAN DIATONIC INTERVALS

interval	in terms of a and $\bar{v}$	ratio (fraction)	ratio (decimal)	size in cents
$\overline{\text{int}}$ (6)	$6\bar{v} - 3a$	$\frac{729}{512}$	1.423828	611.730
$\overline{\text{int}}$ (5)	$5\bar{v} - 2a$	$\frac{243}{128}$	1.898438	1109.775
$\overline{\text{int}}$ (4)	$4\bar{v} - 2a$	$\frac{81}{64}$	1.265625	407.820
$\overline{\text{int}}$ (3)	$3\bar{v} - a$	$\frac{27}{16}$	1.687500	905.865
$\overline{\text{int}}$ (2)	$2\bar{v} - a$	$\frac{9}{8}$	1.125000	203.910
$\overline{\text{int}}$ (1)	$\bar{v}$	$\frac{3}{2}$	1.500000	701.955
octave	a	$\frac{2}{1}$	2.000000	1200.000
$\overline{\text{int}}$ (−1)	$a - \bar{v}$	$\frac{4}{3}$	1.333333	498.045
$\overline{\text{int}}$ (−2)	$2a - 2\bar{v}$	$\frac{16}{9}$	1.777778	996.090
$\overline{\text{int}}$ (−3)	$2a - 3\bar{v}$	$\frac{32}{27}$	1.185185	294.135
$\overline{\text{int}}$ (−4)	$3a - 4\bar{v}$	$\frac{128}{81}$	1.580247	792.180
$\overline{\text{int}}$ (−5)	$3a - 5\bar{v}$	$\frac{256}{243}$	1.053498	90.225
$\overline{\text{int}}$ (−6)	$4a - 6\bar{v}$	$\frac{1024}{729}$	1.404664	588.270

5. Order of notes in the diatonic scale. The definition of diatonic scale (Sec. 1 of this chapter) requires that notes 0, 1, 2, 3, 4, 5, and 6 should be arranged in ascending order in such a manner that the greatest interval between any two of them is less than one octave. For our purposes, it is most convenient to choose note 0 as the starting point, since note x is higher than note 0 by $\overline{\text{int}}$ (x) (Theorem 6), and $\overline{\text{int}}$ $(x) < a$. Thus notes 0 through 6 may be arranged in ascending order in the manner desired simply by arranging intervals (0) through (6) in increasing order. Then if the lower note of each interval is note 0, the higher notes of each interval are the notes of the diatonic scale. By examining the sizes in cents of intervals (0) through (6) (Table 3), we find the arrangement given in Table 4. Thus the order of notes in the diatonic scale is 0, 2, 4, 6, 1, 3, 5, 0.

Different styles throughout music history have treated the scale as beginning and ending with various different notes, and a different name is applied in each case, the names being called *modes*. In particular, the major mode is the one beginning and ending with note 1, which gives the order 1, 3, 5, 0, 2, 4, 6, 1.

TABLE 4

intervals	(0)	(2)	(4)	(6)	(1)	(3)	(5)	(0)
size in cents	000.000	203.910	407.820	611.730	701.955	905.865	1109.775	1200.000

6. Distribution of the adjacent intervals in the diatonic scale. We call the intervals formed by two successive notes of the diatonic scale *adjacent intervals*, and their arrangement may be easily found by Theorem 6 (Sec. 3 of this chapter). Between notes 0 and 2 we have $\overline{\text{int}}$ (2), between notes 2 and 4 we have $\overline{\text{int}}$ $(4 - 2) = \overline{\text{int}}$ (2), and between notes 4 and 6 $\overline{\text{int}}$ $(6 - 4) = \overline{\text{int}}$ (2). Between notes 6 and 1 we find $\overline{\text{int}}$ $(1 - 6) = \overline{\text{int}}$ (-5), between notes 1 and 3 and again between notes 3 and 5 we find $\overline{\text{int}}$ (2), and finally between notes 5 and 0 we have $\overline{\text{int}}$ $(0 - 5) = \overline{\text{int}}$ (-5). Two different interval sizes only are seen to occur—$\overline{\text{int}}$ (2) five times, and $\overline{\text{int}}$ (-5) twice. The statement that the succession of these intervals returns to the initial note is given symbolically by the equation

$$5\,\overline{\text{int}}\ (2) + 2\,\overline{\text{int}}\ (-5) = \text{int}\ (0)$$

The distribution is shown in Table 5.

When the scale is tuned precisely in the manner described, the tuning is said to be *Pythagorean*. In Pythagorean tuning, $\overline{\text{int}}$ (2) is called a *major tone*, and $\overline{\text{int}}$ (-5) is called a *limma*. Recalling the sizes of these intervals in cents (from Table 3), we should have $(5)(203.910) + (2)(90.225) = 1200.000$, and this is the case.

The arrangement of major tones and limmas shown in Table 5 completes the classical definition of Pythagorean tuning. Further insights into the properties of this tuning may be gained from an exploration of the distributional pattern of all the diatonic intervals, and this is the subject of the next chapter.

TABLE 5

			one octave				
notes	0	2	4	6	1	3	5	0
adjacent intervals		(2)	(2)	(2)	(-5)	(2)	(2)	(-5)
ratios		$\frac{9}{8}$	$\frac{9}{8}$	$\frac{9}{8}$	$\frac{256}{243}$	$\frac{9}{8}$	$\frac{9}{8}$	$\frac{256}{243}$

III Names and Distributional Patterns of the Diatonic Intervals

---

Introduction. In this chapter, we take up a systematic investigation of those intricate interconnections among intervals that will eventually be shown to apply to the entire family of recognizable diatonic tunings. The subject is best described by the algebra of congruences and residues, and since this branch of number theory is generally not included in standard texts and the reader is likely to be unfamiliar with it, we give in Section 1 such elementary aspects of the subject as are needed in the theory of diatonic scales. In Section 2 we derive a pair of formulas which relate the scale to the generating array, and vice versa; and in Section 3 this is expanded upon to furnish a means of determining the ordinal number associated with an interval, given how many notes the interval spans on the generating array. Section 4 shows how to form a sequence of notes in which the adjacent intervals are all named by the same given ordinal number, and Section 5 demonstrates that there are two modalities of diatonic intervals associated with ordinal numbers second through seventh, always differing by the same amount. In Section 6 the conventional names for certain notes and intervals are precisely set forth, and we demonstrate a cyclic connection involving the broken circle of fifths, the triads, and the scale. In Section 7 it is revealed that Pythagorean tuning is suited to only a portion of the existing repertoire, owing to its discordant thirds and triads.

1. Congruences and residues. In the following discussion, all numbers are positive or negative integers, or zero.

If $x - a$ is divisible exactly by m, we say "x is congruent to a, modulo m," and write

$$x \equiv a \,(\mathrm{mod}\ m)$$

In this expression, m is called the *modulus* and a is called the *residue*. Since $m\,|\,x - a$ and $x \equiv a \,(\mathrm{mod}\ m)$ have exactly the same meaning,[1] one

---

[1] See Ch. I, note 5.

may wonder why the new notation is introduced. As we shall see, each has its own advantages and in particular, the symbol "$\equiv$" behaves in much the same way as "$=$," so that congruences and equations have much in common.

From the definition, the following properties are immediately deduced:

If $x \equiv a \pmod{m}$, then $a \equiv x \pmod{m}$;

If $x \equiv a \pmod{m}$, then $-x \equiv -a \pmod{m}$;

If $x \equiv a \pmod{m}$ and $y \equiv a \pmod{m}$, then $x \equiv y \pmod{m}$;

If $x \equiv a \pmod{m}$, then $kx \equiv ka \pmod{m}$;

If $x \equiv a \pmod{m}$ and $y \equiv b \pmod{m}$, then $x + y \equiv a + b \pmod{m}$, and $x - y \equiv a - b \pmod{m}$.

The properties listed above are true of equations as well as congruences, but we now come upon a difference: if $kx \equiv ka \pmod{m}$, it is not necessarily true that $x \equiv a \pmod{m}$. For example, $(4)(5) \equiv (4)(2) \pmod{12}$, but $5 \not\equiv 2 \pmod{12}$. The situation is clarified by the following theorem:

THEOREM 8.   *If the greatest common divisor of k and m is d, then $kx \equiv ka \pmod{m}$ implies $x \equiv a \left(\mathrm{mod}\, \dfrac{m}{d} \right)$.* Since $d = (k, m)$,[2] we may define k_1 and m_1 by $k_1 = \dfrac{k}{d}$ and $m_1 = \dfrac{m}{d}$. Now $(k_1, m_1) = 1$ and

$$\frac{k_1 dx - k_1 da}{dm_1} = \frac{k_1(x - a)}{m_1}$$

this last being an integer; and since $(k_1, m_1) = 1$, all the factors of m_1 must also be factors of $x - a$, i.e., $m_1 | x - a$, and this proves the theorem.

A particular case is of especial importance:

THEOREM 9.   *If k and m are coprime, then $kx \equiv ka \pmod{m}$ implies $x \equiv a \pmod{m}$.*

Another essential point of difference between equations and congruences is the following, which has extensive application to music theory:

THEOREM 10.   *Any multiple of the modulus may be added to either side of the congruence.* If $x \equiv a \pmod{m}$, or $m | x - a$, then $m | x + mn - a$ and $m | x - a - mn$ for any n, hence $x + mn \equiv a \pmod{m}$ and $x \equiv a + mn \pmod{m}$.

---

[2] See Ch. I, note 6.

Clearly there corresponds an infinite number of residues to any given x. Of especial importance in application to music theory is the residue for which $0 \leqslant a \leqslant m - 1$, and we call this the *least residue*. Let x be positive; now if $x \equiv a \pmod{m}$ and $0 \leqslant a \leqslant m - 1$, we may write $\dfrac{x - a}{m} = h$ where h is a positive integer or zero, and

$$\frac{x}{m} = h + \frac{a}{m}, \qquad 0 \leqslant a \leqslant m - 1$$

Now if $x \geqslant 0$, the above is equivalent to ordinary long division, i.e., we divide x by m, obtaining a quotient h which is immaterial, and a remainder a which is the least residue. This provides an elementary means of calculating the least residue for a positive x.

Since the principal congruences arising in the theory of diatonic scales are of the form $kx \equiv a \pmod{m}$ where $(k, m) = 1$ and $0 \leqslant a \leqslant m - 1$, we now consider this particular case, which exhibits the following fundamentally important property:

THEOREM 11.   *If k and m are coprime, and $kx \equiv a \pmod{m}$ where a is the least residue, and x takes all integral values from 0 to $m - 1$, then all the residues are different.* In other words, let $kx \equiv a \pmod{m}$ where $(k, m) = 1$ and $0 \leqslant a \leqslant m - 1$, and also let $k(x + n) \equiv b \pmod{m}$ where $0 \leqslant b \leqslant m - 1$; now if $0 < n < m$, then $a \neq b$. We prove the theorem by showing that the assumption that it is false results in a logical contradiction. First assume that $a = b$, or that

$$kx \equiv a \pmod{m}$$

$$k(x + n) \equiv a \pmod{m}$$

also $0 \leqslant a \leqslant m - 1$, $(k, m) = 1$, and $0 < n < m$. Now by definition,

$$m \,|\, kx - a$$

$$m \,|\, kx - a + kn$$

and hence $m \,|\, kn$. But $(k, m) = 1$, hence $m \,|\, n$, or $m \leqslant n$. But this contradicts the hypothesis that $n < m$, and this proves the theorem.

By virtue of the fact that $0 \leqslant a \leqslant m - 1$, the m different residues are the m integers from 0 through $m - 1$.

Example: If $4x \equiv a \pmod 7$, and x goes from 0 to 6, the residues make the sequence 0, 4, 1, 5, 2, 6, 3.

If x continues to increase beyond $m - 1$, the same sequence of residues will recur over and over, as a consequence of Theorem 10.

The situation where $(k, m) > 1$ brings about additional complications, and discussion of this case will be postponed until it is needed (Ch. XI, Sec. 10). Suffice to say here that $(k, m) = 1$ is an essential element of the hypothesis—without it the theorem is false.

Example: If $6x \equiv a \pmod 8$, and x goes from 0 to 7, the residues make the sequence 0, 6, 4, 2, 0, 6, 4, 2.

We conclude this section with a musical example already familiar.[3] The application of the interval size convention (Ch. I, Sec. 5) is a congruence relation "modulo octave." Let the size of $\overline{\text{int}}$ (i) be c cents, so that $c = i\overline{v} + na$, $0 \leqslant c < a$ (Ch. II, Sec. 2). Now we have $i\overline{v} - c = -na$, or $a \mid i\overline{v} - c$, and hence $i\overline{v} \equiv c \pmod a$. Next we substitute $\overline{v} = 701.955$ and $a = 1200$ (Ch. I, Sec. 6), and we have

$$701.955i \equiv c \pmod{1200}, \; 0 \leqslant c < 1200$$

taking c as the least residue. This provides a simple means to obtain the size in cents of $\overline{\text{int}}$ (i) when i is positive, without first obtaining the ratio.

Example: Find the size in cents of $\overline{\text{int}}$ (4). We have $(4)(701.955) \equiv c$ $\pmod{1200}$, and we now divide 2807.820 by 1200, and obtain a quotient 2 which is immaterial, and a remainder 407.820, which is the size in cents.

If i is negative, the remainder is also negative, and out of the range $0 \leqslant c < 1200$. But we may apply Theorem 10:

$$-1200i + 701.955i \equiv c \pmod{1200}$$

$$-498.045i \equiv c \pmod{1200}$$

Now if i is negative, $-498.045i$ is positive, and we may once again find c by ordinary long division.

Example: Find the size in cents of $\overline{\text{int}}$ (-5), We have $(-5)(-498.045) \equiv c \pmod{1200}$, and upon dividing 2490.225 by 1200, we get a remainder of

---

[3] In the rest of this section, the letters a and $\overline{v}$ are used with the same meaning as in Ch. I, Sec. 6.

90.225, which is the size in cents. The reader should now review the two examples of Chapter II, Sec. 2.

2. The diatonic scale regarded as a sequence of least residues. We now return to the array of pitches generating the diatonic scale—the seven pitches numbered 0, 1, 2, 3, 4, 5, 6, each higher than the one immediately preceding by $\bar{v}$. It was shown in Chapter II, Sec. 5 that when these pitches are transposed by some number of octaves so that the greatest distance between any two of them is less than one octave, and then rearranged in ascending order, the new sequence of notes is 0, 2, 4, 6, 1, 3, 5. We observe now that this new sequence is not a haphazard rearrangement of the original, but may be derived from it by a simple rule. If we imagine the notes of the generating array to repeat, and then to return once more to note 0, we may write

$$\underline{0}, 1, \underline{2}, 3, \underline{4}, 5, \underline{6}, 0, \underline{1}, 2, \underline{3}, 4, \underline{5}, 6, \underline{0}$$

The order of notes in the diatonic scale is now seen to result if we start at note 0 and then proceed, taking every other note from the generating array, it being agreed that when we have counted as far as note 6 we go back to note 0 and continue counting, as illustrated by the underlined notes. Let us call the generating sequence j's and the scale sequence i's, and write out the two arrays, one below the other:

generating array of j's   0, 1, 2, 3, 4, 5, 6, 0

scale sequence of i's   0, 2, 4, 6, 1, 3, 5, 0

The relation between the xth j and the xth i is now given by the congruence

$$2j \equiv i \,(\mathrm{mod}\ 7)$$

where i is the least residue, or $0 \leqslant i \leqslant 6$. Or we might say that the order of notes in the scale is the sequence of least residues that are congruent, modulo 7, to the even integers in increasing order. Or again, the order of notes in the scale is the order of the remainders when the numbers 0, 2, 4, 6, 8, 10, 12, 14 are divided by 7.

It will soon be seen that the letters i and j in the congruence $2j \equiv i \,(\mathrm{mod}\ 7)$ admit of a variety of interpretations. They may represent notes, intervals, positions, or numbers in various combinations; and in order to avoid confusion, it is essential to bear constantly in mind which interpretation is being used in any argument.

We may regard the sequence of j's as showing the position in the diatonic scale occupied by note i. Thus note 0 is in position 0, note 2 is in position 1, note 4 is in position 2, and so on; and so we may state that position j in the diatonic scale is occupied by note i where $2j \equiv i \pmod 7$, and $0 \leqslant i \leqslant 6$. It is an elementary matter to calculate i given j—we multiply j by 2, then divide by 7, and the remainder is i.

We may obtain an expression enabling us to calculate j given i by proceeding as follows: we rewrite the congruence first in the form $i \equiv 2j \pmod 7$, and then $4i \equiv 8j \pmod 7$. Since any multiple of the modulus may be added to or subtracted from either side of the congruence (Theorem 10), and since $8j = 7j + j$, we have finally,

$$4i \equiv j \pmod 7$$

Thus the position in the diatonic scale occupied by note i is position j, where $4i \equiv j \pmod 7$, and $0 \leqslant j \leqslant 6$. In order to calculate j given i, we multiply i by 4, divide this product by 7, and the remainder is j.

Example: In what position in the scale is note 6? We have $(4)(6) \equiv j \pmod 7$, and when 24 is divided by 7, the remainder is 3. Hence $j = 3$, and so the answer is that note 6 is in position 3 in the scale.

3. The conventional names of intervals.   As all musicians know, the name of an interval consists of two parts: first, a word such as major, minor, perfect, diminished, or augmented, called the *modality*, and second, an ordinal number—second, fourth, sixth, for example, although we say *unison* rather than first[4] and *octave* rather than eighth. As the two parts exhibit different mathematical behavior, we consider them separately, taking up first the question of the ordinal number.

In the case of an interval formed by notes 0 through 6, the ordinal number relates the interval to the notes of the scale. Specifically, the ordinal number is the number of notes encompassed by the interval, including both the lower note and the higher note. It will be convenient to imagine the scale continuing into the next higher octave, and assign numbers 7

---

[4] Some theorists prefer the word *prime*; this has some advantages, but it is not a commonly used term among musicians in practical situations.

through 13 to these positions, as in the diagram below:

position of note i (j's)   0, 1, 2, 3, 4, 5, 6, 7, 8, 9, 10, 11, 12, 13
notes in scale order (i's)   0, 2, 4, 6, 1, 3, 5, 0, 2, 4, 6, 1, 3, 5

FIGURE 4

Now the intervals between notes 0 and 2, notes 2 and 4, notes 4 and 6, notes 6 and 1, etc. are called *seconds*. And the intervals between notes 0 and 4, notes 2 and 6, notes 4 and 1, etc. are *thirds*; the interval between notes 0 and 6 is a *fourth*, and so on. We are actually considering the interval as being the sum of a number of seconds, and calling it by the ordinal number that exceeds this number by 1. Thus the interval between the note in position 0 and the note in position j is called a $(j + 1)$th. And more generally, the interval between the note in position j_1 and the note in position j_2 ($j_2 > j_1$) is called a $(j + 1)$th where $j = j_2 - j_1$.

Example: The interval between the note in position 4 and the note in position 8—between notes 1 and 2—is an $(8 - 4 + 1)$th, a fifth.

We are now prepared to prove the following fundamental theorem:

THEOREM 12.   *For every interval formed by notes 0 through 6, the number of seconds which adds to* $\overline{\text{int}}$ (i) *depends entirely upon the number i, irrespective of the actual notes forming* $\overline{\text{int}}$ (i). At the same time, we deduce the functional relation connecting i and j in the statement "$\overline{\text{int}}$ (i) is a $(j + 1)$th." The reader will find it helpful to refer to Figure 4 during the proof.

Let there be two notes i_1 and i_2, $0 \leqslant i_1 \leqslant 6$, $0 \leqslant i_2 \leqslant 6$, and $i_1 \neq i_2$, such that i_2 is the higher. (It was pointed out in Ch. II, Sec. 4 that this does not necessarily mean that $i_2 > i_1$.) Now if we call the interval between notes i_1 and i_2 $\overline{\text{int}}$ (i), we have $i = i_2 - i_1$ (Theorem 6; Ch. II, Sec. 3). Now let note i_1 be in position j_1, and let note i_2 be in position j_2 relative to the scale; $\overline{\text{int}}$ (i) is now a $(j + 1)$th where $j = j_2 - j_1$. By what was found in the previous section, we see that $4i_1 \equiv j_1$ (mod 7), and $4i_2 \equiv j_2$ (mod 7). Since i_2 is higher than i_1 by less than one octave, or seven seconds (by virtue of the interval size convention), we have $j_1 < j_2 < j_1 + 7$, or $j_1 < j_2 \leqslant j_1 + 6$, and from this last $0 < j_2 - j_1 \leqslant 6$. Next, $4(i_2 - i_1) \equiv j_2 - j_1$ (mod 7), and if we take $j_2 - j_1$ as the least residue, then $0 < j_2 - j_1 \leqslant 6$, as above.[5] Hence $j_2 - j_1 = j$; and since $i_2 - i_1 = i$, we finally obtain $4i \equiv j$ (mod 7), and $0 < j \leqslant 6$. Thus $\overline{\text{int}}$ (i) is a $(j + 1)$th where $4i \equiv j$ (mod 7), $0 < j \leqslant 6$. It will be observed that the individual notes i_1 and i_2 are not present in

---

[5] It should be noted that the condition $i_1 \neq i_2$ specifically excludes the value zero for i, and consequently for $j_2 - j_1$ in this circumstance.

this relation, and this proves the theorem. If we use the method of Section 1 of this chapter to evaluate j given a positive i, we may say that when i is positive, $\overline{\text{int}}$ (i) is a $(j + 1)$th where j is the remainder that results when $4i$ is divided by 7.

Examples: $\overline{\text{Int}}$ (4) is a $(2 + 1)$th—a third—since $(4)(4)$ divided by 7 gives a remainder of 2. $\overline{\text{Int}}$ (6) is a $(3 + 1)$th—a fourth—since $(4)(6)$ divided by 7 gives a remainder of 3.

When i is negative, the remainder is also negative, and outside the range $0 < j \leqslant 6$. However, we may apply Theorem 10:

$$-7i + 4i \equiv j \,(\text{mod } 7)$$

$$-3i \equiv j \,(\text{mod } 7)$$

When i is negative, $-3i$ is positive, and j may be found again by ordinary division.

Thus when i is negative, $\overline{\text{int}}$ (i) is a $(j + 1)$th where j is the remainder that results when $-3i$ is divided by 7.

Examples: $\overline{\text{Int}}$ (-5) is a $(1 + 1)$th—a second—since $(-3)(-5)$ divided by 7 gives a remainder of 1. $\overline{\text{Int}}$ (-1) is a fourth, since $(-3)(-1)$ divided by 7 gives a remainder of 3.

4. The generating array viewed as a broken circle of fifths.   If we imagine the array of notes that generates the diatonic scale to be followed by the initial note once again, we have between each successive pair of consecutive notes the following adjacent intervals (Theorem 6; Ch. II, Sec. 3):

generating array of notes   0, 1, 2, 3, 4, 5, 6, 0
adjacent intervals   (1) (1) (1) (1) (1) (1)(−6)

The idea of this combination of intervals returning to the original note is conveyed symbolically by the equation

$$6\,\overline{\text{int}} \,(1) + \overline{\text{int}} \,(-6) = \text{int} \,(0)$$

Upon applying Theorem 12, we find that $\overline{\text{int}}$ (-6) is a fifth, as well as $\overline{\text{int}}$ (1). We call a succession of fifths returning to the initial note a *circle of fifths*, and from now on, we refer to the generating array by this more commonly used musical term. When all the fifths are the same size save for one, the circle is said to be *broken*. From Table 3 (Ch. II, Sec. 4), we see that $\overline{\text{int}}$ (1) > $\overline{\text{int}}$ (-6), and hence, using the techniques developed in

Chapter II, Sec. 3, we may write

$$\overline{\text{int}}\,(1) - \overline{\text{int}}\,(-6) = \overline{\text{int}}\,(7)$$

By the method of Chapter II, Sec. 2, we find that the ratio of $\overline{\text{int}}\,(7)$ is $\frac{2187}{2048}$, its complete expression in terms of a and $\bar{v}$ is $7\bar{v} - 4a$, and it contains 113.685 cents. In Pythagorean tuning, $\overline{\text{int}}\,(7)$ is called an *apotome*.

We have already observed how the scale may be evolved from the circle of fifths by taking every second note (Sec. 2 of this chapter), and we now expand upon that principle by considering the properties of the sequence that results upon taking every ith note from the circle. By "taking every ith note," we mean specifically that we start at note 0, count ahead i notes, count ahead i notes once again and repeat the process over and over, it being understood that whenever we reach note 6, we continue with note 0 and go on as before. Thus, from the elementary properties of congruences given in Section 1 of this chapter, the new sequence is given by the successive values of y where

$$ix \equiv y\,(\text{mod } 7), \quad 0 \leqslant y \leqslant 6$$

as x takes the values 0, 1, 2, 3, 4, 5, 6, 7, in this order.

Example: The sequence of notes obtained by taking every fourth note from the circle of fifths is 0, 4, 1, 5, 2, 6, 3, 0, as illustrated below by the underlined notes:

$\underline{0}$, 1, 2, 3, $\underline{4}$, 5, 6, 0, $\underline{1}$, 2, 3, 4, $\underline{5}$, 6, 0, 1, $\underline{2}$, 3, 4, 5, $\underline{6}$, 0, 1, 2, $\underline{3}$, 4, 5, 6, $\underline{0}$

These numbers are the least residues where $4x \equiv y\,(\text{mod } 7)$, and x takes successive integral values from 0 through 7.

It should be observed that since 7 and i are coprime for any i, 7 being prime itself, the new sequence is always a rearrangement of all the notes forming the circle of fifths (Theorem 11).

Now let us consider the sequence resulting from taking every jth note from the scale, i.e., we start at note 0 and count ahead j notes over and over, always counting note 0 directly after note 5 in the scale sequence 0, 2, 4, 6, 1, 3, 5.

Example: The sequence resulting from taking every second note from the scale is 0, 4, 1, 5, 2, 6, 3, 0, as illustrated below:

$\underline{0}$, 2, $\underline{4}$, 6, $\underline{1}$, 3, $\underline{5}$, 0, $\underline{2}$, 4, $\underline{6}$, 1, $\underline{3}$, 5, $\underline{0}$

If we recall once again that taking every second note from the circle of fifths gives the scale, it follows at once that taking every jth note from the scale gives the same sequence of notes as does taking every $2j$th note from the circle. (The last two examples are an illustration of this principle.) But if $2j > 7$, we may replace $2j$ with $2j - 7$, since counting ahead 7 notes brings us back where we started. Hence taking every jth note from the scale gives the same sequence of notes as does taking every ith note from the circle where $2j \equiv i \pmod 7$, and $0 \leqslant i \leqslant 6$. This last is important, for when we count ahead j notes from a particular note in the scale, we find a note higher than the original by j seconds, and so the interval between the two is a $(j + 1)$th. Hence when we take every jth note from the scale, we obtain a sequence of notes in which the interval between any two consecutive notes is a $(j + 1)$th.

In sum, all seven $(j + 1)$ths occur as adjacent intervals in the sequence that results from taking every ith note from the circle of fifths, where $2j \equiv i \pmod 7$, and $0 \leqslant i \leqslant 6$.

Example: Find the sequence of notes in which each note is higher than the one immediately preceding by a sixth. Here $j + 1 = 6$, $j = 5$, and so $10 \equiv i \pmod 7$, hence $i = 3$. The sequence now wanted is all the least residues where $3x \equiv y \pmod 7$ as x takes all integral values from 0 through 7 in increasing order, viz., 0, 3, 6, 2, 5, 1, 4, 0. This may be illustrated by writing out the circle of fifths three times and underlining every third note:

$$\underline{0}, 1, 2, \underline{3}, 4, 5, \underline{6}, 0, 1, \underline{2}, 3, 4, \underline{5}, 6, 0, \underline{1}, 2, 3, \underline{4}, 5, 6, \underline{0}$$

And if we write out the scale twice:

$$\overset{\overset{\displaystyle\frown\text{sixth}\frown\quad\frown\text{sixth}\frown}{}}{0, 2, 4, 6, 1, 3, 5, 0, 2, 4, 6, 1, 3, 5, 0}$$

it may be easily seen that the intervals between notes 0 and 3, notes 3 and 6, notes 6 and 2, notes 2 and 5, etc. are all sixths, i.e., that each is the sum of five seconds.

5. The two modalities of diatonic intervals.

THEOREM 13. *Every ordinal number from second through seventh names two different diatonic intervals.* By Theorem 12, $\overline{\text{int}}\,(i)$ is a $(j + 1)$th where

TABLE 6

intervals	ordinal number
(1) and (-6)	fifth
(2) and (-5)	second
(3) and (-4)	sixth
(4) and (-3)	third
(5) and (-2)	seventh
(6) and (-1)	fourth

$4i \equiv j \pmod 7$ and $0 \leqslant j \leqslant 6$; and since $\overline{\text{int}}\,(i)$ is a diatonic interval, we have also $-6 \leqslant i \leqslant 6$ (Sec. 4 of this chapter). By Theorem 10, it is also true that $4(i-7) \equiv j \pmod 7$; and if $1 \leqslant i \leqslant 6$, then $-6 \leqslant i - 7 \leqslant -1$. Hence the same ordinal number names both $\overline{\text{int}}\,(i)$ and $\overline{\text{int}}\,(i-7)$, and this proves the theorem.

Applying Theorem 12, we find the correspondences given in Table 6.

THEOREM 14. *Two different diatonic intervals named by the same ordinal number differ in every case by* $\overline{\text{int}}\,(7)$. *In addition, the larger corresponds to a positive i, and the smaller to a negative i.* From Table 3 (Ch. II, Sec. 4), we see that $\overline{\text{int}}\,(1) > \overline{\text{int}}\,(-6)$, $\overline{\text{int}}\,(2) > \overline{\text{int}}\,(-5)$, $\overline{\text{int}}\,(3) > \overline{\text{int}}\,(-4)$, $\overline{\text{int}}\,(4) > \overline{\text{int}}\,(-3)$, $\overline{\text{int}}\,(5) > \overline{\text{int}}\,(-2)$, and $\overline{\text{int}}\,(6) > \overline{\text{int}}\,(-1)$; hence when $1 \leqslant i \leqslant 6$, $\overline{\text{int}}\,(i) - \overline{\text{int}}\,(i-7) = \overline{\text{int}}\,(i - i + 7) = \overline{\text{int}}\,(7)$ (Ch. II, Sec. 3). This is the apotome (Sec. 4 of this chapter) of 113.685 cents—sufficiently large that in every case, $\overline{\text{int}}\,(i)$ and $\overline{\text{int}}\,(i-7)$ have a substantially different character which we call the interval's *modality.*

The two different $(j+1)$ths named by the same ordinal number correspond roughly to the distinction of *major* and *minor*, but the precise application of these terms brings about an additional complication. So for the moment, we avoid the conventional musical terms and refer to the two different $(j+1)$ths as the *greater* and the *lesser.*

We may now find a formula that gives the number of lesser $(j+1)$ths in the diatonic scale.

THEOREM 15. *The number of lesser $(j+1)$ths occurring in the diatonic scale is i where* $2j \equiv i \pmod 7$ *and* $0 \leqslant i \leqslant 6$. We recall first (Sec. 4 of this chapter) that all seven $(j+1)$ths occur as adjacent intervals in the sequence that results from taking every ith note from the broken circle of fifths where $2j \equiv i \pmod 7$ and $0 \leqslant i \leqslant 6$, i.e., the least residues where $ix \equiv y \pmod 7$ and x takes successive integral values from 0 through 7. In this sequence of least residues, every time a larger number is followed by a smaller number, we have found a lesser $(j+1)$th (Theorem 6; Ch. II,

Sec. 3). Since $0 \leqslant i \leqslant 6$ and $0 \leqslant y \leqslant 6$, it is clear that each time the product ix exceeds or equals the next multiple of 7, the value of y is less than the y immediately preceding. And since the greatest value for ix is $7i$, this occurs exactly i times.

Example: To find the number of lesser sixths, we have $j + 1 = 6, j = 5$, $10 \equiv i \pmod{7}$, and so $i = 3$; thus the number of lesser sixths is 3, and consequently the number of greater sixths is 4. Referring once again to the example of the previous section, if we write out the sequence of notes in which all the adjacent intervals are sixths:

$$0, 3, 6, 2, 5, 1, 4, 0$$

it is easily seen that a smaller number follows a larger number three times, and that the succession of adjacent intervals is (3), (3), (-4), (3), (-4), (3), (-4).

It is instructive to derive a similar formula giving the number of greater $(j + 1)$ths in the diatonic scale.

THEOREM 16. *The number of greater $(j + 1)$ths occurring in the diatonic scale is h where $5j \equiv h \pmod{7}$ and $0 \leqslant h \leqslant 6$.* Since the number of lesser $(j + 1)$ths is i where $2j \equiv i \pmod{7}$ and $0 \leqslant i \leqslant 6$, we may write $-2j \equiv -i \pmod{7}$, and also $7j - 2j \equiv 7 - i \pmod{7}$ (Theorem 10), and finally $5j \equiv 7 - i \pmod{7}$. Now let h be the number of greater $(j + 1)$ths; clearly $h = 7 - i$, and so $5j \equiv h \pmod{7}$, $0 \leqslant h \leqslant 6$ is the formula wanted. Or, using the methods of Section 1 of this chapter, we may say that the number of greater $(j + 1)$ths in the diatonic scale is the remainder that results when $5j$ is divided by 7.

We now prove a theorem which throws further light on the peculiar asymmetric distribution of greater and lesser intervals within the diatonic scale.

THEOREM 17. *The lower notes of each of the h greater $(j + 1)$ths are notes $0, 1, 2, \ldots h - 1$.* Let the greater $(j + 1)$th be $\overline{\text{int}}$ (i) where $2j \equiv i \pmod{7}$ and $1 \leqslant i \leqslant 6$ (Theorem 12). Now if the lower note of $\overline{\text{int}}$ (i) is note n, the higher note is note $n + i$ (Theorem 7; Ch. II, Sec. 3). But the greatest value that $n + i$ may assume is 6, or $n + i < 7$, and $n < 7 - i$. Since $h = 7 - i$, as described in Theorem 16, we have $n < h$, and hence n may only be $0, 1, 2, \ldots h - 1$.

Example: The number of greater sixths is given by h where $(5)(5) \equiv h \pmod{7}$, $0 \leqslant h \leqslant 6$; so $h = 4$, since 25 divided by 7 gives a remainder of 4. By Theorem 17, the lower notes of the four greater sixths are notes 0, 1, 2, and 3. Since $i = 7 - 4 = 3$, the four greater sixths are found to be between notes 0 and 3, notes 1 and 4, notes 2 and 5, and notes 3 and 6.

TABLE 7

seconds	0	2	4	6	1	3	5	0
		(2)	(2)	(2)	(−5)	(2)	(2)	(−5)
thirds	0	4	1	5	2	6	3	0
		(4)	(−3)	(4)	(−3)	(4)	(−3)	(−3)
fourths	0	6	5	4	3	2	1	0
		(6)	(−1)	(−1)	(−1)	(−1)	(−1)	(−1)
fifths	0	1	2	3	4	5	6	0
		(1)	(1)	(1)	(1)	(1)	(1)	(−6)
sixths	0	3	6	2	5	1	4	0
		(3)	(3)	(−4)	(3)	(−4)	(3)	(−4)
sevenths	0	5	3	1	6	4	2	0
		(5)	(−2)	(−2)	(5)	(−2)	(−2)	(−2)

It is no great labor to write out the sequences of notes in which the adjacent intervals are seconds, thirds, fourths, fifths, sixths, and sevenths. Table 7 will serve to illustrate clearly the principles derived so far in this chapter.

6. The conventional names of notes and intervals. It is perhaps unfortunate that we use letters rather than *sol-fa* syllables to name notes, since it is natural to make the assumption that the "normal" sequence of notes is the alphabetical order. However, this is somewhat misleading, and so we introduce *sol-fa* syllables first, and then replace them by letters. We have at once a direct and precise representation of the notes up to now called by numbers if we substitute the familiar syllables for the numbers as follows:

$$\text{note } 0 = fa \qquad \text{note } 4 = la$$
$$\text{note } 1 = do \qquad \text{note } 5 = mi$$
$$\text{note } 2 = sol \qquad \text{note } 6 = si$$
$$\text{note } 3 = re$$

If we wish to know the name of the interval formed by, say, *la* and *do*, this is the interval between note 4 and note 1, or $\overline{\text{int}}\,(1-4) = \overline{\text{int}}\,(-3)$ (Theorem 6; Ch. II, Sec. 3). Using Theorem 12, we find that $\overline{\text{int}}\,(-3)$ is a third, since $(-3)(-3)$ divided by 7 gives a remainder of 2. Furthermore, since i is negative, $\overline{\text{int}}\,(-3)$ is a lesser third. This result is, of course, thoroughly familiar to all trained musicians, who learn by rote how to answer this and similar questions.

TABLE 8

NAMES OF INTERVALS (-6) THROUGH (6)

$4i \equiv j \pmod 7$	interval (i)	modality	ordinal number
$0 \leqslant j \leqslant 6$	$\overline{\text{int}}$ (6)	augmented	fourth, $j = 3$
	$\overline{\text{int}}$ (5)	major	seventh, $j = 6$
	$\overline{\text{int}}$ (4)	major	third, $j = 2$
	$\overline{\text{int}}$ (3)	major	sixth, $j = 5$
	$\overline{\text{int}}$ (2)	major	second, $j = 1$
	$\overline{\text{int}}$ (1)	perfect	fifth, $j = 4$
	int (0)		octave
	$\overline{\text{int}}$ (-1)	perfect	fourth, $j = 3$
	$\overline{\text{int}}$ (-2)	minor	seventh, $j = 6$
	$\overline{\text{int}}$ (-3)	minor	third, $j = 2$
	$\overline{\text{int}}$ (-4)	minor	sixth, $j = 5$
	$\overline{\text{int}}$ (-5)	minor	second, $j = 1$
	$\overline{\text{int}}$ (-6)	diminished	fifth, $j = 4$

The words "greater" and "lesser" are not used by musicians, but are generally replaced by "major" and "minor," respectively. Exceptions are made in the case of the first two basic intervals (Ch. I, Sec. 5). In the case of the octave, no distinction of modality is made within a diatonic scale.[6] Since $\overline{\text{int}}$ (1) is the generating interval, it is regarded as admitting no distinction of major and minor, and for the sake of consistency, its inversion, $\overline{\text{int}}$ (-1) (Theorem 5; Ch. II, Sec. 3), is similarly regarded. The generating interval—$\overline{\text{int}}$ (1)—is called a *perfect fifth*, and its inversion— $\overline{\text{int}}$ (-1)—is called a *perfect fourth*. The lesser fifth is said to be *diminished*, and the greater fourth is said to be *augmented*.

Table 8 gives the complete names of intervals (-6) through (6), and illustrates the pattern of modality.

In Table 9 we replace the *sol-fa* syllables introduced in this section by a seemingly arbitrary sequence of letters. It thus appears that the fundamental order of notes—the generating array, or the broken circle of fifths—is not the letters in alphabetical order, but is the sequence

---

[6] Different modalities of octaves do exist, but they are not diatonic intervals. See Ch. IV, Sec. 3.

TABLE 9

CORRESPONDENCES AMONG *sol-fa* SYLLABLES, LETTERS, AND NUMBERS

sol-fa syllables	*fa*	*do*	*sol*	*re*	*la*	*mi*	*si*
letters	F	C	G	D	A	E	B
numbers	0	1	2	3	4	5	6

F, C, G, D, A, E, B, corresponding respectively to notes 0, 1, 2, 3, 4, 5, and 6. If we call the broken circle of fifths the *first order of notes*, the scale is logically the *second order of notes*, since it may be derived from the first order by taking every other note (Sec. 2 of this chapter). The alphabetical sequence of letters is thus seen to represent the second order of notes.

If we now continue the process by taking every other note from the scale, we have

$$0, 2, 4, 6, 1, 3, 5, 0, 2, 4, 6, 1, 3, 5, 0$$

$$F, G, A, B, C, D, E, F, G, A, B, C, D, F, F$$

In this sequence of thirds, which we call the *third order of notes*, any three adjacent notes taken together form a *triad*, and triads are the fundamental units of traditional harmony, as is well known to musicians.

If we go through the process again, taking every other note from the third order:

$$0, 4, 1, 5, 2, 6, 3, 0, 4, 1, 5, 2, 6, 3, 0$$

$$F, A, C, E, G, B, D, F, A, C, E, G, B, D, F$$

we see that this *fourth order of notes* is identical to the first order, i.e., the original generating array.

The particular cyclic nature of the orders of notes is rather more special than might be thought. The first order of notes is given by the least residues in the congruence $j \equiv i \pmod 7$ where j goes from 0 through 7. The second order of notes is then the sequence of least residues where $2j \equiv i \pmod 7$, and the third order is the sequence of least residues where $4j \equiv i \pmod 7$, where j again goes from 0 through 7. The fourth order is similarly associated with the congruence $8j \equiv i \pmod 7$; but $8j = 7j + j$, and by Theorem 10, $8j \equiv i \pmod 7$ and $j \equiv i \pmod 7$ must give the same sequence of least residues. The existence of only three orders of notes from the process of evolution described is due to the coincidental fact that the number of notes (7) is one less than the third power of 2 (8). This interconnection among the generating array, the scale, and the triads is an important element in the sensation of harmonic progression and tonality.

If we write out the second order of notes on a conventional five-line staff in treble clef, arbitrarily placing note 2 on line 2, it is clear that the notation reveals at a glance the ordinal number associated with all the diatonic intervals.

sol–fa syllables	do	re	mi	fa	sol	la	si	do	re	mi	fa	sol	la	si	do
letters	C	D	E	F	G	A	B	C	D	E	F	G	A	B	C
numbers	1	3	5	0	2	4	6	1	3	5	0	2	4	6	1

Thus GB and BD, for example, are immediately seen to be thirds. However, the location of the interval on the staff does not reveal its modality. But if we substitute, according to Table 9, 2 for G, 6 for B, and 3 for D, GB is seen to be $\overline{\text{int}}$ $(6 - 2) = \overline{\text{int}}$ (4) (Theorem 6; Ch. II, Sec. 3), which is major (Table 8), and BD is $\overline{\text{int}}$ $(3 - 6) = \overline{\text{int}}$ (-3), which is minor. The logic of this system eludes most students, who simply learn by rote the modality of all possible combinations of two of the seven notes.

The reader will find it helpful at this time to review the contents of this chapter, substituting letters for numbers according to Table 9.

7. Pythagorean thirds and the syntonic comma.

We found earlier (Table 7; Sec. 5 of this chapter) that the diatonic scale generated by notes 0 through 6 contains three major thirds which are formed by notes 0 and 4, notes 1 and 5, and notes 2 and 6. If we now substitute letters according to Table 9, the major thirds are seen to be FA, CE, and GB. The ratio of $\overline{\text{int}}$ (4) was previously found to be $\frac{81}{64}$, and its size to be 407.820 cents (Table 3; Ch. II, Sec. 4). Unfortunately this is somewhat different from the third basic interval, ratio $\frac{5}{4}$, size 386.314 cents (Ch. I, Secs. 5 and 6). The difference is the not inconsiderable quantity $4\bar{v} - 2a - \bar{t} = 21.506$ cents. This interval, whose ratio is $\left(\frac{3}{2}\right)^4 \left(\frac{1}{2}\right)^2 \left(\frac{4}{5}\right) = \frac{81}{80}$ (Theorem 4; Ch. I, Sec. 5), is called a *syntonic comma*. The syntonic comma plays such an important part in the theory of temperaments and just tuning that it will be helpful to ascribe to it the letter $\bar{k}$; accordingly we frame the definition[7]

$$\bar{k} = 4\bar{v} - 2a - \bar{t}$$

We call the interval whose ratio is $\frac{5}{4}$ a *pure major third*, and the one whose ratio is $\frac{81}{64}$ a *Pythagorean major third*. The syntonic comma is small enough that the pure and Pythagorean major thirds sound like two different versions of the same interval.

Since the equation defining $\bar{k}$ may be written $4\bar{v} - 2a = \bar{t} + \bar{k}$, a Pythagorean major third may be represented as $4\bar{v} - 2a$, $\bar{t} + \bar{k}$, or $\overline{\text{int}}$ (4), whichever is more convenient.

In several respects, the addition of a syntonic comma to a pure major third results in undesirable musical consequences. Since the Pythagorean major third is nearly the size of a pure major third, it produces beats through an interaction of the fourth harmonic of the higher pitch with the fifth harmonic of the lower pitch (Ch. I, Sec. 3). If the frequency of the lower pitch is f_1, then the beat frequency is $f_1[(4)(\frac{81}{80}) - 5] = \frac{1}{16}f_1$. Thus the Pythagorean third whose lower pitch is middle C (264 Hz) produces beats at a rate of 16.5 per second. In a subjective sense, the beats impart a distinctly rough quality, which although perhaps not undersirable in any absolute sense, is definitely out of place in a context of smoother sounding perfect fifths and perfect fourths.

Pythagorean minor thirds present similar problems. If we subtract a pure major third from a pure perfect fifth, the result is $\bar{v} - \bar{t}$, ratio $(\frac{3}{2})(\frac{4}{5}) = \frac{6}{5}$, size 315.641 cents. This interval is called a *pure minor third*. Since a Pythagorean minor third is the difference between a pure perfect fifth and a Pythagorean major third, it is equal to $\bar{v} - (4\bar{v} - 2a) = 2a - 3\bar{v}$, or $\bar{v} - \bar{t} - \bar{k}$, and is thus seen to be smaller than its pure counterpart by a syntonic comma. From Table 3 (Ch. II, Sec. 4), its ratio is $\frac{32}{27}$. This interval produces beats between the sixth harmonic of the lower pitch and the fifth harmonic of the higher pitch (see Ch. I, Sec. 3). If the frequency of the lower pitch is f_2, the beat frequency is $f_2[(5)(\frac{32}{27}) - 6] = -\frac{2}{27}f_2$ (the negative sign indicates that the impure interval is smaller than the pure version), or -19.556 Hz if the lower pitch is the standard middle C.

The effect of the beats present in the Pythagorean major third is heightened if the fifth above the lower pitch is added, completing the major

---

[7] The symbol $\bar{k}$ denotes the true version of this comma; k will be used to denote its representation in various temperaments. See also Ch. I, Sec. 5.

triad. This heightened effect is due to the fact that the beats produced by the major and minor thirds reinforce each other periodically. If the lowest pitch of the triad is f_1 and the next higher pitch is f_2, we have $f_2 = \frac{81}{64}f_1$. Hence the minor third between the middle pitch and the highest pitch produces beats at $(-\frac{2}{27})(\frac{81}{64})f_1 = -\frac{3}{32}f_1$ per second. And since the beats produced by the major third are at $\frac{1}{16}f_1$ per second, the two beat frequencies are in the ratio $\frac{3}{2}$. This causes a reinforcement of every second cycle of the slower beat frequency, and every third cycle of the faster beat frequency, resulting in yet another beat whose frequency is one half of that produced by the major third, or $\frac{1}{32}f_1$. This amounts to 8.25 per second if the lowest pitch forming the triad is the standard middle C. Owing to these phenomena, Pythagorean major triads seem peculiarly discordant and unsatisfactory, and so Pythagorean tuning has generally been regarded as unsuitable for music in which major thirds and triads are treated as consonances. However, in music where major thirds are not regarded as consonances—a vast repertoire that spans the eighth through the fourteenth centuries—Pythagorean tuning is not inappropriate, and it seems likely that it was widely practiced as descibed by contemporary theorists.[8]

The problem of the Pythagorean thirds is a general one and has no ideal resolution. The difficulty is that no combination of octaves and pure perfect fifths produces a pure major third. In fact, rather more than this is true, as given in the following theorem:

THEOREM 18. *No combination of octaves and pure perfect fifths produces any other basic interval.* If otherwise, let the basic interval have the ratio $\dfrac{p}{2^n}$ (Ch. I, Sec. 5) where p is a prime greater than 3 and n is an integer. If the combination in question consists of x perfect fifths and y octaves, we must have $\left(\dfrac{3}{2}\right)^x 2^y = \dfrac{p}{2^n}$, where x and y are positive or negative integers, or zero. This last is the same as $3^x 2^{n+y-x} = p$; and if we put $z = n + y - x$ so that $3^x 2^z = p$, it is evident that whether x and z are positive, negative, or zero in any combination, the equation $3^x 2^z = p$ contradicts the assertion that p is a prime greater than 3, and this proves the theorem.

The musical difficulties associated with Pythagorean intervals can be resolved only by *temperament*, and this subject will be treated at length in Chapters VIII, IX, and X.

[8] See also Ch. VII, Sec. 1.

IV   Extended Pythagorean Tuning

Introduction.   We now extend the basic concepts of Pythagorean tuning beyond the confines of notes 0 through 6. In Section 1 we present a precise description of the conventional musical symbols ♯ and ♭, demonstrating that a flat is an inverse sharp, and Section 2 shows how to compute the frequency of any pitch in Pythagorean tuning within the octave starting at middle C, and how to determine its distance from middle C in cents. Section 3 treats extensively the names of certain chromatic intervals, and shows how to derive the name of the interval, given the names of the notes forming it. In Section 4 it is revealed that the techniques used to derive the name of a diatonic interval cannot be totally relied upon in the case of all the chromatic intervals. In Section 5 we touch upon the difference between two notes that many musicians are accustomed to regarding as the same, such as A♭ and G♯, and show that Pythagorean tuning, although generated by pure intervals, produces a variety of intervals that are out of tune. Even though Pythagorean triads are too discordant to be arranged satisfactorily into major and minor keys, the structure of keys is most conveniently explored initially within Pythagorean tuning, and this is the subject of Sections 6 and 7. In Chapter X, Sec. 2, it will be shown that these same properties hold throughout the entire family of recognizable diatonic tunings.

1. The sharp and the flat.   We now return to the concept of the totality of notes named by all the positive and negative integers and zero, where the interval between note n and note $n + 1$ is $\overline{\text{int}}$ (1)—a pure perfect fifth, ratio $\frac{3}{2}$—for all values of n (Ch. II, Sec. 3). We call this endless array of notes (Ch. I, Sec. 4) *extended Pythagorean tuning*; it may be conveniently visualized according to the diagram below, known as the *line of fifths*:

notes   ...−4 −3 −2 −1 0 1 2 3 4 5 6 7 8 9 10 ...
names ...D♭ A♭ E♭ B♭ F C G D A E B F♯ C♯ G♯ D♯...

As before, notes 0 through 6 correspond respectively to the letters F, C, G, D, A, E, and B (Ch. III, Sec. 6). However, we do not use more letters to name notes 7, 8, 9, etc., but repeat the original seven in the same order, adding the symbol ♯—*sharp*—in each case, so that note 7 is called F♯, note 8 is C♯, note 9 is G♯, and so on. When all seven letters have been used up again, we start over with F, this time adding the symbol ✗—*double sharp*—so that note 14 is F✗, note 15 is C✗, and so on. Although in practice notes beyond note 18 (A✗) are hardly ever used, such notes exist theoretically, and are logically named by a continuation of the same principle. Thus as we continue to the right on the line of fifths, we call the notes F, C, G, D, A, E, B, this sequence repeating over and over, and we add another sharp as we encounter notes 7, 14, 21, i.e., notes that are multiples of 7. It is thus apparent that note $n♯$ is note $n + 7$. Hence the interval between note n and note $n♯$ is $\overline{\text{int}}\,(n + 7 - n) = \overline{\text{int}}\,(7)$ (Theorem 6; Ch. II, Sec. 3). This is the apotome, ratio $\frac{2187}{2048}$, size 113.685 cents (Ch. III, Sec. 4).

Since the addition of a sharp effectively moves a note seven positions to the right on the line of fifths, the number 7 is associated with the sharp in much the same way that the numbers 0, 1, 2, 3, 4, 5, 6 are associated with the letters F, C, G, D, A, E, B. From this, it is an elementary matter to determine the number giving the position on the line of fifths occupied by any note whose name includes any number of sharps.

Examples: D♯ is note $3 + 7$, or note 10, and C✗ is note $1 + (2)(7)$, or note 15.

We may easily reverse the process and find the name of a note given its number, when the latter is positive. If we write the given number as $n + 7x$ where $0 \leqslant n \leqslant 6$, the name of the note is the letter associated with n, followed by x sharps.

Examples: Note 12 is note $5 + 7$, or E♯, and note 14 is note $0 + (2)(7)$, or F✗.

If we consider the notes to the left of note 0 on the line of fifths, we have a situation similar to the one just discussed. We do not use new letters for notes -1, -2, -3, etc., but repeat the original seven, this time in reverse order—B, E, A, D, G, C, F—adding the symbol ♭—*flat*—in each case, so that note -1 is B♭, note -2 is E♭, and so on.[1] As before, when all seven letters have been used up, we start over with B once more, this time adding the symbol ♭♭—*double flat*—so that note -8 is B♭♭, note -9 is E♭♭, etc. Thus note $n♭$ is always seven positions to the left of

---

[1] In German, the situation is complicated by the fact that the letter B is used for note -1, note 6 being called H. Thus German B is the same as English B♭, and German B♭ is the same as English B♭♭. German H♯ is the same as English B♯, and in German, B♯ and H♭ are not used.

note n on the line of fifths, and hence -7 is associated with the flat in exactly the same way that 7 is associated with the sharp. We may now determine the number associated with a note whose name includes any number of flats.

Examples: G♭ is note $2 - 7$, or note -5, and A♭♭ is note $4 - (2)(7)$, or note -10.

The process for finding the name of a note whose number is negative is much the same as that when the number is positive. We write the number as $n - 7y$ where $0 \leqslant n \leqslant 6$; the name is now the letter corresponding to n, followed by y flats.

Examples: Note -6 is note $1 - 7$, or C♭, and note -11 is note $3 - (2)(7)$, or D♭♭.

It is understood by musicians that whereas a sharp added to a note raises it, a flat added to a note lowers it. In other words, unless further information is provided, the interval between note n and note $n♭$ is construed as descending. It is important to bear in mind that this constitutes an exception to the interval size convention (Ch. I, Sec. 5). Accordingly, the interval between note $n♭$ and note n is ascending, and is equal to $\overline{\text{int}}\,(n - n + 7) = \overline{\text{int}}\,(7)$. Thus a flat lowers a note by the same amount that a sharp raises it, viz., by an apotome of 113.685 cents. Viewed in this light, a flat is an inverse sharp, and this relation will frequently be useful during the discussion of chromatic intervals and key signatures.

2. Frequencies of pitches in extended Pythagorean tuning. We are now able to calculate the frequencies of all pitches in extended Pythagorean tuning, given their conventional musical names. More specifically, given a fixed reference pitch, such as middle C = 264 Hz or 261.626 Hz,[2] and given the name of a particular note (G♭, C✕, etc.), we may calculate the latter's frequency in such a manner that it is higher than the reference frequency by less than one octave. We first express the interval between C and the note whose frequency is wanted as $\overline{\text{int}}\,(i)$ (Ch. II, Sec. 3), and next find the ratio of this interval (Ch. II, Sec. 2). To calculate the desired frequency, we multiply the ratio by the frequency of middle C.

Example: Given middle C to be 264 Hz, find the frequency of the A♯ next above. By the method of Section 1 of this chapter, A♯ is note 11,

---

[2] The value 261.626 Hz corresponds to middle C in 12-note equal tuning where the A next above is 440 Hz. This may be preferred in some practical situations, since the A associated with a middle C of 264 Hz in Pythagorean tuning is 445.5 Hz, which might be thought too high.

and C is note 1. Hence the interval between C and A♯ is $\overline{\text{int}}$ (10), and the ratio of $\overline{\text{int}}$ (10) is a fraction whose numerator is 3^{10} and whose denominator is the greatest power of 2 less than that number. This amounts to $\frac{59049}{32768} = 1.802032$, and so the frequency of A♯ is $(264)(1.802032) = 475.737$ Hz.

TABLE 10

PYTHAGOREAN TUNING

note	ratio with C	frequency C = 264	frequency C = 261.626	cents up from C
A✗	1.924338	508.025	503.456	1133.235
D✗	1.282892	338.684	335.637	431.280
G✗	1.710523	451.578	447.517	929.325
C✗	1.140349	301.052	298.344	227.370
F✗	1.520465	401.403	397.792	725.415
B♯	1.013643	267.602	265.195	23.460
E♯	1.351524	356.802	353.593	521.505
A♯	1.802032	475.737	471.458	1019.550
D♯	1.201355	317.158	314.305	317.595
G♯	1.601807	422.877	419.074	815.640
C♯	1.067871	281.918	279.382	113.685
F♯	1.423828	375.891	372.510	611.730
B	1.898438	501.188	496.680	1109.775
E	1.265625	334.125	331.120	407.820
A	1.687500	445.500	441.493	905.865
D	1.125000	297.000	294.329	203.910
G	1.500000	396.000	392.438	701.955
C	1.000000	264.000	261.626	0.000
F	1.333333	352.000	348.834	498.045
B♭	1.777778	469.333	465.112	996.090
E♭	1.185185	312.889	310.075	294.135
A♭	1.580247	417.185	413.433	792.180
D♭	1.053498	278.123	275.622	90.225
G♭	1.404664	370.831	367.496	588.270
C♭	1.872885	494.442	489.995	1086.315
F♭	1.248590	329.628	326.663	384.360
B♭♭	1.664787	439.504	435.551	882.405
E♭♭	1.109858	293.002	290.367	180.450
A♭♭	1.479811	390.670	387.156	678.495
D♭♭	1.973081	520.893	516.208	1176.540
G♭♭	1.315387	347.262	344.139	474.585

To find the distance up from middle C in cents, we find the size of $\overline{\text{int}}$ (i) in cents, using either the method of Chapter II, Sec. 2 or Chapter III, Sec. 1, the latter involving the least algebra. In the case just discussed, the size of $\overline{\text{int}}$ (10) is the remainder that results when (10)(701.955) is divided by 1200, or 1019.550 cents.

Table 10 gives the frequencies of all pitches in extended Pythagorean tuning from note -12 (G$\flat\flat$) through note 18 (A$\bm{\times}$) in the octave above and including middle C, based either on C = 264 Hz or C = 261.626 Hz. Also included is the distance in cents of each pitch from middle C, and the ratio (decimal equivalent) of the interval formed by middle C and the pitch in question.

3. Chromatic intervals and their names.   The words augmented, major, minor, perfect, and diminished (Ch. III, Sec. 6) suggest a concept that we call a *level of modality*. In the case of diatonic intervals other than unisons or octave multiples, we have found two levels of modality associated with each ordinal number (Ch. III, Sec. 5). In the case of the fifth, the levels are called perfect and diminished; in the case of the fourth, augmented and perfect; and for seconds, thirds, sixths, and sevenths, the levels are called major and minor. We recall that the difference between the two levels is always $\overline{\text{int}}$ (7) (Theorem 14; Ch. III, Sec. 5), and also that $\overline{\text{int}}$ (7) is the amount by which a sharp raises a note and a flat lowers a note (Sec. 1 of this chapter). Hence the addition of a sharp to the higher note, or a flat to the lower note, converts a minor interval to major, perfect fourth to an augmented fourth, or a diminished fifth to a perfect fifth.

Examples: BF is the interval between notes 6 and 0 (Table 9; Ch. III, Sec. 6), and hence is equal to $\overline{\text{int}}$ (-6) (Theorem 6; Ch. II, Sec. 3). This is a diminished fifth (Table 8; Ch. III, Sec. 6), hence B$\flat$F and BF$\sharp$ are both perfect fifths. Also, since AF is a minor sixth, A$\flat$F and AF$\sharp$ are both major sixths. This shows that diatonic intervals may occur between other notes than those named without sharps or flats.

Now if AF, AF$\sharp$, and A$\flat$F are all called sixths, then it seems logical to call an interval such as A$\flat$F$\sharp$ a sixth as well. The principle is generalized as follows: the addition of any number of sharps or flats to either note forming an interval changes the interval's modality, but does not affect the ordinal number. Hence the difference between any two intervals named by the same ordinal number, but differing in modality, is always a multiple of $\overline{\text{int}}$ (7). Therefore the statement that $\overline{\text{int}}$ (i) is a ($j + 1$)th where $4i \equiv j \pmod{7}$ and $0 \leqslant j \leqslant 6$ (Ch. III, Sec. 3) holds for other values of i

than $-6 \leqslant i \leqslant 6$, since the addition of any multiple of 7 to the number i gives the same residue as before (Theorem 10; Ch. III, Sec. 1), i.e., does not change the ordinal number.[3]

Example: A♭ is note -3 and F♯ is note 7, using the method of Section 1 of this chapter, hence A♭F♯ is $\overline{\text{int}}$ (10) (Theorem 6; Ch. II, Sec. 3). Thus $\overline{\text{int}}$ (10) is a $(j + 1)$th where $40 \equiv j \pmod 7$ and j is the least residue. We now use the method of Chapter III, Sec. 1 to calculate j: when 40 is divided by 7, the remainder is 5, and so $\overline{\text{int}}$ (10) is a $(5 + 1)$th—a sixth—and this is consistent with the principle that was outlined previously in this section.

Clearly under the most general theoretical conditions, the number of levels of modality is without limit; but this does not correspond to practice throughout music history.

The naming of intervals for which i is a multiple of 7 is outside the general scheme, probably owing in part to the literal contradiction inherent in the words "diminished unison" and "augmented unison." Although *apotome* is the classical term for $\overline{\text{int}}$ (7), it is not used by musicians in practical situations. The conventional term is *chromatic semitone*, and this is somewhat unfortunate, for it implies a relation between this interval and certain others that may or may not hold.[4]

The next level of modality larger than major is called *augmented*; and as i increases, we find five intervals beginning with $\overline{\text{int}}$ (6)—an augmented fourth (Ch. III, Sec. 6)—and ending with $\overline{\text{int}}$ (11), but excluding $\overline{\text{int}}$ (7), for which the ordinal number $(j + 1)$th is again given by the congruence $4i \equiv j \pmod 7$ where $0 \leqslant j \leqslant 6$, as shown in Table 11. There is a special situation regarding the name of $\overline{\text{int}}$ (12), and this will be taken up in the next section.

The next larger level of modality is called *doubly augmented*, but in practice, intervals beyond $\overline{\text{int}}$ (13)—a doubly augmented fourth—hardly ever occur.

The next level of modality smaller than minor is called *diminished*, and applies to intervals (-6) through (-11), but not (-7); and once again, the ordinal number is one greater than j where $4i \equiv j \pmod 7$ and $0 \leqslant j \leqslant 6$. In the case of $\overline{\text{int}}$ (-7), the conventional name is *diminished octave* (rather than diminished unison), but the congruence does not give

---

[3] It must not be assumed that the principle is valid for all values of i; an exception will be analyzed in Sec. 4 of this chapter.

[4] The term *semitone* is strictly applicable only to 12-note equal tuning, where both the chromatic semitone and minor second are exactly one half of a major second. See Ch. XI, Sec. 6.

TABLE 11

NAMES OF INTERVALS (8) THROUGH (11)

$4i \equiv j$ (mod 7)	interval (i)	modality	ordinal number
$0 \leqslant j \leqslant 6$	$\overline{\text{int}}$ (11)	augmented	third, $j = 2$
	$\overline{\text{int}}$ (10)	augmented	sixth, $j = 5$
	$\overline{\text{int}}$ (9)	augmented	second, $j = 1$
	$\overline{\text{int}}$ (8)	augmented	fifth, $j = 4$

the correct ordinal number, since the residue is zero. It should also be noted that the interval that exceeds an octave by $\overline{\text{int}}$ (7) is called an *augmented octave*; but in practice, augmented and diminished octaves seldom occur and trained musicians find both terms slightly disturbing. The names of intervals (-8) through (-11) are collected in Table 12. As before, $\overline{\text{int}}$ (-12) requires a separate discussion, and will be dealt with in the next section.

The next smaller level of modality is called *doubly diminished*; but again in practice, intervals beyond $\overline{\text{int}}$ (-13)—a doubly diminished fifth— hardly ever occur.

It is useful to collect together the ranges for i corresponding to the various levels of modality:

LEVEL OF MODALITY	INTERVALS
doubly augmented	(13)
augmented	(6), (8), (9), (10), (11)
major	(2), (3), (4), (5)
perfect	(-1), (1)
minor	(-2), (-3), (-4), (-5)
diminished	(-6), (-8), (-9), (-10), (-11)
doubly diminished	(-13)

TABLE 12

NAMES OF INTERVALS (-8) THROUGH (-11)

$4i \equiv j$ (mod 7)	interval (i)	modality	ordinal number
$0 \leqslant j \leqslant 6$	$\overline{\text{int}}$ (-8)	diminished	fourth, $j = 3$
	$\overline{\text{int}}$ (-9)	diminished	seventh, $j = 6$
	$\overline{\text{int}}$ (-10)	diminished	third, $j = 2$
	$\overline{\text{int}}$ (-11)	diminished	sixth, $j = 5$

All intervals for which i lies outside the range $-6 \leqslant i \leqslant 6$, i.e., that are not diatonic, are called *chromatic*.

We may use the principles developed in this section, along with Theorems 6 and 7 (Ch. II, Sec. 3) and Tables 8 and 9 (Ch. III, Sec. 6), to provide methodical answers to a variety of questions that arise in practical musical situations.

Example: Find the name of the interval between C♯ and B♭. Since C♯ is note $1 + 7 = 8$ and B♭ is note $6 - 7 = -1$, C♯B♭ is $\overline{\text{int}}\,(-1 - 8) = \overline{\text{int}}\,(-9)$, a diminished seventh.

Example: What note is a diminished third above G♯? Since G♯ is note $2 + 7 =$ note 9, the answer will be the conventional name of note $9 + i$ where $\overline{\text{int}}\,(i)$ is a diminished third. A diminished third is $\overline{\text{int}}\,(-10)$, and so the note wanted is note $9 - 10 =$ note -1, and this is note $6 - 7$, or B♭.

We conclude this section by giving in Table 13 the ratios, sizes in cents, and expressions in terms of a and $\bar{v}$ for the Pythagorean chromatic intervals where $7 \leqslant i \leqslant 15$ and $-15 \leqslant i \leqslant -7$. This combined with Table 3

TABLE 13

PYTHAGOREAN CHROMATIC INTERVALS

interval	in terms of a and $\bar{v}$	ratio (fraction)	ratio (decimal)	size in cents	
$\overline{\text{int}}\,(15)$	$15\bar{v} - 8a$	$\frac{14348907}{8388608}$	1.710523	929.325	
$\overline{\text{int}}\,(14)$	$14\bar{v} - 8a$	$\frac{4782969}{4194304}$	1.140349	227.370	
$\overline{\text{int}}\,(13)$	$13\bar{v} - 7a$	$\frac{1594323}{1048576}$	1.520465	725.415	
$\overline{\text{int}}\,(12)$	$12\bar{v} - 7a$	$\frac{531441}{524288}$	1.013643	23.460	comma
$\overline{\text{int}}\,(11)$	$11\bar{v} - 6a$	$\frac{177147}{131072}$	1.351524	521.505	
$\overline{\text{int}}\,(10)$	$10\bar{v} - 5a$	$\frac{59049}{32768}$	1.802032	1019.550	
$\overline{\text{int}}\,(9)$	$9\bar{v} - 5a$	$\frac{19683}{16384}$	1.201355	317.595	
$\overline{\text{int}}\,(8)$	$8\bar{v} - 4a$	$\frac{6561}{4096}$	1.601807	815.640	
$\overline{\text{int}}\,(7)$	$7\bar{v} - 4a$	$\frac{2187}{2048}$	1.067871	113.685	apotome
$\overline{\text{int}}\,(-7)$	$5a - 7\bar{v}$	$\frac{4096}{2187}$	1.872885	1086.315	
$\overline{\text{int}}\,(-8)$	$5a - 8\bar{v}$	$\frac{8192}{6561}$	1.248590	384.360	
$\overline{\text{int}}\,(-9)$	$6a - 9\bar{v}$	$\frac{32768}{19683}$	1.664787	882.405	
$\overline{\text{int}}\,(-10)$	$6a - 10\bar{v}$	$\frac{65536}{59049}$	1.109858	180.450	
$\overline{\text{int}}\,(-11)$	$7a - 11\bar{v}$	$\frac{262144}{177147}$	1.479811	678.495	
$\overline{\text{int}}\,(-12)$	$8a - 12\bar{v}$	$\frac{1048576}{531441}$	1.973081	1176.540	
$\overline{\text{int}}\,(-13)$	$8a - 13\bar{v}$	$\frac{2097152}{1594323}$	1.315387	474.585	
$\overline{\text{int}}\,(-14)$	$9a - 14\bar{v}$	$\frac{8388608}{4782969}$	1.753850	972.630	
$\overline{\text{int}}\,(-15)$	$9a - 15\bar{v}$	$\frac{16777216}{14348907}$	1.169233	270.675	

(Ch. II, Sec. 4) gives pertinent data for all the Pythagorean intervals for which $-15 \leqslant i \leqslant 15$. The reader will find it a useful exercise to verify the results using the methods of Chapter II, Sec. 2 and Chapter III, Sec. 1.

4. Exceptions to the interval size convention. ·The naming of $\overline{\text{int}}(i)$ by the principles of the previous section results in certain cases that are at variance with the interval size convention (Ch. I, Sec. 5). Consider, for example, $\overline{\text{int}}$ (12); since 48 divided by 7 gives a remainder of 6, this interval would be called a seventh. But if we find its size in cents using the method of Chapter III, Sec. 1, which applies the convention, we have $(12)(701.955) = 8423.460$, and when this is divided by 12, the remainder is 23.460, which is the size in cents. This amount—considerably smaller than a minor second—obviously does not correspond to a seventh. If we add $\overline{\text{int}}$ (7)—an apotome—to $\overline{\text{int}}$ (5)—a major seventh—the sum would logically be called an augmented seventh, containing $1109.775 + 113.685 = 1223.460$ cents. An augmented seventh is thus seen to be greater than an octave. Since such an interval clearly exists and is logically named, it is an example of an exception to the interval size convention.

It is also important to observe that the five-line staff notation of this interval is misleading. For example, the note an augmented seventh above $A\flat$, or note -3, is note $-3 + 12$, or note 9, which is $G\sharp$. But if we write this interval on the staff next to an octave, we are given a singu-

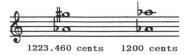

1223.460 cents   1200 cents

larly mistaken impression regarding the relative sizes of the two intervals, as the octave appears larger. In the following case, the notation is equally

misleading, for actually $G\sharp$ is higher than $A\flat$ by 23.460 cents. According to the general plan for naming intervals, $G\sharp A\flat$, which is $\overline{\text{int}}$ (-12), would be called a diminished second; and hence $A\flat G\sharp$, as written on the staff above, would be called a descending diminished second, which is absurd. As the reader is almost certainly aware, many trained musicians are accustomed to regarding A♭ and G♯ as the same note; but this is a predisposition arising from the habit of thinking in terms of 12-note equal tuning.

Repeated augmentation of any interval will ultimately bring about a situation similar to that associated with $\overline{\text{int}}$ (12), since each successive augmentation adds another apotome of 113.685 cents, and this sum must eventually exceed one octave. For example, a triply augmented sixth is greater than a major sixth of 905.865 cents by three apotomes, and $905.865 + (3)(113.685) = 1246.920$ cents, again greater than one octave. This shows that the interval size convention, although helpful in revealing the interconnections among diatonic intervals, cannot be expected to produce similar insights in the case of the chromatic intervals.

5. The Pythagorean comma. Since a Pythagorean augmented seventh is greater than an octave, a special name is needed for the interval that is less than an augmented seventh by one octave. This interval is properly represented by $\overline{\text{int}}$ (12), which effectively applies the interval size convention, discarding the octave. By the method of Chapter II, Sec. 2, the ratio of $\overline{\text{int}}$ (12) is $\dfrac{3^{12}}{2^{19}} = \dfrac{531441}{524288}$, its full expression in terms of a and $\bar{v}$ is $12\bar{v} - 7a$ (using Ch. I, Sec. 7), and it contains 23.460 cents. This interval, called a *Pythagorean comma*, arises so frequently in the discussion of just tuning and temperaments that we assign to it the letter $\bar{p}$; accordingly we have[5]

$$\bar{p} = 12\bar{v} - 7a$$

Recalling that $\overline{\text{int}}$ (1) contains 701.955 cents (Table 3; Ch. II, Sec. 4, also Ch. I, Sec. 6), we have $\overline{\text{int}}$ (1) $> \overline{\text{int}}$ (12), and hence $\overline{\text{int}}$ (1) $- \overline{\text{int}}$ (12) $= \overline{\text{int}}$ (−11) (Ch. II, Sec. 3). Since $\overline{\text{int}}$ (−11) is a diminished sixth (Table 12; Sec. 3 of this chapter), this last equation shows that a diminished sixth is less than a perfect fifth by a Pythagorean comma, and hence is equal to $\bar{v} - \bar{p}$. Like the syntonic comma (Ch. III, Sec. 7), the Pythagorean comma is sufficiently small that $\bar{v}$ and $\bar{v} - \bar{p}$ sound like two different versions of the same interval. But $\bar{v} - \bar{p}$ is discordant—so much so that it sounds badly out of place in a context where pure perfect fifths are the standard. The ratio of this interval is $\frac{262144}{177147} = 1.479811$ (Table 13; Sec. 3 of this chapter),

---

[5] The symbol $\bar{p}$ denotes the true version of this comma; p will be used to denote its representation in various temperaments. See also Ch. I, Sec. 5.

and it produces beats between the third harmonic of its lower pitch and the second harmonic of its higher pitch; and if the lower pitch is the standard middle C of 264 Hz, the beat frequency is $264[(2)(1.479811) - 3] = -10.660$ per second (Ch. I, Sec. 3).

Since $\overline{\text{int}}\,(-11)$ sounds like a discordant perfect fifth, the equation $11\,\overline{\text{int}}\,(1) + \overline{\text{int}}\,(-11) = \text{int}\,(0)$ depicts a broken circle of fifths that has much in common with the one that generates the diatonic scale (Ch. III, Sec. 4). This broken circle of fifths plays an important part in the description of chromatic scales, which will be treated during the discussion of meantone tuning (Ch. IX, Sec. 3).

We are now in a position to provide at least a partial answer to the question so puzzling to musical beginners, concerning the apparent anomaly of there being two names, such as A♭ and G♯, for the same note. All musicians are aware that this is due to temperament, and it is widely believed that temperament is an unavoidable evil made necessary by the practical requirements of keyboard instruments. But as we shall see (Ch. V, Secs. 3 and 4; Ch. VI, Secs. 2, 3, and 4; Ch. VIII, Sec. 1; Ch. IX, Sec. 2; Ch. X, Sec. 6; Ch. XI, Sec. 8; Ch. XII, Sec. 2), this is only one of several considerations that bear upon the subject. The question naturally arises, if A♭ and G♯ are the same in the tempered scale, but not in an untempered or "true" scale, in what way do they actually differ? As far as Pythagorean tuning is concerned, the answer is that G♯ is higher than A♭ by a Pythagorean comma of 23.460 cents; and more generally, this interval separates any two notes whose numbers differ by 12, the note having the greater number being the higher. However, there is really no very good reason to regard Pythagorean tuning as being "true," even though its generating interval is pure; for not only are diminished sixths discordant, but the same is true of major thirds (Ch. III, Sec. 7).

At this point, it must occur to the reader that a slight decrease in the size of each perfect fifth in the broken circle of twelve fifths will enlarge the diminished sixth and reduce the major thirds, thereby making these intervals less discordant. This concept will be a useful aid subsequently to the understanding of certain aspects of temperaments.

6. Major keys, minor keys, and their signatures. The broken circle of fifths (six perfect and one diminished) that generates a diatonic scale may be treated in such a manner as to establish either of two *keys*, one major and one minor, and each is said to be the *relative* of the other. The structural pattern underlying these two keys may be best explored initially

TABLE 14

	major triads					
	sub-dom.	tonic	dom.			
roots	F	C	G	D	A	E	B
				sub-dom.	tonic	dom.
				minor triads		

within the confines of notes 0 through 6, and it will be convenient to refer once again to the concept of the first, second, and third order of notes, as described in Chapter III, Sec. 6.

Each triad formed by three adjacent notes on the third order of notes is said to be in *root position*, the lowest note in each case being the root. In conventional musical terminology, the triads whose outer two notes form a perfect fifth are called major or minor, depending on the modality of the third formed by the root and the note next above. The triad whose outer two notes form a diminished fifth is said to be *diminished*.

If we write out the third order of notes, continuing it into the next octave, and examine the modality of the adjacent intervals (M for major and m for minor)[6]

names	F	A	C	E	G	B	D	F	A...
numbers	0	4	1	5	2	6	3	0	4...
modality	M	m	M	m	M	m	m	M	

it is evident that the triads whose roots are notes 0, 1, and 2 (F, C, and G) are major, and those whose roots are notes 3, 4, and 5 (D, A, and E) are minor. The distinction between a major key and its relative minor key lies in which group is treated as the *primary triads*. In either case, the central primary triad—referring to the location of its root on the first order of notes—is the *tonic*; the triad next left is the *subdominant*, and the one next right is the *dominant*. Table 14 is a convenient visualization. It is customary to call the major or minor key by the same name as the root of the tonic triad. Thus notes 0 through 6 may establish the key of either C major, or its relative minor, A minor. We take up first the question of major keys.

---

[6] See Table 7 (Ch. III, Sec. 5), recalling that a major third is $\overline{\text{int}}$ (4), and a minor third is $\overline{\text{int}}$ (−3).

TABLE 15

notes	C	D	E	F	G	A	B
degrees	I	II	III	IV	V	VI	VII
triad modality	major	minor	minor	major	major	minor	diminished

It is customary to number the notes of the major scale (the second order of notes) in ascending order, using Roman numerals and counting the tonic note as I; the notes so numbered are called *degrees*. The modality of the triads on the seven degrees is shown in Table 15. Observe that the arrangement of Table 14 reveals a symmetric pattern of modality which is not evident in Table 15. Beginning harmony students are often puzzled by the apparently haphazard arrangement of major, minor, and diminished triads on the seven degrees.

From the definition of diatonic scale (Ch. II, Sec. 1), it follows that a major key may be established by any group of seven adjacent notes on the line of fifths, and, as in the key of C major, the note next to the left in each case is the tonic, and the name of the key.

Example: The notes 4, 5, 6, 7, 8, 9, 10 establish the key of 5 major, or E major. And by Section 1 of this chapter, the notes are named as follows:

numbers	4	5	6	$0 + 7$	$1 + 7$	$2 + 7$	$3 + 7$
names	A	E	B	F♯	C♯	G♯	D♯

The E major scale may be derived from this broken circle by starting at the tonic E and taking every other note from the circle to give the sequence 5, 7, 9, 4, 6, 8, 10, 5, corresponding to E, F♯, G♯, A, B, C♯, D♯, E.

It is convenient to represent the family of major keys produced by extended Pythagorean tuning by the following:

$$0 + n \quad 1 + n \quad 2 + n \quad 3 + n \quad 4 + n \quad 5 + n \quad 6 + n$$

where $1 + n$ is the tonic note, and n is any integer. The major scale is the sequence that results from starting at note $1 + n$ and taking every other note from the above:

notes	$1 + n$	$3 + n$	$5 + n$	$0 + n$	$2 + n$	$4 + n$	$6 + n$	$1 + n$
degrees	I	II	III	IV	V	VI	VII	I
adjacent intervals	(2)	(2)	(−5)	(2)	(2)	(2)	(−5)	

As in the case of C major, the adjacent intervals make the sequence (2), (2), (−5), (2), (2), (2), (−5). Hence if this sequence of numbers is added, one after the other, to the number of any given tonic note, the result will be the corresponding major scale.

Example: Write out the scale of B♭ major. Since B♭ is note $6 - 7 =$ note -1, the scale is as follows: -1, 1, 3, -2, 0, 2, 4, -1. Using the method of Section 1 of this chapter, we find the conventional names:

numbers	$6 - 7$	1	3	$5 - 7$	0	2	4	$6 - 7$
names	B♭	C	D	E♭	F	G	A	B♭

Since the relation between the scale and the generating array is the same in all major keys, it follows that the distribution of the two different modalities of intervals associated with each ordinal number must be identical in every major key, irrespective of what the tonic actually is. The reader should now review Chapter III, Sec. 5.

Clearly all major scales, with the exception of C major, involve one or more sharps or flats, and no major scale contains both sharps and flats. In any major key, the sharps or flats, along with the notes they affect, are referred to as the *key signature*, and we now determine the relation between the key signature and the tonic note.

THEOREM 19.   *The key signature for x major is x − 1, meaning* $|x - 1|$ *sharps when x − 1 is positive, and* $|x - 1|$ *flats when x − 1 is negative,*[7] *sharps being written in the order F♯, C♯, G♯, D♯, A♯, E♯, B♯, and flats B♭, E♭, A♭, D♭, G♭, C♭, F♭, however many there are.* Since the key signature for C major is no sharps or flats, it is convenient to use that key as a reference point. If we move the tonic note one place to the right on the line of fifths, we establish the key of G major; this key has six notes in common with C major, and replaces F by F♯ as shown below:

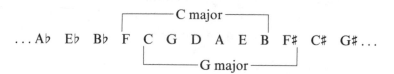

Hence the key signature for G major is one sharp, F♯. And if the process is repeated, the next key encountered will be D major, replacing C by C♯, and having two sharps in its signature, F♯ and C♯. Generally, if we write

---

[7] See Ch. II, note 1.

out the notes for $1 + n$ major and $2 + n$ major

$1 + n$ major	$0 + n$	$1 + n$	$2 + n$	$3 + n$	$4 + n$	$5 + n$	$6 + n$	
$2 + n$ major		$1 + n$	$2 + n$	$3 + n$	$4 + n$	$5 + n$	$6 + n$	$7 + n$

we find that the two keys have six notes in common, and that the notes of $2 + n$ major differ from $1 + n$ major only in that note $0 + n$ is replaced by note $7 + n$, i.e., note n is replaced by note $n\sharp$ (Sec. 1 of this chapter). In other words, each time the tonic note is moved one place to the right on the line of fifths, a new sharp appears in the signature, and the sharps are added in the order F$\sharp$, C$\sharp$, G$\sharp$, D$\sharp$, A$\sharp$, E$\sharp$, B$\sharp$. Hence the number of sharps in the signature of a particular major key is equal to the number of places to the right of C on the line of fifths occupied by its tonic. If the tonic is note x, this last is i where $\overline{\text{int}}\,(i)$ is the interval between C and note x, i being positive; and since C is note 1, we have $i = x - 1$ (Theorem 6; Ch. II, Sec. 3).

Clearly any major key whose tonic lies to the left of C on the line of fifths has a signature involving flats. By a line of reasoning similar to the above, each time the tonic note moves one place to the left of C, another flat appears in the signature, the flats being added in the order B$\flat$, E$\flat$, A$\flat$, D$\flat$, G$\flat$, C$\flat$, F$\flat$, i.e., the sharp sequence reversed. Hence the number of flats in the signature of a particular major key is equal to the number of places to the left of C on the line of fifths occupied by its tonic. If the tonic is note x, this will be i where $\overline{\text{int}}\,(i)$ is the interval between C and note x, and once again $i = x - 1$; but in this case, $x - 1$ is negative. The theorem is easily remembered if we recall that a flat is an inverse sharp (Sec. 1 of this chapter).

Example: What is the key signature for B major? Since B is note 6, there are $6 - 1 = 5$ sharps, viz., F$\sharp$, C$\sharp$, G$\sharp$, D$\sharp$, A$\sharp$, written in that order.

Example: What is the key signature for E$\flat$ major? Since E$\flat$ is note $5 - 7 = -2$, $x - 1 = -3$. The negative sign denotes flats, so there are three flats, viz., B$\flat$, E$\flat$, A$\flat$, written in that order.

It is an elementary matter to develop a similar theorem for minor keys.

THEOREM 20.   *The key signature for x minor is $x - 4$, meaning $|x - 4|$ sharps when $x - 4$ is positive, and $|x - 4|$ flats when $x - 4$ is negative.* We saw earlier that the tonic of the minor key relative to C major is A, three places to the right of C on the line of fifths (Table 14). This admits of the same generalization as that applied to major keys, and so the minor key relative to x major is $x + 3$ minor for all cases. Hence the signature for

x minor is $x - 1 - 3 = x - 4$, to be understood in the same sense as $x - 1$ in Theorem 19.

An additional accidental often occurs in minor keys. The third of the dominant triad—the seventh degree—is frequently raised by a chromatic semitone to convert the dominant harmony from minor to major, which has the effect of canceling a flat, or adding a sharp for the seventh degree. A scale that incorporates this alteration is called a *harmonic minor*. Strictly speaking, a harmonic minor is not a diatonic scale, for the interval between the sixth and seventh degree is $\overline{\text{int}}\ (2 + 7) = \overline{\text{int}}\ (9)$, an augmented second—one of the chromatic intervals.

We may now derive a rule, familiar to trained musicians, establishing the order of letters naming the notes in any major or minor scale.

THEOREM 21. *The notes of any scale are the first seven letters, starting with the tonic, proceeding in alphabetical order with A following G, and with sharps or flats added according to principles just demonstrated.* We first observe that the notes of the C major or A minor scales are the first seven letters, beginning with C or A and proceeding in alphabetical order, with A following G in the case of C major. Since moving the tonic one place to the right on the line of fifths has the effect of replacing note n with note $n + 7$, the order of letters in any two scales whose tonics are so related must be the same, since the same letter names both note n and note $n + 7$ (Sec. 1 of this chapter). For the same reason, the alteration of the seventh degree associated with the harmonic minor has no effect on the sequence of letters. Hence all scales are represented by the same sequence of letters as C major, save for the starting point and the distribution of sharps or flats.

It is a useful exercise to use Theorems 18–20 to derive scales obtained earlier in this section.

Example: Write out the scale of E major. The sequence of letters will be E, F, G, A, B, C, D, E. Since E is note 5, the signature is $5 - 1 = 4$, meaning 4 sharps since 4 is positive, and the sharps are F♯, C♯, G♯, and D♯. Hence the final result is E, F♯, G♯, A, B, C♯, D♯, E.

Example: Write out the scale of B♭ major. The sequence of letters will be B, C, D, E, F, G, A, B. Since B♭ is note $6 - 7 =$ note -1, the signature is $-1 - 1 = -2$, or two flats since the sum is negative. The first two flats are B♭ and E♭, hence the answer is B♭, C, D, E♭, F, G, A, B♭.

In the case of harmonic minors, the procedure is virtually the same, with the additional alteration of the seventh degree up by a chromatic semitone.

Example: Write out the scale of B♭ harmonic minor. The sequence of letters is the same as B♭ major in the previous example, and the signature is $-1 - 4 = -5$, or five flats, viz., B♭, E♭, A♭, D♭, G♭. In addition, the seventh degree must be raised from A♭ to A, and so the final result is B♭, C, D♭, E♭, F, G♭, A, B♭.

Example: Write out the scale of G♯ harmonic minor. The signature consists of $2 + 7 - 4 = 5$ sharps, viz., F♯, C♯, G♯, D♯, A♯. In addition, the seventh degree must be raised from F♯, to F×, and so the answer is G♯, A♯, B, C♯, D♯, E, F×, G♯.

7. Key signatures and transposition.   In the following discussion, "having a signature of x" means $|x|$ sharps in the case of a positive x, and $|x|$ flats in the case of a negative x.[8]

THEOREM 22.   *When a composition having a signature of x is transposed up or down by* $\overline{\mathrm{int}}$ (i), *the new signature is* $x + i$ *if the transposition is up, or* $x - i$ *if the transposition is down.* Let the original key be $x + 1$ major, this key having a signature of x (Theorem 19), so that the new tonic is note $x + 1 + i$ (Theorem 7; Ch. II, Sec. 3); this key has a signature of $x + i$. If the interval of transposition is down, it is properly represented by $-\overline{\mathrm{int}}$ (i), or by $\overline{\mathrm{int}}$ $(-i) + \mathrm{int}$ (0). In this case, we may disregard int (0), since octave transposition does not affect the key signature. Hence the new tonic is now note $x + 1 - i$, and the new signature is $x - i$. The discussion is unchanged if some other note is treated as a tonic, or if there is no tonic at all. In either case, the note we have referred to as the tonic may be regarded as an arbitrary reference point, and hence the relation between the interval of transposition and the change in key signature is unaffected by whatever harmonic or modal treatment may be in effect.

It is helpful to observe that a positive i adds sharps or subtracts flats, and a negative i adds flats or subtracts sharps. This is easily remembered if we bear in mind that a flat is an inverse sharp (Sec. 1 of this chapter).

When the interval of transposition is expressed in conventional musical terminology (modality and ordinal number), it is first necessary to find i from Table 8 (Ch. III, Sec. 6), Table 11, or Table 12 (both Sec. 3 of this chapter), or to use the mathematical procedures by which the tables were constructed.

Example: When a composition having two sharps in its signature is played a minor third higher, what is the new signature? The new signature

[8] See Ch. II, note 1.

will be $2 + i$ where $\overline{\text{int}}$ (i) is a minor third. From Table 8, $i = -3$, and so the signature is $2 - 3 = -1$, or one flat (B♭).

Example: When a composition having four flats in its signature is transposed down a minor second, what is the new signature? Since a minor second is $\overline{\text{int}}$ (-5), the new signature will be $-4 - (-5) = -4 + 5 = 1$, or one sharp (F♯).

Although keys involving more than seven sharps or flats occur infrequently, they clearly exist according to our definition, and are more likely to arise in situations involving transposition or transposing instruments. For example, if a composition having six sharps in its signature is transposed up a major second—by $\overline{\text{int}}$ (2)—the new signature is eight sharps, meaning a double sharp for F, and sharps for C, G, D, A, E, and B. Such situations occur often enough that a practicing musician should feel reasonably secure in all major keys from B♭♭ (nine flats) to D♯ (nine sharps), and their relative minors (G♭ to B♯, respectively).

V   The Diatonic Major Scale
in Just Tuning

Introduction.   Just tuning of the major scale results from an attempt to remove the impurity of the major and minor thirds and sixths produced by Pythagorean tuning (Ch. III, Sec. 7). As in the discussion of Pythagorean tuning, we develop the theory for one diatonic system—C major—and then extend the tuning to include other keys. In Section 1 we extend the conventional nomenclature of notes so as to reveal at a glance differences between pure and Pythagorean intervals. In Section 2 it is shown that pure tuning of the primary triads of C major does not give a tuning in which all the thirds and perfect fifths are pure. In particular, minor third DF is Pythagorean; fifth DA is smaller than pure by a syntonic comma, and in consequence is unacceptably discordant. In Section 3 we show that the addition of a second D, lower than the D already present by a syntonic comma, makes possible the pure tuning of all six major and minor triads of C major. In Section 4 it is demonstrated that in fact there exists no tuning of the seven notes of C major that furnishes pure intervals exclusively. Furthermore, certain elementary progressions of four pure triads require that the two different D's should occur successively in the same part, resulting in an unmusical melodic discontinuity. Examples of such basic progressions are IV-II-V-I, VI-II-V-I, and III-VI-II-V. The reader should study carefully the different just tunings of Tables 23 and 24, along with Theorems 23 and 24, in order to understand why it is impossible to find a just tuning of the progressions cited above within the confines of only seven different notes. In the author's experience, most musicians are quite surprised to learn that no entirely satisfactory just tuning exists for certain elementary diatonic progressions of triads.

In Section 5 we show that the smoothest tuning for a dominant seventh chord requires the addition of another F to the scale, and that this F seems flat in all contexts, melodic and harmonic. In addition, the two F's must occur in succession in the common progressions II^7-V^7 and IV-V^7, resulting in yet another unmusical discontinuity. In Section 6 we find the best tunings for the secondary seventh chords, and show that these harmonies have no entirely satisfactory just tuning. It is also demonstrated that certain diatonic combinations of chord and non-chord notes, e.g., a dominant seventh with a suspended third, have no beat-free tuning.

1. Pure tuning of the primary triads. A major triad is said to be in *pure tuning* when the three pitches forming it are in the ratio 4:5:6. Under these conditions, the triad is composed entirely of pure intervals (Ch. I, Sec. 2)—the perfect fifth, major third, and minor third are in ratios $\frac{3}{2}$, $\frac{5}{4}$, and $\frac{6}{5}$, respectively. This nulls the beats produced by low-order harmonics, and causes difference-tones to converge upon a pitch two octaves lower than the root of the triad,[1] producing the most euphonious possible tuning for a major triad—very substantially different from the peculiar discordance of a Pythagorean triad (Ch. III, Sec. 7).

In the case of a Pythagorean major triad, the interval formed by the root and the third is equal to $\bar{t} + \bar{k}$, and the interval formed by the third and the fifth is $\bar{v} - \bar{t} - \bar{k}$. Now if the third is lowered by a syntonic comma, the interval between the root and third becomes $\bar{t}$, a pure major third, and that between the third and fifth becomes $\bar{v} - \bar{t}$, a pure minor third (Ch. III, Sec. 7), and this puts the triad in pure tuning.

Just tuning of a major key is traditionally defined as that which puts the three primary triads (Ch. IV, Sec. 6) in pure tuning. Hence just tuning of C major may be achieved by starting with Pythagorean tuning of notes F, C, G, D, A, E, and B, and then lowering A, E, and B each by a syntonic comma. This has the effect of including the third basic interval, along with the first and second, as a generating unit of the scale (Ch. I, Sec. 5). For this reason, the description of the relations between notes and intervals in just tuning is rather more complex than in Pythagorean tuning. It will be most convenient to express the just intervals as $\overline{\text{int}}\ (i)$, $\overline{\text{int}}\ (i) + \bar{k}$, or $\overline{\text{int}}\ (i) - \bar{k}$, where $-6 \leqslant i \leqslant 6$.

As regards the letters naming notes, we use F, C, G, D, A, E, B, corresponding to numbers 0, 1, 2, 3, 4, 5, 6, respectively, as in Pythagorean tuning. In addition, we use subscripts to indicate the number of syntonic commas by which a note in just tuning differs from its Pythagorean counterpart—if the just note is the lower, the subscript is negative; if the just note is the higher, the subscript is positive; a zero subscript indicates that

---

[1] At the present writing, the author is unable to find a complete explanation of this phenomenon. See Alexander Wood, *The Physics of Music*, (6th ed.; London: Methuen, 1961), 165–170.

a note is the same in just tuning and the Pythagorean reference tuning. With this modification, a C major Pythagorean scale is written

$$C_0 \quad D_0 \quad E_0 \quad F_0 \quad G_0 \quad A_0 \quad B_0 \quad C_0$$

The proposed just scale replaces A_0, E_0, and B_0 by notes lower than these by a syntonic comma, the new notes being A_{-1}, E_{-1}, and B_{-1}, so that the just scale is written

$$C_0 \quad D_0 \quad E_{-1} \quad F_0 \quad G_0 \quad A_{-1} \quad B_{-1} \quad C_0$$

We shall soon find the need for other subscripts as well.

With this notation at our disposal, the determination of the exact sizes and ratios of all the diatonic just intervals presents no special difficulty.

2. The diatonic intervals in just tuning. We begin by determining the ratios and sizes in cents of the major and minor seconds. If we write out the just scale

$$C_0 \quad D_0 \quad E_{-1} \quad F_0 \quad G_0 \quad A_{-1} \quad B_{-1} \quad C_0$$

it is immediately apparent that seconds $C_0 D_0$ and $F_0 G_0$ are the same as their Pythagorean counterparts, and are equal to $\overline{\text{int}}\ (2)$ (Ch. IV, Sec. 6), ratio $\frac{9}{8}$, size 203.910 cents (Table 3; Ch. II, Sec. 4). This interval also occurs between A_{-1} and B_{-1}, since both these notes are lower than their Pythagorean counterparts by the same amount.

With respect to seconds $D_0 E_{-1}$ and $G_0 A_{-1}$, we find a difference; since the higher note in each case is lower than the same note in Pythagorean tuning by $\bar{k}$, these intervals are less than a Pythagorean major second by that amount, and are thus equal to $\overline{\text{int}}\ (2) - \bar{k}$. Further information about this interval is obtained by finding its complete expression in terms of the first three basic intervals, a, $\bar{v}$, and $\bar{t}$. From Table 3 (Ch. II, Sec. 4), $\overline{\text{int}}\ (2) = 2\bar{v} - a$, and $\bar{k}$ is defined as $4\bar{v} - 2a - \bar{t}$ (Ch. III, Sec. 7). Hence

$$\overline{\text{int}}\ (2) - \bar{k} = (2\bar{v} - a) - (4\bar{v} - 2a - \bar{t})$$
$$= a + \bar{t} - 2\bar{v}$$

The ratio of this interval is $\left(\dfrac{2}{1}\right)\left(\dfrac{5}{4}\right)\left(\dfrac{2}{3}\right)^2 = \dfrac{10}{9}$ (Theorem 4; Ch. I, Sec. 5),

TABLE 16

JUST TUNING OF THE C MAJOR SCALE

notes	numbers	1_0	3_0	5_{-1}	0_0	2_0	4_{-1}	6_{-1}	1_0
	letters	C_0	D_0	E_{-1}	F_0	G_0	A_{-1}	B_{-1}	C_0
adjacent intervals	ratio	$\frac{9}{8}$	$\frac{10}{9}$	$\frac{16}{15}$	$\frac{9}{8}$	$\frac{10}{9}$	$\frac{9}{8}$	$\frac{16}{15}$	
	size in cents	203.910	182.404	111.731	203.910	182.404	203.910	111.731	
	name	major tone	minor tone	diatonic semitone	major tone	minor tone	major tone	diatonic semitone	

and it contains 182.404 cents. Interval $a + \bar{t} - 2\bar{v}$ is called a *minor tone*, the name *major tone* being given to interval $2\bar{v} - a$.

It is also apparent that the two just minor seconds $E_{-1}F_0$ and $B_{-1}C_0$ are larger than the corresponding Pythagorean intervals by $\bar{k}$, since their lower notes E_{-1} and B_{-1} are lower than E_0 and B_0 by $\bar{k}$. Hence each of these intervals is equal to $\overline{\text{int}}\,(-5) + \bar{k}$, and the full expression in terms of a, $\bar{v}$, and $\bar{t}$ is

$$(3a - 5\bar{v}) + (4\bar{v} - 2a - \bar{t}) = a - \bar{v} - \bar{t}$$

The ratio of this interval is $(\frac{2}{1})(\frac{2}{3})(\frac{4}{5}) = \frac{16}{15}$, and it contains 111.731 cents. Interval $a - \bar{v} - \bar{t}$ is called a *diatonic semitone*,[2] the word *limma* being retained for the corresponding Pythagorean interval, $\overline{\text{int}}\,(-5)$. We summarize the above results in Table 16.

An examination of Table 16 suggests that the purity of the primary triads has been achieved at a sacrifice. Although the difference between the major tone and minor tone is only 21.506 cents, this amount is detectable, and the effect of the two different sizes of major seconds can hardly be considered desirable from a melodic standpoint. Rather more disturbing, particularly to players of stringed instruments, is the relatively large interval of 111.731 cents between the leading tone and the tonic.[3] Many musicians find that although E_{-1}, A_{-1}, and B_{-1} provide for an undeniably smooth tuning of the primary triads, they are slightly flat with regard to the scale. This suggests that the scale and the chords have independent requirements

---

[2] The word *semitone* is often applied rather loosely to any minor second. See also Ch. IV, note 4.

[3] We use the term *leading tone* in the usual sense, i.e., the note a minor second below the tonic in a major or minor key.

regarding their respective tunings, and that an improvement in the one causes a deterioration in the other. This point will be amplified later (Sec. 5 of this chapter; Ch. VIII, Sec. 4; Ch. X, Secs. 1 and 4).

In just tuning, the broken circle of fifths is as follows:

$$F_0 \quad C_0 \quad G_0 \quad D_0 \quad A_{-1} \quad E_{-1} \quad B_{-1} \quad F_0$$

and fifths $F_0 C_0$, $C_0 G_0$, and $G_0 D_0$, being the same as in Pythagorean tuning, are each equal to $\overline{\text{int}}$ (1). Similarly, fifths $A_{-1} E_{-1}$ and $E_{-1} B_{-1}$ are also equal to $\overline{\text{int}}$ (1), since the three notes involved differ from their Pythagorean counterparts by the same amount.

In the case of the diminished fifth, the just interval $B_{-1} F_0$ is seen to exceed the corresponding Pythagorean interval $B_0 F_0$ by $\bar{k}$, and is equal to

$$\overline{\text{int}}\,(-6) + \bar{k} = (4a - 6\bar{v}) + (4\bar{v} - 2a - \bar{\imath})$$
$$= 2a - 2\bar{v} - \bar{\imath}$$

This interval, which has no special name, has a ratio equal to $\left(\dfrac{2}{1}\right)^2 \left(\dfrac{2}{3}\right)^2 \left(\dfrac{4}{5}\right) = \dfrac{64}{45}$, and contains 609.776 cents. In Section 5 of this chapter, we shall find that there exists a smoother tuning for a diminished fifth.

In the case of perfect fifth $D_0 A_{-1}$, the just interval is less than pure fifth $D_0 A_0$ by $\bar{k}$, and is equal to

$$\overline{\text{int}}\,(1) - \bar{k} = \bar{v} - (4\bar{v} - 2a - \bar{\imath})$$
$$= 2a - 3\bar{v} + \bar{\imath}$$

The ratio of this fifth is $\left(\dfrac{2}{1}\right)^2 \left(\dfrac{2}{3}\right)^3 \left(\dfrac{5}{4}\right) = \dfrac{40}{27}$, and it contains 680.449 cents. This interval sounds like a perfect fifth, but badly out of tune. If the lower pitch is middle C_0 of 264 Hz, so that the higher pitch is G_{-1}, the beat frequency is $264[(2)(\frac{40}{27}) - 3] = -9.778$ per second (Ch. I, Sec. 3). This shows that interval $\bar{v} - \bar{k}$ is discordant to nearly the same degree as a Pythagorean diminished sixth (Ch. IV, Sec. 5), and like the latter, is inappropriate in a musical context where pure intervals are numerous. In consequence, the arrangement shown in Table 16 is a tuning of the C major scale in which the triad on degree II should be avoided. Since no composer of tonal music has ever systematically avoided the second-degree

TABLE 17

notes	numbers	0_0	1_0	2_0	3_0	4_{-1}	5_{-1}	6_{-1}	0_0
	letters	F_0	C_0	G_0	D_0	A_{-1}	E_{-1}	B_{-1}	F_0
adjacent intervals (fifths)	ratio		$\frac{3}{2}$	$\frac{3}{2}$	$\frac{3}{2}$	$\frac{40}{27}$	$\frac{3}{2}$	$\frac{3}{2}$	$\frac{64}{45}$
	size in cents		701.955	701.955	701.955	680.449	701.955	701.955	609.776
	pure/ impure		pure	pure	pure	impure	pure	pure	impure

triad, it appears that the tuning given in Table 16 is inapplicable to the entire tonal repertoire.

Data pertaining to the fifths in just tuning are summarized in Table 17.

In just tuning, the sequence of notes in which all the adjacent intervals are thirds is as follows:

$$F_0 \quad A_{-1} \quad C_0 \quad E_{-1} \quad G_0 \quad B_{-1} \quad D_0 \quad F_0$$

According to the definition of just tuning (Sec. 1 of this chapter), all thirds occurring in any one of the primary triads are pure, and this accounts for all the thirds except D_0F_0. Unfortunately, this minor third is Pythagorean, since both notes forming it have zero subscripts. Consequently $G_0B_{-1}D_0F_0$ is somewhat less than an ideal tuning for a dominant seventh chord. Table 18 summarizes data pertaining to the thirds.

The failure of just tuning, as defined, to provide a good tuning for both the second-degree triad and the dominant seventh chord is a high price to pay for the purity of the primary triads, especially considering that the progression II-V⁷-I is one of the most basic and commonly used of all harmonic progressions. In order to rectify the situation, it is necessary to add more notes to the seven forming the primary triads.

TABLE 18

notes	numbers	0_0	4_{-1}	1_0	5_{-1}	2_0	6_{-1}	3_0	0_0
	letters	F_0	A_{-1}	C_0	E_{-1}	G_0	B_{-1}	D_0	F_0
adjacent intervals (thirds)	ratio		$\frac{5}{4}$	$\frac{6}{5}$	$\frac{5}{4}$	$\frac{6}{5}$	$\frac{5}{4}$	$\frac{6}{5}$	$\frac{32}{27}$
	size in cents		386.314	315.641	386.314	315.641	386.314	315.641	294.135
	pure/ impure		pure major	pure minor	pure major	pure minor	pure major	pure minor	impure minor

TABLE 19

notes	C_0	D_{-1}	D_0	E_{-1}	F_0	G_0	A_{-1}	B_{-1}	C_0
adjacent intervals (ratios)		$\frac{10}{9}$	$\frac{81}{80}$	$\frac{10}{9}$	$\frac{16}{15}$	$\frac{9}{8}$	$\frac{10}{9}$	$\frac{9}{8}$	$\frac{16}{15}$

3. Rectification of the second-degree triad. We now show that a tuning of the second-degree triad in which all the intervals are pure may be achieved by the addition of one more note to the just scale. We recall that the second-degree triad $D_0F_0A_{-1}$ contains two impure intervals, viz., D_0F_0, a Pythagorean minor third $\bar{v} - \bar{t} - \bar{k}$, and D_0A_{-1}, the mistuned perfect fifth $\bar{v} - \bar{k}$. Since each of these intervals is smaller than the closest pure interval by $\bar{k}$, and since major third F_0A_{-1} is pure, it is clear that replacing D_0 by D_{-1} increases both the minor third and the perfect fifth by $\bar{k}$, giving the pure tuning for both these intervals, while leaving F_0A_{-1} undisturbed. However, we must retain D_0 to serve as the fifth of the dominant triad. With this adjustment, the major scale now contains eight notes, with C_0D_{-1} being a minor tone, ratio $\frac{10}{9}$, and $D_{-1}D_0$ a syntonic comma, ratio $\frac{81}{80}$.

Using the notes of Table 19, we may play six pure major or minor triads, using D_{-1} as the root of the second-degree triad, and D_0 as the fifth of the dominant triad. The effect of the two different D's is a striking disruption and contradiction of established musical habits. In the very commonly occurring progression II-V, it happens frequently that D_0 must follow D_{-1} directly, with both notes occurring in the same part. We give two illustrations of this phenomenon, both of which are standard harmonic progressions of the sort that are described in any elementary textbook. In the first, the six major and minor triads are arranged into a harmonic sequence, their roots proceeding through the broken circle of fifths in the direction E, A, D, G, C, F:

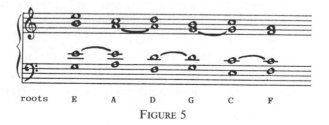

roots   E   A   D   G   C   F

FIGURE 5

TABLE 20

triads	B_{-1}	C_0	D_{-1}	D_0	E_{-1}	F_0
	G_0	A_{-1}	A_{-1}	B_{-1}	C_0	C_0
	E_{-1}	E_{-1}	F_0	G_0	G_0	A_{-1}
degrees	III	VI	II	V	I	IV

The names of the notes, along with the appropriate subscripts, are shown in Table 20, which gives the three notes of each triad and indicates which notes are common to the adjacent triads. The notes used are those of Table 19 with D_{-1} serving as the root of the second-degree triad, and D_0 the fifth of the fifth-degree triad, guaranteeing the purity of all harmonic intervals. Since the second-degree triad is followed directly by the fifth-degree triad, D_0 comes immediately after D_{-1}, and hence in the distribution of Figure 5, the tenor part must rise a syntonic comma at the second D. It is most important to observe that musical notation without the subscripts gives no clue whatever that the two D's are different. Clearly the conventional notation cannot be relied upon to reveal the presence of a syntonic comma.[4]

In the following example, using only four triads, much the same thing occurs.

FIGURE 6

As before, we list the notes in each chord, choosing the subscripts in the same manner (see Table 21). Again the progression II-V requires that D_0 should follow D_{-1} directly, and the arrangement of Figure 6 places both these notes in the soprano part. In the author's opinion, not only is such a use of the syntonic comma as a melodic interval at variance with established musical habits, it produces a positively disagreeable musical effect.

If the soprano part is not allowed to rise a syntonic comma at the fifth-degree chord, and all harmonic intervals are tuned purely, the result

---

[4] See also the second example of Ch. I, Sec. 7.

TABLE 21

triads	G_0	$A_{\overline{1}}$——A_{-1}	B_{-1}	C_0
	$E_{\overline{1}}$——E_{-1}	F_0	$G_{\overline{0}}$——G_0
	$C_{\overline{0}}$——C_0	D_{-1}⌐D_0	E_{-1}
degrees	I	VI	II	V	I

TABLE 22

triads	G_0	$A_{\overline{1}}$——A_{-1}	B_{-2}	C_{-1}
	E_{-1}	E_{-1}	F_0	$G_{\overline{1}}$——G_{-1}
	$C_{\overline{0}}$——C_0	$D_{\overline{1}}$——D_{-1}	E_{-2}
degrees	I	VI	II	V	I

is most peculiar. In the arrangement shown in Table 22, D_{-1} is retained as the fifth of the fifth-degree triad. This necessitates the use of G_{-1} as the root, as fifth $G_0 D_{-1}$ is equal to the unacceptable $\bar{v} - \bar{k}$. Also B_{-1} cannot be used as the third of this triad, as $G_{-1} B_{-1}$ is Pythagorean; hence we use the note lower than B_{-1} by a syntonic comma, or note B_{-2}. And by similar considerations, if G_{-1} is retained in the final C triad, we must take C_{-1} as the root and E_{-2} as the third; hence the final C triad is lower than the initial C triad by a syntonic comma. Under these conditions, if the progression of Figure 6 is played over and over, the pitch drops 21.506 cents with each repetition. The effect of this upon the ears of knowledgeable musicians is the most confounding harmonic disorientation, made all the more perplexing by the smoothness of the tuning of each individual triad.

At this point, the reader might suspect that a satisfactory tuning of the progression of Figure 6 in which all the triads are pure does not exist.

4. Distribution of impure intervals within various just tunings.

THEOREM 23. *Any tuning of the seven-note diatonic scale must contain some impure intervals.* This may be demonstrated in a manner that appeals to musical intuition by considering the arrangement of notes in which all the adjacent intervals are thirds, i.e., F, A, C, E, G, B, D, F. In Pythagorean tuning, thirds FA, CE, and GB are all major and equal to $\overline{int}$ (4), and thirds AC, EG, BD, and DF are all minor and equal to $\overline{int}$ (-3) (Table 7; Ch. III, Sec. 5). The idea of the sum of four minor thirds and three major thirds returning to the original note is conveyed symbolically by the equation

$$4 \; \overline{\text{int}} \; (-3) + 3 \; \overline{\text{int}} \; (4) = \text{int} \; (0)$$

i.e., the initial pitch and the final pitch are separated by some number of octaves, so that the total number of notes is seven. In Pythagorean tuning, all the thirds are impure, the major thirds being greater than a pure major third by $\bar{k}$, and the minor thirds less than a pure minor third by $\bar{k}$. If all the thirds are to be pure, we must decrease each of the major thirds by $\bar{k}$, and increase each of the minor thirds by $\bar{k}$. This adds four syntonic commas and subtracts three syntonic commas, so that the sum of seven pure thirds exceeds the sum of seven Pythagorean thirds by $\bar{k}$. If we write $\overline{\text{int}} \; (4) - \bar{k}$ for the pure major third and $\overline{\text{int}} \; (-3) + \bar{k}$ for the pure minor third, this last is expressed by the equation

$$4[\overline{\text{int}} \; (-3) + k] + 3[\overline{\text{int}} \; (4) - k] = \text{int} \; (0) + \bar{k}$$

meaning that the final note is higher than the initial note by $\bar{k}$, so that the total number of notes is eight. If the number of notes is arbitrarily limited to seven, at least one of the thirds must be impure, and this proves the theorem.

Using a similar technique, we can prove something even more comprehensive than Theorem 23.

THEOREM 24.   *Any tuning of four adjacent notes on the line of fifths must contain impure intervals.* If all the fifths are pure, the notes under the most general conditions are n_0, $(n + 1)_0$, $(n + 2)_0$, and $(n + 3)_0$. The intervals formed by arranging these notes in all possible pairs are intervals (-3), (-2), (-1), (1), (2), and (3) (Theorem 6; Ch. II, Sec. 3). Of these, both $\overline{\text{int}} \; (-3)$ and $\overline{\text{int}} \; (3)$ are impure, being equal to $\bar{v} - \bar{t} - \bar{k}$ and $a - \bar{v} + \bar{t} + \bar{k}$, respectively. Clearly any adjustment made to improve either $\overline{\text{int}} \; (3)$ or $\overline{\text{int}} \; (-3)$ must put at least one of the fifths out of tune, and this proves the theorem.

Many musicians may be surprised to learn that there is no way to tune the four strings of a violin in such a manner that all intervals formed by any pair of strings will be pure. The standard tuning is G_0, D_0, A_0, E_0, with the result that G_0E_0 is Pythagorean. It is an instructive exercise actually to play a syntonic comma on a violin—one has only to compare the tenth harmonic on the G string (B_{-1}) with the third harmonic on the E string (B_0).

It is interesting to explore other tunings of the seven-note diatonic scale with the goal of finding the one that produces the fewest possible impure intervals. When we speak of "other tunings of the seven-note diatonic scale," we mean the ones in which the notes are substantially the same as those of the Pythagorean reference tuning; that is, the seven notes and the twelve diatonic intervals should be named and distributed according to the principles described in Chapter III, Secs. 3–6. In all the tunings we are about to investigate, no note departs from its Pythagorean counterpart by more than two syntonic commas. Since this amounts to only 43.013 cents—less than one half of a Pythagorean minor second (a limma, 90.225 cents)—this difference will not affect the ordinal number naming an interval. Nor are the two levels of modality affected, since the difference between the two diatonic levels in Pythagorean tuning (an apotome, 113.685 cents) is more than four times the size of a syntonic comma.

We begin our investigation with the third order of notes (Ch. III, Sec. 6), since no more than one of the adjacent intervals (thirds) must be impure (Theorem 23). We then consider all the cases in which one of the seven thirds is impure, noting that we have already explored at length the tuning in which DF is impure. Whichever third is impure must be less than the corresponding pure interval by $\bar{k}$; and if we allow any one of the seven thirds to be impure in this manner, we must investigate six other tunings of the seven diatonic notes, each producing a different arrangement of pure and impure intervals. If we write out the third order of notes making all the thirds pure, and continue the array into the next higher octave:

$$
\text{notes} \begin{cases} \text{numbers} & 0 \quad 4 \quad 1 \quad 5 \quad 2 \quad 6 \quad 3 \quad 0 \quad 4 \\ \text{letters} & \quad F \quad A \quad C \quad E \quad G \quad B \quad D \quad F \quad A \end{cases}
$$

$$
\begin{matrix} \text{modality of} \\ \text{third} \end{matrix} \qquad M \quad m \quad M \quad m \quad M \quad m \quad m \quad M
$$

we have a pictorial representation of each fifth as the sum of two thirds. Now if either of the two adjacent thirds adding to a perfect fifth is made smaller by $\bar{k}$, their sum is also made smaller by $\bar{k}$, and becomes $\bar{v} - \bar{k}$, the impure fifth of 680.449 cents, ratio $\frac{40}{27}$. Furthermore, making any one of the seven thirds smaller by $\bar{k}$ will make exactly two of the fifths smaller by $\bar{k}$—the one in which the lower note of the third is the lower note of the fifth, the other in which the higher note of the third is the higher note of the fifth. In other words, the root of one of the impure fifths is the lower note of the impure third, and the root of the other impure fifth is a third (major or minor) lower than that.

If the impure third is BD or DF, one of the fifths affected is diminished fifth BF. In either case, triad BDF is the sum of a pure and a Pythagorean minor third, and is less than ideal as a harmonic combination. If BD and DF are both pure, then diminished fifth BF is the sum of two pure minor thirds, or $2(\bar{v} - \bar{t})$; its ratio is $\left(\dfrac{6}{5}\right)^2 = \dfrac{36}{25}$, and it contains 631.283 cents. In the next section, it will be shown that the smoothest tuning for triad BDF occurs when its three pitches are in the ratio 5:6:7, and so the tuning $2(\bar{v} - \bar{t})$ for BF is also less than ideal.

Since making any one of the seven thirds impure effectively renders two of the fifths unacceptable, it is also clear that no tuning of the seven-note diatonic scale produces more than five pure triads. Furthermore, the most advantageous arrangements occur when the impure third is either BD or DF, since in either case one of the fifths affected is diminished fifth BF, and this fifth is rejected no matter which third is impure. If one of the other five thirds is impure, two additional fifths are thrown out of tune, and the number of pure triads produced by the tuning can be no more than four.

We may now easily determine which triads are pure, given which one of the seven thirds is impure. We simply eliminate the triad whose root is the same as the lower note of the impure third, as well as the one whose root is a third lower than that, and we reject BDF in all cases. Results are given in Table 23.

An examination of Table 23 reveals that just tunings of the seven-note diatonic scale are even more restrictive harmonically than might have been expected. Only two of the tunings give five pure triads, and neither of these contains both the triads on D and G. Nor is this all, for we

TABLE 23

tuning number	impure third	impure fifths	impure triads (roots)	pure triads (roots)
1	FA	DA, FC	D, F, B	C, E, G, A
2	AC	FC, AE	F, A, B	C, D, E, G
3	CE	CG, AE	C, A, B	D, E, F, G
4	EG	CG, EB	C, E, B	D, F, G, A
5	GB	EB, GD	E, G, B	C, D, F, A
6	BD	GD, BF	G, B	C, D, E, F, A
7	DF	DA, BF	D, B	C, E, F, G, A

TABLE 24

| pure triads | | playable in tunings |
degrees	roots	(see Table 23)
I, II, III, IV	C, D, E, F	6
I, II, III, V	C, D, E, G	2
I, II, III, VI	C, D, E, A	6
I, II, IV, V	C, D, F, G	none
I, II, IV, VI	C, D, F, A	5 and 6
I, II, V, VI	C, D, G, A	none
I, III, IV, V	C, E, F, G	7
I, III, IV, VI	C, E, F, A	6 and 7
I, III, V, VI	C, E, G, A	1 and 7
I, IV, V, VI	C, F, G, A	7
II, III, IV, V	D, E, F, G	3
II, III, IV, VI	D, E, F, A	6
II, III, V, VI	D, E, G, A	none
II, IV, V, VI	D, F, G, A	4
III, IV, V, VI	E, F, G, A	7

may show that certain progressions involving only four triads cannot be played in any of the seven-note just tunings of Table 23. Since the total number of combinations of the six triads (all except BDF) taken in groups of four is only fifteen, it is no great labor to list them all, indicating which of the tunings of Table 23, if any, each group may be played in. The results are given in Table 24.

Of the fifteen different groups of four triads, three are found to be duplicated in two of the seven-note just tunings, and three others do not appear in any. Of especial interest are the three unplayable combinations, since each of these represents four triads whose roots are four contiguous notes of the broken circle of fifths—in the first case, notes F, C, G, D; in the second, notes C, G, D, A; and in the third, notes G, D, A, E. Since these are the only such arrangements of four triads (always excluding BDF) within C major, we may conclude that progression of four triads through the circle of fifths in a major key requires the use of eight notes, two of them differing by a syntonic comma. In each case, the use of the eight-note scheme of Table 19 provides the just tuning of all the triads if we use D_{-1} in the triad on II and D_0 in the triad on V. It will be observed that all combinations of three triads (excluding BDF) can be played in one or more of the tunings of Table 23.

TABLE 25

notes	F_0	A_{-1}	C_0	E_{-1}	G_0	B_{-2}	D_{-1}	F_0
adjacent intervals (ratios)		$\frac{5}{4}$	$\frac{6}{5}$	$\frac{5}{4}$	$\frac{6}{5}$	$\frac{100}{81}$	$\frac{6}{5}$	$\frac{6}{5}$

It is also instructive to investigate the scales resulting from the seven just tunings of Table 23. One example will serve to illustrate a technique that is applicable to all the tunings. We arbitrarily select tuning 5, which makes third GB less than the corresponding pure interval by $\bar{k}$. If we start with F_0, and then take A_{-1}, C_0, E_{-1}, and G_0, all the thirds up to $E_{-1}G_0$ are pure. The note a pure major third higher than G_0 is B_{-1}; hence we must use B_{-2} in order that G_0B_{-2} should be less than a pure third by $\bar{k}$. From B_{-2}, we next take D_{-1}, so that $B_{-2}D_{-1}$ exceeds the Pythagorean minor third by $\bar{k}$, and hence is pure, and finally, $D_{-1}F_0$ is pure. Table 25 shows the third order of notes. Major third G_0B_{-2} is equal to $\overline{\text{int}}$ (4) $- 2\bar{k}$, or $\bar{t} - \bar{k}$, so that its complete expression in terms of a, $\bar{v}$, and $\bar{t}$ is

$$\bar{t} - (4\bar{v} - 2a - \bar{t}) = 2a - 4\bar{v} + 2\bar{t}$$

Since $2a - 4\bar{v} + 2\bar{t} = 2(a - 2\bar{v} + \bar{t})$, and $a - 2\bar{v} + \bar{t}$ is a minor tone, ratio $\frac{10}{9}$ (Sec. 2 of this chapter), interval $\bar{t} - \bar{k}$ is the sum of two minor tones, its ratio is therefore $\left(\dfrac{10}{9}\right)^2 = \dfrac{100}{81}$, and it contains 364.807 cents.

The broken circle of fifths is the first order of notes—F, C, G, D, A, E, B—with the addition of the subscripts found above, as given in Table 26. Fifths F_0C_0, C_0G_0, along with fifths $D_{-1}A_{-1}$ and $A_{-1}E_{-1}$ are the same size as the corresponding Pythagorean intervals, and are each equal to $\bar{v}$, ratio $\frac{3}{2}$. Fifths G_0D_{-1} and $E_{-1}B_{-2}$ are smaller than this by $\bar{k}$, and are equal to $\bar{v} - \bar{k}$, ratio $\frac{40}{27}$. $B_{-2}F_0$, being the sum of two pure minor thirds, has a ratio equal to $\frac{36}{25}$, and contains 631.283 cents.

TABLE 26

notes	F_0	C_0	G_0	D_{-1}	A_{-1}	E_{-1}	B_{-2}	F_0
adjacent intervals (ratios)		$\frac{3}{2}$	$\frac{3}{2}$	$\frac{40}{27}$	$\frac{3}{2}$	$\frac{3}{2}$	$\frac{40}{27}$	$\frac{36}{25}$

TABLE 27

notes	C_0	D_{-1}	E_{-1}	F_0	G_0	A_{-1}	B_{-2}	C_0
adjacent intervals (ratios)		$\frac{10}{9}$	$\frac{9}{8}$	$\frac{16}{15}$	$\frac{9}{8}$	$\frac{10}{9}$	$\frac{10}{9}$	$\frac{27}{25}$

The adjacent intervals of the scale are determined by the same method. Table 27 shows the second order of notes.

The interval between B_{-2} and C_0 is greater than its Pythagorean counterpart by two syntonic commas, and is equal to

$$\overline{int}\,(-5) + 2\bar{k} = (3a - 5\bar{v}) + 2(4\bar{v} - 2a - \bar{t})$$
$$= 3\bar{v} - a - 2\bar{t}$$

This interval is called a *maximum semitone;*[5] its ratio is $\left(\frac{3}{2}\right)^3\left(\frac{1}{2}\right)\left(\frac{4}{5}\right)^2 = \frac{27}{25}$, and its size is 133.238 cents. With such a large interval between the leading tone and the tonic, this scale seems even more out of tune than the one of Table 16 (Sec. 2 of this chapter), besides being relatively poor in pure intervals.

The reader is invited to work out the configuration of major tones, minor tones, diatonic semitones, and maximum semitones found in the other seven-note just scales. The results are collected in Table 28 for reference.

5. Rectification of the dominant seventh chord and the seventh-degree triad. We now take up the problem of finding a just tuning for all the diatonic chords associated with C major, irrespective of the number of notes needed. We have seen (Sec. 3 of this chapter) how the addition of D_{-1} to the scale $C_0D_0E_{-1}F_0G_0A_{-1}B_{-1}C_0$ brings about the rectification of the second-degree triad, and we now show that the addition of yet another note makes possible the just tuning of the dominant seventh chord. Since the dominant triad $G_0B_{-1}D_0$ is pure, it is only necessary to find another tuning for F, as the F_0 present in the scale makes a Pythagorean minor third with D_0. When the dominant seventh is tuned so that the frequencies of its pitches are in the ratios $4:5:6:7$, it will be found that all beats between lower-order harmonics are nulled, and that

---

[5] See note 2, supra.

TABLE 28

impure
third

F_0A_{-2}	notes	C_{-1}	D_{-1}	E_{-2}	F_0	G_{-1}	A_{-2}	B_{-2}	C
	adjacent intervals	$\frac{9}{8}$	$\frac{10}{9}$	$\frac{27}{25}$	$\frac{10}{9}$	$\frac{10}{9}$	$\frac{9}{8}$	$\frac{16}{15}$	
$A_{-1}C_{-1}$	notes	C_{-1}	D_{-1}	E_{-2}	F_0	G_{-1}	A_{-1}	B_{-2}	C_{-1}
	adjacent intervals	$\frac{9}{8}$	$\frac{10}{9}$	$\frac{27}{25}$	$\frac{10}{9}$	$\frac{9}{8}$	$\frac{10}{9}$	$\frac{16}{15}$	
C_0E_{-2}	notes	C_0	D_{-1}	E_{-2}	F_0	G_{-1}	A_{-1}	B_{-2}	C_0
	adjacent intervals	$\frac{10}{9}$	$\frac{10}{9}$	$\frac{27}{25}$	$\frac{10}{9}$	$\frac{9}{8}$	$\frac{10}{9}$	$\frac{27}{25}$	
$E_{-1}G_{-1}$	notes	C_0	D_{-1}	E_{-1}	F_0	G_{-1}	A_{-1}	B_{-2}	C_0
	adjacent intervals	$\frac{10}{9}$	$\frac{9}{8}$	$\frac{16}{15}$	$\frac{10}{9}$	$\frac{9}{8}$	$\frac{10}{9}$	$\frac{27}{25}$	
G_0B_{-2}	notes	C_0	D_{-1}	E_{-1}	F_0	G_0	A_{-1}	B_{-2}	C_0
	adjacent intervals	$\frac{10}{9}$	$\frac{9}{8}$	$\frac{16}{15}$	$\frac{9}{8}$	$\frac{10}{9}$	$\frac{10}{9}$	$\frac{27}{25}$	
$B_{-1}D_{-1}$	notes	C_0	D_{-1}	E_{-1}	F_0	G_0	A_{-1}	B_{-1}	C_0
	adjacent intervals	$\frac{10}{9}$	$\frac{9}{8}$	$\frac{16}{15}$	$\frac{9}{8}$	$\frac{10}{9}$	$\frac{9}{8}$	$\frac{16}{15}$	
D_0F_0	notes	C_0	D_0	E_{-1}	F_0	G_0	A_{-1}	B_{-1}	C_0
	adjacent intervals	$\frac{9}{8}$	$\frac{10}{9}$	$\frac{16}{15}$	$\frac{9}{8}$	$\frac{10}{9}$	$\frac{9}{8}$	$\frac{16}{15}$	

all difference-tones reinforce a pitch two octaves below the root of the chord, producing the smoothest possible tuning. Hence we need another F, higher than G_0 by the interval whose ratio is $\frac{7}{4}$. This is the fourth basic interval (Ch. I, Sec. 5) of 968.826 cents; and since the numerator of its ratio contains the prime factor 7, this interval cannot be expressed rationally in terms of a, $\bar{v}$, and $\bar{t}$ (Ch. I, Sec. 7). In order to find comparable expressions for intervals whose ratios include 7 as a factor, it would be necessary to introduce a symbol for $\log \frac{7}{4}$; but this is not necessary for an understanding of the discussion that follows.

We first determine the relation between the new F and the F_0 already present in the scale. We first note that F_0 is higher than G_0 by $\overline{\text{int}}\,(-2)$, ratio $\frac{16}{9}$, and that the new F is higher than G_0 by the interval whose ratio is $\frac{7}{4}$. Hence the difference between the new F and F_0 is the difference

TABLE 29

notes	C_0	D_{-1}	D_0	E_{-1}	F_{-z}	F_0	G_0	A_{-1}	B_{-1}	C_0
adjacent intervals (ratios)		$\frac{10}{9}$	$\frac{81}{80}$	$\frac{10}{9}$	$\frac{21}{20}$	$\frac{64}{63}$	$\frac{9}{8}$	$\frac{10}{9}$	$\frac{9}{8}$	$\frac{16}{15}$

between these two intervals, this being $(\frac{16}{9})(\frac{4}{7}) = \frac{64}{63}$ (Ch. I, Sec. 1). Thus F_0 is higher than the new F by a comma whose ratio is $\frac{64}{63}$, size 27.264 cents.[6] If we denote this comma by $\bar{z}$, we may use the symbol F_{-z} for the new F.

It should be observed that F_{-z} combines very poorly with certain other notes, especially the tonic C_0. The interval between C_0 and F_{-z} is less than the corresponding Pythagorean interval by $\bar{z}$, and is equal to $\overline{\text{int}}\,(-1) - \bar{z}$, ratio $(\frac{4}{3})(\frac{63}{64}) = \frac{21}{16}$, size 470.781 cents. This interval sounds like a badly out-of-tune perfect fourth, and if its lower pitch is middle C of 264 Hz, its beat frequency is $264[(3)(\frac{21}{16}) - 4] = -16.5$ per second (Ch. I, Sec. 3). It is too discordant to be used in a context where pure intervals predominate.

Also of interest is the distance separating E_{-1} and F_{-z}, since this occurs as a melodic interval whenever the dominant seventh resolves to the tonic triad. Clearly $E_{-1}F_{-z}$ is smaller than $E_{-1}F_0$ by $\bar{z}$, and since $E_{-1}F_0$ is a diatonic semitone $a - \bar{v} - \bar{t}$, ratio $\frac{16}{15}$ (Sec. 2 of this chapter), $E_{-1}F_{-z}$ must be equal to $a - \bar{v} - \bar{t} - \bar{z}$; hence its ratio is $(\frac{16}{15})(\frac{63}{64}) = \frac{21}{20}$, and it contains 84.467 cents.

We may now list in ascending order, along with the adjacent intervals they form, the nine notes needed for the triads on degrees I, II, III, IV, and VI, along with the dominant seventh (on V); see Table 29.

The note F_{-z} combines with the other notes of the dominant seventh chord to produce the previously unencountered intervals shown in Table 30. We have already noted that G_0F_{-z} is smaller than G_0F_0 by the comma $\bar{z}$, ratio $\frac{64}{63}$, size 27.264 cents. Whenever the dominant seventh chord is directly preceded by the second- or fourth-degree triad, the note F_{-z} must come just after F_0. This produces the sensation that F_{-z} is flat, even though the dominant seventh is free of beats. When the dominant seventh resolves to the tonic, F_{-z} descends to E_{-1} by the relatively small amount of 84.467 cents. Since E_{-1} seems slightly flat to trained musicians (Sec. 2 of this chapter), the small distance between E_{-1} and F_{-z} makes F_{-z} seem all the more flat.

[6] This comma is sometimes referred to as a septimal comma.

TABLE 30

interval formed by notes	ratio	size in cents
$G_0F_{-\bar{z}}$	$\frac{7}{4}$	968.826
$B_{-1}F_{-\bar{z}}$	$\frac{7}{5}$	582.512
$D_0F_{-\bar{z}}$	$\frac{7}{6}$	266.871
$F_{-\bar{z}}G_0$	$\frac{8}{7}$	231.174
$F_{-\bar{z}}B_{-1}$	$\frac{10}{7}$	617.488
$F_{-\bar{z}}D_0$	$\frac{12}{7}$	933.129

The subjective impression that $F_{-\bar{z}}$ is flat is even stronger when this note is combined with D_0. The interval $D_0F_{-\bar{z}}$, ratio $\frac{7}{6}$, differs from a pure minor third, ratio $\frac{6}{5}$, by an interval whose ratio is $(\frac{6}{5})(\frac{6}{7}) = \frac{36}{35}$. If we compare minor third $D_0F_{-\bar{z}}$ with pure minor third $D_{-1}F_0$, noting that D_{-1} is lower than D_0 by $\bar{k}$, and F_0 is higher than $F_{-\bar{z}}$ by $\bar{z}$, it is obvious that $D_{-1}F_0$ is larger than $D_0F_{-\bar{z}}$ by $\bar{k} + \bar{z}$, and hence this is the size of the interval whose ratio is $\frac{36}{35}$, amounting to 48.770 cents. This departure from the pure tuning is sufficiently great that the interval whose ratio is $\frac{7}{6}$, although still having the sound of a minor third, takes on a special character all its own. All this produces an ambivalent reaction in a trained musician—although $G_0B_{-1}D_0F_{-\bar{z}}$ is unquestionably a smoother tuning for a dominant seventh than $G_0B_{-1}D_0F_0$, there can be no denying the sensation that $F_{-\bar{z}}$ is very flat, relative both to the scale and to certain other notes of the chord itself.

When G_0 is taken away from a dominant seventh chord, leaving notes $B_{-1}D_0F_{-\bar{z}}$, the effect of this combination is only slightly less smooth, being definitely superior in this regard to $B_{-1}D_{-1}F_0$, $B_{-1}D_0F_0$, and $B_{-2}D_{-1}F_0$. Since BF is always combined with G, D, or both, in common harmonic situations, we always take the tuning $B_{-1}F_{-\bar{z}}$ for this interval.

We may now complete the harmonic sequence of Figure 5 (Sec. 3 of this chapter), including in it the seventh degree along with the others. We use the notes of Table 29, selecting D_0 or D_{-1}, F_0 or $F_{-\bar{z}}$ according to the following simple rules, guaranteeing the purity of all triads: D_{-1} serves as the root of the second-degree triad, and D_0 is used in all other situations; $F_{-\bar{z}}$ is the tuning for F whenever this note is combined with B_{-1}, and F_0 is used in all other situations; see Figure 7.

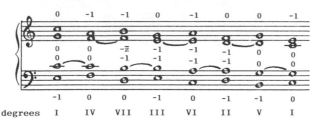

FIGURE 7

Once again, the price paid for harmonic purity is a disruption of one of the individual parts, as $F_{-\bar{z}}$ must follow F_0 in the tenor part at the progression of IV-VII.

In the progression between the triad on II and the dominant seventh, both the commas $\bar{k}$ and $\bar{z}$ may occur simultaneously as melodic intervals, as illustrated in Table 31. Between II and V, F must fall by $\bar{z}$, or 27.264 cents, while D rises by $\bar{k}$, or 21.506 cents. This means that in just tuning, the dominant seventh chord and the second-degree triad have no notes in common. Under these conditions, the subjective impression of the progression II-V^7 is that there is a slight but disturbing discontinuity between the two chords, which in turn attenuates the sensation of cadence associated with these harmonies. In consequence, the progression II-V^7 does not have an ideal just tuning.

TABLE 31

	II	V	I
chords	D_{-1}	B_{-1}	C_0
	A_{-1}	G_0——G_0	
	F_0——$F_{-\bar{z}}$		E_{-1}
	D_{-1}——D_0		C_0
degrees	II	V	I

6. Pure tuning of the major dominant ninth and secondary seventh chords. If we regard the seventh, GF, of a dominant seventh chord as being composed of thirds GB, BD, and DF, it is clear that each of the other six seventh chords, major or minor, may also be regarded as being composed of three thirds. We thus define a seventh chord in the most general sense as being four notes, each higher than the one next below by a third. The diatonic seventh chords in C major may be written out by starting on each of the seven degrees of the scale and adding above each,

TABLE 32

	B	C	D	E	F	G	A
chords	G	A	B	C	D	E	F
	E	F	G	A	B	C	D
	C	D	E	F	G	A	B
degrees	I	II	III	IV	V	VI	VII

three notes, every one higher than the preceding by a third. These chords, with the exception of the dominant seventh, are called *secondary seventh chords*, and they find extensive use in practical situations.

An examination of Table 32 reveals that four different distributions of major and minor thirds must be considered. Two of these are associated with only one chord—the arrangement minor-minor-major (from bottom to top) with the chord on VII, and major-minor-minor with the chord on V. Of the other two arrangements, major-minor-major is associated with chords on I and IV, and minor-major-minor with those on II, III, and VI. The best just tuning of these latter two arrangements is that which assures the purity of all thirds and perfect fifths found between any two notes of the chord.

In the case of the seventh chords on degrees I and IV, each of these may be regarded as a major triad with the addition of one more note a major third above the highest note of the triad. If we take the tuning $C_0E_{-1}G_0B_{-1}$ for the seventh chord on I, the triad $C_0E_{-1}G_0$ is pure, as is major third G_0B_{-1} and perfect fifth $E_{-1}B_{-1}$. In this case, major seventh C_0B_{-1} is the sum of two pure major thirds and one pure minor third, its ratio is $\left(\frac{5}{4}\right)^2\left(\frac{6}{5}\right) = \frac{15}{8}$, and it contains 1088.269 cents. Thus the pure tuning for this particular seventh chord arranges the four pitches in the ratios 8:10:12:15; and the same is true if we take $F_0A_{-1}C_0E_{-1}$ for the fourth-degree seventh chord. The major seventh whose ratio is $\frac{15}{8}$ is the inversion of a diatonic semitone (Ch. II, Sec. 3), and is quite sharply discordant, as is any tuning for a major seventh. In addition, for reasons outlined previously (Sec. 2 of this chapter), many musicians find the higher note to be slightly flat.

Each of the seventh chords on degrees II, III, and VI may be regarded as a minor triad with the addition of one more note a minor third higher than the highest note of the triad. If the sixth-degree seventh chord is tuned $A_{-1}C_0E_{-1}G_0$, all three thirds and both perfect fifths are pure.

Minor seventh $A_{-1}G_0$ is the sum of two pure minor thirds and one pure major third, and its ratio is $\left(\frac{6}{5}\right)^2\left(\frac{5}{4}\right) = \frac{9}{5}$. The four pitches of this chord are thus in the ratios $10:12:15:18$; this is also the tuning for the seventh chords on II and III if they are tuned $D_{-1}F_0A_{-1}C_0$ and $E_{-1}G_0B_{-1}D_0$, respectively. The minor seventh whose ratio is $\frac{9}{5}$ is the inversion of a minor tone, and contains 1017.596 cents. This interval exceeds the minor seventh associated with a dominant seventh chord by an interval whose ratio is $\left(\frac{9}{5}\right)\left(\frac{4}{7}\right) = \frac{36}{35}$; this is the relatively large comma $\bar{k} + \bar{z}$ of 48.770 cents. This quite substantial difference between the two different minor sevenths causes the one to seem too small and the other to seem too large. When taken out of context, the best subjective tuning for a minor seventh is probably ratio $\frac{16}{9}$, making it the inversion of a major tone. But this tuning cannot be applied to any of the seventh chords without making at least one third impure.

The major dominant ninth chord is a dominant seventh with the addition of a fifth note a major third higher than the highest note of the dominant seventh. As the pure tuning for the dominant seventh is $G_0B_{-1}D_0F_{-\bar{z}}$, the note completing the ninth chord is A; and since we must select a tuning for A that does not conflict with D_0 a perfect fifth lower, the only acceptable tuning is A_0, assuring that D_0A_0 is pure. Hence major ninth G_0A_0 is the sum of two perfect fifths, and its ratio is $\left(\frac{3}{2}\right)^2 = \frac{9}{4}$. Thus the five pitches $G_0B_{-1}D_0F_{-\bar{z}}A_0$ are in the ratios $4:5:6:7:9$, and from this it is at once apparent that minor seventh $B_{-1}A_0$ is in the ratio $\frac{9}{5}$, and major third $F_{-\bar{z}}A_0$ is in the ratio $\frac{9}{7}$.

The interval whose ratio is $\frac{9}{7}$, 435.084 cents, is troublesome. It exceeds a pure major third by an interval whose ratio is $\left(\frac{9}{7}\right)\left(\frac{4}{5}\right) = \frac{36}{35}$, once again the large comma $\bar{k} + \bar{z}$ of 48.770 cents. When taken out of context, $F_{-\bar{z}}A_0$ sounds like an extremely distorted major third, and seems very wrong to a musically habituated ear. The same is hardly less true for minor triad $D_0F_{-\bar{z}}A_0$, since its third sounds excessively flat. It is only when $F_{-\bar{z}}A_0$ is combined with B_{-1} that the characteristic smoothness of just tuning appears, and the addition of G_0 results in a further improvement.

We determine the tuning for half-diminished seventh chord BDFA in much the same way as for the other seventh chords. We begin with the tuning $B_{-1}D_0F_{-\bar{z}}$, as derived in the previous section, and select A_0 so that perfect fifth D_0A_0 is pure, making the four pitches $B_{-1}D_0F_{-\bar{z}}A_0$ in the ratios $5:6:7:9$. Even though this tuning is free of beats, its effect

TABLE 33

seventh chords						
B_{-1}	C_0	D_0	E_{-1}	$F_{-\bar{z}}$	G_0	A_0
G_0	A_{-1}	B_{-1}	C_0	D_0	E_{-1}	$F_{-\bar{z}}$
E_{-1}	F_0	G_0	A_{-1}	B_{-1}	C_0	D_0
C_0	D_{-1}	E_{-1}	F_0	G_0	A_{-1}	B_{-1}
degrees						
I	II	III	IV	V	VI	VII

upon a trained musical ear is even more peculiarly alien than a purely tuned dominant seventh chord. It is worthwhile to observe that none of the notes $D_0F_{-\bar{z}}A_0$ is exactly the same as the corresponding $D_{-1}F_0A_{-1}$ of the second-degree triad, also that the major dominant ninth and the seventh-degree seventh chord require the note A_0—not needed in any other triad or seventh chord.

We sum up the preceding by noting that pure tuning of the seven diatonic seventh chords requires ten notes, viz., C_0, D_{-1}, D_0, E_{-1}, $F_{-\bar{z}}$, F_0, G_0, A_{-1}, A_0, and B_{-1}; and we select D_{-1} or D_0, $F_{-\bar{z}}$ or F_0, A_{-1} or A_0 according to the following rules:

1. D_{-1} serves as the root of the second-degree triad or seventh chord, and D_0 is used in all other situations.
2. $F_{-\bar{z}}$ is the tuning for F when this note is combined with B_{-1}, and F_0 is used in all other situations.
3. A_0 serves as the ninth of the major dominant ninth, or the seventh of the seventh-degree seventh chord, and A_{-1} is used in all other situations.

The pure tuning of all diatonic seventh chords is given in Table 33.

It is now possible to expand the harmonic sequence of Figure 5 (Sec. 3 of this chapter) to include seventh chords, using the tunings of Table 33:

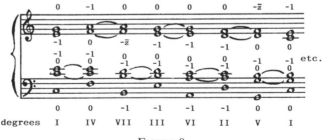

| degrees | I | IV | VII | III | VI | II | V | I |

FIGURE 8

Both the commas $\bar{k}$ and $\bar{z}$ occur simultaneously as melodic intervals at the progressions IV-VII and II-V, resulting in a subtle yet disturbing discontinuity in the smoothness of the progressions. It must be concluded that the beat-free tuning is less than totally satisfactory for the sequence of Figure 8.[7]

We conclude this section by observing that there are some combinations of notes occurring in traditional harmony that cannot be tuned in any way so as to be entirely free of beats. A case in point is a dominant seventh with a suspended third—by no means the rarest of harmonies. In C major, this requires G, C, D, and F; but F, C, G, and D are four adjacent notes on the line of fifths, and it is impossible to tune these notes so that all pairs make pure intervals (Theorem 24; Sec. 5 of this chapter).

[7] This sequence, referred to also in Secs. 3 and 5 of this chapter, is no mere theoretical abstraction. Its persistent use by composers throughout the tonal period in music history is truly remarkable. Examples before 1700 are relatively rare, but see Heinrich Schütz's madrigal, "Itzt blicken durch des Himmels Saal," composed possibly as early as 1629 and surely before 1638; there are numerous occurrences near the end, where the text first reads "hier lass meiner Liebe Pfand." Heinrich Schütz Sämtliche Werke, herausgegeben von Philipp Spitta (Leipzig: Breitkopf und Härtel, 1893), vol. 15, 70–73. Another example will be found in Arcangelo Corelli's Sonata for two violins and continuo, Op. 1, No. 12, c. 1681; see the opening *Grave*, bars 2–3, bars 6–8, and bars 11–13. Les Oeuvres de Arcangelo Corelli (London: Augener Ltd., n.d.), vol. 1, 66. After 1700, the sequence occurs with extraordinary frequency. The following list of examples is by no means complete, but it does serve to illustrate the great variety of styles in which the sequence is idiomatic.

J. S. Bach, Fantasy and Fugue for organ in G minor (1720), at every entry of the subject, also frequent use in the episodes.

J. S. Bach, Fugue in F♯ minor from the Well-Tempered Clavier, Book 2 (1742), at every entry of the first subject.

F. J. Haydn, Symphony No. 44 in E minor (1771), first movement, bars 28–35.

W. A. Mozart, Piano Sonata No. 16 in C major, K. 545 (1788), first movement, bars 18–21.

L. van Beethoven, String Quartet in A major, Op. 18, No. 5 (1801), last movement, bars 23–27 and bars 44–49.

L. van Beethoven, Overture "Die Weihe des Hauses," Op. 124 (1822), numerous examples with variations in the main *Allegro*, especially bars 152–153.

F. Schubert, Impromptu in E♭ major, Op. 90, No. 2, D. 899 (1827), bars 25–32.

F. Chopin, Etude in C major, Op. 10, No. 1 (1830), bars 39–44.

R. Schumann, "Carnaval," Op. 9 (1835), No. 17 ("Paganini") bars 1–3.

R. Schumann, Piano Concerto in A minor, Op. 54 (1846), first movement, bars 221–225.

J. Brahms, Piano Quintet in F minor, Op. 34 (1862), first movement, bars 147–149.

P. I. Tchaikovsky, Symphony No. 4 in F minor, Op. 36 (1878), second movement, bars 14–21.

P. I. Tchaikovsky, Symphony No. 6 in B minor, Op. 74 (1893), first movement, bars 26–27.

A. Scriabin, Piano Sonata No. 3 in F♯ minor, Op. 23 (1898), second movement, bars 39–41.

In Figure 9 the proper tuning for F in the dominant seventh is $F_{-\bar{z}}$; but this note cannot be combined with C_0, nor can C_0 be moved, since it must not clash with G_0. The least discordant arrangement is to take F_0 against C_0; but Pythagorean major sixth F_0D_0 is in the most sensitive register, producing beats at 11 per second. In addition to this, the pitch of the bass part must fall by $\bar{z}$ (27.264 cents) when the suspension resolves from C_0 to B_{-1} in the alto part.

As we shall see (Ch. VII, Secs. 1–4), similar difficulties arise frequently in practical situations.

VI   Extended Just Tuning

Introduction. The question of extended just tuning involves the tuning of the entire family of major and minor keys, the just tuning of chromatic intervals and chords where such exists, and a detailed study of the resulting maze of commas.

In Section 1 we explore the properties of the just tuning of the family of major keys, using the techniques developed during the investigation of extended Pythagorean tuning (Ch. IV, Sec. 6) in conjunction with the subscript notation used to describe the just tuning of C major (Ch. V, Secs. 1–3). Section 2 deals formally with linear relations connecting five commas formed by integral combinations of the first three basic intervals—the Pythagorean comma, syntonic comma, schisma, diaschisma, and diesis. It will be seen that the question of the proximity of A♭ and G♯ in just tuning—or of any two notes separated by twelve positions on the line of fifths—has no simple answer. In Section 3 important relations are derived involving the schisma, which make possible a close approximation to just tuning within the confines of extended Pythagorean tuning. Section 4 deals with the just tuning of minor keys, and shows how the commas of Section 2 may arise in certain practical situations. Section 5 deals with a systematic investigation of the six semitones thus far encountered in Pythagorean tuning and just tuning, and reveals yet further instances of the commas described in Section 2. In Section 6 we take up the question of the just tuning of various chromatic chords occurring in minor keys. It will be found that the just tuning of certain fairly common progressions in minor keys may bring about successions of severely distorted melodic intervals, and that some chromatic chords cannot be tuned so as to be formed entirely by pure intervals. This latter point is expanded upon in Section 7, where it is also shown that only the first, second, third, fourth, and seventh basic intervals (ratios $\frac{2}{1}, \frac{3}{2}, \frac{5}{4}, \frac{7}{4}$, and $\frac{17}{16}$, respectively, see Ch. I, Sec. 5) have conventional musical applications within the framework of extended just tuning. Section 8 collects together in tabular form data pertinent to the intervals and frequencies of extended just tuning. Table 44 lists the intervals thus far encountered; but other intervals may arise in practical situations, as will be seen in Chapter VII, Sec. 5. Tables 45–53

TABLE 34

notes	$(1+n)_0$	$(3+n)_0$	$(5+n)_{-1}$	$(0+n)_0$	$(2+n)_0$	$(4+n)_{-1}$	$(6+n)_{-1}$	$(1+n)_0$
degrees	I	II	III	IV	V	VI	VII	I
ratios	$\frac{9}{8}$	$\frac{10}{9}$	$\frac{16}{15}$	$\frac{9}{8}$	$\frac{10}{9}$	$\frac{9}{8}$	$\frac{16}{15}$	

give numerical data that are sufficient for the illustration of the musical examples in the following chapter.

1. Just tuning of the family of major keys. We first recall (Ch. IV, Sec. 6) that the family of major keys in Pythagorean tuning consists of notes $0 + n$, $1 + n$, $2 + n$, $3 + n$, $4 + n$, $5 + n$, and $6 + n$, where $1 + n$ is the tonic and n is any integer. If we use the modified notations of Chapter V, Sec. 1, and attach a zero subscript to each note, the second order of notes—the scale of $(1 + n)_0$ major (Ch. III, Sec. 6)—becomes

notes	$(1+n)_0$	$(3+n)_0$	$(5+n)_0$	$(0+n)_0$	$(2+n)_0$	$(4+n)_0$	$(6+n)_0$	$(1+n)_0$
degrees	I	II	III	IV	V	VI	VII	I

As in the case of C major, the three major triads on degrees I, IV, and V are Pythagorean (Ch. III, Sec. 7). Pure tuning may be achieved by lowering each of the higher notes of the three major thirds by a syntonic comma (Ch. V, Sec. 1), which amounts to replacing notes $(4 + n)_0, (5 + n)_0$, and $(6 + n)_0$ by notes $(4 + n)_{-1}, (5 + n)_{-1}$, and $(6 + n)_{-1}$, to produce the scale shown in Table 34. As in C major, rectification of the second-degree triad (Ch. V, Sec. 3) requires another second-degree note lower than the one already present by a syntonic comma, this being note $(3 + n)_{-1}$. The eight notes necessary to play three pure major and three pure minor triads in the key of $(1 + n)_0$ major are

$$(0+n)_0 \quad (1+n)_0 \quad (2+n)_0 \quad (3+n)_0 \quad (3+n)_{-1} \quad (4+n)_{-1} \quad (5+n)_{-1} \quad (6+n)_{-1}$$

FIGURE 10

Example: Write out the E♭ major just scale. We give two methods for doing this.

First method: E♭ is note $5 - 7$, or note -2 (Ch. IV, Sec. 1); as this is the tonic of $1 + n$ major, we have $1 + n = -2$, and $n = -3$. Now substituting -3 for n in the expressions of Table 34 gives $-2_0 0_2 2_{-1} - 3_0 - 1_0 1_{-1} 3_{-1} - 2_0$. We get the conventional names by using Chapter IV, Sec. 1, to give $E♭_0 F_0 G_{-1} A♭_0 B♭_0 C_{-1} D_{-1} E♭_0$, with in addition, F_{-1}, serving as the root of the second-degree triad.

Second method: We use Theorems 19 and 21 (Ch. IV, Sec. 6) to find the Pythagorean tuning, and then lower the third-, sixth-, and seventh-degree notes by a syntonic comma. The key signature for E♭ major is $5 - 7 - 1 = -3$, meaning three flats, viz., B♭, E♭, and A♭. The E♭ Pythagorean scale is the letters in alphabetical order beginning with E and with A following G; flats are attached to B, E, and A, all with zero subscripts, viz., $E♭_0 F_0 G_0 A♭_0 B♭_0 C_0 D_0 E♭_0$. The just tuning is the same as this, but with degrees III, VI, and VII (G, C, and D) lowered by a syntonic comma: $E♭_0 F_0 G_{-1} A♭_0 B♭_0 C_{-1} D_{-1} E♭_0$, with the addition of F_{-1} for the root of the second-degree triad.

It is of especial interest to compare the notes required by the keys of $1 + n$ major and $2 + n$ major, i.e., two major keys whose signatures differ by one sharp or flat. The eight notes needed for the key of $(2 + n)_0$ major may be derived from Figure 10 by replacing n by $n + 1$ in the eight expressions, giving

$$(1+n)_0 \quad (2+n)_0 \quad (3+n)_0 \quad (4+n)_0 \quad (4+n)_{-1} \quad (5+n)_{-1} \quad (6+n)_{-1} \quad (7+n)_{-1}$$

$$\text{FIGURE 11}$$

A comparison of the notes found in Figures 10 and 11 reveals that $(2 + n)_0$ major requires two notes not present in $(1 + n)_0$ major, viz., $(7 + n)_{-1}$ and $(4 + n)_0$ to serve as the third and fifth, respectively, of the dominant triad. It will be observed that the lowered second degree, note $(4 + n)_{-1}$, is already present among the notes of $(1 + n)_0$ major. Or we may observe that the key of $(1 + n)_0$ major requires two notes not found in $(2 + n)_0$ major—notes $(0 + n)_0$ and $(3 + n)_{-1}$, the first serving as the root of the fourth-degree triad, and the second needed to effect the rectification of the second-degree triad. In either case, modulation to the most nearly related keys—those having a signature of one sharp or flat more or less than the original—requires the addition of two notes to the notes of the original key.

Example: What notes must be added to those of C_0 major in order to play in the key whose signature is one sharp (G_0 major)? Since C is note 1, we have $1 + n = 1$, and $n = 0$. Transposition is one place to the right on the line of fifths, so that the new notes are $(7 + n)_{-1}$ and $(4 + n)_0$, or notes 7_{-1} and 4_0, corresponding to $F\sharp_{-1}$ and A_0 (Ch. IV, Sec. 1).

We also observe that one of the new notes, $F\sharp_{-1}$, combines with one of the notes already present, F_0, to produce an interval not previously encountered. In the general case, this is the interval between notes $(0 + n)_0$

and $(7 + n)_{-1}$, being equal to $\overline{\text{int}}\,(7) - \overline{k}$ (Theorem 6; Ch. II, Sec. 3, also Ch. V, Sec. 1). The full expression for this interval in terms of a, $\overline{v}$, and $\overline{t}$ is determined by substituting $7\overline{v} - 4a$ for $\overline{\text{int}}\,(7)$ (Ch. III, Sec. 4), and $4\overline{v} - 2a - \overline{t}$ for $\overline{k}$ (Ch. III, Sec. 7), and we obtain

$$(7\overline{v} - 4a) - (4\overline{v} - 2a - \overline{t}) = 3\overline{v} + \overline{t} - 2a$$

Interval $3\overline{v} + \overline{t} - 2a$ is called a *major chroma*; its ratio is $\left(\dfrac{3}{2}\right)^3\left(\dfrac{5}{4}\right)\left(\dfrac{1}{2}\right)^2 = \dfrac{135}{128}$ (Theorem 4; Ch. I, Sec. 5), and it contains 92.179 cents.

It is interesting at this point to write out the ten notes, in ascending order, needed to play the six major or minor triads in C major and G major.

TABLE 35

notes	C_0	D_{-1}	D_0	E_{-1}	F_0	$F\sharp_{-1}$	G_0	A_{-1}	A_0	B_{-1}	C_0
ratios	$\frac{10}{9}$	$\frac{81}{80}$	$\frac{10}{9}$	$\frac{16}{15}$	$\frac{135}{128}$	$\frac{16}{15}$	$\frac{10}{9}$	$\frac{81}{80}$	$\frac{10}{9}$	$\frac{16}{15}$	

Since modulation by one position to the right or left on the line of fifths adds one note having a 0 subscript and another having a -1 subscript, it is clear that the aggregate of notes needed to play the major and minor triads in all major keys consists of the notes named by all the positive or negative integers, with the addition of the 0 and -1 subscripts. In other words, extended just tuning as thus far described may be regarded as two arrays of extended Pythagorean tuning (Ch. IV, Sec. 1), the one a syntonic comma higher than the other. This furnishes a convenient means for the investigation of various other intervals that arise from extended just tuning.

2. The diesis, the schisma, and the diaschisma.[1]   These three commas and the Pythagorean comma all arise if we consider the difference between one octave and the sum of three major thirds, the thirds being Pythagorean or pure in all possible combinations. We begin with the case where all the thirds are Pythagorean; using the expression $4\overline{v} - 2a$ for a Pythagorean major third (Ch. III, Sec. 7), we may write the difference between

---

[1] The etymology of these words is of interest. All three are from Greek roots, *diesis* meaning a discharge and *schisma* a separation, to which the prefix *dia-* adds the notion of division. *Comma* also has a Greek root meaning set apart, and *syntonic* (or *syntonous*) means drawn tight.

one octave and the sum of three Pythagorean major thirds thus:

$$3(4\bar{v} - 2a) - a = 12\bar{v} - 7a$$

This amount, $12\bar{v} - 7a$, is a Pythagorean comma $\bar{p}$ of 23.460 cents, ratio $\frac{531441}{524288}$ (Ch. IV, Sec. 5).

If the three major thirds are all pure, their sum is less than one octave; accordingly we define a comma $\bar{d}$ as one octave less the sum of the thirds, or

$$a - 3\bar{t} = \bar{d}$$

The comma $\bar{d}$ is called a *diesis*;[2] its ratio is $\left(\dfrac{2}{1}\right)\left(\dfrac{4}{5}\right)^3 = \dfrac{128}{125}$ (Theorem 4; Ch. I, Sec. 5), and it contains 41.059 cents.

It remains now to investigate two other cases—one in which two of the thirds are pure and one Pythagorean, and one in which two of the thirds are Pythagorean and one is pure. If we consider the equation $3(4\bar{v} - 2a) - a = \bar{p}$, and depict one of the Pythagorean thirds as $\bar{t} + \bar{k}$, rather than $4\bar{v} - 2a$ (Ch. III, Sec. 7), we have

$$2(4\bar{v} - 2a) + (\bar{t} + \bar{k}) - a = \bar{p}$$

and if $\bar{k}$ is now subtracted from both sides of this equation, the result is

$$2(4\bar{v} - 2a) + \bar{t} - a = \bar{p} - \bar{k}$$

The left-hand side of the above represents the sum of two Pythagorean major thirds and one pure major third, less one octave. The comma $\bar{p} - \bar{k}$ is called a *schisma*, and we assign it the symbol $\bar{s}$ so that $\bar{s} = \bar{p} - \bar{k}$ and $\bar{p} = \bar{k} + \bar{s}$, i.e., *a syntonic comma plus a schisma makes a Pythagorean comma*.[3] The expression for the schisma in terms of a, $\bar{v}$, and $\bar{t}$ is obtained

---

[2] The word *diesis* is found throughout the history of Western music theory and is used very loosely to mean any interval substantially smaller than a limma (90.225 cents). The terms major diesis, minor diesis, greater diesis, lesser diesis, chromatic diesis, and enharmonic diesis may also be found. In reading other works on music theory it is essential to ascertain exactly what interval is meant by any of the above terms. In this book, diesis refers exclusively to the interval whose ratio is $\frac{128}{125}$.

[3] The symbols $\bar{d}$ and $\bar{s}$ denote the true versions of these commas; d and s will be used to denote their representations in various temperaments. See also Ch. I, Sec. 5.

by collecting terms in $2(4\bar{v} - 2a) + \bar{t} - a$ to give

$$8\bar{v} + \bar{t} - 5a = \bar{s}$$

From this its ratio is $\left(\dfrac{3}{2}\right)^8\left(\dfrac{5}{4}\right)\left(\dfrac{1}{2}\right)^5 = \dfrac{32805}{32768}$, and it contains 1.954 cents. The schisma enjoys the distinction of being unusually small in comparison with the other commas.

If in the equation $2(4\bar{v} - 2a) + \bar{t} - a = \bar{p} - \bar{k}$ we replace one Pythagorean major third $4\bar{v} - 2a$ by its equivalent $\bar{t} + \bar{k}$, we have

$$(4\bar{v} - 2a) + (\bar{t} + \bar{k}) + \bar{t} - a = \bar{p} - \bar{k}$$

and if $\bar{k}$ is subtracted from both sides of this equation, the result is

$$(4\bar{v} - 2a) + 2\bar{t} - a = \bar{p} - 2\bar{k}$$

Since $\bar{p}$ contains 23.460 cents and $\bar{k}$ contains 21.506 cents (Ch. III, Sec. 7), it is apparent that $\bar{p} - 2\bar{k}$ is negative; accordingly we reverse signs to obtain

$$a - 2\bar{t} - (4\bar{v} - 2a) = 2\bar{k} - \bar{p}$$

The left-hand side of this equation represents one octave less the sum of two pure major thirds and one Pythagorean major third. The comma $2\bar{k} - \bar{p}$ is called a *diaschisma*, and there is no pressing need for a special letter to represent it. If we recall that $\bar{p} = \bar{k} + \bar{s}$, we have $2\bar{k} - \bar{p} = 2\bar{k} - (\bar{k} + \bar{s}) = \bar{k} - \bar{s}$, i.e., *a schisma plus a diaschisma makes a syntonic comma*. If we collect terms in $a - 2\bar{t} - (4\bar{v} - 2a) = 2\bar{k} - \bar{p}$, we have

$$3a - 4\bar{v} - 2\bar{t} = 2\bar{k} - \bar{p}$$

From this the ratio of the diaschisma is $\left(\dfrac{2}{1}\right)^3\left(\dfrac{2}{3}\right)^4\left(\dfrac{4}{5}\right)^2 = \dfrac{2048}{2025}$, and it contains 19.553 cents.

One further relation may be derived from $a - 2\bar{t} - (4\bar{v} - 2a) = 2\bar{k} - \bar{p}$; we replace $4\bar{v} - 2a$ by $\bar{t} + \bar{k}$ to obtain

$$a - 2\bar{t} - \bar{t} - \bar{k} = 2\bar{k} - \bar{p}$$

and now add $\bar{k}$ to both sides, giving

$$a - 3\bar{t} = 3\bar{k} - \bar{p}$$

TABLE 36

name	letter	in terms of a, $\bar{v}$, and $\bar{t}$	in terms of $\bar{p}$ and $\bar{k}$	ratio	size in cents
Pythagorean comma	$\bar{p}$	$12\bar{v} - 7a$	$\bar{p}$	$\frac{531441}{524288}$	23.460
syntonic comma	$\bar{k}$	$4\bar{v} - 2a - \bar{t}$	$\bar{k}$	$\frac{81}{80}$	21.506
schisma	$\bar{s}$	$8\bar{v} + \bar{t} - 5a$	$\bar{p} - \bar{k}$	$\frac{32805}{32768}$	1.954
diaschisma	—	$3a - 4\bar{v} - 2\bar{t}$	$2\bar{k} - \bar{p}$	$\frac{2048}{2025}$	19.553
diesis	$\bar{d}$	$a - 3\bar{t}$	$3\bar{k} - \bar{p}$	$\frac{128}{125}$	41.059

But $a - 3\bar{t}$ is a diesis $\bar{d}$, as defined earlier in this section, hence

$$\bar{d} = 3\bar{k} - \bar{p}$$

This last may be written $\bar{d} = (2\bar{k} - \bar{p}) + \bar{k}$, which states that *a diaschisma plus a syntonic comma makes a diesis.* Also, replacing $\bar{p}$ by $\bar{k} + \bar{s}$ gives $\bar{d} = 3\bar{k} - (\bar{k} + \bar{s}) = 2\bar{k} - \bar{s}$, another expression for the diesis which is sometimes useful.

Pertinent data relative to the five commas discussed in this section are collected in Table 36.

As we have seen (Ch. IV, Sec. 5), a Pythagorean comma $\bar{p}$ separates any two notes that are distant by twelve positions on the line of fifths, for example, Ab_0 and $G\#_0$. It follows that $Ab_0G\#_{-1}$ is smaller than $Ab_0G\#_0$ by $\bar{k}$, and hence represents a schisma. It is also apparent that $Ab_0G\#_{-2}$ is equal to $\bar{p} - 2\bar{k}$, a descending diaschisma, and that $Ab_{+1}G\#_{-2}$ is equal to $\bar{p} - 3\bar{k}$, a descending diesis. It is essential to bear in mind that the standard notation without subscripts does not reveal which of these four commas is represented by $AbG\#$. We now have a new insight into the nature of the "true" difference between Ab and $G\#$ in any given musical passage. It is first necessary to deduce the proper subscripts from the context; in the author's experience, there is no simple rule covering all cases, and subjective judgment must serve in many situations. Once the comma is determined, it may be safely stated that if it is a Pythagorean comma or a schisma, $G\#$ is higher than Ab by 23.460 cents in the former case, or by 1.954 cents in the latter. If the comma in question is a diaschisma or a diesis, Ab is higher than $G\#$ by 19.553 cents in the former case, or by 41.059 cents in the latter.

3. The schismatic major third. We now return to the visualization of just tuning as two arrays of extended Pythagorean tuning, one having 0

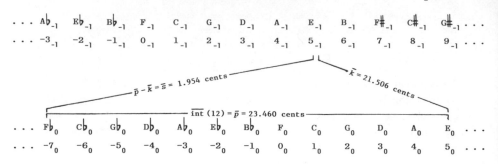

FIGURE 12

subscripts, and the other having -1 subscripts (Sec. 1 of this chapter), as in Figure 12. In Figure 12, both the upper array (-1 subscripts) and lower array (0 subscripts) may be thought of as extending indefinitely in either direction, with all the adjacent intervals equal to $\overline{\text{int}}$ (1) (Ch. IV, Sec. 1). In addition, each -1-subscript note is higher than the 0-subscript note written directly below it by $\overline{\text{int}}$ $(4) - \bar{k}$, a pure major third. If we start at some note on the lower array, say note -7_0 ($F\flat_0$), and count ahead twelve places to note 5_0 (E_0), we find note 5_0 to be higher than note -7_0 by $\overline{\text{int}}$ (12) (Theorem 6; Ch. II, Sec. 3), a Pythagorean comma $\bar{p}$ of 23.460 cents, ratio $\frac{531441}{524288}$ (Ch. IV, Sec. 5). Also note 5_0 (E_0) is higher than note 5_{-1} (E_{-1}) by a syntonic comma $\bar{k}$ of 21.506 cents; hence note 5_{-1} (E_{-1}) is higher than note -7_0 ($F\flat_0$) by $\bar{p} - \bar{k}$, a schisma $\bar{s}$ of 1.954 cents, ratio $\frac{32805}{32768}$. Or we may observe more directly that the interval between note -7_0 and note 5_{-1} is $\overline{\text{int}}$ $(12) - \bar{k} = \bar{p} - \bar{k} = \bar{s}$.

Now if note 1_0 (C_0) is the root of a pure major triad, the notes needed for the third and fifth are notes 5_{-1} (E_{-1}) and 2_0 (G_0), respectively. But since note -7_0 ($F\flat_0$) is lower than note 5_{-1} (E_{-1}) by the very small amount 1.954 cents, it is at once evident that the combination of notes 1_0, -7_0, and 2_0 is a very close approximation of a pure C major triad within the confines of Pythagorean tuning—much better than 1_0, 5_0, and 2_0, which contains a Pythagorean major third. It is thus a singular fact that $C_0F\flat_0G_0$ is much less discordant than $C_0E_0G_0$—a surprising discovery in view of the appearance of the notation. In general, a nearly pure tuning of a major triad may be achieved within extended Pythagorean tuning if we take $\overline{\text{int}}$ (-8), rather than $\overline{\text{int}}$ (4), as the tuning for the major third.

The relation between $\overline{\text{int}}$ (-8) and a pure major third may be further illustrated by observing that $\overline{\text{int}}$ (4) $> \overline{\text{int}}$ (12), and hence $\overline{\text{int}}$ (4) $- \overline{\text{int}}$ (12) =

$\overline{\text{int}}$ (-8) (Ch. II, Sec. 3). Upon substituting $\overline{\text{int}}$ $(4) = \bar{t} + \bar{k}$ and $\overline{\text{int}}$ $(12) = \bar{p}$, we have $\bar{t} + \bar{k} - \bar{p} = \overline{\text{int}}$ (-8); and since $\bar{s} = \bar{p} - \bar{k}$, the final result is $\overline{\text{int}}$ $(-8) = \bar{t} - \bar{s}$. As was found earlier (Table 13; Ch. IV, Sec. 3), the size of $\overline{\text{int}}$ (-8) is 384.360 cents, and its ratio is $\frac{8192}{6561}$. If the lower pitch is the standard middle C of 264 Hz, $\overline{\text{int}}$ (-8) produces beats at a rate of $264[(4)(\frac{8192}{6561}) - 5] = -1.489$ per second (Ch. I, Sec. 3)—far smoother than the Pythagorean third producing 16.5 beats per second (Ch. III, Sec. 7). Since $\overline{\text{int}}$ (-8) is smaller than a pure major third by a schisma, it is some-times called a *schismatic major third*.

If the major third of a triad is tuned $\bar{t} - \bar{s}$, its minor third is equal to $\bar{v} - \bar{t} + \bar{s}$; and since $\overline{\text{int}}$ $(1) > \overline{\text{int}}$ (-8), we have also $\overline{\text{int}}$ $(1) - \overline{\text{int}}$ $(-8) = \overline{\text{int}}$ (9). From this, it follows that $\overline{\text{int}}$ $(9) = \bar{v} - \bar{t} + \bar{s}$, or that a Pythagorean augmented second exceeds a pure minor third by a schisma.

It is of interest to explore briefly the arrangement that results from tuning the primary triads of C major (Ch. IV, Sec. 6) so that their thirds are schismatic. Each triad may be represented by notes n_0, $(n - 8)_0$, and $(n + 1)_0$, where $n = 0, 1,$ or 2, and hence the triads wanted are $F_0 B\flat\flat_0 C_0$, $C_0 F\flat_0 G_0$, and $G_0 C\flat_0 D_0$. This produces the scale $C_0 D_0 F\flat_0 F_0 G_0 B\flat\flat_0 C\flat_0 C_0$, in which $B\flat\flat_0$, $F\flat_0$, and $C\flat_0$ are lower by a schisma than their just counterparts, A_{-1}, E_{-1}, and B_{-1}, respectively. From this it can be seen that $F\flat_0 F_0$ and $C\flat_0 C_0$ are larger than a diatonic semitone (Ch. V, Sec. 2) by $\bar{s}$; and since $F\flat_0 F_0$ and $C\flat_0 C_0$ are apotomes (Ch. IV, Sec. 1), it follows that *an apotome exceeds a diatonic semitone by a schisma*. This may be directly demonstrated by substituting $7\bar{v} - 4a$ for the apotome and $a - \bar{v} - \bar{t}$ for the diatonic semitone to give $(7\bar{v} - 4a) - (a - \bar{v} - \bar{t}) = 8\bar{v} + \bar{t} - 5a$. In this "schismatic tuning," the broken circle of fifths is $F_0 C_0 G_0 D_0 B\flat\flat_0 F\flat_0 C\flat_0 F_0$, showing that the triad on II contains the extremely discordant interval $D_0 B\flat\flat_0$—a Pythagorean diminished sixth, or $\bar{v} - \bar{p}$ (Ch. IV, Sec. 5) Rectification of this triad requires a note lower than $B\flat\flat_0$ by $\bar{v}$, viz., $E\flat\flat_0$. In other words, $E\flat\flat_0$ must serve as the root of the triad on II, while D_0 is the fifth of the triad on V. Since $E\flat\flat_0$ is lower than D_0 by $\bar{p}$, it can be seen that this approximately just con-figuration brings about the same practical disadvantage regarding the progression II-V as was found in true just tuning (Ch. V, Sec. 3).

Another important relation involving the schisma may be discovered by adding to the approximately just scale the note required for the schismatic third of the dominant triad in G_0 major. This is the note higher than D_0 by $\overline{\text{int}}$ (-8), viz., $G\flat_0$, once again lower than the note making a pure third ($F\#_{-1}$) by a schisma. Thus the succession $F_0 G\flat_0 F\#_{-1} G_0$ is ascending

$$\overbrace{\text{major chroma } 3\bar{v} + \bar{t} - 2a}$$

$$\overbrace{\text{limma}} \qquad \overbrace{\text{schisma}} \qquad \overset{\text{diatonic}}{\overbrace{\text{semitone}}}$$

$$F_0 \qquad 3a - 5\bar{v} \qquad G\flat_0 \qquad 8\bar{v} + \bar{t} - 5a \qquad F\sharp_{-1} \qquad a - \bar{v} - \bar{t} \qquad G_0$$

$$\underbrace{\qquad\qquad\qquad \text{apotome } 7\bar{v} - 4a \qquad\qquad\qquad}$$

FIGURE 13

within major tone $F_0 G_0$; more particularly, $F_0 G\flat_0$ is $\overline{\text{int}}\ (-5)$, a limma (Ch. II, Sec. 6); $G\flat_0 F\sharp_{-1}$ is a schisma, as shown in this section, and $F\sharp_{-1} G_0$ is $\overline{\text{int}}\ (-5) + \bar{k}$, a diatonic semitone (Ch. V, Sec. 2). If we recall that $F_0 F\sharp_{-1}$ is a major chroma (Sec. 2 of this chapter), this shows that *a major chroma exceeds a limma by a schisma.* Figure 13 is a helpful visualization in relating the schisma to the limma, major chroma, diatonic semitone, and apotome.

Referring once again to Figure 12, we may easily show that no note of the lower array may occur in the upper array. By Theorem 18 (Ch. III, Sec. 7), no combination of octaves and pure perfect fifths produces any other basic interval. And since each note of the upper array makes a pure major third—the third basic interval—with one of the notes of the lower array, the result follows at once.

4. Just tuning of the family of minor keys. In Pythagorean tuning, the A minor harmonic scale is A, B, C, D, E, F, G♯, A (Theorems 20 and 21; Ch. IV, Sec. 6). In just tuning, we choose subscripts so that the scale has the maximum number of notes in common with its relative major. Hence we take A_{-1} rather than A_0 as the tonic, and the tonic triad is thus $A_{-1} C_0 E_{-1}$. The root of the subdominant triad must be D_{-1} so as not to clash with A_{-1}, and so this triad is tuned $D_{-1} F_0 A_{-1}$—the same tuning as the second-degree triad in the relative major (Ch. V, Sec. 3). In the case of the dominant triad, the G♯ needed must make a pure major third with E_{-1}, and this requires $G\sharp_{-2}$. Thus the just harmonic A minor scale is $A_{-1} B_{-1} C_0 D_{-1} E_{-1} F_0 G\sharp_{-2} A_{-1}$. In this scale, as in C_0 major, $A_{-1} B_{-1}$ and $D_{-1} E_{-1}$ are major tones, $C_0 D_{-1}$ is a minor tone, and $E_{-1} F_0$ is a diatonic semitone (Ch. V, Secs. 2 and 3), as is $G\sharp_{-2} A_{-1}$. Augmented second $F_0 G\sharp_{-2}$ is smaller than $F_0 G\sharp_0$ by two syntonic commas; since $F_0 G\sharp_0$ is $\overline{\text{int}}\ (9)$, or $9\bar{v} - 5a$ (Ch. IV, Sec. 3), the full expression for $F_0 G\sharp_{-2}$ in terms of a, $\bar{v}$, and $\bar{t}$ is

$$(9\bar{v} - 5a) - 2(4\bar{v} - 2a - \bar{t}) = \bar{v} + 2\bar{t} - a$$

TABLE 37

JUST TUNING OF THE A MINOR SCALE

notes	A_{-1}	B_{-1}	C_0	D_{-1}	E_{-1}	F_0	$G\sharp_{-2}$	A_{-1}
adjacent intervals (ratios)		$\frac{9}{8}$	$\frac{16}{15}$	$\frac{10}{9}$	$\frac{9}{8}$	$\frac{16}{15}$	$\frac{75}{64}$	$\frac{16}{15}$

This ratio of this interval is $\left(\dfrac{3}{2}\right)\left(\dfrac{5}{4}\right)^2\left(\dfrac{1}{2}\right) = \dfrac{75}{64}$ (Theorem 4; Ch. I, Sec. 5), and it contains 274.582 cents. The complete scale is given in Table 37.

If we take every other note from the scale, we obtain the following sequence in which all the adjacent intervals are thirds—$A_{-1}C_0E_{-1}G\sharp_{-2}$ $B_{-1}D_{-1}F_0A_{-1}$. In this arrangement, all the thirds are pure except $B_{-1}D_{-1}$, which is Pythagorean. This interval is needed for the major triad whose root is G_0—a triad often used as the dominant of the relative major and in harmonic sequences—and its rectification may be effected by using D_0 rather than D_{-1}. Note that G_0 is also used as the third of the minor triad on V, a commonly occurring alteration. We observe that $G_0G\sharp_{-2}$ makes a previously unencountered interval which is less than $G_0G\sharp_0$ (an apotome, See Ch. IV, Sec. 1) by two syntonic commas, and is equal to

$$(7\bar{v} - 4a) - 2(4\bar{v} - 2a - \bar{t}) = 2\bar{t} - \bar{v}$$

Its ratio is $\left(\dfrac{5}{4}\right)^2\left(\dfrac{2}{3}\right) = \dfrac{25}{24}$, and it contains 70.672 cents. This interval is call a *minor chroma*, and since a major chroma is less than an apotome by one syntonic comma (Sec. 1 of this chapter), we see that *a major chroma exceeds a minor chroma by a syntonic comma*. We have also $2\bar{t} - \bar{v} = \bar{t} - (\bar{v} - \bar{t})$, and since $\bar{v} - \bar{t}$ is a pure minor third (Ch. V, Sec. 1), this shows that *a minor chroma is the difference between a pure major third and a pure minor third*.

The broken circle of fifths is $A_{-1}E_{-1}B_{-1}F_0C_0G\sharp_{-2}D_{-1}A_{-1}$. Augmented fifth $C_0G\sharp_{-2}$ is greater than perfect fifth C_0G_0 by minor chroma $G_0G\sharp_{-2}$ and is equal to

$$\bar{v} + 2\bar{t} - \bar{v} = 2\bar{t}$$

i.e., the sum of two pure major thirds—in this case C_0E_{-1} and $E_{-1}G\sharp_{-2}$. Its ratio is $\left(\dfrac{5}{4}\right)^2 = \dfrac{25}{16}$, and it contains 772.627 cents.

The inversion of $C_0G\sharp_{-2}$ is of interest, and is equal to $\bar{a} - 2\bar{t}$ (Ch. II, Sec. 3). Now if we write $a - 2\bar{t} = a - 3\bar{t} + \bar{t}$, and recall that $a - 3\bar{t}$ is a diesis $\bar{d}$ of 41.059 cents (Sec. 2 of this chapter), we see that $G\sharp_{-2}C_0$ is equal to $\bar{t} + \bar{d}$, ratio $(\frac{5}{4})(\frac{128}{125}) = \frac{32}{25}$, size 427.373 cents. The addition of a diesis to a pure major third results in an even more discordant interval than Pythagorean major third $\bar{t} + \bar{k}$, and should be avoided as a harmonic combination if at all possible.

In C major, we occasionally encounter the minor subdominant triad, and this requires the note a pure minor third higher than F_0 and a pure major third lower than C_0, viz., $A\flat_{+1}$. In Section 2 of this chapter, we showed that $A\flat_{+1}$ is higher than $G\sharp_{-2}$ by a diesis—a very perceptible melodic interval, especially when placed in the highest part. In the following progression, the superior part makes the succession $G_0A\flat_{+1}G_0G\sharp_{-2}A_{-1}$, and the difference between $A\flat_{+1}$ and $G\sharp_{-2}$ is clearly perceptible, even with the intervening G_0:

It also follows that augmented second $F_0G\sharp_{-2}$ is smaller than pure minor third $F_0A\flat_{+1}$ by a diesis, and hence is a discordant harmonic interval.

It is now a simple matter to determine the tuning of any just harmonic minor scale, given its tonic. We first determine the numbers associated with each note of the scale of A minor according to the principles of Chapter IV, Sec. 1, and then attach the subscripts to each degree as found earlier in this section:

names	A_{-1}	B_{-1}	C_0	D_{-1}	E_{-1}	F_0	$G\sharp_{-2}$	A_{-1}
numbers	4_{-1}	6_{-1}	1_0	3_{-1}	5_{-1}	0_0	9_{-2}	4_{-1}

The general harmonic minor scale is shown in Table 38, where $(4 + n)_{-1}$ is the tonic and n is any integer.

Example: Write out the harmonic minor scale whose tonic is C_{-1}. Since C is note 1, we have $4 + n = 1$, and $n = -3$. Hence the scale is $1_{-1}3_{-1}$

TABLE 38

notes	$(4+n)_{-1}$	$(6+n)_{-1}$	$(1+n)_0$	$(3+n)_{-1}$	$(5+n)_{-1}$	$(0+n)_0$	$(9+n)_{-1}$	$(4+n)_{-1}$
degrees	I	II	III	IV	V	VI	VII	I
ratios	$\frac{9}{8}$	$\frac{16}{15}$	$\frac{10}{9}$	$\frac{9}{8}$	$\frac{16}{15}$	$\frac{75}{64}$	$\frac{16}{15}$	

$-2_0 0_{-1} 2_{-1} - 3_0 6_{-2} 1_{-1}$, corresponding to $C_{-1}D_{-1}E\flat_0F_{-1}G_{-1}A\flat_0B_{-2}$ C_{-1}.

Another method is to determine first the sequence of letters and distribution of accidentals by Theorems 20 and 21 (Ch. IV, Sec. 6), and then to attach 0 subscripts to degrees III and VI, -1 subscripts to degrees I, II, IV, and V, and a -2 subscript to degree VII.

It is also of interest to observe that $A\flat_0$ (degree VI in C_{-1} minor) is higher than $G\sharp_{-2}$ (degree VII in A_{-1} minor) by a diaschisma (Sec. 2 of this chapter), and that more generally, this comma separates the sixth degree of n minor from the seventh degree of $n + 3$ minor.

5. Minor seconds, chromatic semitones, and commas. At this point, it will be helpful to make some observations regarding the smaller just intervals composed of the first three basic intervals only (Ch. I, Sec. 5). We have thus far encountered six just intervals that are smaller than the major seconds and larger than the commas. Three of these—the maximum semitone, diatonic semitone, and limma—appear in the notation as minor seconds, and the others—the apotome, major chroma, and minor chroma—are written as chromatic semitones (Ch. IV, Sec. 3). These intervals are listed in Table 39, along with characteristics needed for the discussion to follow.

It will be observed that the intervals vary in size over a considerable range, and it is of interest to determine the commas by which any two

TABLE 39

name of interval	expressed as $\overline{\text{int}}\,(i) + n\bar{k}$	ratio	size in cents	defined in
maximum semitone	$\overline{\text{int}}\,(-5) + 2\bar{k}$	$\frac{27}{25}$	133.238	Ch. V, Sec. 4
apotome	$\overline{\text{int}}\,(7)$	$\frac{2187}{2048}$	113.685	Ch. III, Sec. 4
diatonic semitone	$\overline{\text{int}}\,(-5) + \bar{k}$	$\frac{16}{15}$	111.731	Ch. V, Sec. 2
major chroma	$\overline{\text{int}}\,(7) - \bar{k}$	$\frac{135}{128}$	92.179	Ch. VI, Sec. 1
limma	$\overline{\text{int}}\,(-5)$	$\frac{256}{243}$	90.225	Ch. II, Sec. 6
minor chroma	$\overline{\text{int}}\,(7) - 2\bar{k}$	$\frac{25}{24}$	70.672	Ch. VI, Sec. 4

TABLE 40

name of interval	in terms of $\overline{\text{int}}\,(-5)$, $\bar{p}$, and $\bar{k}$
maximum semitone	$\overline{\text{int}}\,(-5) + 2\bar{k}$
apotome	$\overline{\text{int}}\,(-5) + \bar{p}$
diatonic semitone	$\overline{\text{int}}\,(-5) + \bar{k}$
major chroma	$\overline{\text{int}}\,(-5) + \bar{p} - \bar{k}$
limma	$\overline{\text{int}}\,(-5)$
minor chroma	$\overline{\text{int}}\,(-5) + \bar{p} - 2\bar{k}$

of them differ. The answers may be easily obtained in a manner that throws further light on the behavior of the commas defined in Section 2 of this chapter. We begin with the expressions of the intervals of Table 39 as $\overline{\text{int}}\,(i) + n\bar{k}$, and note that either $i = 7$, or $i = -5$. Now since $\overline{\text{int}}\,(7) > \overline{\text{int}}\,(-5)$, as shown above, we have $\overline{\text{int}}\,(7) - \overline{\text{int}}\,(-5) = \overline{\text{int}}\,(12)$ (Ch. II, Sec. 3); and upon substituting $\bar{p}$ for $\overline{\text{int}}\,(12)$ (Ch. IV, Sec. 5), this becomes $\overline{\text{int}}\,(7) = \overline{\text{int}}\,(-5) + \bar{p}$. Now substituting $\overline{\text{int}}\,(-5) + \bar{p}$ for $\overline{\text{int}}\,(7)$ in the expressions of Table 39 gives the results shown in Table 40. The above intervals thus differ from each other by commas which may be expressed in terms of $\bar{p}$ and $\bar{k}$ only. It is an elementary matter to obtain these expressions, and the names of the commas may then be found in Table 36 (Sec. 2 of this chapter). The results are listed below.

1. A limma exceeds a minor chroma by $-(\bar{p} - 2\bar{k}) = 2\bar{k} - \bar{p}$, a diaschisma (19.553 cents).
2. A major chroma exceeds a limma by $\bar{p} - \bar{k}$, a schisma (1.954 cents).
3. A major chroma exceeds a minor chroma by $(\bar{p} - \bar{k}) - (\bar{p} - 2\bar{k}) = \bar{k}$, a syntonic comma (21.506 cents).
4. A diatonic semitone exceeds a major chroma by $\bar{k} - (\bar{p} - \bar{k}) = 2\bar{k} - \bar{p}$, a diaschisma (19.553 cents).
5. A diatonic semitone exceeds a limma by $\bar{k}$, a syntonic comma (21.506 cents).
6. A diatonic semitone exceeds a minor chroma by $\bar{k} - (\bar{p} - 2\bar{k}) = 3\bar{k} - \bar{p}$, a diesis (41.059 cents).
7. An apotome exceeds a diatonic semitone by $\bar{p} - \bar{k}$, a schisma (1.954 cents).
8. An apotome exceeds a major chroma by $\bar{p} - (\bar{p} - \bar{k}) = \bar{k}$, a syntonic comma (21.506 cents).

9. An apotome exceeds a limma by $\bar{p}$, a Pythagorean comma (23.460 cents).

10. An apotome exceeds a minor chroma by $\bar{p} - (p - 2\bar{k}) = 2\bar{k}$, two syntonic commas (43.013 cents).

11. A maximum semitone exceeds an apotome by $2\bar{k} - \bar{p}$, a diaschisma (19.553 cents).

12. A maximum semitone exceeds a diatonic semitone by $2\bar{k} - \bar{k} = \bar{k}$, a syntonic comma (21.506 cents).

13. A maximum semitone exceeds a major chroma by $2\bar{k} - (\bar{p} - \bar{k}) = 3\bar{k} - \bar{p}$, a diesis (41.059) cents.

14. A maximum semitone exceeds a limma by $2\bar{k}$, two syntonic commas (43.013 cents).

There is one more case to consider—a maximum semitone exceeds a minor chroma by $2\bar{k} - (\bar{p} - 2\bar{k}) = 4\bar{k} - p$. This new comma is greater than a diesis by $\bar{k}$, and its full expression in terms of a, $\bar{v}$, and $\bar{t}$ is

$$4(4\bar{v} - 2a - \bar{t}) - (12\bar{v} - 7a) = 4\bar{v} - 4\bar{t} - a$$

From this, its ratio is $\left(\dfrac{3}{2}\right)^4\left(\dfrac{4}{5}\right)^4\left(\dfrac{1}{2}\right) = \dfrac{648}{625}$ (Theorem 4; Ch. I, sec. 5), and it contains 62.565 cents. If we write $4\bar{v} - 4\bar{t} - a = 4(\bar{v} - \bar{t}) - a$, the comma $4\bar{k} - \bar{p}$ is seen to be the amount by which the sum of four pure minor thirds exceeds one octave.

The comma $4\bar{k} - \bar{p}$ is a very large one, being only slightly smaller than a minor chroma. The difference is of some interest; if we recall that a minor chroma is equal to $2\bar{t} - \bar{v}$ (Sec. 4 of this chapter), the difference amounts to

$$(2\bar{t} - \bar{v}) - (4\bar{v} - 4\bar{t} - a) = a - 5\bar{v} + 6\bar{t}$$

The ratio of this comma is $\left(\dfrac{2}{1}\right)\left(\dfrac{2}{3}\right)^5\left(\dfrac{5}{4}\right)^6 = \dfrac{15625}{15552}$, and its size is 8.107 cents.

Yet another comma results from subtracting a diesis from a minor chroma, giving

$$(2\bar{t} - \bar{v}) - (a - 3\bar{t}) = 5\bar{t} - a - \bar{v}$$

Its ratio is $\left(\dfrac{5}{4}\right)^5\left(\dfrac{1}{2}\right)\left(\dfrac{2}{3}\right) = \dfrac{3125}{3072}$, and it contains 29.614 cents. The reader will find it a useful exercise to show that this comma is greater than the one preceding by $\bar{k}$.

Of course, there is no end to the number of commas formed by combinations of the first three basic intervals.

6. Augmented triads, diminished sevenths, half-diminished sevenths, and secondary dominants.

We return now to our investigation of the triads and seventh chords produced by the notes of the harmonic minor scale. As in the case of the major scale, the harmonic minor is constructed upon principles that guarantee the purity of the triads on degrees I, IV, and V, but say nothing directly about either the modality or tuning of the other four triads. It will be convenient to refer to the key of A_{-1} minor; transposition to any other minor key may be effected by the method described in Section 4 of this chapter.

We first recall the A_{-1} minor scale—A_{-1} B_{-1} C_0 D_{-1} E_{-1} F_0 $G\#_{-2}$ A_{-1}; of the triads on degrees II, III, VI, and VII, it is apparent that only $F_0A_{-1}C_0$ is pure and major. Two of the others—$G\#_{-2}B_{-1}D_{-1}$ and B_{-1} $D_{-1}F_0$—are diminished, each being composed of two adjacent minor thirds with a diminished fifth between the outer two notes. Neither diminished triad is in the smoothest possible tuning, for both contain the Pythagorean minor third $B_{-1}D_{-1}$. In the case of G#BD, we observe that these notes are the third, fifth, and seventh of the dominant seventh chord whose root is E. If this dominant seventh is tuned purely by putting its notes in the ratios 4:5:6:7, we must take a D lower than D_{-1} by the comma $\bar{z}$, ratio $\frac{64}{63}$, size 27.264 cents (Ch. V, Sec. 5). This note is lower than D_0 by the comma $\bar{k} + \bar{z}$, ratio $\frac{36}{35}$, size 48.770 cents, and we denote it by $D_{-(\bar{k}+\bar{z})}$.

When dominant seventh $E_{-1}G\#_{-2}B_{-1}D_{-(\bar{k}+\bar{z})}$ resolves normally to $E_{-1}A_{-1}C_0$ in conformity with the usual voice-leading conventions, C_0 must come directly after $D_{-(\bar{k}+\bar{z})}$. The interval $C_0D_{-(\bar{k}+\bar{z})}$ is smaller than major tone C_0D_0 by $\bar{k} + \bar{z}$, and hence its ratio is $\left(\frac{9}{8}\right)\left(\frac{35}{36}\right) = \frac{35}{32}$, and its size is 155.140 cents. This is only 21.902 cents larger than a maximum semitone (Ch. V, Sec. 4), and is far smaller than desirable, even when heard as a melodic interval; consequently $D_{-(\bar{k}+\bar{z})}$ seems exceedingly flat in this context.

There exist conventional harmonic progressions of which Figure 14 is an illustration, where just tuning brings about the succession D_0D_{-1} $D_{-(k+\bar{z})}$ in the soprano part if the triad V/III is tuned as suggested in

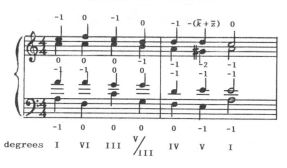

FIGURE 14

Section 4 of this chapter. The purity of the individual harmonies does not conceal the bizarre melodic contour of the superior part.

In the case of diminished triad BDF, we may obtain the pure tuning 5:6:7 by taking either $B_{-1}D_0F_{-\bar{z}}$, or the same thing lower by a syntonic comma, viz., $B_{-2}D_{-1}F_{-(\bar{k}+\bar{z})}$. In the absence of other considerations, there is no really good reason to prefer one tuning to the other.

Rather more troublesome is third-degree triad CEG♯. If we take the tuning directly from the scale, viz., $C_0E_{-1}G\sharp_{-2}C_0$, we are confronted with the problem of diminished fourth $G\sharp_{-2}C_0$, which amounts to discordant interval $\bar{t}+\bar{d}$ of 427.373 cents (Sec. 4 of this chapter); and so this tuning is considerably less than ideal. An improvement results from the tuning $C_0E_{-1}G\sharp_{-1}C_0$, requiring only one note not found in the A harmonic minor scale ($G\sharp_{-1}$). In this arrangement, C_0E_{-1} is pure, and $E_{-1}G\sharp_{-1}$ is Pythagorean. And since Pythagorean diminished fourth $G\sharp_0C_0$ is $\overline{\text{int}}\,(-8)$, which is equal to $\bar{t}-\bar{s}$, (Sec. 3 of this chapter), it is clear that $G\sharp_{-1}C_0$ is equal to $\bar{t}+\bar{k}-\bar{s}$, so that $G\sharp_{-1}C_0$ exceeds a pure major third by $\bar{k}-\bar{s}$, a diaschisma of 19.553 cents, ratio $\frac{2048}{2025}$ (Sec. 2 of this chapter). Hence the ratio of $G\sharp_{-1}C_0$ is $(\frac{5}{4})(\frac{2048}{2025}) = \frac{512}{405}$, and it contains 405.866 cents.

It is clearly impossible to tune CE, EG♯, and G♯C so that each of these intervals will be entirely free of beats, since at least one of them must exceed a pure major third by an amount not less than one third of a diesis, or 13.686 cents. Hence a completely smooth tuning for an augmented triad cannot be found.

The question of the tuning of half-diminished seventh chord BDFA is complex. If we put this chord in the ratios 5:6:7:9, and take B_{-1} as the root, we need notes $B_{-1}D_0F_{-\bar{z}}A_0$, giving the same tuning as the relative major (Ch. V, Sec. 6). But in A minor, this brings about disadvantages.

In the progression II^7-V^7, as shown below,

$$A_0 \qquad \qquad G\sharp_{-2}$$
$$F_{-\bar{z}} \qquad \qquad E_{-1}$$
$$D_0 \qquad \qquad D_{-(\bar{k}+\bar{z})}$$
$$B_{-1} \qquad \qquad B_{-1}$$

A_0 descends 133.238 cents (a maximum semitone, see Ch. V, Sec. 4) to $G\sharp_{-2}$, and D_0 descends 48.770 cents to $D_{-(\bar{k}+\bar{z})}$. Both these intervals are perceived as being very large, especially the comma $\bar{k}+\bar{z}$. If the half-diminished seventh is tuned a syntonic comma lower,

$$A_{-1} \qquad \qquad G\sharp_{-2}$$
$$F_{-(\bar{k}+\bar{z})} \qquad \qquad E_{-1}$$
$$D_{-1} \qquad \qquad D_{-(\bar{k}+\bar{z})}$$
$$B_{-2} \qquad \qquad B_{-1}$$

the subjective effect is distinctly better. However, if $B_{-2}D_{-1}F_{-(\bar{k}+\bar{z})}A_{-1}$ is preceded directly by the sixth-degree triad $F_0A_{-1}C_0$, this again brings about a succession of two notes that differ by 48.770 cents—F_0 and $F_{-(\bar{k}+\bar{z})}$. It can be seen that the two tunings exchange one set of disadvantages for another, and that there is no firm theoretical foundation that establishes either version as superior.

Of the other seventh chords in the A_{-1} harmonic minor scale, it may be said that ACEG$\sharp$ and CEG$\sharp$B have no ideal tuning, since both contain the inherently impure combination CEG$\sharp$. As to the seventh chords whose roots are D and F, the minor scale suggests the tunings $D_{-1}F_0A_{-1}C_0$ and $F_0A_{-1}C_0E_{-1}$—both the same as the corresponding chords in C_0 major, and consisting entirely of pure intervals (Ch. V, Sec. 6).

Diminished seventh chord G$\sharp$BDF is another troublesome chord. If we consider this chord according to its most common use as a dominant, and add to it the root E, it is clear that the tuning $E_{-1}G\sharp_{-2}B_{-1}D_{-(\bar{k}+\bar{z})}$ should be retained for these notes, leaving only the tuning of F in question. The smoothest tuning is the one that causes all the difference-tones to converge upon the root of the chord,[4] and this occurs when the five pitches are in the ratios 8:10:12:14:17. If we apply the interval size convention (Ch. I, Sec. 5) to the interval between E_{-1} and the new F, this being greater than one octave in the chord as tuned above, the ratio is seen to be $\frac{17}{16}$; this is the seventh basic interval (Ch. I, Sec. 5) of 104.955 cents. Since $E_{-1}F_0$ is a diatonic semitone of 111.731 cents, ratio $\frac{16}{15}$ (Sec. 4 of this chapter), the new F is lower than F_0 by a comma which is the dif-

---

[4] See Ch. V, note 1.

TABLE 41

interval formed by notes	ratio	size in cents
$E_{-1}F_{-\bar{y}}$	$\frac{17}{16}$	104.955
$G\sharp_{-2}F_{-\bar{y}}$	$\frac{17}{10}$	918.642
$B_{-1}F_{-\bar{y}}$	$\frac{17}{12}$	603.000
$D_{-(\bar{k}+\bar{z})}F_{-\bar{y}}$	$\frac{17}{14}$	336.130
$F_{-\bar{y}}E_{-1}$	$\frac{32}{17}$	1095.045
$F_{-\bar{y}}G\sharp_{-2}$	$\frac{20}{17}$	281.358
$F_{-\bar{y}}B_{-1}$	$\frac{24}{17}$	597.000
$F_{-\bar{y}}D_{-(\bar{k}+\bar{z})}$	$\frac{28}{17}$	863.870

ference between these intervals; its ratio is thus $(\frac{16}{15})(\frac{16}{17}) = \frac{256}{255}$, and it contains 6.776 cents. If we denote this comma by $\bar{y}$, and the new F by $F_{-\bar{y}}$, we may observe that $F_{-\bar{y}}$ combines with the other notes of the chord to produce the intervals shown in Table 41.[5]

Of the intervals listed in Table 41, several are quite discordant and should be used only when combined with each other according to certain specific arrangements within the diminished seventh chord. Minor third $D_{-(\bar{k}+\bar{z})}F_{-\bar{y}}$ of 336.130 cents, ratio $\frac{17}{14}$, is greater than a pure minor third (315.641 cents) by a comma whose ratio is $(\frac{17}{14})(\frac{5}{6}) = \frac{85}{84}$, and it contains 20.488 cents—very nearly the same as a syntonic comma (21.506 cents). Thus minor third $D_{-(\bar{k}+\bar{z})}F_{-\bar{y}}$ is impure to very nearly the same degree as a Pythagorean minor third.

Augmented second $F_{-\bar{y}}G\sharp_{-2}$, ratio $\frac{20}{17}$, size 281.358 cents, is also nearly the size of a pure minor third. The difference is a comma whose ratio is $(\frac{6}{5})(\frac{17}{20}) = \frac{51}{50}$, containing 34.283 cents. Thus an augmented second in ratio $\frac{20}{17}$ is smaller than a pure minor third by an amount considerably greater than a syntonic comma, and hence is quite discordant.

Of the remaining intervals of Table 41, $B_{-1}F_{-\bar{y}}$ and $F_{-\bar{y}}B_{-1}$ of 603.000 cents and 597.000 cents, respectively, are not excessively discordant—they fall within the rather wide range of tuning permissible for diminished fifths

[5] Several of the numbers of Table 41 involve coincidences that may be misleading. Since the interval whose ratio is $\frac{24}{17}$ is the difference between a pure perfect fifth (ratio $\frac{3}{2}$) and the seventh basic interval (ratio $\frac{17}{16}$), it appears at first glance that its size in cents must be $701.955 - 104.955 = 597$ cents exactly, and that its inversion (ratio $\frac{17}{12}$) must contain 603 cents exactly. But this is not the case; in order to reveal the true situation, it is necessary to carry the calculations out to more decimal places, and we obtain $\log \frac{3}{2} = 701.955001$, $\log \frac{17}{16} = 104.955410$, $\log \frac{24}{17} = 596.999591$, and $\log \frac{17}{12} = 603.000409$.

and augmented fourths. The same is also true for minor second $E_{-1}F_{-\bar{y}}$, whose size falls between a limma (90.225 cents) and a diatonic semitone (111.731 cents).

When a diminished seventh chord is distributed so that intervals whose ratios are $\frac{7}{6}$, $\frac{12}{7}$, $\frac{17}{14}$, $\frac{28}{17}$, $\frac{17}{10}$, or $\frac{20}{17}$, are placed between the two lower pitches, they are quite prominent, and give the chord a distinctly rough character. This can be improved by retuning the impure interval so that its ratio is $\frac{6}{5}$ or $\frac{5}{3}$, whatever are the notes involved. This suggests that the pure tuning of a diminished seventh chord should be chosen according to its distribution, irrespective of its harmonic function in a given context.

When dominant sevenths or ninths function as secondary dominants, it is usually best if the same subscript is attached to the root of the dominant and the root of its resolution. Thus the roots of secondary dominants will usually be notes with either -1 subscripts or 0 subscripts. For example, in A major we take A_0 as the tonic, rather than A_{-1} (Sec. 4 of this chapter), and so the minor dominant ninth in that key is tuned a syntonic comma higher than the corresponding chord in A minor. Hence the notes needed are E_0, $G\sharp_{-1}$, B_0, $D_{-\bar{z}}$, and one other note higher than $F_{-\bar{y}}$ by $\bar{k}$, and we call this note $F_{+(\bar{k}-\bar{y})}$. The comma $\bar{k}-\bar{y}$ has a ratio equal to $(\frac{81}{80})(\frac{256}{255}) = \frac{4131}{4096}$, and contains 14.730 cents. It is also of interest to show that this comma is the difference between the seventh basic interval and a limma, for we have $(\frac{17}{16})(\frac{243}{256}) = \frac{4131}{4096}$.

Thus far, our discussion of just tuning has brought about no fewer than eight different tunings for any note having one conventional name. These correspond to notes having subscripts $+1$ (Sec. 4 of this chapter), 0, -1 (Ch. V, Sec. 1), -2 (Ch. V, Secs. 3 and 4, and Sec. 4 of this chapter), $-\bar{z}$ (Ch. V, Sec. 5), also $-(\bar{k}+\bar{z})$, $-\bar{y}$, and $(\bar{k}-\bar{y})$, described in this section. The choice of a particular subscript is best illustrated by actual musical examples, and will be dealt with in the next chapter.

7. The fifth and sixth basic intervals and their relation to altered dominant seventh chords and whole-tone scales.   Since we have so far found uses in just tuning for basic intervals up to the seventh (ratio $\frac{17}{16}$), but not yet for the fifth and sixth (ratios $\frac{11}{8}$ and $\frac{13}{8}$, respectively), it is natural to explore the harmonic and melodic properties associated with these latter two.

We first recall that the third, fourth, and seventh basic intervals are harmonically preferable versions of certain Pythagorean diatonic intervals from which they depart by relatively small commas. In particular, the third basic interval (ratio $\frac{5}{4}$) exceeds $\overline{\text{int}}$ (4) by $\overline{k} = 21.506$ cents (Ch. III, Sec. 7); the fourth basic interval (ratio $\frac{7}{4}$) is less than $\overline{\text{int}}$ (-2) by $\overline{z} = 27.264$ cents (Ch. V, Sec. 5); and the seventh basic interval (ratio $\frac{17}{16}$) exceeds $\overline{\text{int}}$ (-5) by $\overline{k} - \overline{y} = 14.730$ cents (Sec. 6 of this chapter). It seems logical to investigate the fifth and sixth basic intervals in this regard, and we begin with the latter.

The interval whose ratio is $\frac{13}{8}$ contains 840.528 cents (Ch. I, Secs. 6 and 8), and an examination of Table 3 (Ch. II, Sec. 4) reveals that no diatonic Pythagorean interval is nearly this size, the closest being $\overline{\text{int}}$ (-4), a minor sixth, which is smaller by 48.348 cents. However, $\overline{\text{int}}$ (8), an augmented fifth (Table 13; Ch. IV, Sec. 3), is smaller by 24.888 cents, and so the sixth basic interval might possibly be a just tuning for $\overline{\text{int}}$ (8) in certain contexts. As an example, let us consider, say, notes 2 and 10 forming $\overline{\text{int}}$ (8), the conventional names for these notes being G and D♯, respectively (Ch. IV, Sec. 1). This interval, when tuned $\frac{13}{8}$, produces the smooth, beat-free effect of just tuning only when combined with the pure major third and the pure minor seventh, as is the case with the seventh basic interval (Sec. 6 of this chapter). This leads us to consider the dominant seventh with a raised fifth, such as GBFD♯, when tuned in the ratios 4:5:7:13. Voice-leading conventions of traditional harmony generally require that the raised fifth should be in the soprano part; this is fortunate, for if the raised fifth is in the bass and the root is directly above, the resulting diminished fourth (ratio $\frac{16}{13}$) contains 359.472 cents, roughly midway between a major and minor third and very discordant indeed in this particular distribution. Equally discordant is BD♯, ratio $\frac{13}{10}$, size 454.214 cents, approximately halfway between a major third and a perfect fourth.

More peculiar is the character of augmented sixth FD♯ when tuned in the ratio $\frac{13}{7}$. This is best revealed by investigating its inversion D♯F, whose ratio is $(\frac{2}{1})(\frac{7}{13}) = \frac{14}{13}$ (Ch. I, Sec. 3). The size of this interval is 128.298 cents—less than a maximum semitone (ratio $\frac{27}{25}$, size 133.238 cents, see Ch. V, Sec. 4) by 4.939 cents. Hence D♯F sounds like a large minor second, and FD♯ (1071.702 cents) is perceived as a small major seventh—very different from what is normally associated with an augmented sixth. This alien character is especially noticeable when the chord occurs in third inversion, placing the augmented sixth between the two outer parts.

When a dominant seventh with a raised fifth resolves normally to a major triad, as for example,

GE of the resolution must be a pure major sixth, ratio $\frac{5}{3}$. If GD♯ is in the ratio $\frac{13}{8}$, the melodic interval between D♯ and E must be the difference between the intervals whose ratios are $\frac{5}{3}$ and $\frac{13}{8}$, or $(\frac{5}{3})(\frac{8}{13}) = \frac{40}{39}$, amounting to 43.831 cents. It should be observed that this is less than one half of a limma (90.225 cents), and only slightly greater than a diesis (41.059 cents), and hence is not a good tuning for a minor second, even from purely melodic considerations. We must conclude that the sixth basic interval is out of tune in relation to both scales and most chords, and cannot be considered a just tuning for any diatonic or chromatic Pythagorean interval. It should be observed that there is no truly pure tuning for a dominant seventh with a raised fifth, since the root, third, and raised fifth form an augmented triad (Sec. 6 of this chapter).

The fifth basic interval, ratio $\frac{11}{8}$, size 551.318 cents, is also considerably different from any of the Pythagorean diatonic or chromatic intervals; the closest is $\overline{\text{int}}$ (-6), a diminished fifth of 588.270 cents, being larger by 36.952 cents. Even more particularly, it is larger than a pure perfect fourth by an interval whose ratio is $(\frac{11}{8})(\frac{3}{4}) = \frac{33}{32}$, amounting to only 53.273 cents. When heard in isolation, its sound is somewhere between that of a perfect fourth and a diminished fifth, and in addition to being intensely discordant, it produces an ambiguous reaction. If the lower note of $\overline{\text{int}}$ (-6) is note 2 (G), the higher note is note -4, or D♭; but if the tuning is $\frac{11}{8}$, a trained musical ear has difficulty deciding whether to call the higher note D♭ or C.

Since the normal just tuning for a diminished fifth is $\frac{7}{5}$ (Ch. V, Sec. 5), or occasionally $\frac{17}{12}$ (Sec. 6 of this chapter), any conventional use for the interval whose ratio is $\frac{11}{8}$ must be outside the framework of dominant sevenths, diminished sevenths, or diminished triads occurring in major and minor scales. Proceeding upon the principles that were applied to the sixth and seventh basic intervals, we might consider D♭ as a note placed above a dominant seventh—in this case as a lowered fifth—and investigate the properties of the chord GBFD♭ when tuned 4:5:7:11. Unlike the raised fifth, there is no voice-leading convention restricting the lowered fifth to a particular part, and this brings about extreme discords in certain fairly common situations. For example, if the distribution is D♭GBF so that D♭G is tuned $\frac{16}{11}$, size 648.682 cents, this interval sounds like a severely distorted perfect fifth, rather than an augmented fourth as notated. If the distribution is D♭FBG and D♭F is tuned $\frac{14}{11}$, size 417.508 cents, its effect is that of a major third badly out of tune. Both these intervals are especially disturbing when placed between the two lower parts.

In the following resolution,

if GD♭ is tuned $\frac{11}{8}$ and G is the same in both chords, the distance from
D♭ to C is the difference between the interval whose ratio is $\frac{11}{8}$ and a
pure perfect fourth, viz., $(\frac{11}{8})(\frac{3}{4}) = \frac{33}{32}$, size 53.273 cents—too small for
a minor second, especially in the superior part, even if not quite as dis-
turbing as the situation brought about by the resolution of the raised fifth
described earlier in this section. This combination of factors precludes the
use of $\frac{11}{8}$ as the just tuning for a diminished fifth in any conventional
harmonic situation; and so the fifth basic interval, like the sixth, is not a
good just tuning for any of the diatonic or chromatic Pythagorean
intervals.

An interesting situation arises if we consider a major dominant ninth
chord in just tuning, in combination with both the raised and lowered
fifth, but missing the perfect fifth—for example GBFAD♭D♯, with D♭ and
D♯ making ratios $\frac{11}{8}$ and $\frac{13}{8}$, respectively, with G. Under these conditions, the six notes are in ratios 4:5:7:9:11:13. If these notes are
rearranged in ascending order in such a manner that the greatest interval
formed by any two of them is less than one octave, the resulting array
forms what is commonly called a *whole-tone scale*. The rearrangement is
accomplished by applying the interval size convention (Ch. I, Sec. 5) to the
intervals formed by each of the notes with the initial G, and then listing
them in increasing order. Thus the order of notes in the whole-tone scale
is G followed by the higher note of each of the intervals of Table 42 in that
order, viz., G, A, B, D♭, D♯, F, G. The ratios of the adjacent intervals may
now be obtained by simple arithmetic—for example, BD♭ is GD♭ less GB,
so that the ratio of BD♭ is $(\frac{11}{8})(\frac{4}{5}) = \frac{11}{10}$, and the other adjacent intervals may be worked out by the same process. The final result is shown in
Table 43. An examination of Table 43 reveals that a considerable effort of

TABLE 42

interval	GA	GB	GD♭	GD♯	GF	GG
ratio	$\frac{9}{8}$	$\frac{5}{4}$	$\frac{11}{8}$	$\frac{13}{8}$	$\frac{7}{4}$	$\frac{2}{1}$
size in cents	203.910	386.314	551.318	840.528	968.826	1200.000

TABLE 43

notes	G		A		B		D♭		D♯		F		G
ratio		$\frac{9}{8}$		$\frac{10}{9}$		$\frac{11}{10}$		$\frac{13}{11}$		$\frac{14}{13}$		$\frac{8}{7}$	
size in cents		203.910		182.404		165.004		289.210		128.298		231.174	

imagination would be required to construe all six adjacent intervals as "whole tones." Presumably, a "whole tone" would be an interval reasonably near the size of a major tone—such as a minor tone (ratio $\frac{10}{9}$), or the interval whose ratio is $\frac{8}{7}$, both of which are so construed in the diatonic just scale. In the same category is the somewhat smaller interval BD♭ of 165.004 cents, which is smaller than a major tone by 38.906 cents. On the other hand, D♭D♯, containing 289.210 cents, is much larger than a major tone, being in fact less than a pure minor third (ratio $\frac{6}{5}$) by 26.432 cents, and less than a Pythagorean minor third (ratio $\frac{32}{27}$) by only 4.925 cents. In consequence, this interval sounds like a minor third, not a whole tone. Also D♯F of 128.298 cents is smaller than a maximum semitone (ratio $\frac{27}{25}$) by only 4.939 cents, and hence sounds like a minor second. In sum, the array of Table 43 possesses musical characteristics vastly different from a whole-tone scale, as the term is commonly understood.

The lack of correspondence between the fifth and sixth basic intervals and the common Pythagorean intervals reveals to a certain extent what is meant by the subjective phrases "in tune" and "out of tune." It seems reasonable to state that a given interval can be exactly in tune only if its Pythagorean tuning and just tuning are exactly the same. This strongly suggests that only octaves, perfect fifths, and perfect fourths can be put exactly in tune. All the other common Pythagorean intervals depart from one of the basic intervals, or from one of the pure intervals by a small amount—one of the commas—and hence are out of tune, since they produce beats between low-order harmonics. And since the beat-free just tuning causes the commas to occur as melodic intervals, it too sounds out of tune, but in quite a different way. Also, as has already been noted (Ch. V, Secs. 2 and 5), the higher notes of the pure major third and the pure minor seventh are flat in relation to the scale.

When an interval such as the fifth or sixth basic interval departs from the nearest common Pythagorean interval by a comma in excess of 45 cents or so, it begins to take on an alien character. Although there is, at present, no use musically for such intervals, there is no reason to discard them as musically worthless. They are simply incompatible with an organization of notes that assumes, as does the conventional notation, that all intervals are formed by combinations of octaves and perfect fifths.

All the higher-order basic intervals are either out of tune by virtue of being nearly equal to one of the pure intervals, thereby producing beats between low-order harmonics, or alien, if they are sufficiently different from the common Pythagorean intervals. It should be remembered that no basic interval beyond the second can be equal to any Pythagorean interval (Theorem 18; Ch. III, Sec. 7). The fact that nearly all musical intervals are either out of tune or alien may be difficult for seekers of perfection to accept; but it is indeed fortunate that the ear is not disturbed unduly by slight imperfections in tuning, for if this were not the case, the development of Western music along the lines we are familiar with could not have taken place.

8. Résumé of the intervals and frequencies of just tuning. For the sake of reference, we collect here, in table form, information pertaining to the intervals that have so far been discussed under the head of just tuning. Table 44 gives their ratios, sizes in cents, and names where names exist, and refers to the chapter and section of the text where the interval in question and its use in just tuning are described. Included are the first seven basic intervals, all the pure intervals, all the diatonic Pythagorean intervals, and various combinations of all these, including a multitude of commas. It has not been thought necessary to list the inversions in all cases, especially of the commas.

Tables 45–53 give frequencies of all notes likely to be needed in any practical just tuning situation, and are sufficient to illustrate most of the examples in this and the following chapter, using either electronic musical or scientific instruments, or computer techniques. Tables 45–49 give frequencies of all notes from A✗ through G♭♭ with $+1, 0, -1, -2$, and -3 subscripts—the subscripts referring to the number of syntonic commas (ratio $\frac{81}{80}$) that the given note departs from the 0-subscript tuning, with the $+1$ subscripts being higher and the negative subscripts lower. The 0-subscript tuning is identical to the Pythagorean tuning of Table 10 (Ch. IV, Sec. 2), and is repeated here for convenience (Table 46).

Table 50 gives frequencies of notes that have $-\bar{z}$ subscripts and are lower than the notes of Table 46 by the comma $\bar{z}$ (ratio $\frac{64}{63}$). These notes furnish the minor sevenths of dominant seventh chords whose roots have 0 subscripts.

TABLE 44

ratio	size in cents	name(s) (if any)	essential characteristics
commas (17)			
$\frac{32805}{32768}$	1.954	schisma	Ch. VI, Sec. 2
$\frac{256}{255}$	6.776		Ch. VI, Sec. 6
$\frac{15625}{15552}$	8.107		Ch. VI, Sec. 5
$\frac{4131}{4096}$	14.730		Ch. VI, Sec. 6
$\frac{2048}{2025}$	19.553	diaschisma	Ch. VI, Sec. 2
$\frac{85}{84}$	20.488		Ch. VI, Sec. 6
$\frac{81}{80}$	21.506	syntonic comma	Ch. III, Sec. 7
$\frac{531441}{524288}$	23.460	Pythagorean comma	Ch. IV, Sec. 5
$\frac{64}{63}$	27.264	septimal comma	Ch. V, Sec. 5
$\frac{3125}{3072}$	29.614		Ch. VI, Sec. 5
$\frac{51}{50}$	34.283		Ch. VI, Sec. 6
$\frac{128}{125}$	41.059	diesis	Ch. VI, Sec. 2
$\frac{6561}{6400}$	43.013		Ch. VI, Sec. 5
$\frac{40}{39}$	43.831		Ch. VI, Sec. 7
$\frac{36}{35}$	48.770		Ch. V, Sec. 5
$\frac{33}{32}$	53.273		Ch. VI, Sec. 7
$\frac{648}{625}$	62.565		Ch. VI, Sec. 5
minor seconds and chromatic semitones (9)			
$\frac{25}{24}$	70.672	minor chroma	Ch. VI, Sec. 4
$\frac{21}{20}$	84.467		Ch. V, Sec. 5
$\frac{256}{243}$	90.225	limma, Pythagorean minor second	Ch. II, Secs. 4 & 6
$\frac{135}{128}$	92.179	major chroma	Ch. VI, Sec. 1
$\frac{17}{16}$	104.955	seventh basic interval	Ch. VI, Sec. 6
$\frac{16}{15}$	111.731	diatonic semitone	Ch. V, Sec. 2
$\frac{2187}{2048}$	113.685	apotome	Ch. III, Sec. 4
$\frac{14}{13}$	128.298		Ch. VI, Sec. 7
$\frac{27}{25}$	133.238	maximum semitone	Ch. V, Sec. 4
major seconds (5)			
$\frac{35}{32}$	155.140		Ch. VI, Sec. 6
$\frac{11}{10}$	165.004		Ch. VI, Sec. 7
$\frac{10}{9}$	182.404	minor tone	Ch. V, Sec. 2

TABLE 44 (Continued)

ratio	size in cents	name(s) (if any)	essential characteristics
[*major seconds, cont.*]			
$\frac{9}{8}$	203.910	major tone, Pythagorean major second	Ch. II, Sec. 6 Ch. V, Sec. 2
$\frac{8}{7}$	231.174		Ch. V, Sec. 5
minor thirds and augmented seconds (7)			
$\frac{7}{6}$	266.871		Ch. V, Sec. 5
$\frac{75}{64}$	274.582		Ch. VI, Sec. 4
$\frac{20}{17}$	281.358		Ch. VI, Sec. 6
$\frac{13}{11}$	289.210		Ch. VI, Sec. 7
$\frac{32}{27}$	294.135	Pythagorean minor third	Ch. III, Sec. 7
$\frac{6}{5}$	315.641	pure minor third	Ch. III, Sec. 7
$\frac{17}{14}$	336.130		Ch. VI, Sec. 6
major thirds and diminished fourths (10)			
$\frac{16}{13}$	359.472		Ch. VI, Sec. 7
$\frac{100}{81}$	364.807		Ch. V, Sec. 4
$\frac{8192}{6561}$	384.360	schismatic major third, Pythagorean diminished fourth	Ch. V, Sec. 3 Ch. IV, Sec. 3
$\frac{5}{4}$	386.314	pure major third, third basic interval	Ch. I, Secs. 2 & 5 Ch. III, Sec. 7
$\frac{512}{405}$	405.866		Ch. VI, Sec. 6
$\frac{81}{64}$	407.820	Pythagorean major third	Ch. III, Sec. 7
$\frac{14}{11}$	417.508		Ch. VI, Sec. 7
$\frac{32}{25}$	427.373		Ch. VI, Sec. 4
$\frac{9}{7}$	435.084		Ch. V, Sec. 6
$\frac{13}{10}$	454.214		Ch. VI, Sec. 7
perfect fourths (2)			
$\frac{21}{16}$	470.781		Ch. V, Sec. 5
$\frac{4}{3}$	498.045	pure perfect fourth	Ch. II, Sec. 4

TABLE 44 (Continued)

ratio	size in cents	name(s) (if any)	essential characteristics
augmented fourths and diminished fifths (10)			
$\frac{11}{8}$	551.318	fifth basic interval	Ch. VI, Sec. 7
$\frac{7}{5}$	582.512		Ch. V, Sec. 5
$\frac{1024}{729}$	588.270	Pythagorean diminished fifth	Ch. II, Sec. 4
$\frac{24}{17}$	597.000		Ch. VI, Sec. 6
$\frac{17}{12}$	603.000		Ch. VI, Sec. 6
$\frac{64}{45}$	609.776		Ch. V, Sec. 2
$\frac{729}{512}$	611.730	Pythagorean augmented fourth	Ch. II, Sec. 4
$\frac{10}{7}$	617.488		Ch. V, Sec. 5
$\frac{36}{25}$	631.283		Ch. V, Sec. 4
$\frac{16}{11}$	648.682		Ch. VI, Sec. 7
perfect fifths and diminished sixths (3)			
$\frac{262144}{177147}$	678.495	Pythagorean diminished sixth	Ch. IV, Sec. 5
$\frac{40}{27}$	680.449		Ch. V, Sec. 2
$\frac{3}{2}$	701.955	pure perfect fifth, second basic interval	Ch. I, Secs. 2 & 5
minor sixths and augmented fifths (9)			
$\frac{25}{16}$	772.627		Ch. VI, Sec. 4
$\frac{128}{81}$	792.180	Pythagorean minor sixth	Ch. II, Sec. 4
$\frac{8}{5}$	813.686		Ch. V, Sec. 2
$\frac{13}{8}$	840.528	sixth basic interval	Ch. VI, Sec. 7
$\frac{28}{17}$	863.870		Ch. VI, Sec. 6
$\frac{5}{3}$	884.359	pure major sixth	Ch. V, Sec. 2
$\frac{27}{16}$	905.865	Pythagorean major sixth	Ch. II, Sec. 4
$\frac{17}{10}$	918.642		Ch. VI, Sec. 6
$\frac{12}{7}$	933.129		Ch. V, Sec. 5

TABLE 44 (Continued)

ratio	size in cents	name(s) (if any)	essential characteristics
minor sevenths (3)			
$\frac{7}{4}$	968.826	fourth basic interval	Ch. V, Sec. 5
$\frac{16}{9}$	996.090	Pythagorean minor seventh	Ch. II, Sec. 4
$\frac{9}{5}$	1017.596		Ch. V, Sec. 6
major sevenths (4)			
$\frac{13}{7}$	1071.702		Ch. VI, Sec. 7
$\frac{15}{8}$	1088.269		Ch. V, Sec. 5
$\frac{32}{17}$	1095.045		Ch. VI, Sec. 6
$\frac{243}{128}$	1109.775	Pythagorean major seventh	Ch. II, Sec. 4
octave (1)			
$\frac{2}{1}$	1200.000	octave, first basic interval	Ch. I, Sec. 2

Table 51 gives frequencies of notes lower than those of Table 46 by the comma $\bar{z} + \bar{k}$ (ratio $\frac{36}{35}$). These notes furnish the minor sevenths of dominant seventh chords whose roots have -1 subscripts.

Table 52 gives frequencies of notes lower than those of Table 46 by the comma $\bar{y}$ (ratio $\frac{256}{255}$). These notes furnish the minor ninths of dominant ninth chords whose roots have -1 subscripts, also the higher note of a diminished seventh whose lower note has a -2 subscript.

Table 53 gives frequencies of notes higher than those of Table 46 by the comma $\bar{k} - \bar{y}$ (ratio $\frac{4131}{4096}$). These notes furnish the minor ninths of dominant ninth chords whose roots have 0 subscripts, also the higher note of a diminished seventh whose lower note has a -1 subscript.

Frequencies are given for both $C_0 = 264$ Hz and $C_0 = 261.626$ Hz.[6] In just tuning, the recommended standard is $C_0 = 264$ Hz, giving $A_{-1} = 440$ Hz. All frequencies are given in the octave above and including middle C. The other columns are self-explanatory.

[6] See Ch. IV, note 2.

TABLE 45

note	ratio with C_0	frequency $C_0 = 264$	frequency $C_0 = 261.626$	cents up from C_0
A$\times_{+1}$	1.948393	514.376	509.749	1154.741
D$\times_{+1}$	1.298928	342.917	339.833	452.786
G$\times_{+1}$	1.731905	457.223	453.111	950.831
C$\times_{+1}$	1.154603	304.815	302.074	248.876
F$\times_{+1}$	1.539471	406.420	402.765	746.921
B$\sharp_{+1}$	1.026314	270.947	268.510	44.966
E$\sharp_{+1}$	1.368418	361.262	358.013	543.011
A$\sharp_{+1}$	1.824558	481.683	477.351	1041.056
D$\sharp_{+1}$	1.216372	321.122	318.234	339.101
G$\sharp_{+1}$	1.621829	428.163	424.312	837.146
C$\sharp_{+1}$	1.081219	285.442	282.875	135.191
F$\sharp_{+1}$	1.441626	380.589	377.166	633.236
B$_{+1}$	1.922168	507.452	502.888	1131.281
E$_{+1}$	1.281445	338.302	335.259	429.326
A$_{+1}$	1.708594	451.069	447.012	927.371
D$_{+1}$	1.139063	300.713	298.008	225.416
G$_{+1}$	1.518750	400.950	397.344	723.461
C$_{+1}$	1.012500	267.300	264.896	21.506
F$_{+1}$	1.350000	356.400	353.195	519.551
B$\flat_{+1}$	1.800000	475.200	470.926	1017.596
E$\flat_{+1}$	1.200000	316.800	313.951	315.641
A$\flat_{+1}$	1.600000	422.400	418.601	813.686
D$\flat_{+1}$	1.066667	281.600	279.067	111.731
G$\flat_{+1}$	1.422222	375.467	372.090	609.776
C$\flat_{+1}$	1.896296	500.622	496.120	1107.821
F$\flat_{+1}$	1.264198	333.748	330.746	405.866
B$\flat\flat_{+1}$	1.685597	444.998	440.995	903.911
E$\flat\flat_{+1}$	1.123731	296.665	293.997	201.956
A$\flat\flat_{+1}$	1.498308	395.553	391.996	700.001
D$\flat\flat_{+1}$	1.997744	527.404	522.661	1198.046
G$\flat\flat_{+1}$	1.331829	351.603	348.441	496.091

TABLE 46

note	ratio with C_0	frequency $C_0 = 264$	frequency $C_0 = 261.626$	cents up from C_0
A𝄪$_0$	1.924338	508.025	503.456	1133.235
D𝄪$_0$	1.282892	338.684	335.637	431.280
G𝄪$_0$	1.710523	451.578	447.517	929.325
C𝄪$_0$	1.140349	301.052	298.344	227.370
F𝄪$_0$	1.520465	401.403	397.792	725.415
B♯$_0$	1.013643	267.602	265.195	23.460
E♯$_0$	1.351524	356.802	353.593	521.505
A♯$_0$	1.802032	475.737	471.458	1019.550
D♯$_0$	1.201355	317.158	314.305	317.595
G♯$_0$	1.601807	422.877	419.074	815.640
C♯$_0$	1.067871	281.918	279.382	113.685
F♯$_0$	1.423828	375.891	372.510	611.730
B$_0$	1.898438	501.188	496.680	1109.775
E$_0$	1.265625	334.125	331.120	407.820
A$_0$	1.687500	445.500	441.493	905.865
D$_0$	1.125000	297.000	294.329	203.910
G$_0$	1.500000	396.000	392.438	701.955
C$_0$	1.000000	264.000	261.626	0.000
F$_0$	1.333333	352.000	348.834	498.045
B♭$_0$	1.777778	469.333	465.112	996.090
E♭$_0$	1.185185	312.889	310.075	294.135
A♭$_0$	1.580247	417.185	413.433	792.180
D♭$_0$	1.053498	278.123	275.622	90.225
G♭$_0$	1.404664	370.831	367.496	588.270
C♭$_0$	1.872885	494.442	489.995	1086.315
F♭$_0$	1.248590	329.628	326.663	384.360
B♭♭$_0$	1.664787	439.504	435.551	882.405
E♭♭$_0$	1.109858	293.002	290.367	180.450
A♭♭$_0$	1.479811	390.670	387.156	678.495
D♭♭$_0$	1.973081	520.893	516.208	1176.540
G♭♭$_0$	1.315387	347.262	344.139	474.585

TABLE 47

note	ratio with C_0	frequency $C_0 = 264$	frequency $C_0 = 261.626$	cents up from C_0
A$\times_{-1}$	1.900581	501.753	497.241	1111.729
D$\times_{-1}$	1.267054	334.502	331.494	409.774
G$\times_{-1}$	1.689405	446.003	441.992	907.819
C$\times_{-1}$	1.126270	297.335	294.661	205.864
F$\times_{-1}$	1.501694	396.447	392.881	703.909
B$\sharp_{-1}$	1.001129	264.298	261.921	1.954
E$\sharp_{-1}$	1.334839	352.397	349.228	499.999
A$\sharp_{-1}$	1.779785	469.863	465.637	998.044
D$\sharp_{-1}$	1.186523	313.242	310.425	296.089
G$\sharp_{-1}$	1.582031	417.656	413.900	794.134
C$\sharp_{-1}$	1.054688	278.438	275.933	92.179
F$\sharp_{-1}$	1.406250	371.250	367.911	590.224
B$_{-1}$	1.875000	495.000	490.548	1088.269
E$_{-1}$	1.250000	330.000	327.032	386.314
A$_{-1}$	1.666667	440.000	436.043	884.359
D$_{-1}$	1.111111	293.333	290.695	182.404
G$_{-1}$	1.481481	391.111	387.593	680.449
C$_{-1}$	1.975309	521.481	516.791	1178.494
F$_{-1}$	1.316872	347.654	344.527	476.539
B$\flat_{-1}$	1.755830	463.539	459.370	974.584
E$\flat_{-1}$	1.170553	309.026	306.247	272.629
A$\flat_{-1}$	1.560738	412.035	408.329	770.674
D$\flat_{-1}$	1.040492	274.690	272.219	68.719
G$\flat_{-1}$	1.387322	366.253	362.959	566.764
C$\flat_{-1}$	1.849763	488.337	483.945	1064.809
F$\flat_{-1}$	1.233175	325.558	322.630	362.854
B$\flat\flat_{-1}$	1.644234	434.078	430.174	860.899
E$\flat\flat_{-1}$	1.096156	289.385	286.782	158.944
A$\flat\flat_{-1}$	1.461541	385.847	382.377	656.989
D$\flat\flat_{-1}$	1.948722	514.463	509.835	1155.034
G$\flat\flat_{-1}$	1.299148	342.975	339.890	453.079

TABLE 48

note	ratio with C_0	frequency $C_0 = 264$	frequency $C_0 = 261.626$	cents up from C_0
A$\times_{-2}$	1.877117	495.559	491.102	1090.222
D$\times_{-2}$	1.251411	330.373	327.401	388.267
G$\times_{-2}$	1.668549	440.497	436.535	886.312
C$\times_{-2}$	1.112366	293.665	291.023	184.357
F$\times_{-2}$	1.483154	391.553	388.031	682.402
B$\sharp_{-2}$	1.977539	522.070	517.375	1180.447
E$\sharp_{-2}$	1.318359	348.047	344.917	478.492
A$\sharp_{-2}$	1.757813	464.063	459.889	976.537
D$\sharp_{-2}$	1.171875	309.375	306.592	274.582
G$\sharp_{-2}$	1.562500	412.500	408.790	772.627
C$\sharp_{-2}$	1.041667	275.000	272.527	70.672
F$\sharp_{-2}$	1.388889	366.667	363.369	568.717
B$_{-2}$	1.851852	488.889	484.492	1066.762
E$_{-2}$	1.234568	325.926	322.995	364.807
A$_{-2}$	1.646091	434.568	430.659	862.852
D$_{-2}$	1.097394	289.712	287.106	160.897
G$_{-2}$	1.463192	386.283	382.808	658.942
C$_{-2}$	1.950922	515.043	510.411	1156.987
F$_{-2}$	1.300615	343.362	340.274	455.032
B$\flat_{-2}$	1.734153	457.816	453.699	953.077
E$\flat_{-2}$	1.156102	305.211	302.466	251.122
A$\flat_{-2}$	1.541469	406.948	403.288	749.167
D$\flat_{-2}$	1.027646	271.299	268.859	47.212
G$\flat_{-2}$	1.370195	361.731	358.478	545.257
C$\flat_{-2}$	1.826927	482.309	477.971	1043.302
F$\flat_{-2}$	1.217951	321.539	318.647	341.347
B$\flat\flat_{-2}$	1.623935	428.719	424.863	839.392
E$\flat\flat_{-2}$	1.082623	285.813	283.242	137.437
A$\flat\flat_{-2}$	1.443498	381.083	377.656	635.482
D$\flat\flat_{-2}$	1.924663	508.111	503.541	1133.527
G$\flat\flat_{-2}$	1.283109	338.741	335.694	431.572

TABLE 49

note	ratio with C_0	frequency $C_0 = 264$	frequency $C_0 = 261.626$	cents up from C_0
$A\times_{-3}$	1.853943	489.441	485.039	1068.716
$D\times_{-3}$	1.235962	326.294	323.359	366.761
$G\times_{-3}$	1.647949	435.059	431.146	864.806
$C\times_{-3}$	1.098633	290.039	287.430	162.851
$F\times_{-3}$	1.464844	386.719	383.241	660.896
$B\#_{-3}$	1.953125	515.625	510.987	1158.941
$E\#_{-3}$	1.302083	343.750	340.658	456.986
$A\#_{-3}$	1.736111	458.333	454.211	955.031
$D\#_{-3}$	1.157407	305.556	302.807	253.076
$G\#_{-3}$	1.543210	407.407	403.743	751.121
$C\#_{-3}$	1.028807	271.605	269.162	49.166
$F\#_{-3}$	1.371742	362.140	358.883	547.211
B_{-3}	1.828989	482.853	478.510	1045.256
E_{-3}	1.219326	321.902	319.007	343.301
A_{-3}	1.625768	429.203	425.343	841.346
D_{-3}	1.083846	286.135	283.562	139.391
G_{-3}	1.445127	381.514	378.082	637.436
C_{-3}	1.926837	508.685	504.110	1135.481
F_{-3}	1.284558	339.123	336.073	433.526
$B\flat_{-3}$	1.712744	452.164	448.098	931.571
$E\flat_{-3}$	1.141829	301.443	298.732	229.616
$A\flat_{-3}$	1.522439	401.924	398.309	727.661
$D\flat_{-3}$	1.014959	267.949	265.539	25.706
$G\flat_{-3}$	1.353279	357.266	354.052	523.751
$C\flat_{-3}$	1.804372	476.354	472.070	1021.796
$F\flat_{-3}$	1.202915	317.569	314.713	319.841
$B\flat\flat_{-3}$	1.603886	423.426	419.618	817.886
$E\flat\flat_{-3}$	1.069257	282.284	279.745	115.931
$A\flat\flat_{-3}$	1.425677	376.379	372.993	613.976
$D\flat\flat_{-3}$	1.900902	501.838	497.325	1112.021
$G\flat\flat_{-3}$	1.267268	334.559	331.550	410.066

TABLE 50

note	ratio with C_0	frequency $C_0 = 264$	frequency $C_0 = 261.626$	cents up from C_0
A$\times_{-\frac{7}{2}}$	1.894271	500.087	495.590	1105.971
D$\times_{-\frac{7}{2}}$	1.262847	333.392	330.393	404.016
G$\times_{-\frac{7}{2}}$	1.683796	444.522	440.524	902.061
C$\times_{-\frac{7}{2}}$	1.122531	296.348	293.683	200.106
F$\times_{-\frac{7}{2}}$	1.496708	395.131	391.577	698.151
B♯$_{-\frac{7}{2}}$	1.995610	526.841	522.103	1196.196
E♯$_{-\frac{7}{2}}$	1.330407	351.227	348.068	494.241
A♯$_{-\frac{7}{2}}$	1.773876	468.303	464.091	992.286
D♯$_{-\frac{7}{2}}$	1.182584	312.202	309.394	290.331
G♯$_{-\frac{7}{2}}$	1.576778	416.270	412.526	788.376
C♯$_{-\frac{7}{2}}$	1.051186	277.513	275.017	86.421
F♯$_{-\frac{7}{2}}$	1.401581	370.017	366.689	584.466
B$_{-\frac{7}{2}}$	1.868774	493.356	488.919	1082.511
E$_{-\frac{7}{2}}$	1.245850	328.904	325.946	380.556
A$_{-\frac{7}{2}}$	1.661133	438.539	434.595	878.601
D$_{-\frac{7}{2}}$	1.107422	292.359	289.730	176.646
G$_{-\frac{7}{2}}$	1.476563	389.813	386.306	674.691
C$_{-\frac{7}{2}}$	1.968750	519.750	515.075	1172.736
F$_{-\frac{7}{2}}$	1.312500	346.500	343.384	470.781
B♭$_{-\frac{7}{2}}$	1.750000	462.000	457.845	968.826
E♭$_{-\frac{7}{2}}$	1.166667	308.000	305.230	266.871
A♭$_{-\frac{7}{2}}$	1.555556	410.667	406.973	764.916
D♭$_{-\frac{7}{2}}$	1.037037	273.778	271.315	62.961
G♭$_{-\frac{7}{2}}$	1.382716	365.037	361.754	561.006
C♭$_{-\frac{7}{2}}$	1.843621	486.716	482.338	1059.051
F♭$_{-\frac{7}{2}}$	1.229081	324.477	321.559	357.096
B♭♭$_{-\frac{7}{2}}$	1.638775	432.636	428.745	855.141
E♭♭$_{-\frac{7}{2}}$	1.092516	288.424	285.830	153.186
A♭♭$_{-\frac{7}{2}}$	1.456689	384.566	381.107	651.231
D♭♭$_{-\frac{7}{2}}$	1.942251	512.754	508.143	1149.276
G♭♭$_{-\frac{7}{2}}$	1.294834	341.836	338.762	447.321

TABLE 51

note	ratio with C_0	frequency $C_0 = 264$	frequency $C_0 = 261.626$	cents up from C_0
$A\boldsymbol{\times}_{-(\bar{k}+\bar{z})}$	1.870885	493.914	489.471.	1084.465
$D\boldsymbol{\times}_{-(\bar{k}+\bar{z})}$	1.247256	329.276	326.314	382.510
$G\boldsymbol{\times}_{-(\bar{k}+\bar{z})}$	1.663008	439.034	435.086	880.555
$C\boldsymbol{\times}_{-(\bar{k}+\bar{z})}$	1.108672	292.689	290.057	178.600
$F\boldsymbol{\times}_{-(\bar{k}+\bar{z})}$	1.478230	390.253	386.743	676.645
$B\sharp_{-(\bar{k}+\bar{z})}$	1.970973	520.337	515.657	1174.690
$E\sharp_{-(\bar{k}+\bar{z})}$	1.313982	346.891	343.771	472.735
$A\sharp_{-(\bar{k}+\bar{z})}$	1.751976	462.522	458.362	970.780
$D\sharp_{-(\bar{k}+\bar{z})}$	1.167984	308.348	305.574	268.825
$G\sharp_{-(\bar{k}+\bar{z})}$	1.557312	411.130	407.433	766.870
$C\sharp_{-(\bar{k}+\bar{z})}$	1.038208	274.087	271.622	64.915
$F\sharp_{-(\bar{k}+\bar{z})}$	1.384277	365.449	362.162	562.960
$B_{-(\bar{k}+\bar{z})}$	1.845703	487.266	482.883	1061.005
$E_{-(\bar{k}+\bar{z})}$	1.230469	324.844	321.922	359.050
$A_{-(\bar{k}+\bar{z})}$	1.640625	433.125	429.229	857.095
$D_{-(\bar{k}+\bar{z})}$	1.093750	288.750	286.153	155.140
$G_{-(\bar{k}+\bar{z})}$	1.458333	385.000	381.537	653.185
$C_{-(\bar{k}+\bar{z})}$	1.944444	513.333	508.716	1151.230
$F_{-(\bar{k}+\bar{z})}$	1.296296	342.222	339.144	449.275
$B\flat_{-(\bar{k}+\bar{z})}$	1.728395	456.296	452.192	947.320
$E\flat_{-(\bar{k}+\bar{z})}$	1.152263	304.198	301.462	245.365
$A\flat_{-(\bar{k}+\bar{z})}$	1.536351	405.597	401.949	743.410
$D\flat_{-(\bar{k}+\bar{z})}$	1.024234	270.398	267.966	41.455
$G\flat_{-(\bar{k}+\bar{z})}$	1.365645	360.530	357.288	539.500
$C\flat_{-(\bar{k}+\bar{z})}$	1.820861	480.707	476.384	1037.545
$F\flat_{-(\bar{k}+\bar{z})}$	1.213907	320.471	317.589	335.590
$B\flat\flat_{-(\bar{k}+\bar{z})}$	1.618543	427.295	423.452	833.635
$E\flat\flat_{-(\bar{k}+\bar{z})}$	1.079029	284.864	282.301	131.680
$A\flat\flat_{-(\bar{k}+\bar{z})}$	1.438705	379.818	376.402	629.725
$D\flat\flat_{-(\bar{k}+\bar{z})}$	1.918273	506.424	501.869	1127.770
$G\flat\flat_{-(\bar{k}+\bar{z})}$	1.278849	337.616	334.579	425.815

TABLE 52

note	ratio with C_0	frequency $C_0 = 264$	frequency $C_0 = 261.626$	cents up from C_0
$A\times_{-\bar{y}}$	1.916821	506.041	501.489	1126.459
$D\times_{-\bar{y}}$	1.277881	337.361	334.326	424.504
$G\times_{-\bar{y}}$	1.703841	449.814	445.768	922.549
$C\times_{-\bar{y}}$	1.135894	299.876	297.179	220.594
$F\times_{-\bar{y}}$	1.514526	399.835	396.239	718.639
$B\#_{-\bar{y}}$	1.009684	266.557	264.159	16.684
$E\#_{-\bar{y}}$	1.346245	355.409	352.212	514.729
$A\#_{-\bar{y}}$	1.794993	473.878	469.616	1012.774
$D\#_{-\bar{y}}$	1.196662	315.919	313.077	310.819
$G\#_{-\bar{y}}$	1.595550	421.225	417.437	808.864
$C\#_{-\bar{y}}$	1.063700	280.817	278.291	106.909
$F\#_{-\bar{y}}$	1.418266	374.422	371.055	604.954
$B_{-\bar{y}}$	1.891022	499.230	494.740	1102.999
$E_{-\bar{y}}$	1.260681	332.820	329.826	401.044
$A_{-\bar{y}}$	1.680908	443.760	439.769	899.089
$D_{-\bar{y}}$	1.120605	295.840	293.179	197.134
$G_{-\bar{y}}$	1.494141	394.453	390.905	695.179
$C_{-\bar{y}}$	1.992188	525.938	521.207	1193.224
$F_{-\bar{y}}$	1.328125	350.625	347.471	491.269
$Bb_{-\bar{y}}$	1.770833	467.500	463.295	989.314
$Eb_{-\bar{y}}$	1.180556	311.667	308.864	287.359
$Ab_{-\bar{y}}$	1.574074	415.556	411.818	785.404
$Db_{-\bar{y}}$	1.049383	277.037	274.545	83.449
$Gb_{-\bar{y}}$	1.399177	369.383	366.060	581.494
$Cb_{-\bar{y}}$	1.865569	492.510	488.081	1079.539
$Fb_{-\bar{y}}$	1.243713	328.340	325.387	377.584
$Bbb_{-\bar{y}}$	1.658284	437.787	433.849	875.629
$Ebb_{-\bar{y}}$	1.105523	291.858	289.233	173.674
$Abb_{-\bar{y}}$	1.474030	389.144	385.644	671.719
$Dbb_{-\bar{y}}$	1.965373	518.859	514.192	1169.764
$Gbb_{-\bar{y}}$	1.310249	345.906	342.795	467.809

EXTENDED JUST TUNING

TABLE 53

note	ratio with C_0	frequency $C_0 = 264$	frequency $C_0 = 261.626$	cents up from C_0
$A\boldsymbol{\times}_{+(\bar{k}-\bar{y})}$	1.940782	512.366	507.758	1147.965
$D\boldsymbol{\times}_{+(\bar{k}-\bar{y})}$	1.293854	341.578	338.505	446.010
$G\boldsymbol{\times}_{+(\bar{k}-\bar{y})}$	1.725139	455.437	451.341	944.055
$C\boldsymbol{\times}_{+(\bar{k}-\bar{y})}$	1.150093	303.625	300.894	242.100
$F\boldsymbol{\times}_{+(\bar{k}-\bar{y})}$	1.533457	404.833	401.192	740.145
$B\sharp_{+(\bar{k}-\bar{y})}$	1.022305	269.888	267.461	38.190
$E\sharp_{+(\bar{k}-\bar{y})}$	1.363073	359.851	356.615	536.235
$A\sharp_{+(\bar{k}-\bar{y})}$	1.817431	479.802	475.486	1034.280
$D\sharp_{+(\bar{k}-\bar{y})}$	1.211620	319.868	316.991	332.325
$G\sharp_{+(\bar{k}-\bar{y})}$	1.615494	426.490	422.655	830.370
$C\sharp_{+(\bar{k}-\bar{y})}$	1.076996	284.327	281.770	128.415
$F\sharp_{+(\bar{k}-\bar{y})}$	1.435995	379.103	375.693	626.460
$B_{+(\bar{k}-\bar{y})}$	1.914660	505.470	500.924	1124.505
$E_{+(\bar{k}-\bar{y})}$	1.276440	336.980	333.949	422.550
$A_{+(\bar{k}-\bar{y})}$	1.701920	449.307	445.266	920.595
$D_{+(\bar{k}-\bar{y})}$	1.134613	299.538	296.844	218.640
$G_{+(\bar{k}-\bar{y})}$	1.512817	399.384	395.792	716.685
$C_{+(\bar{k}-\bar{y})}$	1.008545	266.256	263.861	14.730
$F_{+(\bar{k}-\bar{y})}$	1.344727	355.008	351.815	512.775
$B\flat_{+(\bar{k}-\bar{y})}$	1.792969	473.344	469.086	1010.820
$E\flat_{+(\bar{k}-\bar{y})}$	1.195313	315.563	312.724	308.865
$A\flat_{+(\bar{k}-\bar{y})}$	1.593750	420.750	416.966	806.910
$D\flat_{+(\bar{k}-\bar{y})}$	1.062500	280.500	277.977	104.955
$G\flat_{+(\bar{k}-\bar{y})}$	1.416667	374.000	370.636	603.000
$C\flat_{+(\bar{k}-\bar{y})}$	1.888889	498.667	494.182	1101.045
$F\flat_{+(\bar{k}-\bar{y})}$	1.259259	332.444	329.454	399.090
$B\flat\flat_{+(\bar{k}-\bar{y})}$	1.679012	443.259	439.273	897.135
$E\flat\flat_{+(\bar{k}-\bar{y})}$	1.119342	295.506	292.848	195.180
$A\flat\flat_{+(\bar{k}-\bar{y})}$	1.492455	394.008	390.464	693.225
$D\flat\flat_{+(\bar{k}-\bar{y})}$	1.989941	525.344	520.619	1191.270
$G\flat\flat_{+(\bar{k}-\bar{y})}$	1.326627	350.230	347.080	489.315

VII   Musical Examples in Just Tuning

Introduction.   If just tuning is taken to mean the most euphonious possible arrangement of all simultaneous combinations of notes, then it follows that any musical passage has a just tuning. On the other hand, as we have seen, certain chords, or combinations of notes, cannot be tuned in such a manner as to consist solely of pure intervals (Ch. V, Sec. 6; Ch. VI, Secs. 6 and 7).

The problem of determining the just tuning for a given musical fragment is generally solvable by the application of principles developed in Chapters V and VI, and involves attaching the appropriate subscripts to the notes as originally notated. However, actual situations present unexpected problems which can only be met by subjective judgment. How a solution may be arrived at is best illustrated by working out the just tuning of actual compositions. After studying a few examples, the reader will see that solutions are not as simple as might have been thought. We present several examples taken from different periods in music history, from the fourteenth, sixteenth, eighteenth, and nineteenth centuries.

In Section 5 the conclusion is drawn that a perfect tuning for a given musical composition cannot be found.

1. Guillaume de Machaut (1284–1370), *Kyrie* from *Messe de Nostre Dame*.[1]

An inspection of the short passage from the *Kyrie* of Machaut's *Messe de Nostre Dame* reveals that by and large, all harmonies are either major or minor triads, or consist of perfect fourths, perfect fifths, and octaves, but without thirds. We recall that the just tuning of such combinations involves the following principles:

  1. Perfect fifths, perfect fourths, and octaves must all be pure; hence two notes forming any of these intervals must have the same subscripts.

---

[1] Guillaume de Machaut, Musicalische Werke (Leipzig: Breitkopf und Härtel, 1943), vol. 4, 2.

GUILLAUME DE MACHAUT (1284–1370), *Kyrie* FROM *Messe de Nostre Dame*

2. Major triads must all be pure; hence the third of a major triad must have a subscript one less than that of the root and fifth.

3. Minor triads must all be pure; hence the third of a minor triad must have a subscript one greater than that of the root and fifth.

4. Thirds and sixths in which both notes have the same subscripts are Pythagorean, and should be avoided if possible.

5. The root and fifth of a major triad should generally have 0 subscripts; the root and fifth of a minor triad should generally have -1 subscripts. This arrangement tends to minimize the occurrence of the syntonic comma as a melodic interval.

The application of the fifth principle above to the present example requires that the modality of combinations containing a root and fifth, but no third, must be deduced from the context. This is aided by observing that the example, as originally notated, uses only nine notes, occupying nine adjacent positions on the line of fifths, viz., F, C, G, D, A, E, B, F♯, and C♯. The absence of A♭, E♭, and B♭ suggests that FC, CG, and GD should be construed as the root and fifth of major triads, and should be tuned F_0C_0, C_0G_0, and G_0D_0, respectively. And since G♯ is not used, we assume EB to be the root and fifth of a minor triad, and prefer the tuning $E_{-1}B_{-1}$. This leaves only DA and AE in any doubt, and the question may always be resolved by considerations of the text. A bar-by-bar discussion of the example follows.

Bar 1. The tuning $D_{-1}A_{-1}$ is suggested by the fact that F is combined with these notes in bar 2. On the fourth quarter, A_{-1} is retained in the soprano part to avoid the occurrence of a melodic syntonic comma. The minor triad on the fifth quarter is best tuned $E_{-1}G_0B_{-1}$; and for the major triad on the sixth quarter, $C_0E_{-1}G_0$ is preferred.

Bar 2. The fourth quarter presents a special problem. If the bass is tuned G_0, the soprano must be tuned D_0, and the alto C_0. But when the bass moves down to F_0, the soprano must change to D_{-1} to avoid Pythagorean major sixth F_0D_0, thus causing a melodic syntonic comma to occur in the soprano. More generally, the combination GCD requires that all three notes should have the same subscripts. In the case of FCD, however, F and C must have the same subscripts; but D must have a subscript one less than F so that FD will be pure. Consequently D must have a subscript one less than C in the combination FCD, regardless of what subscripts are actually chosen. In other words, CD must be a major tone when combined with G, and a minor tone when combined with F—hence a melodic syntonic comma is unavoidable in the text as given. The best tuning for the text is the one shown—$G_{-1}C_{-1}D_{-1}$ followed by $F_0C_0D_{-1}$—placing the melodic syntonic comma in the alto part rather than in the soprano. We might also consider $G_0C_0D_0$ followed by $F_{+1}C_{+1}D_0$ as a possibility; but this causes the bass to progress from F_{+1} down to E_{-1}, a maximum semitone of 133.238 cents (Ch. V, Sec. 4)—larger than one would desire for a minor second. On the fifth quarter, $E_{-1}B_{-1}$ is preferred for the reasons stated above; and on the sixth quarter, the minor triad is tuned $B_{-1}D_0F♯_{-1}$.

Bar 3. The tuning of this bar follows directly from the principles listed at the beginning of this section, save for D in the alto. Here D_0 is preferred so that $B_{-1}D_0$ will be pure.

Bar 4. On the second quarter, we take E_{-1} so that $E_{-1}G_0$ is pure. On the fifth quarter, the combination FCD occurs once again, and for the same reason as before, the best tuning is $F_0C_0D_{-1}$. As a consequence of this, the fourth quarter is best tuned $A_{-1}E_{-1}$ followed by $G_{-1}A_{-1}D_{-1}$, thereby avoiding a melodic syntonic comma or a maximum semitone.

Bar 5. This bar presents no special difficulty. On the fourth quarter, the best tuning is $A_{-1}E_{-1}$, retaining A_{-1} which occurred earlier in minor triad $D_{-1}F_0A_{-1}$.

Bar 6. The tuning of the first three quarters is determined by what is necessary given F_0 in the tenor—C_0, A_{-1}, and G_0, so that C_0G_0 will be pure. On the fourth quarter, E_{-1} is chosen for the alto so that $E_{-1}G_0$ will be pure; and on the sixth quarter, E_{-1} makes a pure perfect fourth with A_{-1}.

Bars 7 and 8 are straightforward and present no problems.

Concerning the melodic intervals, an investigation of the individual voices reveals the following:

There is one syntonic comma, as noted above (alto, bar 2).

All minor seconds are diatonic semitones, ratio $\frac{16}{15}$, size 111.731 cents (Ch. V, Sec. 2).

Major seconds are either major tones, ratio $\frac{9}{8}$, size 203.910 cents, or minor tones, ratio $\frac{10}{9}$, size 182.404 cents.

Major and minor thirds are all pure.

There is one Pythagorean major sixth (bar 5, in the bass, $D_{-1}B_{-1}$).

Perfect fourths and fifths are pure with two exceptions—the first in the soprano in bar 3 ($E_{-1}A_0$), and the second in the alto in bar 6 ($A_{-1}D_0$). Impure melodic perfect fourths and fifths are not unduly disturbing if they depart from the pure tuning by no more than a syntonic comma.

It is of interest to note that only the 0 and -1 subscripts are needed for the just tuning of this example, the actual notes required being $F_0C_0G_0D_0A_0C_{-1}G_{-1}D_{-1}A_{-1}E_{-1}B_{-1}F\sharp_{-1}$ and $C\sharp_{-1}$—a total of thirteen. Of these, A_0, C_{-1}, and $C\sharp_{-1}$ occur only once.

Although the smoothness of the individual harmonies is undeniably agreeable, it is achieved at a sacrifice. In the tuning of the individual parts, the melodic syntonic comma, the rather large minor second and the two different major seconds are clearly less than ideal arrangements of the given text. In addition, the pure tuning of major and minor triads is at odds with the style of the fourteenth century, in which these harmonies were treated as dissonances. It will be observed that no triad occurs on the first beat of any bar.

If the example is played in Pythagorean tuning, the awkward contours of the individual parts are corrected—there are no melodic commas, all the minor seconds are the smaller limmas, and all the major seconds are major tones. Since the tonal quality of voices effectively masks the beats associated with slightly impure intervals, the Pythagorean triads are not disturbing in this context; in fact, their more acute sound is advantageous, given their treatment as dissonances. It must be concluded that the example is more idiomatic in Pythagorean tuning than in just tuning.[2] We shall return to this fragment during the discussion of 12-note equal tuning (Ch. XI, Sec. 6).

2. Orlando di Lasso (1530–1594), Motet _Ave regina coelorum_.[3]

ORLANDO DI LASSO (1530–1594),
MOTET _Ave regina coelorum_

In the first example from di Lasso's motet _Ave regina coelorum_, the tuning follows from the principles set forth at the beginning of the previous section—major triads are tuned so that their roots and fifths have 0 subscripts and their thirds have −1 subscripts, and minor triads are tuned so that their roots and fifths have −1 subscripts and their thirds have

---

[2] See also Ch. III, Sec. 7.
[3] Orlando di Lasso, Sämtliche Werke (Leipzig: Breitkopf und Härtel, 1894), vol. 1, 79–80.

0 subscripts. The example contains several instances of combinations of notes that are not triads, and a discussion of these cases follows.

Bar 3. On the third beat, the alto has G, functioning as a suspension which resolves to the root of the F major triad on the fourth beat. Since this major triad should be tuned $F_0A_{-1}C_0$, the G must be tuned G_0 so that C_0G_0 will be pure. However, the same G serves as the root of a G minor triad on the second beat, and G_{-1} is the correct tuning at this point. If G_{-1} is retained on the third beat, the tenor and bass must be tuned C_{-1}; and if C_{-1} is retained on the fourth beat, the F major triad there would be tuned $F_{-1}A_{-2}C_{-1}$, a syntonic comma lower than the F major triad in the second bar. If this anomaly is to be avoided, as clearly it must, then a melodic syntonic comma will occur somewhere in bar 2 or bar 3, since each harmony has one note in common with the preceding harmony.

Bar 4. On the first beat, F in the alto is a suspension resolving to the third of major triad $C_0E_{-1}G_0$, and is tuned F_0 so that C_0F_0 will be pure. The eighth note D in the alto is tuned D_0 owing to the presence of G_0 in the soprano. On the third beat, A in the soprano is a suspension resolving to the root of major triad $G_0B_{-1}D_0$, and must be tuned A_0 so as not to clash with D_0. However, A_{-1} is needed for the second beat, since it is the root of a minor triad. Thus there occurs another melodic syntonic comma at this point, unavoidable for the same reasons as in bar 3.

Bar 5. G in the soprano is tuned G_0 to combine with the root of major triad $D_0F\sharp_{-1}A_0$, and we take E_0 so that A_0E_0 will be pure.

If the melodic syntonic commas are eliminated, retaining G_{-1} in the alto on the third beat of bar 3 and keeping the same A in the soprano on the second and third beats of bar 4, the tuning must be as shown below, by virtue of the fact that two successive harmonies always have one note in common. In this version, the pitch falls by two syntonic commas—from G_0 to G_{-2}, amounting to 43.013 cents—within five bars. This difference

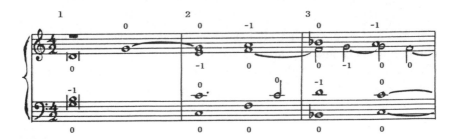

is sufficiently large to be perceived as a modulation, and represents a distortion of the intent, which is clearly that the initial chord and the final chord should be the same.

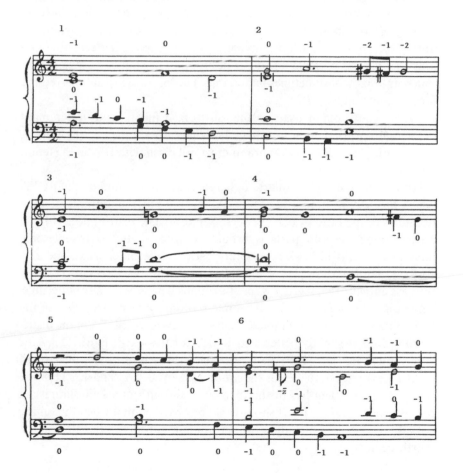

By and large, the just tuning of the last nine bars of di Lasso's *Ave regina coelorum*, as shown above, is achieved by applying the same principles. Tuning of non-chord notes (suspensions, passing notes and neighboring notes) follows from the necessity of avoiding impure perfect fifths and fourths—always possible—and the desirability of avoiding Pythagorean thirds and sixths—sometimes impossible. The following situations require further comment:

Bar 2. The E major triad on the fourth beat functions as a dominant of the A minor triad in the next bar, and hence is best tuned $E_{-1}G\sharp_{-2}B_{-1}$. Neighboring note F$\sharp$ in the soprano must not clash with B_{-1} in the tenor, and hence is tuned $F\sharp_{-1}$.

Bar 5. On the eighth quarter, there occurs the combination BDFA which has a pure tuning $B_{-1}D_0F_{-\bar{z}}A_0$, where $\bar{z}$ is the septimal comma of 27.264 cents, ratio $\frac{64}{63}$ (Ch. V, Secs. 5 and 6). The distribution of these notes among the four parts is peculiarly problematic, as troublesome interval $F_{-\bar{z}}A_0$ (Ch. V, Sec. 6) occurs between the outer parts, and discordant major sixth $F_{-\bar{z}}D_0$ of 933.129 cents (Ch. V, Sec. 5) occurs between the bass and alto in a register where its rough effect is especially noticeable. Any other tuning for F makes a more discordant interval with B_{-1} in the tenor, and so there is no completely smooth tuning for BDFA in the distribution given. A slightly better distribution for the text is $F_0B_{-1}D_{-1}A_{-1}$; even though $B_{-1}D_{-1}$ is Pythagorean and F_0B_{-1} is not pure, the overall effect is less undesirable than that produced by $F_{-\bar{z}}A_0$ and $F_{-\bar{z}}D_0$. The heart of the problem lies in the placing of the fifth of a half-diminished seventh chord in the bass. It should also be observed that when the tuning is $F_0B_{-1}D_{-1}A_{-1}$, a melodic syntonic comma appears in the alto on the fourth beat.

Bar 6. The eighth note F in the alto is the seventh of a dominant seventh chord whose root is G_0, and consequently the tuning $F_{-\bar{z}}$ is preferred. This tuning is much less of a problem than in the previous case, since A is not present, and $D_0 F_{-\bar{z}}$ is a minor tenth—an interval much less sensitive to impure tuning than a major sixth. On the sixth quarter, a difficult choice must be made regarding B in the soprano. If Pythagorean intervals are to be avoided, B_{-2} is the choice, so that $D_{-1}B_{-2}$ will be pure. Note that D_{-1} is necessary owing to A_{-1} in the bass. Under these conditions, the soprano descends from C_0 to B_{-2}, a maximum semitone of 133.238 cents, ratio $\frac{27}{25}$ (Ch. V, Sec. 4). Since the combination ACDB (reading from bottom to top—observe that the alto and tenor parts are crossed) is discordant in any tuning owing to major seventh CB, there can be little objection to the use of Pythagorean major sixth $D_{-1}B_{-1}$, bringing about the smaller descending diatonic semitone $C_0 B_{-1}$ in the soprano.

Bar 7. On the fourth quarter, there occurs the combination DGAE. These four notes, when rearranged GDAE, are seen to be four consecutive notes on the line of fifths, and so the Pythagorean tuning of GE cannot be avoided without disturbing at least one of the fifths—a worse alternative (Theorem 24; Ch. V, Sec. 4). On the second quarter, we might consider E_{-2} for the soprano; but E_{-1} is preferable in spite of Pythagorean major sixth $G_{-1}E_{-1}$, as it avoids the maximum semitone between F_0 and E_{-2} which otherwise would occur as a melodic interval in the superior part.

Bar 8. Major triad DF♯A on the fourth beat serves as a dominant to both a G minor chord (second beat) and a G major chord (bar 9). Since bar 5 contains a D major chord followed by a G major chord, with tunings $D_0 F\sharp_{-1}A_0$ and $G_0 B_{-1}D_0$, this tuning should be retained in bars 8 and 9 in order to avoid a modulation down by a syntonic comma. It seems best that the G minor chord on the second beat of bar 8 should contain the same G as the final chord, hence the preferred tuning $G_0 B\flat_{+1}D_0$ at this point—an exception to the principle that roots of minor triads should have -1 subscripts. On the first beat of bar 8, the soprano must be tuned A_0 to combine with D_0 in the alto. But the fourth beat of bar 7 requires A_{-1} and D_{-1}; hence a melodic syntonic comma occurs in both the soprano and alto between bars 7 and 8.

As in the Kyrie of Machaut, in the individual parts major seconds are either major tones or minor tones, and minor seconds are diatonic semitones. There are two exceptions involving the note $F_{-\bar{z}}$ (bar 6): minor second $E_{-1}F_{-\bar{z}}$ is in the ratio $\frac{21}{20}$, containing 84.467 cents (Ch. V, Sec. 5); major second $F_{-\bar{z}}G_0$ is greater than a major tone by $\bar{z}$, its ratio being $\left(\frac{9}{8}\right)\left(\frac{64}{63}\right) = \frac{8}{7}$, and it contains 231.174 cents. Impure melodic intervals occur in the tenor in bar 3 ($A_{-1}D_0$), and in the tenor and bass parts between bars 7 and 8 ($F_0B\flat_{+1}$ and $D_{-1}B\flat_{+1}$, respectively).

Notes needed for the nine-bar fragment are the following: $G\#_{-2}G_{-1}$ $D_{-1}A_{-1}E_{-1}B_{-1}F\#_{-1}F_0C_0G_0D_0A_0E_0B\flat_{+1}$ and $F_{-\bar{z}}$—a total of fifteen. Of these, five are used only once or twice in special situations:

$F_{-\bar{z}}$ is the seventh of a dominant seventh chord whose root is G_0 (bar 6);

$G\#_{-2}$ is the third of a major triad whose root is E_{-1} (bar 2);

$B\flat_{+1}$ is the third of a minor triad whose root is G_0 (bar 8);

E_0 is used only as a neighboring note to the third of a major triad whose root is D_0 (bars 4 and 8);

G_{-1} is needed as a passing note over D_{-1} in the bass (bar 7).

Of especial interest are the tunings of D and A, since both the 0 subscripts and -1 subscripts occur frequently. In bars 1 and 2, and halfway through bar 3, D_{-1} and A_{-1} are used, as they occur in D minor, A minor, and F major harmonies. From the latter half of bar 3 through the first half of bar 5, D and A occur in G major and D major harmonies, requiring D_0 and A_0. From the latter half of bar 5 through bar 7, D minor and A minor harmonies again require D_{-1} and A_{-1}, while the D major and G major harmonies of the last two bars need D_0 and A_0.

We observe that this example, like the preceding, can be tuned so that nearly all harmonies consist entirely of pure intervals. Exceptions noted above occur very briefly, and never at points of rhythmic stress. The disruption of the tuning of the scales is more noticeable, since scale passages occur frequently in individual parts. The effect of a scale in just tuning has been noted and commented upon earlier (Ch. V, Sec. 2). In addition, it is interesting to observe that in bar 6, the bass has the descending scale E, D, C, B, A, which is imitated in the tenor; but the bass uses D_0, while the tenor uses D_{-1}. Also in bars 6 and 7, the soprano makes a descending scale from A to D, and then ascends to A again, using first G_0, and then G_{-1}. Such artifacts, including the melodic syntonic commas noted, are clearly outside the stylistic framework of this composition. In later discussions, we shall give evidence that there exist temperaments that are more in keeping with the style of the motet (Ch. IX, Sec. 6; Ch. X, Sec. 6; Ch. XI, Sec. 6).

3. J. S. Bach (1685–1750), Prelude in E♭ major, Book 1, Well-Tempered Clavier.[4]

[4] The example follows the text of the Bach Gesellschaft (Leipzig: Breitkopf und Härtel, 1866), vol. 14, 26.

J. S. Bach (1685–1750), Prelude in E♭ major,
Book 1, Well-Tempered Clavier

We observe that the passage from J. S. Bach's Prelude in E♭ major—Book 1 of the Well-Tempered Clavier—makes extensive use of secondary seventh chords. The tuning for such chords in C major will be found in Table 33 (Ch. V, Sec. 6). Transposition into E♭ major—a matter of second nature to trained musicians—is accomplished formally by noting that E♭ is three positions to the left of C on the line of fifths (Ch. IV, Sec. 1). Hence we replace each note of Table 33 by the one lying three positions to its left on the line of fifths, and retain the same subscripts associated with each degree.[5] This gives a total of ten notes, viz., $E\flat_0 F_{-1} F_0 G_{-1} A\flat_{-\bar{z}} A\flat_0 B\flat_0 C_{-1} C_0$ and D_{-1}. It will be observed that F_{-1} is used as the root of the chord on the second degree, and F_0 is used in all other situations; $A\flat_{-\bar{z}}$ is used when A♭ is combined with D_{-1}, and $A\flat_0$ is used in all other situations; finally, C_0 is used when C is combined with $A\flat_{-\bar{z}}$, and C_{-1} is used in all other situations. But this is not enough to work out the just tuning of the passage, for there are instances of secondary dominants, viz., V/IV (bars 3 and 13), V/II (bar 7), V/VI (bar 7), and V/V (bars 10, 11, and 15). In accord with the principle that the root

[5] See also the examples of Ch. VI, Sec. 1, and Table 54.

TABLE 54

	I	II	III	IV	V	VI	VII
seventh chords	D_{-1}	Eb_0	F_0	G_{-1}	$Ab_{-\bar{z}}$	Bb_0	C_0
	Bb_0	C_{-1}	D_{-1}	Eb_0	F_0	G_{-1}	$Ab_{-\bar{z}}$
	G_{-1}	Ab_0	Bb_0	C_{-1}	D_{-1}	Eb_0	F_0
	Eb_0	F_{-1}	G_{-1}	Ab_0	Bb_0	C_{-1}	D_{-1}
degrees	I	II	III	IV	V	VI	VII

of a secondary dominant should have the same subscript as the degree of which it is the dominant (Ch. VI, Sec. 6), the roots of dominants of the major degrees (IV and V) are given 0 subscripts, and the roots of dominants of the minor degrees (II and VI) are given -1 subscripts, and thus we have:

function	tuning
V/IV	$Eb_0 G_{-1} Bb_0 Db_{-\bar{z}}$
V/V	$F_0 A_{-1} C_0 Eb_{-\bar{z}}$
V/II	$C_{-1} E_{-2} G_{-1} Bb_{-(\bar{k}+\bar{z})}$
V/VI	$G_{-1} B_{-2} D_{-1} F_{-(\bar{k}+\bar{z})}$

All that remains is the question of non-chord notes, and this is resolved by tuning them so that they do not make either impure perfect fifths or fourths, or Pythagorean thirds or sixths with any other note present. It will be found that this does not require the addition of any further notes. The notes needed for the entire passage are thus $E_{-2} B_{-2} F_{-1}$ $C_{-1} G_{-1} D_{-1} A_{-1} Ab_0 Eb_0 Bb_0 F_0 C_0 Db_{-\bar{z}} Ab_{-\bar{z}} Eb_{-\bar{z}} Bb_{-(\bar{k}+\bar{z})}$ and $F_{-(\bar{k}+\bar{z})}$ — a total of seventeen.

In this example, frequent melodic commas may be expected to occur in individual parts. The septimal comma $\bar{z}$, 27.264 cents, ratio $\frac{64}{63}$, will occur each time the seventh of a dominant seventh chord is present in the same part in the preceding chord—the rule rather than the exception. It will be observed that $\bar{z}$ occurs as a melodic interval no fewer than thirteen times, seven of them in the superior part. The syntonic comma $\bar{k}$, 21.506 cents, ratio $\frac{81}{80}$, will occur melodically in the progression II-V (bars 3 and 4), or when a minor triad is followed by a major triad having the same root (bars 11 and 12), and in other situations as well (bars 7, 8, 14, and 15). All in all, there are eight instances of melodic syntonic commas, and three of these occur simultaneously (bar 12). There is also one occurrence melodically of the large comma $\bar{k} + \bar{z}$, 48.770 cents, ratio $\frac{36}{35}$ (bars 6 and 7). The harmony on the fourth beat of bar 6 is V^7, requiring Bb_0 in the bass, while that on the first beat of bar 7 is V/II, with the seventh tuned $B\flat_{-(\bar{k}+\bar{z})}$.

Subjectively speaking, the effect of this example in just tuning is very peculiar. Although a beat-free tuning is possible for every harmony, the overall sensation is that the passage is badly out of tune, especially the sevenths of dominant seventh chords, which seem very flat. In addition, a disturbing harmonic discontinuity occurs between bars 6 and 7, caused by the large melodic comma in the bass. Clearly a more satisfactory tuning for this example would be one in which the seventh of a dominant seventh chord were the same as the root of the triad a major second lower, and in which the root of the triad on II were the same as the fifth of the triad on V.

4. César Franck (1822–1890), Symphony in D minor.[6]

In the following example from Franck's D minor Symphony, which makes extensive use of diminished seventh and altered chords, determination of the ratios of the various intervals is a rather more complex process than in the preceding examples. It is sometimes necessary to determine first, by the method of Chapter IV, Sec. 1, numbers associated with the notes relative to note 0 (F) on the line of fifths. We next use Theorem 6 (Ch. II, Sec. 3) to find the Pythagorean interval between two consecutive notes, disregarding subscripts, and then find the ratio from Table 3 (Ch. II, Sec. 4), or Table 13 (Ch. IV, Sec. 3). Finally we multiply or divide the Pythagorean ratio by the ratio of the comma by which the actual interval differs from the Pythagorean version, recalling that the commas $\bar{k}$, $\bar{z}$, $\bar{k} + \bar{z}$, $\bar{y}$, and $\bar{k} - \bar{y}$ have ratios $\frac{81}{80}$, $\frac{64}{63}$, $\frac{36}{35}$, $\frac{256}{255}$, and $\frac{4131}{4096}$, respectively (Ch. III, Sec. 7; Ch. V, Sec. 5; Ch. VI, Sec. 6). As before, the actual choice of subscripts is determined so as to put every harmony in the smoothest possible tuning, while at the same time avoiding unduly large melodic commas, especially in the superior part. A bar-by-bar analysis follows.

Bar 1, first beat. This D minor triad is tuned $D_{-1}F_0A_{-1}$ in accord with the principle that the roots of minor triads should normally have -1 subscripts (Sec. 1 of this chapter).

Bar 1, second beat, first eighth. The normal tuning for a half-diminished

---

[6] The example is taken from the first movement, bars 17–21.

César Franck (1822–1890), Symphony in D minor

seventh chord on the second degree of a minor key is for the root to have either a -1 subscript or a -2 subscript (Ch. VI, Sec. 6), and in the present case, this would be either $E_{-1}G_0Bb_{-\bar{z}}D_0$, or $E_{-2}G_{-1}Bb_{-(\bar{k}+\bar{z})}D_{-1}$. But in either case, the interval between Bb and D in the two lower parts would be $\overline{\text{int}}$ (4) $+ \bar{z}$, ratio $(\frac{81}{64})(\frac{64}{63}) = \frac{9}{7}$, and this is the intensely discordant major third of 435.084 cents (Ch. V, Sec. 6). It is better that the interval between the two lower parts should be pure, and so the preferred tuning for these notes is Bb_0D_{-1}, retaining D_{-1} from the previous harmony. Hence the tuning for the complete chord is $E_{-2}G_{-1}Bb_0D_{-1}$, making Bb_0G_{-1} pure as well. To be sure, Bb_0E_{-2} is impure, being smaller than its pure counterpart $Bb_{-(\bar{k}+\bar{z})}E_{-2}$ by the large comma $\bar{k} + \bar{z}$ of 48.770 cents. Fortunately the distribution is such that the rough character of this interval is effectively masked; but even so, there is no completely smooth tuning for this harmony as given.

Bar 1, second beat, second eighth. The composer's notation of this diminished seventh chord is C#EGB♭, representing it according to convention as an incomplete minor dominant ninth chord whose root is A. Since this dominant resolves to a chord whose root has a -1 subscript, the first tuning to consider construes the chord as having A_{-1} for a root, viz., $C\#_{-2}E_{-1}G_{-(\bar{k}+\bar{z})}B\flat_{-\bar{y}}$, which puts the four notes in the ratios $10:12:14:17$. But this is not satisfactory in the distribution given, since $B\flat_{-\bar{y}}C\#_{-2}$ would occur between the two lower parts. Since $C\#_{-2}B\flat_{-\bar{y}}$ is in the ratio $\frac{17}{10}$, its inversion is in the ratio $(\frac{2}{1})(\frac{10}{17}) = \frac{20}{17}$ (Ch. II, Sec. 3). This interval of 281.358 cents is discordant, being smaller than a pure minor third by 34.283 cents (Ch. VI, Sec. 6). It is better that the interval between the two lower parts should be pure, and this suggests either $A\#_{-3}C\#_{-2}$, or $A\#_{-2}C\#_{-1}$. In the case of the former, the bass must descend from $B\flat_0$ to $A\#_{-3}$, amounting to $\overline{\text{int}}\,(12) - 3\bar{k} = \bar{p} - 3\bar{k}$, a diesis of 41.059 cents (Ch. VI, Sec. 2). This is larger than desirable for a melodic comma, and so we prefer the latter tuning. In this case, the bass descends from $B\flat_0$ to $A\#_{-2}$, which is $\overline{\text{int}}\,(12) - 2\bar{k} = \bar{p} - 2\bar{k}$, a diaschisma of 19.553 cents (Ch. VI, Sec. 2). Under these conditions, the chord is tuned as though it were built over a missing root $F\#_{-1}$, and the complete preferred tuning is $A\#_{-2}C\#_{-1}E_{-(\bar{k}+\bar{z})}G_{-\bar{y}}$. We observe that there are melodic commas in the two upper parts, viz., $\bar{k} - \bar{y}$ ascending in the superior part (14.730 cents), and $\bar{z} - \bar{k}$ descending in the part next below. The ratio of this comma is $(\frac{64}{63})(\frac{80}{81}) = \frac{5120}{5103}$, and it contains 5.758 cents. Since the highest part rises and the lowest part falls, and all the melodic commas are less than 20 cents, it appears that the preferred tuning brings about a fairly uniform distribution of the commas among the parts.

Bar 1, third beat. The composer's notation of this German sixth chord is B♭DFG#, in conformity with the usual convention. The smoothest tuning for a German sixth chord is the same as that for a dominant seventh, putting the four notes in the ratios $4:5:6:7$. This suggests the tuning $B\flat_0D_{-1}F_0A\flat_{-\bar{z}}$, replacing the composer's G# by A♭. From a harmonic standpoint, $A\flat_{-\bar{z}}$ is ideal, although this note seems rather flat within the melodic progression of the superior part. The reason will be taken up later in this section.

Bar 2, first beat. The composer's notation of this diminished seventh chord is G#BDF, indicating its harmonic function as V/V, built over a missing root E. Hence we consider first the tuning $G\#_{-2}B_{-1}D_{-(\bar{k}+\bar{z})}F_{-\bar{y}}$, taking E_{-1} rather than E_0 as the root in accord with the principle that the root of a secondary dominant should have the same subscript as the root of its resolution—in this case A_{-1} (Ch. VI, Sec. 6). Once again, however, the two lower parts are unsatisfactory in the tuning first suggested. The ratio of $G\#_{-2}F_{-\bar{y}}$ is $\frac{17}{10}$, and this is the discordant interval of 918.642 cents, larger than a pure major sixth by 34.283 cents (Ch. VI, Sec. 6). Pure tuning of this interval requires that the higher note should be tuned $E\#$ instead of F, and this suggests that the chord should be regarded as built over the root $C\#_{-1}$ or $C\#_0$, rather than E_{-1}. We are thus led to the two possibilities $E\#_{-2}G\#_{-1}B_{-(\bar{k}+\bar{z})}D_{-\bar{y}}$ and $E\#_{-1}G\#_0B_{-\bar{z}}D_{+(\bar{k}-\bar{y})}$. Since both tunings are identical save for a difference in register amounting to a syntonic comma, the final choice turns upon the sizes of the melodic commas and the subjective impression of how sharp or how flat the entire harmony is. If the latter tuning is adopted, $D_{+(\bar{k}-\bar{y})}$ in the middle part must come directly after D_{-1}, the difference amounting to $2\bar{k} - \bar{y}$, or 36.237 cents. This very considerable raising of the tonic note makes the entire harmony seem too high. In the case of the former tuning, the difference between the two D's becomes $\bar{k} - \bar{y}$, or 14.730 cents—a much better arrangement. Hence the preferred tuning is $E\#_{-2}G\#_{-1}B_{-(\bar{k}+\bar{z})}D_{-\bar{y}}$.

The tuning for the second beat of bar 2 depends mainly upon what follows, and so we postpone this discussion for the moment.

Bar 2, third and fourth beats. The tonic chord on the fourth beat is tuned as in Bar 1 $(D_{-1}F_0A_{-1})$, and since the root of its dominant should also have a -1 subscript (Ch. VI, Sec. 4), the preferred tuning for the third beat is $A_{-1}C\#_{-2}E_{-1}G_{-(\bar{k}+\bar{z})}$.

Bar 2, second beat. There are two tunings to consider for the dominant seventh chord on the second eighth of this beat, viz., $C_0E_{-1}G_0B\flat_{-\bar{z}}$ and $C_{-1}E_{-2}G_{-1}B\flat_{-(\bar{k}+\bar{z})}$. Once again, the choice depends upon the size and placement of the melodic commas. In the former tuning, the bass would descend from G_0 to $G_{-(\bar{k}+\bar{z})}$ by $\bar{k} + \bar{z}$, or 48.770 cents—much larger than desirable—hence we take the latter arrangement. This in effect distributes the large comma between two parts, the bass falling by $\bar{z}$ (27.264 cents), and the middle part rising by $\bar{k}$ (21.506 cents) from E_{-2} to E_{-1}. On the first eighth, non-chord note F is tuned F_{-1} so as not to clash with C_{-1} in the highest part, and hence the part next below is best tuned $B\flat_{-1}$ so as not to make a severe discord with F_{-1}. It should be noted that this combination includes $B\flat$, F, C, and G—four adjacent notes on the line of fifths—an arrangement for which there is no completely pure tuning (Theorem 24; Ch. V, Sec. 4; see also Ch. V, Sec. 6). Between the first and second beats of bar 2, the higher part on the bottom staff makes a comma between $E\#_{-2}$ and F_{-1}; since $F_{-1}E\#_{-2}$ is $\overline{\text{int}}$ $(12) - \bar{k} = \bar{p} - \bar{k}$, the comma is a descending schisma of 1.954 cents (Ch. VI, Sec. 2)—virtually an undetectable amount.

Bar 3, first beat. The composer's notation is F#ACEb, implying D as a root. However, from a standpoint of just tuning, it is preferable that the interval between the two lower parts should be in the ratio $\frac{7}{5}$ or $\frac{10}{7}$, rather than $\frac{17}{12}$, which would result from the tuning $F\sharp_{-1}A_0C_{-\bar{z}}Eb_{+(\bar{k}-\bar{y})}$ or $F\sharp_{-2}A_{-1}C_{-(\bar{k}+\bar{z})}Eb_{-\bar{y}}$. Hence a better tuning results from construing the chord as built over F_0 as a root, and so we have $A_{-1}C_0Eb_{-\bar{z}}Gb_{+(\bar{k}-\bar{y})}$. This puts the interval between the two lower parts in the ratio $\frac{7}{5}$, and retains A_{-1} from the previous harmony.

Bar 3, second beat. The sensitive interval in this distribution is GE between the two lower parts, and to make this interval pure, we tune the chord as though built over a missing root C_{-1}, and so we have $E_{-2}G_{-1}Bb_{-(k+\bar{z})}Db_{-\bar{y}}$, replacing the composer's C# in the highest part by a Db.

Bar 3, third beat. The harmonic function here is V/IV, resolving to minor triad $G_{-1}Bb_0D_{-1}$ on the first beat of bar 4, and hence built over the root D_{-1}. The tuning to consider first is thus $F\sharp_{-2}A_{-1}C_{-(\bar{k}+\bar{z})}Eb_{-\bar{y}}$, and this is a satisfactory just tuning for the chord, since the interval between the two lower parts is in the ratio $\frac{10}{7}$. It is true that $C_{-(\bar{k}+\bar{z})}$ in the lowest part seems slightly flat, as is usually the case when the seventh of a dominant chord is placed in the bass. This effect is heightened in the present case by the melodic progression from G_{-1} to $C_{-(k+\bar{z})}$—a perfect fourth reduced by $\bar{z}$. Note that this would be made worse if the chord on the second beat were tuned higher by a syntonic comma.

Bar 3, fourth beat. The composer's notation is the conventionally correct BbF#CD, showing that the chord is dominant seventh DF#C in combination with passing note Bb. Unfortunately this harmony cannot be tuned purely, since it contains augmented triad BbDF# (Ch. VI, Sec. 6). In the distribution given, it is best to place the impure interval in the least conspicuous register, and put in pure tuning the intervals between the two outer parts and between the two lower parts. In the case of the former, we consider first Bb_0D_{-1}; but if this tuning were chosen, the bass would descend from $C_{-(\bar{k}+\bar{z})}$ to Bb_0. This interval is smaller than a major tone by $\bar{k}+\bar{z}$, hence its ratio is $(\frac{9}{8})(\frac{35}{36})=\frac{35}{32}$, and it contains 155.140 cents. This is too small for a major second, being larger than a maximum semitone (133.238 cents) by only 21.902 cents, and so we prefer $Bb_{-1}D_{-2}$, making the melodic major second in the lowest part less than a major tone by $\bar{z}$. The ratio of this interval is $(\frac{9}{8})(\frac{63}{64}) = \frac{567}{512}$, and it contains 176.646 cents—still rather small for a major second, but acceptable as a melodic interval. We note also that the superior part descends from $E\flat_{-\bar{y}}$ to D_{-2}, an interval that exceeds a diatonic semitone (111.731 cents) by $\bar{k} - \bar{y}$ (14.730 cents), amounting to 126.462 cents, which is less than a maximum semitone by 6.776 cents and hence an acceptable tuning for a melodic minor second. In order to make the minor sixth between the two lower parts pure, we tune the higher note $G\flat_0$, replacing the composer's F♯ by G♭. This puts the extremely discordant augmented fifth $G\flat_0 D_{-2}$ in a register where its rough effect is somewhat concealed. The addition of C to this harmony brings about further problems. The best tuning for this note in the given context is C_{-1}, which combines satisfactorily with $B\flat_{-1}$ and D_{-2}. However, $G\flat_0 C_{-1}$ is less than the corresponding pure interval $G\flat_{-\bar{z}} C_{-1}$ (ratio $\frac{10}{7}$) by $\bar{z}$, hence its ratio is $(\frac{10}{7})(\frac{63}{64}) = \frac{45}{32}$, and it contains 590.224 cents—a tolerable tuning for an augmented fourth or diminished fifth. Upon the resolution of B♭ to A in the lowest part, the chord becomes a dominant seventh whose root might be either D_{-1} or D_{-2}. In the case of D_{-2}, the third would be $F\sharp_{-3}$, and the part on the middle staff would descend from $G\flat_0$ to $F\sharp_{-3}$, or $\overline{\text{int}}\ (12) - 3\bar{k} = \bar{p} - 3\bar{k}$. This is a diesis of 41.059 cents—larger than desirable for a melodic comma, and so we take the tuning $D_{-1}F\sharp_{-2}A_{-1}C_{-(\bar{k}+\bar{z})}$. Thus on the fourth beat of bar 3, there occur three simultaneous melodic commas—the highest part rises by $\bar{k}$ (21.506 cents), the part next below falls by $\bar{z}$ (27.264 cents), and the part on the middle staff falls by $2\bar{k} - \bar{p}$, a diaschisma (19.553 cents, see Ch. VI, Sec. 2). The preferred tuning brings about a relatively uniform distribution of the melodic commas among three parts.

Bar 4, first and second beats. These two triads are tuned in the usual manner (Sec. 1 of this chapter).

Bar 4, third beat. If we retain G_{-1} in the lowest part, and arrange the diminished seventh chord so that it is built over a missing root $E\flat_0$, we have $G_{-1}B\flat_0 D\flat_{-\bar{z}}F\flat_{+(\bar{k}-\bar{y})}$. This puts the interval between the two lower parts in the ratio $\frac{10}{7}$, and hence is a good tuning for this harmony. The composer's notation is inconsistent at this point, the second violins reading C♯, and the first horn D♭.

Bar 4, fourth beat. There is no problem retaining $G_{-1}B\flat_0 D\flat_{-\bar{z}}$ from the previous harmony and adding F_0, so that $B\flat_0 F_0$ will be pure.

Bar 5, first beat. This minor triad is tuned in the usual manner, i.e., its root and fifth have -1 subscripts, and its third has a 0 subscript. It is of interest to determine the ratio and size of the melodic comma $D\flat_{-\bar{z}}C\sharp_{-1}$: this amounts to $\overline{\text{int}}\ (12) - \bar{k} + \bar{z} = \bar{p} - \bar{k} + \bar{z} = \bar{s} + \bar{z}$ (Ch. VI, Sec. 2), the ratio being $(\frac{32805}{32768})(\frac{64}{63}) = \frac{3645}{3584}$, size 29.218 cents.[7]

The question of the melodic intervals, already partly dealt with, is especially interesting in the highly chromatic superior part. The following results may be obtained by using the method described at the beginning of this section.

F_0G_{-1} is $\overline{\text{int}}\ (2) - \bar{k}$, ratio $(\frac{9}{8})(\frac{80}{81}) = \frac{10}{9}$, size 182.404 cents. This is a minor tone (Ch. V, Sec. 2).

$G_{-1}G_{-\bar{y}}$ is $\bar{k} - \bar{y}$, ratio $\frac{4131}{4096}$, size 14.730 cents.

$G_{-\bar{y}}A\flat_{-\bar{z}}$ is $\overline{\text{int}}\ (-5) - \bar{z} + \bar{y}$, ratio $(\frac{256}{243})(\frac{63}{64})(\frac{256}{255}) = \frac{7168}{6885}$, size 69.737 cents.

$A\flat_{-\bar{z}}A\natural_{-1}$ is $\overline{\text{int}}\ (7) - \bar{k} + \bar{z}$, ratio $(\frac{2187}{2048})(\frac{80}{81})(\frac{64}{63}) = \frac{15}{14}$, size 119.443 cents.

$A_{-1}B_{-(\bar{k}+\bar{z})}$ is $\overline{\text{int}}\ (2) - \bar{z}$, ratio $(\frac{9}{8})(\frac{63}{64}) = \frac{567}{512}$, size 176.646 cents.

$B_{-(\bar{k}+\bar{z})}C_{-1}$ is $\overline{\text{int}}\ (-5) + \bar{z}$, ratio $(\frac{256}{243})(\frac{64}{63}) = \frac{16384}{15309}$, size 117.489 cents.

$C_{-1}C\sharp_{-2}$ is $\overline{\text{int}}\ (7) - \bar{k}$, ratio $(\frac{2187}{2048})(\frac{80}{81}) = \frac{135}{128}$, size 92.179 cents. This is a major chroma (Ch. VI, Sec. 1).

$C\sharp_{-2}D_{-1}$ is $\overline{\text{int}}\ (-5) + \bar{k}$, ratio $(\frac{256}{243})(\frac{81}{80}) = \frac{16}{15}$, size 111.731 cents. This is a diatonic semitone (Ch. V, Sec. 2).

$D_{-1}C_0$: since the notes in the given registers form a descending interval, we consider C_0D_{-1} instead. This is $\overline{\text{int}}\ (2) - \bar{k}$, a minor tone, ratio $\frac{10}{9}$, size 182.404 cents, as found above in the case of F_0G_{-1}.

$C_0D\flat_{-\bar{y}}$ is $\overline{\text{int}}\ (-5) - \bar{y}$, ratio $(\frac{256}{243})(\frac{255}{256}) = \frac{85}{81}$, size 83.449 cents.

$D\flat_{-\bar{y}}E\flat_{-\bar{y}}$ is $\overline{\text{int}}\ (2)$, ratio $\frac{9}{8}$, size 203.910 cents. This is a major tone (Ch. V, Sec. 2).

$E\flat_{-\bar{y}}D_{-2}$: again we reverse the order of the notes as given, so that the interval will be ascending. $D_{-2}E\flat_{-\bar{y}}$ is $\overline{\text{int}}\ (-5) - \bar{y} + 2\bar{k}$, ratio $(\frac{256}{243})(\frac{255}{256})(\frac{81}{80})(\frac{81}{80}) = \frac{1377}{1280}$, size 126.462 cents.

$D_{-2}D_{-1}$ is a syntonic comma, ratio $\frac{81}{80}$, size 21.506 cents.

$D_{-1}E\flat_0$ is $\overline{\text{int}}\ (-5) + \bar{k}$, a diatonic semitone, ratio $\frac{16}{15}$, size 111.731 cents, as found above in the case of $C\sharp_{-2}D_{-1}$.

$E\flat_0F\flat_{+(\bar{k}-\bar{y})}$ is $\overline{\text{int}}\ (-5) + \bar{k} - \bar{y}$, ratio $(\frac{256}{243})(\frac{81}{80})(\frac{255}{256}) = \frac{17}{16}$, size 104.955 cents.

---

[7] When the ratios consist of large integers, it will be most convenient to factor them into primes before reducing the product to its lowest terms. In the present case, we have
$$\left(\frac{32805}{32768}\right)\left(\frac{64}{63}\right) = \left[\frac{(3^8)(5)}{2^{15}}\right]\left[\frac{2^6}{(3^2)(7)}\right] = \frac{(3^6)(5)}{(2^9)(7)} = \frac{3645}{3584}.$$

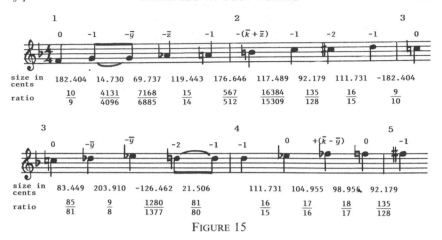

FIGURE 15

$Fb_{+(\bar{k}-\bar{y})}F\natural_0$ is $\overline{int}\ (7) - \bar{k} + \bar{y}$, ratio $(\frac{2187}{2048})(\frac{80}{81})(\frac{256}{255}) = \frac{18}{17}$, size 98.955 cents.

$F_0F\sharp_{-1}$ is $\overline{int}\ (7) - \bar{k}$, a major chroma, ratio $\frac{135}{128}$, size 92.179 cents, as found above in the case of $C_{-1}C\sharp_{-2}$.

The results are summarized in Figure 15, using musical notation as an aid to visualization.

As for the notation without subscripts, there are only three different melodic intervals—major seconds, minor seconds, and chromatic semitones. However, in just tuning, the variations in size between intervals having the same name are extraordinary. Of the four major seconds, there are three different sizes, viz., one major tone of 203.910 cents ($Db_{-\bar{y}}Eb_{-\bar{y}}$), two minor tones of 182.404 cents (F_0G_{-1} and C_0D_{-1}), and one other of 176.646 cents ($A_{-1}B_{-(\bar{k}+\bar{z})}$). Regarding minor seconds and chromatic semitones, an even greater variety is found. Of the eleven such intervals in the example, there are no fewer than nine different versions. These are listed in Table 55 in order of size.

It will be observed that all these intervals are essentially within the permissible limits for minor seconds or chromatic semitones—roughly between a minor chroma and a maximum semitone. Even so, the largest is nearly twice the size of the smallest.

In general, the melodic progression of the superior part is not unduly disturbing. The most awkward succession occurs in bar 1, where small minor second $G_{-\bar{y}}Ab_{-\bar{z}}$ followed directly by large chromatic semitone $Ab_{-\bar{z}}A\natural_{-1}$ makes $Ab_{-\bar{z}}$ seem quite noticeably flat.

TABLE 55

notes	ratio	size in cents
$G_{-\bar{y}}A\flat_{-\bar{z}}$	$\frac{7168}{6885}$	69.737
$C_0 D\flat_{-\bar{y}}$	$\frac{85}{81}$	83.449
$\begin{cases} C_{-1}C\#_{-2} \\ F_0 F\#_{-1} \end{cases}$	$\frac{135}{128}$	92.179
$F\flat_{+(\bar{k}-\bar{y})}F_0$	$\frac{18}{17}$	98.955
$E\flat_0 F\flat_{+(\bar{k}-\bar{y})}$	$\frac{17}{16}$	104.955
$\begin{cases} C\#_{-2}D_{-1} \\ D_{-1}E\flat_0 \end{cases}$	$\frac{16}{15}$	111.731
$B_{-(\bar{k}+\bar{z})}C_{-1}$	$\frac{16384}{15309}$	117.489
$A\flat_{-\bar{z}}A_{-1}$	$\frac{15}{14}$	119.443
$D_{-2}E\flat_{-\bar{y}}$	$\frac{1377}{1280}$	126.462

The entire passage in just tuning requires no fewer than thirty-six different notes. These are listed in Table 56 in ascending order, along with the size in cents of the interval formed by each adjacent pair.

In view of the great variety of notes and intervals, and the fact that a number of the harmonies have no pure tuning, we must conclude that just tuning is not the ideal for this example. In a later discussion, we shall show that the passage is especially well suited to 12-note equal tuning (Ch. XI, Sec. 6).

5. Other examples and conclusions. It must not be assumed that the preceding examples of Machaut, di Lasso, Bach, and Franck represent typical problems with respect to their just tuning. On the contrary, they were chosen with a view to presenting relatively simple and straightforward situations. Since just tuning is designed to present every chord in the smoothest possible arrangement, it follows that musical textures most amenable to just tuning are in three or more parts, in a slow tempo, and contain a relatively small number of non-chord notes. In fact, the musical repertoire yields relatively few examples conforming to these criteria. More common are passages characterized by rapid ornamentation and running scales, frequently in fewer than three parts. The inappropriateness of just tuning for such textures is illustrated by the following example (p. 152)[8]:

[8] W. A. Mozart, Piano Sonata in F major, K. 533 (1788) and K. 494, (1786) third movement, bars 126–127.

TABLE 56

notes	intervals	notes	intervals
$C_{-(\bar{k}+\bar{z})}$		$E\sharp_{-2}$	
	27.264		19.553
C_{-1}		F_0	
	21.506		70.672
C_0		$F\sharp_{-2}$	
	62.961		19.553
$D\flat_{-\bar{z}}$		$G\flat_0$	
	7.712		1.954
$C\sharp_{-2}$		$F\sharp_{-1}$	
	12.777		12.777
$D\flat_{-\bar{y}}$		$G\flat_{+(\bar{k}-\bar{y})}$	
	8.730		50.184
$C\sharp_{-1}$		$G_{-(\bar{k}+\bar{z})}$	
	68.719		27.264
D_{-2}		G_{-1}	
	21.506		14.730
D_{-1}		$G_{-\bar{y}}$	
	14.730		69.737
$D_{-\bar{y}}$		$A\flat_{-\bar{z}}$	
	69.737		29.218
$E\flat_{-\bar{z}}$		$G\sharp_{-1}$	
	20.488		90.225
$E\flat_{-\bar{y}}$		A_{-1}	
	6.776		21.506
$E\flat_0$		A_0	
	64.915		41.455
$E_{-(\bar{k}+\bar{z})}$		$B\flat_{-(\bar{k}+\bar{z})}$	
	5.758		27.264
E_{-2}		$B\flat_{-1}$	
	21.506		1.954
E_{-1}		$A\sharp_{-2}$	
	12.777		19.553
$F\flat_{+(\bar{k}-\bar{y})}$		$B\flat_0$	
	77.448		64.915
F_{-1}		$B_{-(\bar{k}+\bar{z})}$	
	1.954		90.225
$[E\sharp_{-2}]$		$[C_{-(\bar{k}+\bar{z})}]$	

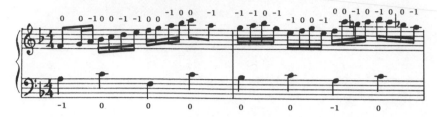

The harmonic implication of the first bar is I, and so we use the standard just tuning for the scale, i.e., degrees I, II, IV, and V have 0 subscripts, and degrees III, VI, VII have -1 subscripts (Ch. V, Sec. 1 and Ch. VI, Sec. 1). In the second bar, the harmonic implication of the first two beats is V^7, hence we consider first the tuning $C_0 E_{-1} G_0 B\flat_{-\bar{z}}$ for these notes. But this brings about disadvantages in the present case, for melodic minor second $A_{-1} B\flat_{-\bar{z}}$ is less than a diatonic semitone by $\bar{z}$—the small minor second of 84.467 cents, ratio $\frac{21}{20}$ (Ch. V, Sec. 5), which makes $B\flat_{-\bar{z}}$ seem too low. In addition, melodic major second $B\flat_{-\bar{z}} C_0$ exceeds a diatonic semitone by $\bar{z}$, its ratio is $(\frac{9}{8})(\frac{64}{63}) = \frac{8}{7}$, and it contains 231.174 cents—quite large for this interval in a melodic context—and this reinforces the sensation that $B\flat_{-\bar{z}}$ is flat. Hence a better tuning for this note is $B\flat_0$, making $B\flat_0 C_0$ a major tone. Note that this requires G_{-1} in the higher part on the first beat in order to avoid Pythagorean interval $B\flat_0 G_0$. But on the second beat, the corresponding note must be tuned G_0 so as not to clash with C_0 in the lower part. The two different G's coming close together, the alternation of major and minor tones, and the rather large diatonic semitones are clearly not the ideal tuning for the superior part in the absence of supporting harmonies.

A slightly different situation is illustrated by the following example.[9] Subscripts have been chosen so that each simultaneous interval is tuned purely, producing the ratio $\frac{5}{4}$ for a major third, $\frac{8}{5}$ for a minor sixth, $\frac{7}{5}$

[9] L. van Beethoven, Piano Sonata in E♭ major, Op. 7, first movement, bars 147–149.

for a diminished fifth, $\frac{10}{7}$ for an augmented fourth, $\frac{9}{8}$ for a major second, and $\frac{16}{9}$ for a minor seventh, discounting all octaves. But the scale is not good, for both minor seconds are different, and there are three different versions of major seconds. In the case of the minor seconds, we find that $G_{-1}Ab_0$ is a diatonic semitone of 111.731 cents, and $C_{-1}Db_{-\bar{z}}$ is the smaller version of 84.467 cents (ratio $\frac{21}{20}$). Regarding the major seconds, Ab_0Bb_0 and Eb_0F_0 are major tones, Bb_0C_{-1} and F_0G_{-1} are minor tones, and $Db_{-\bar{z}}Eb_0$ is the larger interval of 231.174 cents (ratio $\frac{8}{7}$). Since the passage is in a rapid tempo, in two parts only, and the generally wide distribution makes the simultaneous intervals relatively insensitive to impure tuning, it is clear that the distortion of the scale outweighs any meager benefits that might result from pure tuning of the harmonic combinations.

It is hoped that after a careful study of the examples presented in this chapter, the reader will be persuaded—as is the author—that the quest for perfection in tuning of a given musical fragment is the pursuit of an *ignis fatuus*. The author has been unable to discover any major composer whose style conforms to the inherent limitations and properties of just tuning. Nor are there any theoretical writings giving practical instruction as to how to sing or play just intervals, or how to compose with them. It must be concluded that at present, just tuning is of no practical use with regard to the existing Western repertoire.

Although it is not the purpose of this book to give instruction to composers of the future, a few remarks should be added concerning the style that might emerge from using exclusively pure intervals in compositions. Such music would be harmonic rather than melodic, and generally in a slow tempo. Owing to the presence of the syntonic and septimal commas, the usual forces associated with the subdominant, dominant, and tonic harmonies would be somewhat weakened, imparting a more static character to all harmonies (see Ch. V, Sec. 5). Use of the discordant, higher-order basic intervals would be desirable only if they were placed in upper voices, and then only in conjunction with the pure basic intervals in the lower parts. It seems highly doubtful that such a style would be expressive in the manner that Western ears have become accustomed to. To appreciate such music would require a degree of infatuation with sheer sound quality, and a disregard for harmonic progression, that does not presently characterize our musical culture.

VIII   The Diatonic Scale in
Meantone Tuning

Introduction.   Meantone tuning, like just tuning, is a device whose purpose is to correct the unmusical impurities associated with Pythagorean triads. Unlike just tuning, in which the triads are pure, meantone tuning allows a slight impurity, which makes possible the elimination of the disturbing melodic discontinuities associated with the syntonic and septimal commas. In Section 1 we see how a slight but noticeable distortion of perfect fifths CG, GD, DA, and AE produces pure tuning of major third CE, and also removes the distinction of the major and minor tones of just tuning. Section 2 defines the diatonic scale in a manner that parallels the definition set forth during the discussion of Pythagorean tuning, as described in Chapter II, Secs. 1–3. In Section 3 we develop further correspondences between meantone and Pythagorean tuning, showing that all the diatonic intervals have the same names and exhibit the same distributional patterns in both tunings. It is also demonstrated that the cyclic nature of the first, second, and third orders of notes applies to meantone as well as Pythagorean tuning. In Section 4 we take up the question of the meantone diatonic seventh chords and the major scale, showing that the meantone chords are superior to their Pythagorean counterparts, although many contemporary musicians find the Pythagorean scale more satisfactory than the meantone version.

Before continuing, the reader should review carefully the contents of Chapters II and III.

1. The meantone perfect fifth.   We first recall that in Pythagorean tuning C, G, D, A, and E are tuned $C_0 G_0 D_0 A_0 E_0$, making perfect fifths $C_0 G_0$, $G_0 D_0$, $D_0 A_0$, and $A_0 E_0$ pure, and major third $C_0 E_0$ Pythagorean (Ch. II, Sec. 1; Ch. III, Secs. 6 and 7). In just tuning, A_0 and E_0 are replaced by A_{-1} and E_{-1}, so that $C_0 G_0$, $G_0 D_0$, and $A_{-1} E_{-1}$ are pure, and major third $C_0 E_{-1}$ is also pure; but $D_0 A_{-1}$ is impure, being equal to $\bar{v} - \bar{k}$ (Ch. V, Secs. 1 and 2). In other words, the impurity associated with third $C_0 E_0$ has been eliminated by distorting one of the fifths by the same amount—in the present case D_0A_{-1}. Clearly a better situation would result if the amount of distortion—a syntonic comma of 21.506 cents—were distributed uniformly over the four fifths CG, GD, DA, and AE, rather than allowing it all to accumulate on DA. The idea of the distribution of a comma uniformly over a number of intervals is called *temperament*. We are thus led to the idea of four adjacent fifths, each reduced by one fourth of a syntonic comma, and we call the interval $\bar{v} - \frac{1}{4}\bar{k}$ a *meantone fifth*. If we adapt the subscript notation of Chapter V, Sec. 1 to the new situation, so that a subscript indicates by what fraction of a syntonic comma a given note departs from its Pythagorean counterpart, the notes forming the four fifths between C_0 and E_{-1} are tuned $C_0G_{-1/4}D_{-1/2}A_{-3/4}E_{-1}$. It will be observed that $C_0D_{-1/2}$ is equal to $\overline{int}\,(2) - \frac{1}{2}\bar{k}$, and that $D_{-1/2}E_{-1}$ is also equal to $\overline{int}\,(2) - \frac{1}{2}\bar{k}$. This shows that $D_{-1/2}$ is exactly midway between C_0 and E_{-1}, and it is this feature, in contradistinction to the major tone and minor tone of just tuning, that gives rise to the term *meantone*.

The ratio of a meantone fifth may be deduced directly from the following consideration:

If all the intervals of the left-hand combination in the above example are pure, the ratio of middle C to the E two octaves and a major third higher is $\left(\dfrac{2}{1}\right)^2\left(\dfrac{5}{4}\right) = 5$. If all the perfect fifths of the right-hand combination are pure, the ratio of middle C to the E four fifths higher is $\left(\dfrac{3}{2}\right)^4 = \dfrac{81}{16}$, the right-hand E being higher than the left-hand E by $\bar{k}$ (ratio $\frac{81}{80}$). Clearly if each fifth is made smaller by $\frac{1}{4}\bar{k}$, the two E's will be exactly the same. This shows that a meantone fifth is one fourth of the interval whose ratio is 5, and consequently the ratio of a meantone fifth is $5^{1/4} = 1.495349$.

The following approach is also of musical interest: since the sum of two octaves plus a pure major third amounts to $2a + \bar{t}$, it is evident that a meantone fifth is equal to $\frac{1}{4}(2a + \bar{t})$. By definition, $4\bar{v} - 2a - \bar{t} = \bar{k}$ (Ch. III, Sec. 7), or $\bar{t} = 4\bar{v} - 2a - \bar{k}$; substituting this expression for $\bar{t}$ gives

$$\tfrac{1}{4}(2a + \bar{t}) = \tfrac{1}{4}(2a + 4\bar{v} - 2a - \bar{k})$$
$$= \bar{v} - \tfrac{1}{4}\bar{k}$$

The amount of tempering, $\frac{1}{4}\bar{k}$, is not inconsiderable, amounting to $\frac{21.506}{4}$ = 5.377 cents; the size of a meantone fifth is thus 701.955 − 5.377 = 696.578 cents. A meantone fifth whose lower pitch is middle C of 264 Hz produces beats at a rate of $264[(2)(1.495349) − 3] = −2.456$ per second (Ch. I, Sec. 3). Produced by low-order harmonics, the beats are usually audible although their subjective effect varies, depending on what instrument plays the interval. In the case of the harpsichord, with its complex array of higher harmonics, the beats detract very little from the overall consonance of the fifth. On the organ, the relatively slow beat in the mid register is not unlike a slow vibrato of the sort deliberately introduced by céleste ranks, and is not disagreeable. In an ensemble, where the sound comes from spread-out sources, the beats disappear entirely. On a modern piano, however, a meantone fifth seems to have an unpleasant, nasal quality aside from the beats. This may be due to other discordant clashes between harmonics and difference-tones produced by the strings. Whatever the reason, meantone tuning is not a satisfactory tuning for a modern piano, at least to the author's ears.

If a major triad is made up of a pure major third and a meantone fifth, the minor third formed by its third and fifth is also reduced by $\frac{1}{4}\bar{k}$. In practical situations, the slight impurity of this interval is masked by the more noticeably impure meantone fifth. Such a triad produces very nearly the same subjective effect as the just version, with the addition of the beats produced by the fifth. There can be no doubt that a meantone triad is much more euphonious than a Pythagorean triad, but a little less so than a pure triad.

2. The diatonic meantone intervals expressed as int (i). We construct a diatonic scale in meantone tuning by a method that parallels the one used in Chapter II, Sec. 1 on Pythagorean tuning. The essential difference is the size of the generating interval—a pure perfect fifth (ratio $\frac{3}{2}$, size 701.955 cents) in the case of Pythagorean tuning, and a meantone fifth (ratio $5^{1/4}$, size 696.578 cents) in the present case. The definition otherwise is the same: we begin at some arbitrary pitch, then find the pitch higher than that by a meantone fifth, and continue the process until we have a total of seven pitches, each higher than the one immediately preceding by a meantone fifth. We next transpose these pitches up or down some number (not excluding zero) of octaves, this number being immaterial, in such a manner that the greatest interval formed by any two of the new pitches is less than one octave. When the new pitches are rearranged in ascending order, the result is a meantone diatonic scale.

As in Pythagorean tuning, all the meantone diatonic intervals are produced by forming pairs of the seven diatonic notes in all possible ways, and hence may be expressed in terms of integral combinations of octaves and meantone fifths. We are thus led to an extension of the idea developed during the discussion of Pythagorean tuning (Ch. II, Sec. 2), where it was shown that an interval of the form $i\bar{v} + na$ is uniquely determined by the number i upon application of the interval size convention (Ch. I, Sec. 5), the interval then being called $\overline{\text{int}}$ (i). All that is needed to adapt this notation to the new situation is a symbol for the tempered fifth to replace $\bar{v}$ $(=\log \frac{3}{2})$, and a broadening of the definition of $\overline{\text{int}}$ (i) to cover cases in which the generating interval is tempered. For the more general situation, we denote a tempered fifth by v, reserving the symbol $\bar{v}$ for a pure fifth. Later we shall show that it is possible to temper by somewhat more or less than $\frac{1}{4}\bar{k}$ (Ch. X, Secs. 1 and 2), and so we define v to denote any tempered fifth; in this and the next chapter, $v = \bar{v} - \frac{1}{4}\bar{k}$. Similarly, when the generating interval is tempered, we denote an interval by the symbol int (i), reserving $\overline{\text{int}}$ (i) specifically for Pythagorean tuning in which the generating interval is pure.

Now let the ratio of any tempered fifth be r; then the ratio of $iv + na$ is $r^i 2^n$. Since the symbol int (i) applies the interval size convention, we see that the ratio of int (i) is $r^i 2^n$ where n is chosen so that $1 < r^i 2^n < 2$. Now let i be positive; then n must be negative or zero. Let $-n = m$, and then

$$r^i 2^n = \frac{r^i}{2^m} \text{ and } 1 < \frac{r^i}{2^m} < 2, \text{ or } 2^m < r^i < 2^{m+1}. \text{ Hence the ratio of int } (i) \text{ for}$$

a positive i is $\frac{r^i}{2^m}$, where m is a positive integer chosen so that 2^m is the

greatest power of 2 less than r^i. Since $\frac{r^i}{2^m} = r^i 2^{-m}$, and this is the ratio of

$iv + na$, we have $\log r^i 2^{-m} = iv + na$ (Ch. I, Sec. 1); from this, it follows that $-m$ is the coefficient of a. This affords a convenient means of finding the size of int (i)—we simply substitute the size in cents for v (696.578 cents for meantone tuning) in the expression $iv - 1200m$.

Example: Find the ratio and size in cents of meantone int (6). Substituting $5^{1/4}$ for r, we see that the ratio is $\dfrac{5^{6/4}}{2^m} = \dfrac{11.180340}{2^m}$, and the greatest

power of 2 less than 11.180340 is $2^3 = 8$, hence the ratio is $\dfrac{11.180340}{8} =$

1.397542. The coefficient of a is -3, hence the size in cents is $6v - 3a =$ (6)(696.578) $- 3600 = 579.471$ cents.[1]

Now assume i to be negative, or let $i = -h$ where h is positive; the ratio of $-hv + na$ is $r^{-h}2^n = \dfrac{2^n}{r^h}$. If $1 < \dfrac{2^n}{r^h} < 2$, then n is zero or positive.

Now taking reciprocals and reversing inequality signs, we have $1 > \dfrac{r^h}{2^n} > \dfrac{1}{2}$, and $2^n > r^i > 2^{n-1}$. Thus the ratio of int (i) for a negative i is $\dfrac{2^n}{r^{|i|}}$,[2] where n is a positive integer chosen so that 2^n is the least power of 2 greater than $r^{|i|}$. In this case, $\log r^{-h}2^n = -hv + na$, and so n is the coefficient of a, and i $(= -h)$ is the coefficient of v.

Example: Find the ratio and size in cents of meantone int (-3). Again substituting $5^{1/4}$ for r, we find the ratio to be $\dfrac{2^n}{5^{3/4}} = \dfrac{2^n}{3.343702}$, and the least power of 2 greater than 3.343702 is $2^2 = 4$, hence the ratio is $\dfrac{4}{3.343702} =$ 1.196279. The coefficient of a is 2, and so the size in cents is $2a - 3v =$ $2400 - (3)(696.578) = 310.265$ cents.[3]

In Chapter II, Sec. 3, we derived a number of important relations connecting Pythagorean intervals expressed as $\overline{\text{int}}$ (i). Since the actual size of the generating interval never enters into the demonstrations, the same relations hold for a tempered fifth as for a pure fifth. For the sake of convenience, they are listed below:[4]

If int (x) + int $(y) < a$, then int (x) + int (y) = int $(x + y)$;

If int (y) > int (x), then int (y) − int (x) = int $(y - x)$;

If y int $(x) < a$, then y int (x) = int (xy); and

If $y > 0$, $y|x$, and int $\left(\dfrac{x}{y}\right) <$ int (x), then $\dfrac{\text{int }(x)}{y} =$ int $\left(\dfrac{x}{y}\right)$.

---

[1] The apparent discrepancy in the multiplication is due to an accumulation of rounding errors. If this is to be avoided, the value for v must be carried out to more decimals, and we have $\log 5^{1/4} = 696.578428$. When the fifth is pure, the rounding error is much less, since the fourth and fifth decimal places are zeros, the value to six places being $\log \frac{3}{2} = 701.955001$.

[2] See Ch. II, note 1.

[3] The reader will note that this process is slightly different from the one used to calculate the ratios of Pythagorean intervals (Ch. II, Sec. 2). If $5^{1/4}$ is replaced by $\frac{3}{2}$, the method of this section computes the ratio of the corresponding Pythagorean interval. The reason for the difference is simply that large powers of 3 are more readily computed than large powers of 1.5.

[4] See Ch. I, note 5.

Recalling that int (0) means some number of octaves not excluding zero, up or down (Ch. II, Sec. 2), we have more generally:

int (x) + int (y) = int $(x + y)$ + int (0);

int (y) − int (x) = int $(y − x)$ + int (0);

y int (x) = int (xy) + int (0);

and if $y > 0$ and $y\,|\,x$, then $\dfrac{\text{int } (x) + \text{int } (0)}{y} = \text{int} \left(\dfrac{x}{y}\right)$.

It will be convenient to number the notes forming the meantone diatonic scale in the order in which they occur in the generating array, starting with 0 and ending with 6. As before, notes 0, 1, 2, 3, 4, 5, and 6 correspond to F, C, G, D, A, E, and B, respectively (Ch. III, Sec. 6).

We also note that the size of the generating interval does not enter into the proofs of Theorems 6 and 7 (Ch. II, Sec. 3), hence it is also true in meantone tuning that the interval between note x and note y is int $(y − x)$, and that the note higher than note x by int (i) is note $x + i$. This shows that the diatonic meantone intervals—the intervals that occur when notes 0 through 6 are taken in pairs—are expressible as int (i) where $−6 \leqslant i \leqslant 6$. Ratios and sizes in cents of all the diatonic meantone intervals are given in Table 57 (p. 160).

3. The major scale and the names of the diatonic meantone intervals. The order of notes in the meantone diatonic scale may be found from Table 57 in exactly the same way that the Pythagorean scale was obtained from Table 3 (Ch. II, Secs. 4 and 5). We have only to arrange intervals (0) through (6) in ascending order; if the lower note of each interval is note zero, the higher notes form the diatonic scale as defined in Section 2 of this chapter. The results are given in Table 58 (p. 160).

As in Pythagorean tuning, the notes of the scale in ascending order are 0, 2, 4, 6, 1, 3, 5, 0, corresponding to F, G, A, B, C, D, E, F, i.e., the notes of the scale may be evolved from the generating array by taking every other note (Ch. III, Sec. 2). Hence the statement "position j in the diatonic scale is occupied by note i where $2j \equiv i \pmod{7}$ and $4i \equiv j \pmod{7}$, $0 \leqslant i \leqslant 6$ and $0 \leqslant j \leqslant 6$" holds for meantone as well as Pythagorean tuning. We use the former congruence to calculate i given j, and the latter to calculate j given i. Also, since any two notes occupy the same relative positions in the Pythagorean and meantone diatonic scale, the ordinal number naming a diatonic meantone interval between two given notes is the same as that naming the corresponding Pythagorean interval, and so

TABLE 57

DIATONIC MEANTONE INTERVALS

interval	in terms of a and v	ratio (fraction)	ratio (decimal)	size in cents
int (6)	$6v - 3a$	$\dfrac{5^{3/2}}{8}$	1.397542	579.471
int (5)	$5v - 2a$	$\dfrac{5^{5/4}}{4}$	1.869186	1082.892
int (4)	$4v - 2a$	$\dfrac{5}{4}$	1.250000	386.314
int (3)	$3v - a$	$\dfrac{5^{3/4}}{2}$	1.671851	889.735
int (2)	$2v - a$	$\dfrac{5^{1/2}}{2}$	1.118034	193.157
int (1)	v	$\dfrac{5^{1/4}}{1}$	1.495349	696.578
octave	a	$\dfrac{2}{1}$	2.000000	1200.000
int (−1)	$a - v$	$\dfrac{2}{5^{1/4}}$	1.337481	503.422
int (−2)	$2a - 2v$	$\dfrac{4}{5^{1/2}}$	1.788854	1006.843
int (−3)	$2a - 3v$	$\dfrac{4}{5^{3/4}}$	1.196279	310.265
int (−4)	$3a - 4v$	$\dfrac{8}{5}$	1.600000	813.686
int (−5)	$3a - 5v$	$\dfrac{8}{5^{5/4}}$	1.069984	117.108
int (−6)	$4a - 6v$	$\dfrac{16}{5^{3/2}}$	1.431084	620.529

TABLE 58

intervals	(0)	(2)	(4)	(6)	(1)	(3)	(5)	(0)
size in cents	000.000	193.157	386.314	579.471	696.578	889.735	1082.892	1200.000

the statement "int (i) is a $(j + 1)$th where $4i \equiv j \pmod 7$ and $0 \leqslant j \leqslant 6$" (Theorem 12; Ch. III, Sec. 3) also holds for meantone tuning. The practical methods for calculating i given j are identical to those described in Chapter III, Sec. 3.

Since Theorem 13 (Ch. III, Sec. 5) is based on Theorem 10 (Ch. III, Sec. 1)[5] and Theorem 12 (Ch. III, Sec. 3), it is true in meantone tuning that the same ordinal number names both int (i) and int $(i - 7)$ where $1 \leqslant i \leqslant 6$, and consequently the correspondences of Table 6 remain valid.

The proof of Theorem 14 depends upon the inequalities int $(i) >$ int $(i - 7)$ for $1 \leqslant i \leqslant 6$; and an examination of Table 57 shows that these also hold for meantone tuning. Hence two different diatonic meantone intervals named by the same ordinal number differ in every case by int (7). Using the methods described in Section 2 of this chapter, we find that the ratio of meantone int (7) is $\dfrac{5^{7/4}}{2^n} = \dfrac{16.718508}{2^n}$; the greatest power of 2 less than 16.718508 is $2^4 = 16$, and so the ratio is $\dfrac{16.718508}{16} = 1.044907$, and the size is 76.049 cents. Although this is considerably less than an apotome of 113.685 cents, the modality can be distinguished with no difficulty.[6]

In sum, the meantone interval between notes i_1 and i_2 ($0 \leqslant i_1 \leqslant 6$, $0 \leqslant i_2 \leqslant 6$) is int (i) where $i = i_2 - i_1$, and this interval is called a $(j + 1)$th where $4i \equiv j \pmod 7$. Furthermore, if i is positive, int (i) is a greater $(j + 1)$th, and if i is negative, int (i) is a lesser $(j + 1)$th. Since this is also true of Pythagorean intervals, it follows that the distribution of greater and lesser $(j + 1)$ths within the diatonic scale is exactly the same in both meantone and Pythagorean tuning, as described in Chapter III, Sec. 4. It is thus also true for meantone tuning that the number of lesser $(j + 1)$ths contained by the scale is i where $2j \equiv i \pmod 7$, $0 \leqslant i \leqslant 6$ (Theorem 15), and that the number of greater $(j + 1)$ths is h where $5j \equiv h \pmod 7$, $0 \leqslant h \leqslant 6$ (Theorem 16), the lower notes of each greater $(j + 1)$th being notes $0, 1, 2 \ldots h - 1$ (Theorem 17). The proofs are identical to those given in Chapter III, Sec. 5.

The convention regarding the words augmented, major, perfect, minor, and diminished, as described in Chapter III, Sec. 6 is also applied to meantone tuning, with the consequence that Table 8 (Ch. III, Sec. 6) gives the

---

[5] It should be observed that Theorem 10 is an abstraction in number theory, and is true without reference to anything having to do with tunings.

[6] The general term for int (7) is *chromatic semitone*; the word *apotome* is reserved specifically for Pythagorean tuning. See also Ch. IV, note 4.

names of the meantone diatonic intervals, these being identical in every
case to the corresponding Pythagorean intervals.

It is also true that the cyclic interconnection among the generating
array, the scale and the triads—the first, second, and third order of notes—
holds for meantone tuning as well, for all that is required is that the notes
of the scale should be in the order 0, 2, 4, 6, 1, 3, 5, 0, i.e., that the congruence $2j \equiv i \pmod 7$ should be valid.

The reader may be puzzled by this rather lengthy demonstration that
the names and structural interconnections associated with the intervals
of C major are the same in both meantone and Pythagorean tuning—a
fact that may seem intuitively obvious. However, it is equally obvious
that if the generating interval departs sufficiently from a pure fifth, the
notes of the scale 0, 2, 4, 6, 1, 3, 5, 0 will no longer be in ascending order.
For example, let the generating interval contain 725 cents, and compare
int (3) with int (5). We have (3)(725) = 2175 and (5)(725) = 3625; upon application of the interval size convention, int (3) = 2175 − 1200 = 975 cents,
and int (5) = 3625 − 3600 = 25 cents. Under these conditions, notes 3 (D)
and 5 (E) are no longer in ascending order. If intervals (1) through (6) are
calculated on the basis of a generating interval of 725 cents and arranged
in increasing order, we have the following:

intervals	(5)	(2)	(4)	(1)	(6)	(3)
size in cents	25	250	500	725	750	975

The notes in ascending order are now 0, 5, 2, 4, 1, 6, 3, 0, viz., F, E, G, A,
C, B, D, F. In this arrangement, the ordinal number naming an interval
between two notes may be different from that of Pythagorean tuning. For
example, in the above scale, FA is a fourth, not a third.

As another example, let the generating interval contain 680 cents, and
compare int (4), a major third, with int (−3), a minor third. We have
(4)(680) = 2720 and (−3)(680) = −2040, and so int (4) = 2720 − 2400 =
320 cents, and int (−3) = −2040 + 2400 = 360 cents. But now a minor
third (360 cents) is greater than a major third (320 cents), in effect reversing
the two levels of modality. In a later discussion (Ch. X, Sec. 2), we shall
determine the maximum and minimum values for v that yield diatonic
intervals and notes in the order of Pythagorean tuning.

4. Diatonic seventh chords and the major scale. The character of the
diatonic seventh chords in meantone tuning depends to a considerable
extent on the timbre of the instrument that plays them, and does not

admit of a precise description. Nevertheless, it is useful to attempt a characterization of the meantone seventh chords, and a comparison with their Pythagorean counterparts.

The addition of a major seventh to a major triad results in a rather discordant harmony no matter what the tuning, owing to the inherent roughness of a major seventh. This interval has a rather different character in meantone tuning and Pythagorean tuning, containing 1082.892 cents in the former and 1109.775 cents in the latter—a difference of 26.883 cents. Even though the difference is quite noticeable, it is difficult to prefer one version to the other. In the case of the complete chord, the principal point of difference is actually the tuning of the thirds, and the Pythagorean thirds impart a shrill quality that is lacking in the meantone version. Much the same is true in the case of minor seventh chords, although a meantone minor seventh (1006.843 cents) is very slightly more discordant than a Pythagorean minor seventh (996.090 cents), owing to the greater departure of the meantone interval from the pure version (ratio $\frac{7}{4}$, size 968.826 cents).

Dominant seventh chords in meantone tuning are somewhat discordant owing to a considerable departure from pure tuning of the diminished fifth. The meantone version (620.529 cents) is greater than the pure version (ratio $\frac{7}{5}$, size 582.512 cents) by 38.017 cents, whereas the Pythagorean diminished fifth (588.270 cents) is larger than pure by only 5.758 cents. But the discordance of the Pythagorean thirds outweighs that of the meantone diminished fifth, and consequently a dominant seventh chord is more satisfactory in meantone tuning than in Pythagorean tuning. The same is true for a half-diminished seventh chord, although the difference is less substantial than in the case of the other seventh chords.

If we play a sequence of seventh chords over the degrees I-IV-VII-III-VI-II-V-I, as distributed in Figure 8 (Ch. V, Sec. 6), first in meantone and then in Pythagorean tuning, there can be little doubt that the meantone version is far mellower, and consequently considerably more satisfactory. In the author's opinion, the meantone version is also superior to the just version, mainly owing to the elimination of the syntonic and septimal commas as melodic intervals.

The effect melodically of a meantone major scale is considerably different from that of a Pythagorean scale. If we construct a meantone major scale as described in Section 2 of this chapter, taking C_0 as the tonic and using the subscript notation of Section 1, the generating array is written $F_{+1/4}C_0G_{-1/4}D_{-1/2}A_{-3/4}E_{-1}B_{-5/4}$. From this, the scale is seen to be

TABLE 59

Pythagorean	C_0	D_0	E_0	F_0	G_0	A_0	B_0	C_0
meantone	C_0	$D_{-1/2}$	E_{-1}	$F_{+1/4}$	$G_{-1/4}$	$A_{-3/4}$	$B_{-5/4}$	C_0
difference in cents	0.000	−10.753	−21.506	+5.377	−5.377	−16.130	−26.883	0.000

$C_0 D_{-1/2} E_{-1} F_{+1/4} G_{-1/4} A_{-3/4} B_{-5/4} C_0$. If we compare this with the Pythagorean scale, we observe that every degree of the scale save the fourth is flat with reference to Pythagorean tuning, with the difference increasing as we go from the first to the third degree, and again from the fifth to the seventh degree, as illustrated in Table 59. The greatest difference occurs in the case of the leading tone, and this is somewhat disadvantageous, for many contemporary musicians are accustomed to preferring a tuning that places the leading tone relatively close to the tonic. It is certainly the case that the expressive force normally associated with the leading tone in melodic situations is quite substantially different in the two tunings, and the difference is especially noticeable in musical styles where scale figurations are prominent.

It appears that Pythagorean tuning favors the scale at the expense of the triads, whereas the opposite is true of meantone tuning. Viewed in this light, neither can be regarded as superior to the other without reference to the repertoire.

IX   Extended Meantone Tuning

Introduction. The theory of extended meantone tuning is a matter of great practical importance, for there is abundant historical evidence that meantone tuning was the preferred tuning for keyboard instruments during the period 1550 to 1650. As in the case of the diatonic intervals, we develop the theory of the meantone chromatic intervals and chromatic scale from what was discovered with regard to extended Pythagorean tuning. Before continuing, the reader should review the contents of Chapter IV.

In Section 1 we extend the notion of the unending line of pure perfect fifths to meantone fifths, and show how to calculate the frequency of any note and the size of any interval from the names of the notes involved. Section 2 develops a systematic method for comparing the musical character of a meantone interval with that of its Pythagorean counterpart. It is also shown that intervals formed by notes that are distant by more than eleven positions on the line of fifths exhibit a completely different musical character or behavior in the two tunings. In Section 3 it is shown that a chromatic scale and a diatonic scale have important structural similarities that are best described using the algebra of congruences and residues, as set forth and applied in Chapter III, Secs. 1 and 2. Section 4 shows that only eight major triads, eight minor triads, six major keys, and three minor keys are available on a 12-note keyboard instrument in meantone tuning, and Section 5 gives a practical method for setting up the tuning by ear. The applicability of meantone tuning to a portion of the existing repertoire is explored in Section 6, where it is shown that certain boldly chromatic compositions conform strictly to the inherent limitations of the tuning. Finally in Section 7, we describe and analyze a 12-note tuning that gives something near meantone tuning for the common triads, and Pythagorean tuning for the more remote triads, with a smooth transition from one to the other as roots proceed along the line of fifths.

1. Names of notes and numerical data. Extension of meantone tuning is accomplished by the same method as extension of Pythagorean tuning

(Ch. IV, Sec. 1). We consider all the notes named by the positive and negative integers and zero, the interval between notes n and $n + 1$ being in each case int (1) $= \bar{v} - \frac{1}{4}\bar{k}$, a meantone fifth. The notes are named by the same means as in Pythagorean tuning, and the same number correspondences hold. Thus numbers 0, 1, 2, 3, 4, 5, and 6 correspond to F, C, G, D, A, E, and B, respectively; in addition, each sharp adds 7 and each flat subtracts 7.

Examples: G♭ is note $2 - 7$, or note -5; F✗ is note $0 + (2)(7)$, or note 14.

Visualization of the entire aggregate is the same line of fifths that is shown in Chapter IV, Sec. 1, with meantone fifths replacing pure fifths.

The question naturally arises whether any two notes on the line of meantone fifths are the same. If this were to be the case, the sum of an integral number of meantone fifths would be equal to the sum of an integral number of octaves, and we should have $5^{n/4} = 2^m$, or $5^n = 2^{4m}$, where m and n are positive integers. But this requires that there should exist a number which is both a power of 2 and a power of 5, and this is impossible (Theorem 1; Ch. I, Sec. 4). Consequently the line of fifths, in meantone as in Pythagorean tuning, extends indefinitely in both directions, and all the notes are different.

We may readily calculate the frequency of any note in the octave above middle C in extended meantone tuning, given its conventional name. We first express the interval between C and the note in question as int (i), and then calculate the ratio of int (i) by the method of Chapter VIII, Sec. 2, which is valid for all values of i given the definition of int (i). To obtain the frequency wanted, we multiply this ratio by the frequency of middle C—264 Hz or 261.626 Hz.[1] The size of int (i) is best found by determining the coefficient of a in the expression $iv + na$, as described in Chapter VIII, Sec. 2, and then substituting 1200 for a and 696.5784 for v, taking care to use a sufficiently accurate value for v to avoid an accumulation of rounding errors.

Example: Find the relevant data for A♯. C is note 1, and A♯ is note $4 + 7 = 11$, hence CA♯ is int $(11 - 1) = $ int (10) (Theorem 6; Ch. II, Sec. 3). We next have $(5^{1/4})^{10} = 5^{5/2} = 55.901699$, and the greatest power of 2 less than that number is $2^5 = 32$. Hence the ratio of int (10) is $\dfrac{55.901699}{32} = $ 1.746928, and the frequency of A♯ is $(1.746928)(264) = 461.189$ Hz, or

---

[1] See Ch. I, note 2 and Ch. IV, note 2.

TABLE 60

MEANTONE TUNING

note	ratio with C	frequency C = 264	frequency C = 261.626	cents up from C
A𝄪	1.825377	481.900	477.565	1041.833
D𝄪	1.220703	322.266	319.367	345.255
G𝄪	1.632667	431.024	427.147	848.676
C𝄪	1.091830	288.243	285.651	152.098
F𝄪	1.460302	385.520	382.052	655.520
B♯	1.953125	515.625	510.987	1158.941
E♯	1.306133	344.819	341.718	462.363
A♯	1.746928	461.189	457.041	965.784
D♯	1.168241	308.416	305.642	269.206
G♯	1.562500	412.500	408.790	772.627
C♯	1.044907	275.855	273.374	76.049
F♯	1.397542	368.951	365.633	579.471
B	1.869186	493.465	489.027	1082.892
E	1.250000	330.000	327.032	386.314
A	1.671851	441.369	437.399	889.735
D	1.118034	295.161	292.506	193.157
G	1.495349	394.772	391.221	696.578
C	1.000000	264.000	261.626	0.000
F	1.337481	353.095	349.919	503.422
B♭	1.788854	472.258	468.010	1006.843
E♭	1.196279	315.818	312.977	310.265
A♭	1.600000	422.400	418.601	813.686
D♭	1.069984	282.476	279.935	117.108
G♭	1.431084	377.806	374.408	620.529
C♭	1.914046	505.308	500.763	1123.951
F♭	1.280000	337.920	334.881	427.373
B♭♭	1.711975	451.961	447.896	930.794
E♭♭	1.144867	302.245	299.526	234.216
A♭♭	1.531237	404.247	400.611	737.637
D♭♭	1.024000	270.336	267.905	41.059
G♭♭	1.369580	361.569	358.317	544.480

$(1.746928)(261.626) = 457.041$ Hz. Since the denominator of the ratio is 2^5, the full expression of int (10) in terms of a and v is $10v - 5a$, and its size in cents is $(10)(696.5784) - (5)(1200) = 965.784$ cents.

Table 60 gives numerical data for all notes on the line of fifths from G♭♭ to A𝄪.

Table 61 gives ratios, sizes in cents, and full expressions in terms of a and v ($= \bar{v} - \frac{1}{4}\bar{k}$) for meantone intervals (7) through (13), and (−7) through (−13). Calculations are done by the method of Chapter VIII, Sec. 2.

TABLE 61

CHROMATIC MEANTONE INTERVALS

interval	in terms of a and v	ratio (fraction)	ratio (decimal)	size in cents
int (13)	$13v - 7a$	$\dfrac{5^{13/4}}{128}$	1.460302	655.520
int (12)	$12v - 6a$	$\dfrac{125}{64}$	1.953125	1158.941
int (11)	$11v - 6a$	$\dfrac{5^{11/4}}{64}$	1.306133	462.363
int (10)	$10v - 5a$	$\dfrac{5^{5/2}}{32}$	1.746928	965.784
int (9)	$9v - 5a$	$\dfrac{5^{9/4}}{32}$	1.168241	269.206
int (8)	$8v - 4a$	$\dfrac{25}{16}$	1.562500	772.627
int (7)	$7v - 4a$	$\dfrac{5^{7/4}}{16}$	1.044907	76.049
int (−7)	$5a - 7v$	$\dfrac{32}{5^{7/4}}$	1.914046	1123.951
int (−8)	$5a - 8v$	$\dfrac{32}{25}$	1.280000	427.373
int (−9)	$6a - 9v$	$\dfrac{64}{5^{9/4}}$	1.711975	930.794
int (−10)	$6a - 10v$	$\dfrac{64}{5^{5/2}}$	1.144867	234.216
int (−11)	$7a - 11v$	$\dfrac{128}{5^{11/4}}$	1.531237	737.637
int (−12)	$7a - 12v$	$\dfrac{128}{125}$	1.024000	41.059
int (−13)	$8a - 13v$	$\dfrac{256}{5^{13/4}}$	1.369580	544.480

2. Chromatic intervals in meantone tuning. In meantone tuning as in Pythagorean tuning, int (i) is called *chromatic* if $i \geqslant 7$ or if $i \leqslant -7$. From Table 57 (Ch. VIII, Sec. 3) and Table 61, we see that int $(8) >$ int (1), int $(9) >$ int (2), int $(10) >$ int (3), and int $(11) >$ int (4). Hence int $(8) -$ int $(1) =$ int (7), int $(9) -$ int $(2) =$ int (7), int $(10) -$ int $(3) =$ int (7), and int $(11) -$ int $(4) =$ int (7) (Ch. II, Sec. 3). We recall that for intervals (1) through (4), the ordinal number is given by $j + 1$ where $4i \equiv j$ (mod 7) (Ch. VIII, Sec. 3); since it is also true that $4(i + 7) \equiv j$ (mod 7) (Theorem 10; Ch. III, Sec. 1), the same is true for intervals (8) through (11). Hence these intervals are named as in Pythagorean tuning (Table 11; Ch. IV, Sec. 3), the difference in level of modality being in each case int (7). The reader should have no difficulty showing that a similar situation exists regarding intervals (-8) through (-11), and consequently these are also named as in Pythagorean tuning (Table 12; Ch. IV, Sec. 3). In sum, int (i) has the same name in Pythagorean and meantone tuning for any i between -11 and 11.

There is a convenient method for making a general comparison between a meantone interval and its Pythagorean counterpart. We recall that in Pythagorean tuning, $\overline{\text{int}}\,(i) = i\bar{v} + n_1 a$, and in meantone tuning, int $(i) = i(\bar{v} - \frac{1}{4}\bar{k}) + n_2 a$, with n_1 and n_2 being determined by the interval size convention. Now $\overline{\text{int}}\,(i) -$ int $(i) = \frac{1}{4}i\bar{k} + a(n_1 - n_2)$, and if $n_1 = n_2$, we have

$$\overline{\text{int}}\,(i) - \text{int}\,(i) = \tfrac{1}{4}i\bar{k}$$

This relation is very useful, for it shows that a Pythagorean interval exceeds its meantone counterpart when i is positive, and vice versa when i is negative $(-11 \leqslant i \leqslant 11)$. Or we might say that the perfect fifth, major intervals, and augmented intervals are larger in Pythagorean than in meantone tuning, and that the perfect fourth, minor intervals, and diminished intervals are larger in meantone than in Pythagorean tuning. Furthermore, the difference varies directly with i; in musical terms, the difference increases as we go from perfect to major to augmented intervals, or from perfect to minor to diminished intervals. The difference mounts up rather rapidly—in the case of int (13), it amounts to $\frac{13}{4}\bar{k} = 69.895$ cents, only slightly smaller than a chromatic semitone (76.049 cents) and nearly the same as a minor chroma (70.672 cents; Ch. VI, Sec. 4). Thus the Pythagorean and meantone versions of int (13) differ by nearly a semitone, and hence have quite different characters. This may help to explain why there are no strongly established habits or predispositions among theorists

regarding the size or character of intervals formed by notes that are more
remote on the line of fifths.

It is interesting to make a more detailed investigation of intervals (8)
through (11), along with their respective inversions.

1. Intervals (8) and (−8), augmented fifth and diminished fourth. We
found earlier that Pythagorean $\overline{\text{int}}$ (−8) is the nearly pure schismatic major
third $\overline{t} - \overline{s}$ (Ch. VI, Sec. 3). Since i is negative, the meantone interval
will be greater than this by $\frac{8}{4}\overline{k}$, or $2\overline{k}$, and hence meantone int (−8) =
$\overline{t} - \overline{s} + 2\overline{k}$. By virtue of the relation $\overline{d} = 2\overline{k} - \overline{s}$ (Ch. VI, Sec. 2), this last
becomes $\overline{t} + \overline{d}$, and thus a meantone diminished fourth exceeds a pure
major third by a diesis of 41.059 cents. This exceedingly discordant interval
and its inversion are usable only in augmented triads, and may not occur
between the two outer parts, or between the two lower parts. If an augmented triad is distributed as shown below,

the discordance of B♭F♯ is masked to a considerable degree by pure intervals DF♯ and DB♭ between the two outer parts and the two lower
parts, respectively. Even so, an augmented triad as arranged in this example
has a peculiar discordance which is not unattractive, but which contrasts
very sharply with the relatively smooth major and minor triads.

2. Intervals (9) and (−9), augmented second and diminished seventh. In
Pythagorean tuning, int (9) is the nearly pure $\overline{v} - \overline{t} + \overline{s}$ of 317.595 cents—
greater than a pure minor third by a schisma (Ch. VI, Sec. 3). The meantone
interval is smaller than this by $\frac{9}{4}\overline{k}$, and hence is equal to $\overline{v} - \overline{t} - (\frac{9}{4}\overline{k} - \overline{s}) =$
269.206 cents. This interval is quite discordant, being smaller than a pure
minor third by 46.435 cents—in fact, it is only 2.335 cents larger than the
pure interval whose ratio is $\frac{7}{6}$ (size 266.871 cents). Like the latter, it has
a peculiar character all its own and is not a satisfactory substitute for a
minor third in a triad. Its inversion is discordant to at least the same
degree.

3. Intervals (10) and (−10), augmented sixth and diminished third. A
meantone augmented sixth contains 965.784 cents—only 3.042 cents less
than a pure minor seventh (ratio $\frac{7}{4}$) of 968.826 cents, and consequently the
two intervals are practically indistinguishable. Hence an Italian sixth chord
in meantone tuning, such as CEA♯, is much smoother than a dominant

seventh with its fifth missing, such as CEB♭. In fact, meantone Italian
sixth chords are a bit too euphonious, given the conventional dissonant
treatment of augmented sixth chords. The much larger Pythagorean augmented sixth of 1019.550 cents is considerably more discordant than the
meantone version.

4. Intervals (11) and (-11), augmented third and diminished sixth. We
have already shown that $\overline{\text{int}}\,(11) = \bar{v} - \bar{p}$, and described the characteristics
of this discordant interval (Ch. IV, Sec. 5). A meantone diminished sixth
exceeds its Pythagorean counterpart by $\frac{11}{4}\bar{k}$, and hence is equal to
$\bar{v} - \bar{p} + \frac{11}{4}\bar{k} = 737.637$ cents. This interval—larger than a pure perfect fifth
by 35.682 cents—is even more discordant than a Pythagorean diminished
sixth, and is totally unsatisfactory as a harmonic combination, even in
dissonant harmonies.

At this point, it is useful to note that intervals (8) through (11) and (-8)
through (-11) exhibit the same musical characteristics and structural
behavior in both meantone and Pythagorean tuning. In every case, the
meantone and Pythagorean tunings sound like two different versions of
the same thing. However, the differences are not inconsiderable—in the
cases of intervals (8), (-8), (9), and (-9), the Pythagorean versions are
smoother than the meantone versions; intervals (10) and (-10) are
smoother in meantone than in Pythagorean tuning, and intervals (11) and
(-11) are discordant in both tunings, but worse in meantone tuning.

In the case of intervals (12) and (-12), we come upon more substantial
differences. According to the general scheme of naming intervals (Ch. IV,
Sec. 3), int (12) would be called an augmented seventh, and int (-12) a
diminished second. We saw earlier (Ch. IV, Sec. 4) that these names lead
to contradictory situations in Pythagorean tuning; but this is not the case
in meantone tuning. The ratio of meantone int (12) is $\dfrac{(5^{1/4})^{12}}{2^m} = \dfrac{5^3}{2^m} = \dfrac{125}{2^m}$;
the greatest power of 2 less than 125 is $2^6 = 64$, hence the ratio is $\frac{125}{64}$
and the size is 1158.941 cents. The essential difference is that a Pythagorean augmented seventh exceeds an octave, but a meantone augmented
seventh does not. In meantone tuning, we have also int (12) > int (5),
hence int (12) $-$ int (5) = int (7) (Ch. VIII, Sec. 2), and this shows that
int (12) is larger than a major seventh by one level of modality (Ch. IV,
Sec. 3), hence the name augmented seventh is fully and consistently applicable. Since the denominator of the ratio is 2^6, we see that the full
expression for meantone int (12) is $12v - 6a$, whereas in Pythagorean
tuning, the corresponding expression for $\overline{\text{int}}\,(12)$ is $12\bar{v} - 7a$ (Ch. IV, Sec.

5). If we imagine the generating interval decreasing at a uniform rate from 701.955 cents (pure) to 696.578 cents (meantone), int (12) decreases from 23.460 cents to zero, jumps an octave upward, then decreases once more from 1200 cents to 1158.941 cents. The jump discontinuity occurs at the point where the coefficient of a changes from 7 to 6.

It should also be noted that in meantone tuning, $12v - 7a$ is a descending diesis, for we have $12v - 7a = 12(\bar{v} - \frac{1}{4}\bar{k}) - 7a = 12\bar{v} - 7a - 3\bar{k} = \bar{p} - 3\bar{k} = -\bar{d}$ (Ch. VI, Sec. 2).

In the case of int (-12), using the method of Chapter VIII, Sec. 2, we find the ratio to be $\frac{128}{125}$, again a diesis of 41.059 cents (Ch. VI, Sec. 2). We have also int $(-5) >$ int (-12), hence int $(-5) -$ int $(-12) =$ int (7). This shows that int (-12) is smaller than a minor second by one level of modality, hence the name diminished second applies without the inconsistency found in Pythagorean tuning. If this interval is written on a conventional five-line staff, as for example,

its true nature is apparent, in that A♭ is higher than G♯ by 41.059 cents. The reader should carefully compare this aspect with the corresponding situation in Pythagorean tuning, where the direction of the interval is reversed (Ch. IV, Sec. 4).

A meantone diminished second is too small to be satisfactory as a melodic interval, and both intervals (12) and (-12) are excessively discordant as harmonic combinations. These intervals have never found any use in the existing repertoire.

It must be concluded that meantone tuning is not an ideal tuning for music in which chromatic intervals occur frequently as harmonic combinations.

3. The meantone chromatic scale. The idea of a broken circle of eleven perfect fifths and one diminished sixth has already been suggested (Ch. IV, Sec. 5), and is represented symbolically by the equation 11 int (1) + int $(-11) =$ int (0). We may evolve a scale from this broken circle by a process analogous to that used to generate a diatonic scale from a broken circle of seven fifths. To this end, we start at some arbitrary point—say note 0 (F) in any register—and construct a total of twelve pitches, each higher than the one immediately preceding by a

TABLE 62

interval	(0)	(7)	(2)	(9)	(4)	(11)
size in cents	0.000	76.049	193.157	269.206	386.314	462.363
interval	(6)	(1)	(8)	(3)	(10)	(5)
size in cents	579.471	696.578	772.627	889.735	965.784	1082.892

TABLE 63

notes	F	F♯	G	G♯	A	A♯	B	C	C♯	D	D♯	E	F
	0	7	2	9	4	11	6	1	8	3	10	5	0
adjacent intervals	(7)	(−5)	(7)	(−5)	(7)	(−5)	(−5)	(7)	(−5)	(7)	(−5)	(−5)	

meantone fifth. We next transpose these pitches up or down some number (not excluding zero) of octaves, this number being immaterial, in such a manner that the greatest interval formed by any two of the new pitches is less than one octave. When these pitches are rearranged in ascending order, the result is called a *chromatic scale*. We thus wish to arrange notes 0 through 11 in ascending order within one octave. Since note x is higher than note 0 by int (x) (Theorem 6; Ch. II, Sec. 3), and int $(x) < a$, the desired arrangement may be effected first by arranging intervals (1) through (11) in increasing order; then if the lower note of each interval is note 0, the higher notes of each interval are the notes of the chromatic scale. From Tables 57 (Ch. VIII, Sec. 3) and 61 (Sec. 1 of this chapter), we find the order to be that given in Table 62. Thus the order of notes in the 12-note chromatic scale is 0, 7, 2, 9, 4, 11, 6, 1, 8, 3, 10, 5, 0, corresponding to F, F♯, G, G♯, A, A♯, B, C, C♯, D, D♯, E, F.

By Theorem 6 (Ch. II, Sec. 3), the successive differences give the adjacent intervals. From Table 63, we see that the chromatic scale consists of an asymmetric arrangement of seven minor seconds and five chromatic semitones. The idea of this sum returning to the initial note is conveyed symbolically by the equation 7 int $(-5) + 5$ int $(7) = $ int (0).

As in the case of the diatonic scale, the rearrangement of the notes of the generating array is not haphazard, but conforms to a simple rule. The rule is suggested if we observe that the notes forming perfect fifths FC,

F♯C♯, GD, G♯D♯, and AE are in each case separated by seven positions on the chromatic scale, indicating that the chromatic scale might be evolved from the generating array by taking every seventh note, always counting note 0 directly after note 11. A brief investigation reveals that the principle is consistently carried out, hence we may say that note i is in position j of the chromatic scale where $7i \equiv j \pmod{12}$, and $0 \leqslant j \leqslant 11$. This result is of interest in that it shows a connection between the evolution of the diatonic and chromatic scales that is by no means obvious.

We may transform the congruence $7i \equiv j \pmod{12}$ in a manner that reveals another cyclic aspect connecting the chromatic scale and the generating array. Using the relations described in Chapter III, Sec. 1, we have

$$j \equiv 7i \pmod{12}$$

$$7j \equiv 49i \pmod{12}$$

$$7j \equiv 48i + i \pmod{12}$$

and finally, applying Theorem 10 (Ch. III, Sec. 1),

$$7j \equiv i \pmod{12}$$

From this, we see that the broken circle of fifths may be evolved from the chromatic scale in exactly the same way that the scale is derived from the circle, viz., by taking every seventh note.

Although the chromatic scale comprising notes 0 through 11 is the most convenient to deal with theoretically, its practical application to the keyboard repertoire requires a slight modification. The reason is that keyboard repertoire that is suited to meantone tuning generally uses the twelve notes from -2 (E♭) through 9 (G♯), rather than from 0 (F) through 11 (A♯). We may write the new chromatic scale by adding -2 to the numbers of the scale previously derived, as shown in Table 64.[2] As it is customary among musicians to regard C as the starting and ending points, we write the keyboard chromatic scale in the order C, C♯, D, E♭, E, F, F♯, G, G♯, A, B♭, B, C. In this arrangement, CC♯, E♭E, FF♯, GG♯, and

---

[2] Other chromatic scales are occasionally needed, viz., B♭ through D♯ and A♭ through C♯. In the former case, the new numbers are given by $i - 1$, and in the latter case by $i - 3$. The asymmetric arrangement of chromatic semitones and minor seconds is the same in all three chromatic scales.

TABLE 64

old numbers (*i*)	0	7	2	9	4	11	6	1	8	3	10	5	0
new numbers (*i* − 2)	−2	5	0	7	2	9	4	−1	6	1	8	3	−2
new names		E♭	E	F	F♯	G	G♯	A	B♭	B	C	C♯	D	E♭

B♭B depict the five chromatic semitones, while the seven minor seconds are written C♯D, DE♭, EF, F♯G, G♯A, AB♭, and BC.

Since a minor second (117.108 cents) is larger than a chromatic semitone (76.049 cents), the difference is given by int (-5) − int (7) = int (-12) = $\bar{d} = 41.059$ cents (Sec. 2 of this chapter)—an amount large enough that the difference between the two intervals is clearly perceptible when a chromatic scale is played slowly. For this reason, a meantone chromatic scale is sometimes loosely referred to as *unequal temperament*.

4. Major keys, minor keys, triads, and wolves. That there exist several diatonic scales within the 12-note chromatic scale is apparent from Figure 16. In Figure 16, the twelve notes of the chromatic scale are laid out in the order in which they occur on the line of fifths. Since a major scale may be evolved from any seven adjacent notes on the line of fifths, the second note from the left being the tonic (Ch. IV, Sec. 6), it is apparent that the first seven notes (under the upper bracket of Figure 16) establish the key of B♭ major, and the last seven notes (under the lower bracket) establish the key of A major. Clearly the keys in between exist as well, and so a meantone chromatic scale furnishes six major keys whose tonics are B♭, F, C, G, D, and A, each having exactly the same size and distribution of the diatonic intervals as does C major. The remaining six notes cannot be tonics of major keys as defined, because in each case one of the perfect fifths of the generating array is replaced by diminished sixth G♯E♭.

A closely related question concerns the number of consonant major and minor triads playable within a 12-note meantone chromatic scale. Since

FIGURE 16

a major triad requires notes higher than its root by intervals (4) and (1), it consists generally of notes n, $n + 4$, and $n + 1$, where n is any integer. Hence the meantone chromatic scale furnishes consonant major triads whose roots are E♭, B♭, F, C, G, D, A, and E. There is no major triad on B, however, for D♯ a major third above B is not present. The nearest note to D♯ within the chromatic scale is E♭, 41.059 cents higher; but diminished fourth BE♭ is the very discordant interval $\bar{t} + \bar{d}$, and cannot serve satisfactorily as a major third. The same situation characterizes the major triads whose roots are F♯ and C♯, for the scale furnishes neither A♯ nor E♯, and their nearest equivalents—B♭ and F—are higher than the respective roots by $\bar{t} + \bar{d}$. Similarly, in the case of the triad whose root is G♯, there is no B♯; but in this case the situation is worse, for there is no D♯ to make a perfect fifth with G♯. The discordance of G♯CE♭ takes on a nearly comical aspect.

The four combinations that are nearly major triads—BE♭F♯, F♯B♭C♯, C♯FG♯, and G♯CE♭—are called *wolves*, a quaint name suggested by a fancied similarity between their sound and that of a pack of howling wolves. Lest the reader think that the bad effect of the wolves has been exaggerated, he is invited to tune a keyboard instrument accurately in meantone tuning (a procedure is given in the next section), and then to play "Silent Night" very slowly in D♭ major.

A minor triad requires notes higher than its root by intervals (-3) and (1), consisting of notes n, $n - 3$, and $n + 1$. Hence the chromatic scale furnishes minor triads whose roots are C, G, D, A, E, B, F♯, and C♯. However, the remaining four are wolves, for E♭F♯B♭, B♭C♯F, and FG♯C each contain an augmented second in place of the required minor third, and G♯BE♭ contains diminished sixth G♯E♭.

The chromatic scale contains relatively few usable harmonic minors. If the tonic is note n, the subdominant root is note $n - 1$, and its minor third is note $n - 4$; also, the dominant root is note $n + 1$, and its major third is note $n + 5$. A harmonic minor thus requires two notes that are separated by nine positions on the line of fifths, viz., notes $n - 4$ and $n + 5$. Consequently the array of Figure 16 contains only three harmonic minors—those whose tonics are G, D, and A.

5. Procedure for putting a harpsichord or an organ in meantone tuning. In any tempered tuning, the main difficulty lies in setting the temperament within the first octave. This can only be done by insuring that the beating intervals produce their beats at precisely the correct rate. In the author's

TABLE 65

BEATS IN MEANTONE TUNING

interval	beats per second	beats per minute
middle CG	−2.46	−147
C♯G♯	−2.57	−154
DA	−2.75	−165
E♭B♭	−2.94	−176
EB	−3.07	−184
middle CF	3.28	197
C♯F♯	3.43	206
DG	3.67	220
EA	4.11	246
FB♭	4.39	264
F♯B	4.59	275

experience, beats are most readily heard and counted when they occur at a rate of two to seven per second, suggesting, quite by coincidence, that the octave above and including middle C is the most convenient in which to set the temperament. Once the pitches within this octave have been tuned, these notes may be duplicated in other registers by tuning octaves accurately against the pitches already established.

Table 65 gives the beat frequencies per second and per minute for the perfect fifths and fourths in the octave above and including middle C of 264 Hz. If a different middle C is wanted, another table should be computed. It is first necessary to determine the frequencies of the pitches C♯, D, E♭, E, F, and F♯; this may be done by multiplying the frequency of middle C by the appropriate numbers in the ratio column of Table 60 (Sec. 1 of this chapter). The beat frequency per second of each perfect fifth is then the frequency of the lower pitch multiplied by $(2)(5^{1/4}) - 3 = -.00930$, and that of each perfect fourth is the frequency of the lower pitch multiplied by $(3)\left(\dfrac{2}{5^{1/4}}\right) - 4 = .01244$ (Ch. I, Sec. 3). The beat frequency per minute is the beat frequency per second multiplied by 60. The reader will find it a useful exercise to verify Table 65.

The most critical part of the process is the tuning of the first five notes— C, G, D, A, and E. After C is accurately tuned to a fork or any other standard, tune G next above, making CG pure, i.e., free of beats. Next begin to lower G almost imperceptibly so that a slow beat becomes faintly audible, and adjust the tuning of G until the rate of 2.46 per second, or 147 per minute is achieved. It may be helpful to count against a stopwatch, or set a metronome to 147 for comparison. Now tune D next below G, first making DG pure and then slowly and carefully lowering D until the beats are at 3.67 per second, or 220 per minute. A metronome set to 110—one half the beat frequency—provides a helpful aid to accuracy. The next step is to tune A against D, first making this fifth pure and then lowering A slightly until DA beats at 2.75 per second, or 165 per minute. At this point, compare CG and DA; the difference in beat frequencies should be slight but perceptible. Next tune E below A, first making EA pure and then lowering E until a beat frequency of 4.11 per second (246 per minute) is attained. Now check major third CE; this interval should be absolutely pure and free of beats. If CE is not pure, the whole procedure should be done over. Experience indicates that a beginner is inclined to apply too much temperament, making fifths too small and fourths too large so that the major third comes out too small. With a little practice, the process becomes more accurate.

Once the first five notes are tuned, the rest follows more easily. The method is to continue along the line of fifths with B, F♯, C♯, and G♯, in each case tuning a pure major third with a note already present and then checking the beat frequency of the new perfect fifth or fourth for a final adjustment. Start by tuning B a major third higher than G; fifth EB should now beat at 3.07 per second (184 per minute). Now check CG, DA, and EB; the beat frequency should exhibit a slight but uniform increase. Now tune F♯ above D, making this major third pure, and compare DG, EA, and F♯B. The increase in beat frequency should be slight and uniform, with F♯B beating at 4.59 per second (275 per minute). Next tune C♯ above A, making AC♯ pure. This C♯ is more than one octave above middle C; the C♯ a chromatic semitone above middle C should be tuned next by tuning an octave lower than the C♯ just obtained. Now check perfect fourth C♯F♯, which should produce 3.43 beats per second (206 per minute), and compare DG which beats at 3.67 per second (220 per minute); the difference should be nearly imperceptible. Next tune G♯ above E, making EG♯ pure; perfect fifth C♯G♯ should beat at 2.57 per second (154 per minute). Beats on CG, C♯G♯, and DA should increase at a practically uniform rate and almost imperceptibly.

Tuning of the notes to the left of C on the line of fifths may be achieved by a similar process. First tune F below A, making FA pure. Perfect fourth CF should now beat at 3.28 per second (197 per minute). A practically uniform and nearly imperceptible increase in beat frequency should be audible upon playing CF, C♯F♯, and then DG. Next tune D a major ninth above middle C by tuning one octave higher than the D already present, then tune B♭ a pure major third lower than the higher D. Perfect fourth FB♭ should now beat at 4.39 per second (264 per minute), and fourths EA, FB♭, and F♯B should exhibit a nearly uniform and almost imperceptible increase in beat frequency. Finally tune E♭ a pure major third below G; perfect fifth E♭B♭ should now beat at 2.94 per second (176 per minute) and DA, E♭B♭, and EB should exhibit a nearly uniform and almost imperceptible increase in beat frequency.

As a final test, play the intervals in the order in which they are given in Table 65; if any interval beats more slowly than the one immediately preceding, further adjustments are needed.

In some instances, a different chromatic scale is needed, for a substantial number of keyboard compositions that are suited to meantone tuning use D♯ but not E♭, and a smaller number use A♭ but not G♯. In the former case, make BD♯ pure and check the beat frequency of D♯G♯, which should be 3.84 per second, or 230 per minute. In the latter case, make A♭C pure, and check the beat frequency of E♭A♭, which should be 3.93 per second, or 236 per minute.

6. Musical examples in meantone tuning. As might be expected, the limitations of 12-note meantone tuning impose substantial restrictions on the style of keyboard compositions. Most obvious is the availability of only twelve notes, the most frequent choice being E♭ through G♯ on the line of fifths. Less common is B♭ through D♯, and rarer still is A♭ through C♯. It is probably the case that keyboard compositions using notes outside the range of A♭ through D♯ were not intended for meantone tuning. The same is true for a composition using both E♭ and D♯, or A♭ and G♯, especially if both notes are used in triads. Exceptions are possible if one note occurs only in a dissonant harmony, but examples are very rare.

As we have seen, only sixteen triads are available—eight major and eight minor. But this restriction is not as severe as might be thought, for even lengthy chromatic compositions very seldom use all the available triads.

Owing to the rather sharp discordance of augmented fourths and diminished fifths, diminished triads and dominant seventh chords occur relatively infrequently. The seventh is usually either a passing note, or treated as a suspension, i.e., prepared in the previous harmony and resolved down a second. Other types of suspensions are quite pleasing and occur frequently—even piquantly discordant ones involving minor seconds and major sevenths.

The only discordant chromatic intervals that have any common use as harmonies are diminished fourths and augmented fifths, and these occur only in augmented triads. In the usual arrangements, the discordant interval is placed neither between the two outer parts nor between the two lowest parts. Augmented seconds and diminished sevenths are found as harmonic combinations only exceedingly rarely, and the same is true of augmented sixths and diminished thirds. Augmented thirds and diminished sixths are never used in any chord.

Although the discordance of a minor second is not unpleasant, the same cannot be said of the considerably smaller chromatic semitone (Sec. 3 of this chapter). This latter interval occurs as a simultaneous combination only briefly and on unstressed beats, and then only if the two pitches are in different registers. Its use is unusual, and it occurs mainly in the keyboard works of English composers.

In view of these special rules, it is not difficult to identify keyboard compositions for which meantone tuning is appropriate. It is important to bear in mind that this may be done simply by examining the composer's notation of the work in question. Neither number analogies nor mathematical techniques are needed. The keyboard works of William Byrd (1543–1623), Girolamo Frescobaldi (1583–1643), Samuel Scheidt (1587–1654), and Jan Pieterszoon Sweelinck (1562–1621) all conform to the rules and restrictions just described, with only the rarest of exceptions.

There also exists a large polyphonic vocal repertoire that conforms to the limitations of 12-note meantone tuning. This is rather surprising considering that there appears to be no practical reason for the imposition of such a stylistic restriction. It may be that composers of the period had the habit of thinking in terms of meantone tuning no matter what the performing medium, or that they composed or rehearsed with the aid of a keyboard instrument. Whatever the reason, the choral works of Giovanni Gabrieli (1553–1612), Hans Leo Hassler (1564–1612), Orlando di Lasso (1532–1594),[3] Giovanni Pierluigi da Palestrina (1526–1594), Tomás Luis de Victoria (1548–1611), and Adriani Willaert (1490–1562), among others, may all be played satisfactorily on a keyboard instrument in meantone tuning.

---

[3] It will be observed that the portion of the di Lasso motet quoted earlier (Ch. VII, Sec. 2) conforms to the restrictions of 12-note meantone tuning.

It must not be assumed that the presence of chromaticism indicates that a work is unsuited to meantone tuning. On the contrary, certain composers during the first half of the seventeenth century appear to have been intrigued by the chromatic possibilities within the tuning, and to have explored them to the uttermost limits. The style thus generated is characterized by various harmonizations of portions of chromatic scales, and relatively frequent use of augmented triads, diminished triads, dominant seventh chords, and a variety of suspensions. A striking example, taken from an organ work of Samuel Scheidt,[4] is worth a detailed study.

[4]Samuel Scheidt, *Werke* (Hamburg: Ugrino Verlag, 1953), vol. 6, part 1, 106. The fragment is the sixth verse of the twelfth psalm, entitled "Da Jesus an dem Kreuz stund."

The example uses all the notes on the line of fifths from B♭ through
D♯; E♭ and A♭ are entirely avoided. It is interesting to note that all twelve
notes may be found in bars 4 through 7 in the lower two parts. But even
in this example, only twelve of the available sixteen triads are used; those
missing are B♭DF, and the minor triads whose roots are B, F♯, and C♯.
The use of a G♯ minor triad in bar 22 is highly unusual.

There are four diminished triads, occurring in bars 6, 13, 22, and 24.
It will be observed that there is preparation in each case. Dominant
sevenths are found only twice—in bar 21 the seventh is a passing note,
and in bar 30 the seventh is prepared and resolved down a major second.
Suspensions are also prepared and resolved strictly, and occur in bars 6,
7, 13, and 24.

Three augmented triads are found, occurring in bars 5, 21, and 29. It
will be observed that preparation is not thought necessary, and that one
instance occurs on the first beat (bar 21). In each case, the discordant
diminished fourth is placed neither between the two outer parts nor
between the two lower parts. No other discordant chromatic intervals are
used as simultaneous combinations. It is most unusual to find augmented
sixth chord B♭DG♯ in bar 7, taking advantage of the nearly pure tuning
of this harmony in meantone tuning (Sec. 2 of this chapter), and coming
directly after the more discordant BDA.

From the beginning, a listener is immediately struck by the peculiarly
poignant expression resulting from the melodic alternation of the small
chromatic semitone (76.049 cents) and the large minor second (117.108

cents) in the individual parts. Equally noteworthy is the contrast between the characteristic mellow sweetness of the triads and the relative sharpness of the various dissonances. These elements combine to produce an exotic charm which is lost when the example is played in the familiar 12-note equal tuning—at least to the author's ears.

Perhaps the most extreme example of meantone dissonant chromaticism is a remarkable work of Frescobaldi, most aptly entitled "Toccata di Durezze e Legature." The entire work is too long to be quoted here, but let it suffice to say that all the restrictions cited earlier in this section are scrupulously observed. The Toccata uses the twelve notes between Eb and G#; but even this radical example uses only fourteen of the sixteen triads—F# minor and C# minor are not used. It is worthwhile to examine the last seven bars.[5]

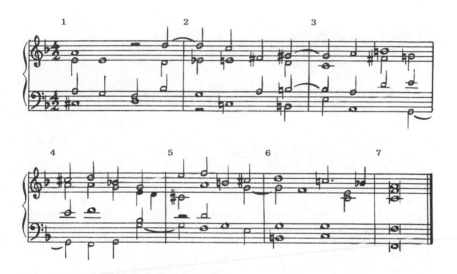

It will be noted that all twelve notes occur in the first two bars. We find four diminished triads; two are attacked without preparation—bars 2 and 4—while the remaining two in bar 5 are approached more strictly. Of the four dominant sevenths, two are prepared and resolved (first two beats of bar 4 and the first two beats of bar 6), and the other two result from passing notes (bar 1 and the second two beats of bar 6). Suspensions

[5] Girolamo Frescobaldi, Opere Complete (Milano: Edizioni Suvini Zerboni, 1979), vol. 5, 32–33.

abound, and are found in every bar except the last. Two involve harmonic major sevenths—FE in bar 1, and E♭D in bar 2. The most extreme example is the combination EBCG♯ in bar 3—an augmented triad with an additional dissonant note—containing both minor second BC and augmented fifth CG♯. The distribution of this latter interval between the two upper parts is in accord with the rule governing placement of augmented fifths and diminished fourths. The melodic contour of the superior part is also unusual and contains two descending diminished fifths (bars 2 and 5). The reader is urged to study the entire work; the rest is hardly less ingenious than the fragment quoted.

Chromaticism that is possible within the confines of meantone tuning may also be found in vocal works. An especially successful example is the motet *Ad dominum, cum tribularer, clamavi* of Hassler,[6] of which the last eight bars are quoted.

---

[6] Hans Leo Hassler, Sämtliche Werke (Wiesbaden: Breitkopf und Härtel, 1961), vol. 5/6, 51–53.

The motet uses the twelve notes from B♭ through D♯, and again we find all twelve occurring in close proximity (bars 5 and 6). The special, expressive character of meantone chromatic scales is very prominent in this example. Particularly noteworthy is the harmonization of melodic chromatic semitones by an agreeably surprising succession of chromatically related triads. Thus in bar 2, we find B major followed directly by D minor; in bar 4, B major is followed by G major, and in bar 6, E minor is followed by G minor. Unlike the two previous examples, this one uses neither diminished triads nor dominant seventh chords, and only one augmented triad occurs very briefly (bar 3). Two unusual suspensions are found, both using minor ninths as simultaneous intervals—BD♯F♯C in bar 4, and EG♯FB in bar 7. Even more remarkable is the harmonic use of diminished sevenths D♯C and G♯F—hardly possible without the presence of the dissonant minor ninths. Like the previous examples, this one adheres strictly to the rules and limitations described earlier in this section.

The choral compositions of Carlo Gesualdo di Venosa (1561–1613) have long been admired for their bold chromaticism; but even the most extreme examples conform rigorously to the rules and limitations of meantone tuning, with one exception—they frequently use more than twelve notes. It should not be surprising that a composer of vocal music should find it unnecessary to heed a restriction associated solely with the limitations of keyboard instruments. This makes possible even more imaginative successions of chromatically related triads.

Gesualdo, *Già piansi nel dolore*.

The fragment above from Gesualdo's *Già piansi nel dolore*,[7] makes use of the fourteen notes from E♯ through E♭, excepting D♯, within a progression of only seven triads. The chromatic successions of F♯ major

---

[7]Carlo Gesualdo di Venosa, *Sämtliche Madrigale für fünf Stimmen* (Hamburg: Ugrino Verlag, 1958). First example, vol. 6, 99; second example, vol. 6, 61; third example, vol. 5, 51.

to D minor, E♭ major to G major, and C major to A major are enhanced by the melodic interplay between the large minor second and the small chromatic semitone.

Gesualdo, *Ardita Zanzaretta.*

The example above from *Ardita Zanzaretta* makes liberal use of the standard dissonances that are idiomatic in meantone tuning.

Thus we find one diminished triad (bar 3), one dominant seventh chord (bar 1), and three suspensions (bars 2 and 4). One of the suspensions involves simultaneous minor second CD♭ (bar 2); and in bar 3, we find a major seventh chord bringing together D♭ and C between the two outer parts. The augmented triad on the first beat of bar 4 places the augmented fifth according to the rule given earlier in this section. The contrasting effect of the melodic chromatic semitones and minor seconds is very noticeable in this fragment, especially when the two intervals occur at the same time (bars 3 and 4). The example uses the thirteen notes from G♭ through F♯.

The availability of more than twelve notes makes possible the placement in close proximity of two notes that differ by a diesis (41.059 cents). This unusual and expressive melodic device is strikingly used in *Mercè grido piangendo*.

In bars 1 and 2, the soprano makes the succession C-B-B♯, and a listener hears at once that B♯ is very substantially lower than C. In fact, the entire harmony on the first beat of bar 2 sounds like an A♭ major triad that is flat by a diesis. The same thing happens again, transposed a perfect fifth lower, in bars 2 and 3; the C♯ major triad in bar 3 sounds like a lowered D♭ major triad. Subjectively, this device is perceived as an expressive

Gesualdo, *Mercè grido piangendo.*

inflection of a sort totally impossible within the confines of conventional 12-note equal tuning. The rest of the example features a variety of harmonizations of melodic chromatic semitones and minor seconds. The fragment uses the notes from E♭ through B♯, with the exception of D♯—a total of fifteen.

The examples quoted in this section may all be played satisfactorily in temperaments where the impurity of the perfect fifth is something slightly different from $\frac{1}{4}\bar{k}$; but a small change in the amount of tempering makes a larger change in the musical character of the examples. We shall return to this problem during the discussion of various other temperaments (Ch. X, Sec. 6; Ch. XI, Secs. 6 and 8).

7. Werckmeister's tuning.   Many attempts have been made to find a 12-note tuning generated by some combination of pure and tempered perfect fifths that might make possible the use of all the major and minor triads. While most of these "mixed tunings" are of more historical than theoretical interest and hence outside the scope of the present discussion, the technique used in their analysis is important for our purposes, and is best illustrated by an example. The following tuning ascribed to Werckmeister (1645–1706) is a good illustration of the process.[8]

Werckmeister's goal is a 12-note tuning which will give something near meantone tuning for the common triads, or Pythagorean tuning for the infrequent triads. Two elements suggest a tuning containing pure fifths in combination with fifths reduced by one fourth of a Pythagorean comma. First, since a Pythagorean comma is larger than a syntonic comma by a schisma of only 1.954 cents (Ch. VI, Sec. 2), it is clear that a fifth equal to $\bar{v} - \frac{1}{4}\bar{p}$ is virtually indistinguishable from a true meantone fifth of $\bar{v} - \frac{1}{4}\bar{k}$.

We find the ratio of $\bar{v} - \frac{1}{4}\bar{p}$ to be $\left(\dfrac{3}{2}\right)\left(\dfrac{524288}{531441}\right)^{1/4} = \left(\dfrac{3}{2}\right)\left(\dfrac{2^{19}}{3^{12}}\right)^{1/4} = \dfrac{2^{15/4}}{3^2} = \dfrac{8}{9}\sqrt[4]{8} = 1.494927$, and it contains 696.090 cents. Middle CG beats at $264[(2)(1.494927) - 3] = -2.679$ per second, in comparison with a true meantone fifth which beats at -2.456 per second. In addition, from the equation $12\bar{v} - 7a = \bar{p}$ (Ch. IV, Sec. 5), we may write $12\bar{v} - \bar{p} = 7a$, $8\bar{v} + (4\bar{v} - \bar{p}) = 7a$, and finally $8\bar{v} + 4(\bar{v} - \frac{1}{4}\bar{p}) = 7a$. This shows that the sum of eight pure fifths and four of Werckmeister's tempered fifths makes seven octaves exactly. Werckmeister's suggested arrangement is that fifths CG, GD, DA, and BF♯ should be $\bar{v} - \frac{1}{4}\bar{p}$, the other eight being pure. We thus arrive at the following, showing the amount by which each note differs from its counterpart in Pythagorean tuning:

$$C_0 G_{-\bar{p}/4} D_{-\bar{p}/2} A_{-3\bar{p}/4} E_{-3\bar{p}/4} B_{-3\bar{p}/4} \begin{cases} F\sharp_{-\bar{p}} & C\sharp_{-\bar{p}} & G\sharp_{-\bar{p}} & D\sharp_{-\bar{p}} & A\sharp_{-\bar{p}} & E\sharp_{-\bar{p}} & B\sharp_{-\bar{p}} \\ G\flat_0 & D\flat_0 & A\flat_0 & E\flat_0 & B\flat_0 & F_0 & C_0 \end{cases}$$

FIGURE 17

The equivalences $G\flat_0 = F\sharp_{-\bar{p}}$, $D\flat_0 = C\sharp_{-\bar{p}}$, etc., follow directly from the definition $\overline{int}\,(12) = \bar{p}$ (Ch. IV, Sec. 5).

Frequencies in the octave above and including middle C may be calculated in the order of the line of fifths by starting at middle C = 264 Hz, and multiplying by $\dfrac{8}{9}\sqrt[4]{8}$ or $\frac{3}{2}$, corresponding respectively to a tempered

[8] J. Murray Barbour, *Tuning and Temperament* (2nd ed.; Michigan, 1953), 161–162.

fifth and a pure fifth, according to Werckmeister's arrangement, always dividing by 2 whenever the accumulated product exceeds 528 (twice the frequency of middle C). The results are:

TABLE 66

WERCKMEISTER'S TUNING

note	frequency	note	frequency
C	264.000	F♯	370.831
C♯	278.123	G	394.661
D	294.994	G♯	417.185
E♭	312.889	A	440.995
E	330.746	B♭	469.333
F	352.000	B	496.120

We next determine the sizes of the major thirds, expressing them as $\bar{t}$ plus commas or fractional parts of commas to reveal their degree of impurity and discordance. We first observe from Figure 17 that major thirds FA and CE are composed of three tempered fifths and one pure fifth, and hence are less than a Pythagorean third by three fourths of a Pythagorean comma. These thirds are thus equal to $\bar{t} + \bar{k} - \frac{3}{4}\bar{p}$, and contain 390.225 cents. There are three thirds—GB, DF♯, and B♭D—composed of two pure fifths and two tempered fifths; these thirds are thus equal to $\bar{t} + \bar{k} - \frac{1}{2}\bar{p}$, and contain 396.090 cents. Four other thirds—AC♯, EG♯, BD♯, and E♭G—are composed of three pure fifths and one tempered fifth, and are equal to $\bar{t} + \bar{k} - \frac{1}{4}\bar{p}$, or 401.955 cents. The remaining three thirds—G♭B♭, D♭F, and A♭C—are composed of four pure fifths, and hence are Pythagorean, containing 407.820 cents.

Sizes of the perfect fifths and major thirds are listed in Table 67 in the order in which roots occur on the line of fifths. This furnishes essential information regarding distribution of the relative discordance associated with the major triads.

It will be observed that triad FAC is the most consonant, containing a pure fifth and a major third larger than pure by only 5.865 cents. Next comes triad CEG, having the same major third and a tempered fifth; this triad is nearest to meantone tuning in Werckmeister's arrangement. Triads GBD and DF♯A contain tempered fifths and slightly larger major thirds; these triads seem slightly more consonant than B♭DF, which has the same

TABLE 67

perfect fifths	size in cents	major thirds	size in cents
CG	696.090	CE	390.225
GD	696.090	GB	396.090
DA	696.090	DF♯	396.090
AE	701.955	AC♯	401.955
EB	701.955	EG♯	401.955
BF♯	696.090	BD♯	401.955
F♯C♯	701.955	F♯A♯	407.820
D♭A♭	701.955	D♭F	407.820
A♭E♭	701.955	A♭C	407.820
E♭E♭	701.955	E♭G	401.955
B♭F	701.955	B♭D	396.090
FC	701.955	FA	390.225

major third, but a pure fifth. The slowly beating tempered fifth tends to mask the slight discordance of the third. Triads AC♯E, EG♯B, and E♭GB♭, containing pure fifths and major thirds that are less than Pythagorean by 5.865 cents, have nearly the character of Pythagorean triads, although their slightly better major thirds make a noticeable difference. The remaining triads are more problematic. In the case of BD♯F♯, we note from Figure 17 that D♯ and F♯ both differ from their Pythagorean counterparts by $-\bar{p}$, and hence minor third D♯F♯ is Pythagorean. In consequence, this triad is rather more discordant than one would like. Finally, triads F♯A♯C♯, D♭FA♭, and A♭CE♭ are Pythagorean in every aspect. This means that all three primary triads in D♭ (or C♯) are Pythagorean, hence tuning of that key is Pythagorean. From this, it can be seen that Werckmeister's tuning is unsuited to compositions in D♭ (or C♯), especially if the tempo is slow. More generally, the major keys of E, B, F♯, D♭, A♭, and E♭ contain at least one Pythagorean third, either major or minor, with D♭ (or C♯) being the worst in this regard.

Sizes of the adjacent intervals in the chromatic scale may be calculated by first arranging the notes of Figure 17 in the order of the chromatic scale:

$$C_0 \, {}^{C\sharp}_{D\flat_0}{}_{-\bar{p}} D_{-\bar{p}/2} \, {}^{D\sharp}_{E\flat_0}{}_{-\bar{p}} E_{-3\bar{p}/4} \, {}^{E\sharp}_{F_0}{}_{-\bar{p}} \, {}^{F\sharp}_{G\flat_0}{}_{-\bar{p}} G_{-\bar{p}/4} \, {}^{G\sharp}_{A\flat_0}{}_{-\bar{p}} A_{-3\bar{p}/4} \, {}^{A\sharp}_{B\flat_0}{}_{-\bar{p}} B_{-3\bar{p}/4} C_0$$

From this, all the adjacent intervals may now be expressed as $\overline{\text{int}}\,(-5)$, or as $\overline{\text{int}}\,(-5)$ increased by a fractional part of a Pythagorean comma. Their sizes in cents may then be found by substituting 90.225 for $\overline{\text{int}}\,(-5)$, and 23.460 for $\bar{p}$. The results are given in Table 68.

TABLE 68

C_0Db_0	$= \overline{\text{int}}\,(-5)$	$= 90.225$	$F\#_{-\bar{p}}G_{-\bar{p}/4}$	$= \overline{\text{int}}\,(-5) + \tfrac{3}{4}\bar{p}$	$= 107.820$
$C\#_{-\bar{p}}D_{-\bar{p}/2}$	$= \overline{\text{int}}\,(-5) + \tfrac{1}{2}\bar{p}$	$= 101.955$	$G_{-\bar{p}/4}Ab_0$	$= \overline{\text{int}}\,(-5) + \tfrac{1}{4}\bar{p}$	$= 96.090$
$D_{-\bar{p}/2}Eb_0$	$= \overline{\text{int}}\,(-5) + \tfrac{1}{2}\bar{p}$	$= 101.955$	$G\#_{-\bar{p}}A_{-3\bar{p}/4}$	$= \overline{\text{int}}\,(-5) + \tfrac{1}{4}\bar{p}$	$= 96.090$
$D\#_{-\bar{p}}E_{-3\bar{p}/4}$	$= \overline{\text{int}}\,(-5) + \tfrac{1}{4}\bar{p}$	$= 96.090$	$A_{-3\bar{p}/4}Bb_0$	$= \overline{\text{int}}\,(-5) + \tfrac{3}{4}\bar{p}$	$= 107.820$
$E_{-3\bar{p}/4}F_0$	$= \overline{\text{int}}\,(-5) + \tfrac{3}{4}\bar{p}$	$= 107.820$	$A\#_{-\bar{p}}B_{-3\bar{p}/4}$	$= \overline{\text{int}}\,(-5) + \tfrac{1}{4}\bar{p}$	$= 96.090$
F_0Gb_0	$= \overline{\text{int}}\,(-5)$	$= 90.225$	$B_{-3\bar{p}/4}C_0$	$= \overline{\text{int}}\,(-5) + \tfrac{3}{4}\bar{p}$	$= 107.820$

From the above, we see that the interval separating the leading tone from the tonic varies from 90.225 cents (in Db and Gb) to 107.820 cents (in Bb, F, C, and G).

It is also of interest to find the size in cents of the intervals between C and each note of the chromatic scale (see Table 69). Each interval is equal

TABLE 69

C_0Db_0	$= \overline{\text{int}}\,(-5)$	$= 90.225$	$C_0G_{-\bar{p}/4}$	$= \overline{\text{int}}\,(1) - \tfrac{1}{4}\bar{p}$	$= 696.090$
$C_0D_{-\bar{p}/2}$	$= \overline{\text{int}}\,(2) - \tfrac{1}{2}\bar{p}$	$= 192.180$	C_0Ab_0	$= \overline{\text{int}}\,(-4)$	$= 792.180$
C_0Eb_0	$= \overline{\text{int}}\,(-3)$	$= 294.135$	$C_0A_{-3\bar{p}/4}$	$= \overline{\text{int}}\,(3) - \tfrac{3}{4}\bar{p}$	$= 888.270$
$C_0E_{-3\bar{p}/4}$	$= \overline{\text{int}}\,(4) - \tfrac{3}{4}\bar{p}$	$= 390.225$	C_0Bb_0	$= \overline{\text{int}}\,(-2)$	$= 996.090$
C_0F_0	$= \overline{\text{int}}\,(-1)$	$= 498.045$	$C_0B_{-3\bar{p}/4}$	$= \overline{\text{int}}\,(5) - \tfrac{3}{4}\bar{p}$	$= 1092.180$
C_0Gb_0	$= \overline{\text{int}}\,(-6)$	$= 588.270$			

to a Pythagorean interval, or a Pythagorean interval decreased by a fractional part of a Pythagorean comma. Sizes of the Pythagorean diatonic intervals are given in Table 3 (Ch. II, Sec. 4).

The tuning may be readily set up by ear. The recommended method is to tune by perfect fourths and fifths within the octave, starting at middle C and proceeding in the left-hand direction on the line of fifths. The beat frequencies given in Table 70 must be accurately established.

TABLE 70

interval	beats per second	beats per minute
middle CG	−2.68	−161
DG	4.00	240
DA	−2.99	−180
EA	0	0
EB	0	0
F♯B	5.03	302
C♯F♯	0	0
C♯G♯	0	0
E♭A♭	0	0
E♭B♭	0	0
FB♭	0	0
middle CF	0	0

If there has been any tendency to temper the impure intervals too much, the final perfect fifth (CG) will beat too slowly, indicating that adjustments are needed. In fact, the tuning is not as critical as might be expected, and may be done quickly after a little practice.

Since Werckmeister's tuning produces major triads that vary from nearly pure to Pythagorean, it appears to be unsuited to styles in which all triads may be expected to occur with equal frequency. The tuning is most effectively applied to repertoire that uses the discordant triads relatively rarely. Such works are characterized by generally conforming to the limitations imposed by meantone tuning, but occasionally using notes not available on a standard meantone keyboard, viz., D♭, A♯, E♯, and B♯. The keyboard and ensemble works of Arcangelo Corelli (1675–1737), François Couperin (1668–1733), Johann Joseph Fux (1660–1741), and Henry Purcell (1659–1695) are representative examples.

X The General Family of Recognizable Diatonic Tunings

Introduction. In this chapter, we determine the range over which the generating interval may vary to produce a diatonic tuning that exhibits the same subjective character and structural organization as Pythagorean tuning and meantone tuning. This also serves to frame precise definitions of the names and symbols associated with notes and intervals. In Section 1 it is shown how a small change in the size of the generating interval affects the triads and the scale, and suggests that an improvement in the former causes a deterioration in the latter, and vice versa. Section 2 determines that the range over which the generating interval may vary within the family of recognizable diatonic tunings is $\frac{4}{7}a < v < \frac{3}{5}a$, and that this is equivalent to the requirement that expressions in terms of a and v for the minor second and chromatic semitone should both be positive numbers. It is also shown that these conditions are both necessary and sufficient for the preservation of the structural elements discovered to exist in Pythagorean tuning and meantone tuning, as set forth in Chapter III, Secs. 2–6, and Ch. IV, Secs. 1, 3, 6, and 7—especially Theorems 12–17 and 19–22. These elements taken together represent the structure of recognizable diatonic tunings, since requirements for the existence of the structural interconnections and requirements for subjective recognizability are the same. We also explore the range over which the generating interval may vary to produce a tuning that provides an acceptable scale in combination with sufficiently consonant triads.

In Section 3 we derive a representation of intervals in terms of the major second (w) and the minor second (h). This has the advantage of revealing the ordinal number naming the interval more readily than the interval's depiction as int (i). The interval's expression in terms of w and h may also be found directly from its name, simply by calling upon established musical habits. Section 4 develops a system of analyzing a recognizable diatonic tuning in terms of a number that reveals the character of the scale, viz., the ratio of the size of the major second to the size of the minor second, which is $\dfrac{w}{h} = R$. It is also shown that within the acceptable range, the relation between R and the size of the generating interval is nearly linear. In Section 5 definitions are framed in terms of R for notes and commonly occurring intervals. These definitions are especially easy for musicians to learn, and greatly facilitate computation. This method is particularly important in the case of recognizable diatonic tunings in which the circle of fifths is ultimately closed, and will be used extensively during the discussion of those particular cases (Ch. XI, Secs. 5, 8, and 10; Ch. XII). In Section 6 we use the techniques developed in Sections 2–5 to analyze a particular diatonic tuning that is important historically, and we examine its applicability to the repertoire that heeds the restrictions inherent in 12-note meantone tuning.

1. Change in size of the diatonic intervals relative to the amount of tempering applied to the perfect fifth. It is interesting to investigate how the diatonic intervals change as the size of the perfect fifth decreases at a uniform rate from pure $(\bar{v})$ to meantone $(\bar{v} - \frac{1}{4}\bar{k})$. To this end, let $v = \bar{v} + x$, with x being the amount of tempering applied, and now imagine x to vary uniformly from 0 to $-\frac{1}{4}\bar{k}$. We now recall that when the fifth is pure, $\overline{\text{int}}\,(i) = i\bar{v} + n_1 a$, and when the fifth is tempered, $\text{int}\,(i) = iv + n_2 a$, with n_1 and n_2 being determined by the interval size convention (Ch. VIII, Sec. 2). Hence $\text{int}\,(i) = i(\bar{v} + x) + n_2 a$, and $\overline{\text{int}}\,(i) - \text{int}\,(i) = i\bar{v} + n_1 a - (i\bar{v} + ix + n_2 a) = a(n_1 - n_2) - ix$, where $-\frac{1}{4}\bar{k} \leqslant x \leqslant 0$. For every diatonic interval $(-6 \leqslant i \leqslant 6)$, we have $n_1 = n_2$ if the amount of tempering is no more than $-\frac{1}{4}\bar{k}$, and so $\overline{\text{int}}\,(i) - \text{int}\,(i) = -ix$, and finally

$$\text{int}\,(i) = \overline{\text{int}}\,(i) + ix$$

This shows that the rate at which $\text{int}\,(i)$ changes is i times the rate at which the perfect fifth changes. For example, as the perfect fifth decreases by one cent, int (4)—the major third (Table 8; Ch. III, Sec. 6; Ch. VIII, Sec. 3)—decreases by four cents. In other words, a small change in the perfect fifth produces a change four times as great in the major third, resulting in a correspondingly greater change in the nature of the major triads. As another example, if the perfect fifth decreases by one cent, int (2)—the major second—decreases by two cents, and int (-5)—the minor second—increases by five cents. Thus an almost unnoticeable change in the perfect fifth produces a very perceptible change in the nature of the scale.

More information concerning the change in the scale relative to a change in the fifth follows from the intervals made by each degree of the scale

TABLE 71

notes	C	D	E	F	G	A	B	C
degrees	I	II	III	IV	V	VI	VII	VIII
intervals	(0)	(2)	(4)	(−1)	(1)	(3)	(5)	(0)

with the tonic, using C major as a reference.[1] If C is fixed and v changes by x cents, the degrees of the scale change by the following amounts:

TABLE 72

notes	C	D	E	F	G	A	B	C
degrees	I	II	III	IV	V	VI	VII	VIII
change	0	$2x$	$4x$	$-x$	x	$3x$	$5x$	0

Table 72 shows that as the perfect fifth decreases uniformly from $\bar{v}$ to $\bar{v} - \frac{1}{4}\bar{k}$, all degrees of the scale except the fourth go flat, with the difference becoming greater as we proceed from the first to the third degree, and again from the fifth to the seventh degree. To a musician who prefers a relatively small interval between the leading tone and the tonic, this seems subjectively to cause a deterioration in the tuning of the scale. On the other hand, the triads improve as their major thirds go from Pythagorean to pure, providing further evidence that the tuning of the scale and the tuning of the triads come from separate considerations, which tend to be mutually exclusive.[2]

It is important to bear in mind that any generating interval between $\bar{v}$ and $\bar{v} - \frac{1}{4}\bar{k}$ yields diatonic scales and chords that differ only slightly from Pythagorean and from meantone tuning, and exhibit the same arrangement of diatonic intervals.

2. The range of recognizability and its relation to the size of the perfect fifth. We are naturally led to wonder over what range the perfect fifth may vary to produce a diatonic tuning that is recognizable as such by ear. It should be expected that certain of these tunings will contain intervals that, although recognizable, are unacceptably out of tune, as for example, Pythagorean major thirds.

[1] Table 71 is constructed by using first the correspondences 0, 1, 2, 3, 4, 5, and 6 for notes F, C, G, D, A, E, and B, respectively, and then the principle that the interval between note x and note y is int $(y - x)$. See Ch. VIII, Sec. 2.

[2] See Ch. V, Sec. 2, and other references cited there.

In the previous section, it was shown how a decrease in the size of the perfect fifth results in a decrease in the major second and an increase in the minor second. If the fifth is made progressively smaller than the mean-tone version, there must come a point at which the major and minor seconds are equal. At this point, the diatonic scale actually becomes a division of the octave into seven equal parts, and under such conditions, any two diatonic intervals named by the same ordinal number are equal.

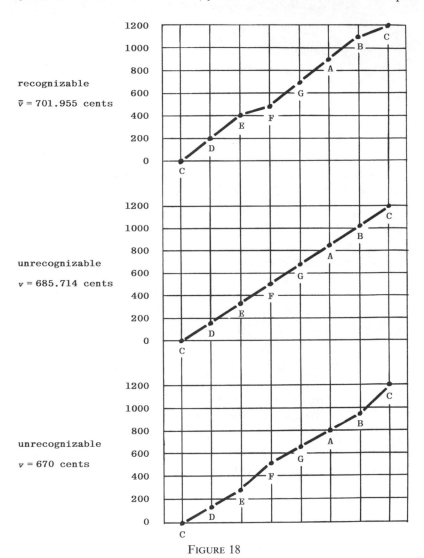

FIGURE 18

This obliterates the distinction of modality, in particular making a minor triad indistinguishable from a major triad. The equal division of the octave also makes it impossible to ascribe a particular function—tonic, dominant, etc.—to an individual note, this being dependent on the asymmetrical arrangement of the major and minor seconds, or the location of the diminished fifth relative to the perfect fifths. It is thus clear that a division of an octave into seven equal parts is not recognizable as a diatonic scale, nor can the usual harmonic behavior associated with major and minor triads be perceived.

If the major and minor seconds are equal, we have $2v - a = 3a - 5v$, $7v = 4a$, and $v = \frac{4}{7}a = 685.714$ cents. The value $\frac{4}{7}a$ is also apparent from the position of the fifth relative to the four equal seconds in the division of the octave into seven equal parts.

If v is made even smaller than $\frac{4}{7}a$, the minor seconds continue to increase, and become greater than the major seconds. Moreover, the two modalities of the diatonic intervals associated with each ordinal number from second through seventh are reversed in order of size, since their difference in every case is int $(7) = 7v - 4a$ (Ch. III, Sec. 5), and $7v - 4a$ is negative when $v < \frac{4}{7}a$. In consequence, triads on degrees I, IV, and V are minor, and triads on degrees II, III, and VI are major. Thus a scale in which $v < \frac{4}{7}a$ is not a recognizable diatonic tuning. It should also be noted that the condition $7v - 4a > 0$ is equivalent to the requirement that the chromatic semitone should be ascending.

The transformation of the scale from recognizable to unrecognizable is illustrated in Figure 18, using Pythagorean tuning, the special case where $v = \frac{4}{7}a$, and one in which $v = 670$ cents.

Now let the perfect fifth be made gradually larger than pure, so that the major seconds increase while the minor seconds decrease. If the process is continued, there must come a point at which the two minor seconds vanish. At this point, the octave is divided into five equal parts where degrees III and IV coincide, as do degrees VII and I. Since the leading tone and tonic are indistinguishable under this condition, such a tuning is not recognizable as a diatonic scale. If the minor seconds vanish, we have $3a - 5v = 0$, and $v = \frac{3}{5}a = 720$ cents.

If the perfect fifth is increased beyond $\frac{3}{5}a$ and the notes of the scale are retained in their original order, the corresponding increase in the major seconds causes the minor seconds to become negative, i.e., descending intervals. Under these conditions, the leading tone is higher than the tonic—a situation that totally destroys the dominant sensation normally

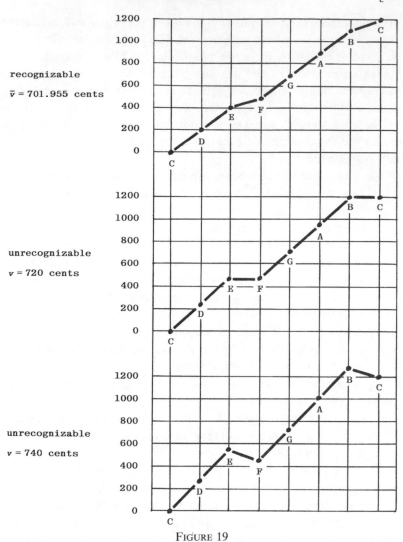

recognizable

$\bar{v} = 701.955$ cents

unrecognizable

$v = 720$ cents

unrecognizable

$v = 740$ cents

FIGURE 19

associated with the fifth-degree triad. Hence a tuning in which $v > \frac{3}{5}a$ is not a recognizable diatonic scale. Thus a recognizable diatonic scale is one where we must have $v < \frac{3}{5}a$, or $3a - 5v > 0$, i.e., the minor second must be ascending. The transition from recognizable to unrecognizable is illustrated in Figure 19, using Pythagorean tuning, the special case where $v = \frac{3}{5}a$, and one in which $v = 740$ cents.

Thus the actual range over which the generating interval may vary is

$$\tfrac{4}{7}a < v < \tfrac{3}{5}a$$

From now on, we shall refer to these fundamentally important inequalities as the *range of recognizability*.[3]

The actual threshold of recognizability in humans can only be determined by a carefully controlled experiment, and considerable differences among individuals are to be expected. It is clearly necessary that the chromatic semitone should be large enough so that the two different levels of modality can be distinguished, and also that the minor second should be large enough so that the leading tone can be distinguished from the tonic. According to the author's experience, a difference of 25 cents is sufficient in either case to identify a major scale as such. In the former case, we have $7v - 4a = 25$, and $v = 689.286$ cents; and in the latter, $3a - 5v = 25$, and $v = 715$ cents. Table 73 gives the sizes of all the diatonic intervals for these two particular values of v.[4] These numbers show that the

TABLE 73

interval	size where $v = 689.286$ cents	size where $v = 715$ cents
minor second	153.571	25
major second	178.571	230
minor third	332.143	255
major third	357.143	460
perfect fourth	510.714	485
augmented fourth	535.714	690
diminished fifth	664.286	510
perfect fifth	689.286	715
minor sixth	842.857	740
major sixth	867.857	945
minor seventh	1021.429	970
major seventh	1046.429	1175

[3] See Ch. XII, Sec. 4 for a brief analysis of two particular unrecognizable diatonic scales (Tables 101 and 102).

[4] The table may be calculated by first expressing each interval as int (*i*) as given in Table 8 (Ch. III, Sec. 6), and then finding the size in cents by the method of Ch. VIII, Sec. 2. As a consequence of Theorem 26, the correspondences of Table 8 hold throughout the range of recognizability.

elements bearing on recognizability of a particular interval are more complex than might have been expected. For example, an interval of 510 cents might be construed as either a diminished fifth or a perfect fourth, depending on the size of the generating interval. It is undeniably true that certain harmonies—especially seventh chords—may become so distorted that they can be identified only within a context of common harmonic progressions.

We now prove a fundamentally important theorem describing structural elements common to all diatonic scales generated by a perfect fifth within the range of recognizability. The proof is an extension of the principles that were developed in Chapter VIII, Sec. 3.

THEOREM 25.   *The structural interconnections described by Theorems* 12 *through* 17 (Ch. III, Secs. 3 and 5) *hold for all recognizable diatonic tunings.* Theorem 12 simply requires that the arrangement of notes 0 through 6 in ascending order should be 0, 2, 4, 6, 1, 3, 5, 0. This means that the major second and minor second are ascending, i.e., that $2v - a > 0$ and $3a - 5v > 0$, which is the same as $v > \frac{1}{2}a$ and $v < \frac{3}{5}a$, or $\frac{1}{2}a < v < \frac{3}{5}a$. But the range of recognizability is $\frac{4}{7}a < v < \frac{3}{5}a$—more restrictive than $\frac{1}{2}a < v < \frac{3}{5}a$. Hence Theorem 12 holds for all recognizable diatonic tunings, and so it is generally true that int (i) is a $(j + 1)$th where $4i \equiv j \pmod 7$ and $0 < j \leqslant 6$. Similarly, in the case of Theorem 13, the same ordinal number names both int (i) and int $(i - 7)$ where $1 \leqslant i \leqslant 6$, for it is always true that if $4i \equiv j \pmod 7$, then $4(i - 7) \equiv j \pmod 7$ (Theorem 10; Ch. III, Sec. 1). As was noted before (Ch. VIII, Sec. 3), the cyclic interconnection among the first, second, and third order of notes requires only that the major second and minor second should be ascending, and hence holds throughout the range of recognizability.

Theorems 14 through 17 require further that the difference between int (i) and int $(i - 7)$ $(1 \leqslant i \leqslant 6)$ should be positive; and since this difference is int $(7) = 7v - 4a$, we have $7v - 4a > 0$, or $v > \frac{4}{7}a$. If $\frac{1}{2}a < v < \frac{4}{7}a$, Theorems 14 through 17 would hold if the words "greater" and "lesser" were interchanged at every occurrence. It is also apparent that if $v < \frac{4}{7}a$, the effects of the sharp and flat are reversed, i.e., a sharp lowers a note by the same amount that a flat raises it.

We may now frame a precise definition of a perfect fifth. The word "perfect" requires that the levels of modality should be in the same order as in Pythagorean tuning, or that $7v - 4a > 0$. "Fifth" requires that the notes of the scale should be ascending, viz., $2v - a > 0$ and $3a - 5v > 0$. Hence a "perfect fifth" is any interval lying between $\frac{4}{7}a$ and $\frac{3}{5}a$ (but not equal to $\frac{4}{7}a$ or $\frac{3}{5}a$) that generates a diatonic scale.

We may extend any recognizable diatonic tuning by starting with the generating array of six adjacent perfect fifths and then continuing in both directions on the line of fifths in such a manner that every adjacent interval is equal to the original generating interval. Any succession of seven notes may generate a diatonic scale, and relations between these scales are described by the following theorem:

THEOREM 26.   *The principles regarding scales, notes, key signatures, and transposition as set forth in Theorems 19 through 22 (Ch. IV, Secs. 6 and 7) hold throughout the range of recognizability.* Since all scales are generated by the same-size perfect fifth in any extended diatonic tuning, it follows that all scales exhibit the same tuning except for differences in register. Since all the scales are recognizable, the chromatic semitone is positive, and hence the sharp and flat behave as in Pythagorean tuning, viz., note $n\flat$ is lower than note n by the same amount $(7v - 4a)$ that note $n\sharp$ is higher than note n, and so the results follow.

The behavior of a chromatic scale within the range of recognizability is clarified by the following theorem:

THEOREM 27.   *The arrangement of intervals* (1) *through* (11) *in increasing order is the same throughout the range of recognizability.* We have already seen (Ch. IX, Sec. 3) that in meantone tuning, this arrangement is (7), (2), (9), (4), (11), (6), (1), (8), (3), (10), (5), the difference between any two adjacent intervals being either int (7) = $7v - 4a$ or int $(-5) = 3a - 5v$. Hence, for this order to hold, a necessary and sufficient condition is simply that both differences should be positive—that $7v - 4a > 0$ and $3a - 5v > 0$, or that $\frac{4}{7}a < v < \frac{3}{5}a$, i.e., that the size of the generating interval should lie within the range of recognizability. An immediate consequence of Theorem 27 is that the notes of the ascending chromatic scale are in the same order throughout the range of recognizability.

Further properties of intervals (1) through (11) and their inversions are revealed by the following:

THEOREM 28.   *In the complete expression for* int (i) *as* $iv + na$, *for any particular i where* $1 \leqslant i \leqslant 11$ *or* $-11 \leqslant i \leqslant -1$, *the coefficient of a is the same throughout the range of recognizability.* If we start at some fixed reference point and then add successively $7v - 4a$ and $3a - 5v$ in the order in which these intervals occur in a chromatic scale, we find the array of intervals shown in Table 74. By Theorem 27, each expression on the right-hand side of these equations is positive and less than a if v lies within the range of recognizability. But it is always true that $0 < $ int $(i) < a$ $(i \neq 0)$, hence in every case, the identity int $(i) = iv + na$ $(1 \leqslant i \leqslant 11)$ holds throughout the range of recognizability. By virtue of the equation int $(-i) = a - $ int (i), we see that the same holds when $-11 \leqslant i \leqslant -1$, and this proves Theorem 28.

Now let the ratio of a perfect fifth be r; then the ratio of an interval expressed as $iv + na$ is $r^i 2^n$. We may use this relation in combination with Table 74 to find the ratio of int (i) where $1 \leqslant i \leqslant 11$, and this ratio will be valid throughout the range of recognizability.

TABLE 74

$$0 + (7v - 4a) = 7v - 4a$$
$$(7v - 4a) + (3a - 5v) = 2v - a$$
$$(2v - a) + (7v - 4a) = 9v - 5a$$
$$(9v - 5a) + (3a - 5v) = 4v - 2a$$
$$(4v - 2a) + (7v - 4a) = 11v - 6a$$
$$(11v - 6a) + (3a - 5v) = 6v - 3a$$
$$(6v - 3a) + (3a - 5v) = v$$
$$v + (7v - 4a) = 8v - 4a$$
$$(8v - 4a) + (3a - 5v) = 3v - a$$
$$(3v - a) + (7v - 4a) = 10v - 5a$$
$$(10v - 5a) + (3a - 5v) = 5v - 2a$$

Example: Find the ratio of int (2). We have int $(2) = 2v - a$, hence its ratio is $\dfrac{r^2}{2}$.

If $-11 \leqslant i \leqslant -1$, we first use the equation int $(-i) = a - $ int (i), and then continue as before.

Example: Find the ratio of int (-5). We have int $(5) = 5v - 2a$, hence int $(-5) = a - (5v - 2a) = 3a - 5v$, and its ratio is thus $\dfrac{8}{r^5}$.

It is important to remember that Theorem 28 does not hold for every i. For example, in Pythagorean tuning, $\overline{\text{int}}$ $(12) = 12\bar{v} - 7a$ (Ch. IV, Sec. 5); but in meantone tuning, int $(12) = 12v - 6a$ (Ch. IX, Sec. 2).

Since some of the recognizable diatonic tunings produce scales that are excessively distorted, or diatonic intervals that are inordinately discordant, it is important to investigate the range over which the generating interval may vary to produce tunings that are satisfactory for music in which triads are treated as consonances. Since an untempered fifth gives a good scale but major thirds that are too large to be acceptable in consonant harmonies, it is clear that the upper limit to the perfect fifth depends on how large a major third we are willing to tolerate. If we arbitrarily set this at

406 cents (round numbers being most convenient),[5] the largest permissible fifth is v where $4v - 2400 = 406$, and $v = 701.5$ cents.

Determination of the size of the smallest acceptable generating interval involves several interrelated elements. Since a meantone minor third is smaller than pure by $\frac{1}{4}\bar{k}$ (Ch. VIII, Sec. 1), we see that if the fifth is made progressively smaller than the meantone value $(\bar{v} - \frac{1}{4}\bar{k})$, there must come a point at which the minor third is pure and the major third is smaller than pure. If the fifth continues to decrease, both the fifth and the major third become increasingly smaller than pure, while the minor third becomes increasingly larger than pure, resulting in a progressive deterioration in the tuning of the triad. If the minor third is pure, we have int $(-3) = \bar{v} - \bar{t}$ (Ch. III, Sec. 7), or $2a - 3v = \bar{v} - \bar{t}$, and $3v = 2a - \bar{v} + \bar{t}$. Next, substituting $4\bar{v} - 2a - \bar{k}$ for $\bar{t}$, we obtain $3v = 2a - \bar{v} + 4\bar{v} - 2a - \bar{k} = 3\bar{v} - \bar{k}$, and finally $v = \bar{v} - \frac{1}{3}\bar{k}$. The ratio of this interval is $\left(\frac{3}{2}\right)\left(\frac{80}{81}\right)^{1/3} = 1.493802$, and it contains 694.786 cents. If the lower pitch is middle C, the beat frequency is $264[(2)(1.493802) - 3] = -3.273$ per second (Ch. I, Sec. 3). This interval is not excessively discordant; but even if the beats are entirely masked, its higher pitch seems distinctly flat. The size of the major third is $4(\bar{v} - \frac{1}{3}\bar{k}) - 2a = 4\bar{v} - 2a - \frac{4}{3}\bar{k} = \bar{t} + \bar{k} - \frac{4}{3}\bar{k} = \bar{t} - \frac{1}{3}\bar{k} = 379.145$ cents. Its ratio is $\left(\frac{5}{4}\right)\left(\frac{80}{81}\right)^{1/3} = 1.244835$, and middle CE beats at $264[(4)(1.244835) - 5] = -5.455$ per second—not an excessive rate. A major triad generated by a fifth equal to $\bar{v} - \frac{1}{3}\bar{k}$ is hardly less smooth than the meantone version.

The major scale is somewhat more open to question, for the minor second is quite large, containing $3600 - (5)(694.786) = 126.069$ cents. Musicians who are troubled by the rather large minor second of meantone tuning (117.108 cents) find one of 126.069 cents even more disturbing, for it makes the leading tone seem very flat.

The chromatic semitone contains $(7)(694.786) - 4800 = 63.504$ cents—smaller than a minor chroma and hardly larger than the comma $4\bar{k} - \bar{p}$ of 62.565 cents (Ch. VI, Sec. 5). In a chromatic scale, the asymmetric succession of minor seconds and chromatic semitones—the former virtually twice the size of the latter—produces a distinctly ungainly effect. In the author's opinion, the chromatic examples of Scheidt and Hassler analyzed earlier with reference to meantone tuning (Ch. IX, Sec. 6), are not satisfactory under such conditions. In addition, the diminished fourths

---

[5] This is about two cents smaller than the discordant Pythagorean major third of 407.820 cents.

of $6000 - (8)(694.786) = 441.710$ cents are too discordant, even when used in augmented triads or other dissonant harmonies.

It must be concluded that music making extensive use of chromatic intervals, either melodically or in harmonies, demands a more restricted range of tunings than music largely confined to diatonic intervals. In the latter case, the permissible extremes for the generating interval are roughly 695 cents to 701.5 cents—at least, according to the author's taste. It must be observed, however, that none of the existing polyphonic repertoire is entirely confined to the notes and intervals of only one diatonic scale.

3. Expressions for intervals and for the range of recognizability in terms of the major second and the minor second.   As we have seen, the modality of an interval expressed as int (i) is immediately known from the number i, but not the ordinal number (Ch. III, Secs. 5 and 6; Ch. IV, Sec. 3). It is also possible to find expressions that reveal at a glance an interval's ordinal number. Since the ordinal number associated with any interval formed by any two of the notes C, D, E, F, G, A, and B is one greater than the number of seconds (major or minor) that the interval contains, we begin by finding expressions for these intervals in terms of the major and minor second. As we shall see, the process is readily extended to include all notes and the chromatic intervals as well.

We now introduce the symbols w for the major second and h for the minor second,[6] so that

$$w = 2v - a$$
$$h = 3a - 5v$$

and now solve these equations for a and v. Multiplying the first equation throughout by 3, and adding this to the second equation gives

$$
\begin{aligned}
3w &= 6v - 3a \\
h &= -5v + 3a \\
\hline
3w + h &= v
\end{aligned}
$$

[6] The choice of the letters w and h follows from the predilection on the part of musicians for calling a major second a "whole step" and a minor second a "half step." It must be emphasized that the use of these letters does not necessarily imply that a major second is the sum of two minor seconds.

Substituting this value for v in the first equation gives

$$w = 2(3w + h) - a$$
$$a = 2(3w + h) - w$$
$$a = 5w + 2h$$

Thus we have

$$v = 3w + h$$
$$a = 5w + 2h$$

These expressions are obvious intuitively and taken for granted by trained musicians.

We may now express int (i) in terms of w and h by first finding the full expression for int (i) in terms of a and v, using the method developed in the previous section, and then replacing a and v by the above expressions and simplifying.

Example: Find an expression in terms of w and h for int (5). Using Theorem 28 and Table 74, the full expression is $5v - 2a$; hence int (5) $= 5(3w + h) - 2(5w + 2h) = 5w + h$.

Example: Find an expression in terms of w and h for int (-9). The full expression for int (9) is $9v - 5a$; hence int $(-9) = a - (9v - 5a) = 6a - 9v$, and finally int $(-9) = 6(5w + 2h) - 9(3w + h) = 3w + 3h$.

If the interval in the first example is, say, CB, it is clear that its ordinal number is one more than the sum of the coefficients of w and h, viz., 7. It is not immediately apparent, however, that the same principle applies to int (-9), since this chromatic interval cannot be found between any two of the seven notes of C major. The situation is explained by the following theorem:

THEOREM 29. *The ordinal number naming an interval expressed as* $pw + qh$ *is* $p + q + 1$ *if* $p + q + 1 \geqslant 2$, *irrespective of the notes forming the interval.* We first recall that a sharp raises and a flat lowers a note by int (7) (Ch. IV, Sec. 1), and that this interval is also the difference between any two adjacent levels of modality associated with the same ordinal number (Ch. IV, Sec. 3). This holds whenever $7v - 4a > 0$, and hence is valid throughout the range of recognizability. We next have

$$7v - 4a = 7(3w + h) - 4(5w + 2h) = w - h$$

Thus if the distance of a note from C is given as $pw + qh$, the addition of a sharp to the note adds $w - h$, and the addition of a flat adds $h - w$. Now imagine an interval formed by any two of the notes of C major, and let this interval be altered by attaching some number of sharps or flats to either or both notes. Both intervals now differ only in modality, the ordinal number naming them being the same. By definition, the ordinal number naming the original interval is $p + q + 1$. If the original interval is now expressed as $pw + qh$, the altered interval has the form $pw + qh + x(w - h) = w(p + x) + h(q - x)$. The sum of the coefficients of w and h is now $p + x + q - x = p + q$, the same as in the case of the unaltered interval. This extends the principle to all intervals expressed as $pw + qh$, whatever may be the actual notes forming them. The restriction $p + q + 1 \geqslant 2$ is in accord with the convention that no interval is named by an ordinal number less than "second."

We may readily determine the modality of an interval expressed as $pw + qh$ from the numbers p and q. We find i by noting first that

$$
\begin{aligned}
iv + na &= pw + qh \\
&= p(2v - a) + q(3a - 5v) \\
&= v(2p - 5q) + a(3q - p)
\end{aligned}
$$

Equating coefficients of v, we have

$$i = 2p - 5q$$

The modality now follows from the correspondences developed in Chapter III, Sec. 6, and Chapter IV, Sec. 3, which are repeated here for convenience.

LEVEL OF MODALITY	$i = 2p - 5q$
doubly augmented	13
augmented	6, 8, 9, 10, and 11
major	2, 3, 4, and 5
perfect	−1 and 1
minor	−2, −3, −4, and −5
diminished	−6, −8, −9, −10, and −11
doubly diminished	−13

Example: Determine the modality of seventh $5w + h$. We have $i = (2)(5) - 5 = 5$, hence $5w + h$ is major.

Example: Determine the modality of seventh $3w + 3h$. In this case, $i = (2)(3) - (5)(3) = -9$, hence $3w + 3h$ is diminished.

It is also easy to express an interval in terms of w and h, given its name. If we take the notes of C major and examine the intervals formed by C with each of the other six notes in ascending order, we have:

$$\begin{array}{cccccc}
\text{CD} & \text{CE} & \text{CF} & \text{CG} & \text{CA} & \text{CB} \\
\text{int (2)} & \text{int (4)} & \text{int (}-1\text{)} & \text{int (1)} & \text{int (3)} & \text{int (5)}
\end{array}$$

It will be noted that all these intervals are either major or perfect. It is a matter of simple memory now, using established musical habits, to express any perfect or major interval in terms of w and h.

Example: Find an expression in terms of w and h for a major seventh. Major seventh CB contains minor second EF in addition to five major seconds (CD, DE, FG, GA, and AB), and thus is equal to $5w + h$.

Other modalities may be determined by adding the appropriate multiple of $w - h$ for each level of modality different from perfect or major.

Example: Find an expression in terms of w and h for a diminished seventh. This interval is smaller by two levels of modality than a major seventh, and is therefore equal to $5w + h - 2(w - h) = 3w + 3h$. The reader should now review all the examples given in this section.

A direct expression for the range of recognizability may be found in terms of w and h. This comes from the fact (demonstrated in the previous section) that the range of recognizability results from the requirement that both the minor second and chromatic semitone should be positive. This means that $h > 0$ and $w - h > 0$, and when these inequalities are combined, we have

$$0 < h < w$$

This is a much more immediately comprehensible expression for the range of recognizability than $\frac{4}{7}a < v < \frac{3}{5}a$.

Names and expressions in terms of w and h for int (i) where $-11 \leqslant i \leqslant 11$ are given in Table 75. As a consequence of Theorem 28, these results are valid throughout the range of recognizability.

TABLE 75

int (i)	in terms of w and h	name
int (11)	$3w - h$	augmented third
int (10)	$5w$	augmented sixth
int (9)	$2w - h$	augmented second
int (8)	$4w$	augmented fifth
int (7)	$w - h$	chromatic semitone
int (6)	$3w$	augmented fourth
int (5)	$5w + h$	major seventh
int (4)	$2w$	major third
int (3)	$4w + h$	major sixth
int (2)	w	major second
int (1)	$3w + h$	perfect fifth
octave	$5w + 2h$	octave
int (-1)	$2w + h$	perfect fourth
int (-2)	$4w + 2h$	minor seventh
int (-3)	$w + h$	minor third
int (-4)	$3w + 2h$	minor sixth
int (-5)	h	minor second
int (-6)	$2w + 2h$	diminished fifth
int (-7)	$4w + 3h$	diminished octave
int (-8)	$w + 2h$	diminished fourth
int (-9)	$3w + 3h$	diminished seventh
int (-10)	$2h$	diminished third
int (-11)	$2w + 3h$	diminished sixth

4. The nature and character of a diatonic tuning as a function of the ratio of the size of the major second to the size of the minor second. Many musicians, especially singers and players of stringed instruments, are accustomed to thinking of the various possible tunings of a diatonic scale in terms of how near they bring the leading tone to the tonic. For this reason, it is desirable to find a parameter that reveals this important musical characteristic more immediately than the size of the perfect fifth relative to the range $\frac{4}{7}a < v < \frac{3}{5}a$. To a certain extent, the proximity of the leading tone to the tonic is simply the size of the minor second; but this does not take into account the interrelation between the minor second and the major second. A more comprehensible measure is one that expresses the size of the minor second relative to the size of the major second, i.e., the ratio of the size of the larger interval to that of the smaller. Accordingly we introduce a new symbol R, defined by

$$R = \frac{w}{h} = \frac{2v - a}{3a - 5v} = \frac{2v - 1200}{3600 - 5v}$$

The range of recognizability may be very neatly expressed in terms of R alone. If we start with $w > h > 0$, and divide throughout by h (noting that the value zero for h is specifically excluded), we have $\frac{w}{h} > 1$, or

$$R > 1$$

Now if $R = 1$, it is clear that the resulting scale is the special, unrecognizable case where the major and minor seconds are equal. In Section 2 of this chapter, we saw that as $v \to 720$ cents, $h \to 0$; hence as $v \to 720$ cents, R increases without bound, i.e., the actual upper limit for R is a function of the refinement of human perception. If the actual maximum value for R is taken to be 715 cents (as suggested in Sec. 2), the upper limit for R is $\frac{(2)(715) - 1200}{3600 - (5)(715)} = 9.2$. The actual lower limit, corresponding to $v = 689.286$ cents as suggested, is $R = 1.162791$.

It is sometimes more convenient to compute R directly from the ratios of the higher to the lower pitch of the major and minor second, respectively. Using the method of Section 2 of this chapter, the ratio of the major second is $\frac{r^2}{2}$, and that of the minor second is $\frac{8}{r^5}$, where r is the ratio of the perfect fifth. Remembering that the size of an interval is the logarithm of its ratio (Ch. I, Sec. 1), we find that[7]

$$R = \frac{\log \dfrac{r^2}{2}}{\log \dfrac{8}{r^5}} = \frac{\ln \dfrac{r^2}{2}}{\ln \dfrac{8}{r^5}}$$

[7] It will be recalled that $\log x = \dfrac{1200}{\ln 2} \ln x$ (Ch. I, Sec. 8), and hence

$$\frac{\log \dfrac{r^2}{2}}{\log \dfrac{8}{r^5}} = \frac{\dfrac{1200}{\ln 2} \ln \dfrac{r^2}{2}}{\dfrac{1200}{\ln 2} \ln \dfrac{8}{r^5}} = \frac{\ln \dfrac{r^2}{2}}{\ln \dfrac{8}{r^5}}$$

Examples: For Pythagorean tuning,

$$R = \frac{\ln \dfrac{9}{8}}{\ln \dfrac{256}{243}} = \frac{.117783}{.052116} = 2.260017$$

For meantone tuning,

$$R = \frac{\ln \dfrac{5^{1/2}}{2}}{\ln \dfrac{8}{5^{5/4}}} = \frac{.111572}{.067644} = 1.649393$$

Since an increase in v results in an increase in w and a decrease in h, it is clear that an increase in v results in an increase in R throughout the range of recognizability, and vice versa. But the relation between v and R cannot be linear, since R increases without bound as $v \to 720$. In order to discover the exact nature of the relation, we call upon two well-known theorems from elementary analytic geometry and the theory of conic sections. The first states that the graph in rectangular coordinates of any equation having the form $xy = -c$ is an equilateral hyperbola whose center is at the origin and whose asymptotes are the x and y axes, one branch of the hyperbola being in the second quadrant and the other branch in the fourth quadrant. The second theorem states that the graph of $(x - a)(y - b) = -c$ is the same curve, but translated so that its center is at the point (a, b),[8] and its asymptotes are the lines $x = a$ and $y = b$.

We now transform the equation defining R as follows:

$$R = \frac{2v - 1200}{3600 - 5v}$$

$$3600R - 5vR = 2v - 1200$$

$$5vR + 2v - 3600R - 1200 = 0$$

$$vR + \tfrac{2}{5}v - 720R - 240 = 0$$

$$vR + \tfrac{2}{5}v - 720R - 288 = -48$$

$$(v - 720)(R + \tfrac{2}{5}) = -48$$

[8] In this context, the symbol (a, b) denotes the coordinates of a point and is not to be confused with the meaning of the same symbol in number theory (see Ch. I, Sec. 6).

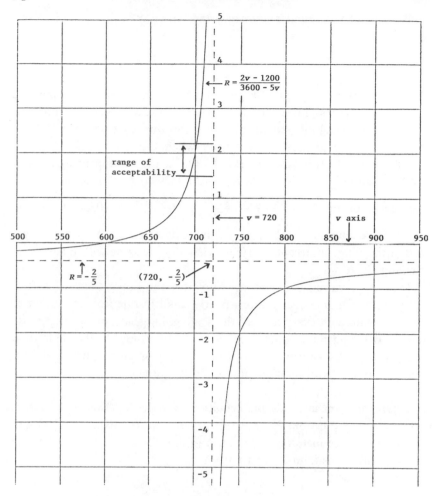

Thus the graph of this equation is an equilateral hyperbola whose center is at $(720, -\frac{2}{5})$, and whose asymptotes are the lines $v = 720$ and $R = -\frac{2}{5}$. The graph is shown in Figure 20; the v axis is horizontal and the R axis is vertical.

In the first section of this chapter, it was suggested that the acceptable range for v is approximately $695 \leqslant v \leqslant 701.5$ cents; to this corresponds the range for R of $1.52 \leqslant R \leqslant 2.194595$. Since the range of acceptability is dependent on both repertoire and subjective judgment, it will be more convenient to use rounder numbers, and so we take the range in terms of R to be

$$1.5 \leqslant R \leqslant 2.2$$

An inspection of the graph of Figure 20 reveals that within this range the curve is nearly straight, so that for purposes of rough estimates, no great error is introduced by assuming that v varies directly with R. Under this assumption, the greatest error occurs when the perfect fifth contains 698.079 cents, the true value for R is 1.789652, and the approximate value for R—assuming the linear relation—is 1.843934. At this point, the percentage error on R is $\dfrac{(100)(1.843934 - 1.789652)}{1.789652} = 3.033089$ percent.

Hence the changes that take place in the scale and the triads as v changes within the range of acceptability are virtually the same with reference to a change in R.

Thus as R varies at a uniform rate over the range $1.649393 \leqslant R \leqslant 2.260017$, the tuning changes at a nearly uniform rate from meantone to Pythagorean, with every note of the scale going sharp except the fourth degree, bringing the leading tone closer to the tonic. At the same time, the perfect fifths improve, going from slightly small to pure, while the major thirds deteriorate from pure to Pythagorean.

5. Expressions for intervals and definitions of notes in terms of R. Easily remembered expressions for intervals in terms of R may be found, closely resembling those in terms of w and h (Table 75; Sec. 3 of this chapter). These expressions follow directly from

$$5w + 2h = a$$

$$\frac{w}{h} = R$$

Upon substituting $w = Rh$ in the former equation, we obtain $5Rh + 2h = a$, then $h(5R + 2) = a$, and finally

$$h = \frac{a}{5R + 2}$$

$$w = \frac{Ra}{5R + 2}$$

Now if an interval is expressed as $pw + qh$, we have

$$pw + qh = \frac{pRa}{5R + 2} + \frac{qa}{5R + 2}$$

$$= (pR + q)\left(\frac{a}{5R + 2}\right)$$

In this last expression, the factor $\frac{a}{5R + 2}$ is a number depending on R,
but not on the interval. We may derive the coefficient $pR + q$ directly
from the interval's representation as $pw + qh$ by replacing w by R and h
by 1.

Examples: Find expressions in terms of R for a perfect fifth and a major
third. A perfect fifth is equal to $3w + h = (3R + 1)\left(\frac{a}{5R + 2}\right)$. A major

third is equal to $2w = \frac{2Ra}{5R + 2}$.

If we rearrange $(pR + q)\left(\frac{a}{5R + 2}\right)$ in the form $\frac{pR + q}{5R + 2}\, a$, we see that
this expresses the interval as a fractional part of an octave; hence the ratio

of such an interval is $2 \exp \frac{pR + q}{5R + 2}$ (Theorem 4; Ch. I, Sec. 5).[9]

Example: The ratio of a perfect fifth is $2 \exp \dfrac{3R + 1}{5R + 2}$. If $R = 2.260017$

(Pythagorean value), the value of the expression is $2 \exp \dfrac{7.780050}{13.300084} =$

$2 \exp .584963 = 1.500000$.

Example: The ratio of a major third is $2 \exp \dfrac{2R}{5R + 2}$. If $R = 1.649393$

(meantone value), the value of the expression is $2 \exp \dfrac{3.298786}{10.246964} =$

$2 \exp .321928 = 1.250000$.

Expressions for the diatonic and commonly occurring chromatic intervals in terms of R follow from Table 75 if we replace w by R and h by 1
throughout. The resulting expressions are the coefficients of the factor

---

[9] The expression $2 \exp x$ means the same as 2^x, and serves to present a more readable
format.

$\dfrac{1200}{5R + 2}$, and the product of the factor and the coefficient give the interval's size in cents. Its ratio, as shown above, is $2 \exp \dfrac{pR + q}{5R + 2}$. The expressions are collected for convenience in Table 76.

TABLE 76

int (i)	$pR + q$	name
int (11)	$3R - 1$	augmented third
int (10)	$5R$	augmented sixth
int (9)	$2R - 1$	augmented second
int (8)	$4R$	augmented fifth
int (7)	$R - 1$	chromatic semitone
int (6)	$3R$	augmented fourth
int (5)	$5R + 1$	major seventh
int (4)	$2R$	major third
int (3)	$4R + 1$	major sixth
int (2)	R	major second
int (1)	$3R + 1$	perfect fifth
octave	$5R + 2$	octave
int (-1)	$2R + 1$	perfect fourth
int (-2)	$4R + 2$	minor seventh
int (-3)	$R + 1$	minor third
int (-4)	$3R + 2$	minor sixth
int (-5)	1	minor second
int (-6)	$2R + 2$	diminished fifth
int (-7)	$4R + 3$	diminished octave
int (-8)	$R + 2$	diminished fourth
int (-9)	$3R + 3$	diminished seventh
int (-10)	2	diminished third
int (-11)	$2R + 3$	diminished sixth

Remarkably simple and easily remembered definitions of the symbols C, D, E, F, G, A, B, ♯, and ♭ may be obtained in terms of R. We first derive expressions in terms of w and h that give the distance from C to the note in question, and then replace w by R and h by 1 to obtain the coefficients of the factor $\dfrac{1200}{5R + 2}$, or the numerator of the fraction in the expression $2 \exp \dfrac{pR + q}{5R + 2}$. The distance from C to the note in question is

TABLE 77

note	C	D	E	F	G	A	B
distance from C	0	w	$2w$	$2w + h$	$3w + h$	$4w + h$	$5w + h$

found by replacing the intervals of Table 71 (Sec. 1 of this chapter) by the expressions given in Table 75 (Sec. 3); results are shown in Table 77. We have already seen that a sharp adds $w - h$ and a flat adds $h - w$ to any note (Sec. 3 of this chapter), hence the definitions of Table 78. The product of the numbers $pR + q$ and $\dfrac{1200}{5R + 2}$ gives the note's distance from C in cents. If the note's frequency is wanted, we multiply the frequency of middle C (264 Hz) by $2 \exp \dfrac{pR + q}{5R + 2}$.

TABLE 78

symbol	C	D	E	F	G	A	B	♯	♭
$pR + q$	0	R	$2R$	$2R + 1$	$3R + 1$	$4R + 1$	$5R + 1$	$R - 1$	$1 - R$

Example: If $R = 2.260017$, where is B♭♭ in relation to C? We have $pR + q = (5R + 1) + 2(1 - R) = 3R + 3$, hence B♭♭ is higher than C by

$$(3R + 3)\left(\frac{1200}{5R + 2}\right) = (9.780050)\left(\frac{1200}{13.300084}\right) = 882.405 \text{ cents.}$$

Example: If $R = 1.649393$ and the frequency of middle C is 264 Hz, what is the frequency of F♭? We have $pR + q = (2R + 1) + (1 - R) = R + 2$, hence the frequency is

$$(264)\left(2 \exp \frac{R + 2}{5R + 2}\right) = (264)\left(2 \exp \frac{3.649393}{10.246964}\right)$$

$$= (264)(2 \exp .356144)$$

$$= (264)(1.280000) = 337.920 \text{ Hz}$$

The reader should compare this method with that used to find the same results during the discussion of Pythagorean tuning (Ch. IV, Sec. 2) and meantone tuning (Ch. IX, Sec. 1).

6. Silbermann's one-sixth comma temperament. It is instructive to use the techniques developed in this chapter to make a thorough analysis of a particular acceptable diatonic tuning. Of especial historic interest is the tuning attributed to Gottfried Silbermann (1683–1753), in which the perfect fifth is made smaller than pure by one sixth of a syntonic comma.[10] The salient features of any acceptable diatonic tuning are the beat frequencies produced by perfect fifth middle CG and major third middle CE, the character of the major scale as given by R, and the size of the chromatic semitone. A complete analysis also includes the distance of each note of the chromatic scale from C, the ratio of the frequency of each pitch to the frequency of middle C, the frequency of each pitch in the octave starting with middle C, and the beat frequencies produced by the perfect fifths, perfect fourths, and major thirds.

We begin by finding the ratio of v, and this is

$$r = \left(\frac{3}{2}\right)\left(\frac{80}{81}\right)^{1/6} = 1.496898$$

The beat frequency produced by middle CG is $264\left[(2)(1.496898) - 3\right] = -1.638$ per second (Ch. I, Sec. 3).

We next compute R:

$$R = \frac{\ln \dfrac{r^2}{2}}{\ln \dfrac{8}{r^5}} = \frac{\ln 1.120351}{\ln 1.064461} = \frac{.113642}{.062468} = 1.819204$$

We next determine the expressions $pR + q$ associated with each note of the chromatic scale, using the correspondences of Table 78, and compute these numbers. The ratio with middle C is then given in each case by $2 \exp \dfrac{pR + q}{5R + 2} = 2 \exp \dfrac{pR + q}{11.096018}$, and the distance from C is equal to $(pR + q)\left(\dfrac{1200}{5R + 2}\right) = (108.147)(pR + q)$. The frequency of each note is obtained by multiplying each ratio by 264 (or whatever the frequency of middle C is chosen to be). Note that it is not necessary to compute the

---

[10] Georg Andres Sorge, *Gespräch zwischen einem Musico theoretico und einem Studio musices* (*Lobenstein*, 1748), 19–20.

TABLE 79

SILBERMANN'S TUNING

note	$pR + q$		cents up from C	ratio with C	frequency $C = 264$
C		0	0	1.000000	264.000
C♯	$R - 1 =$	.819204	88.594	1.052506	277.862
D	$R =$	1.819204	196.741	1.120351	295.773
D♯	$2R - 1 =$	2.638407	285.336	1.179176	311.303
E♭	$R + 1 =$	2.819204	304.888	1.192570	314.838
E	$2R =$	3.638407	393.482	1.255187	331.369
F	$2R + 1 =$	4.638407	501.629	1.336097	352.730
F♯	$3R =$	5.457611	590.224	1.406250	371.250
G	$3R + 1 =$	6.457611	698.371	1.496898	395.181
G♯	$4R =$	7.276814	786.965	1.575494	415.930
A♭	$3R + 2 =$	7.457611	806.518	1.593388	420.655
A	$4R + 1 =$	8.276814	895.112	1.677051	442.741
B♭	$4R + 2 =$	9.276814	1003.259	1.785155	471.281
B	$5R + 1 =$	10.096018	1091.853	1.878886	496.026

results in any particular order. Table 79 gives data for all notes on the line of fifths from A♭ through D♯.

We find the beat frequency produced by major third middle CE to be $264[(4)(1.255187) - 5] = 5.477$ per second—faster than fifth middle CG, but much slower than Pythagorean major third middle CE (16.5 per second). Unfortunately, however, the diminished fourths in Silbermann's tuning are wolves. Each diminished fourth contains $(108.147)(R + 2) = (108.147)(3.819204) = 413.035$ cents—slightly larger than a Pythagorean major third. The diminished sixth contains $(108.147)(2R + 3) = (108.147)(6.638407) = 717.923$ cents, and is thus also a wolf. Hence Silbermann's tuning imposes the same restrictions on the style of keyboard compositions as does meantone tuning (Ch. IX, Sec. 6), if only a little less emphatically.

The scale produced by Silbermann's tuning is considerably different from the meantone scale. In Silbermann's temperament, $w = 196.741$ cents and $h = 108.147$ cents, the corresponding meantone values being 193.157 cents and 117.108 cents, respectively. Modern musicians generally prefer the smaller minor second of Silbermann's scale, with its correspondingly higher leading tone. Silbermann's chromatic scale is more markedly different from the meantone chromatic scale, owing to the smaller difference between the minor second and the chromatic semitone.

In Silbermann's tuning, the quantity $12v - 7a$ (the interval formed by two notes separated by twelve positions on the line of fifths, such as A♭G♯) is negative, being equal to $12(\bar{v} - \frac{1}{6}\bar{k}) - 7a = 12\bar{v} - 7a - 2\bar{k} = \bar{p} - 2\bar{k} = -19.553$ cents. This descending interval is the diaschisma of just tuning (Ch. VI, Sec. 2).

Since Silbermann's triads are only a little less smooth than meantone triads, it can be safely stated that any composition that heeds the restrictions imposed by 12-note meantone tuning may be played satisfactorily in Silbermann's tuning. If the composition is largely confined to diatonic intervals, such as, for example, the di Lasso fragment analyzed earlier with reference to just tuning (Ch. VII, Sec. 2), the choice turns upon whether one prefers the smoother meantone triads or Silbermann's scale with its smaller minor second. In compositions making extensive use of chromatic intervals (see the examples of Ch. IX, Sec. 6), there are other factors to consider. In meantone tuning, one is very conscious of the unusual expressiveness associated with the noticeably unequal chromatic scale and the contrast between the euphonious triads and the piquant dissonances. In Silbermann's tuning, the more nearly equal chromatic scale is less expressive, the triads are less smooth, and the dissonances are milder. In view of this, the chromatic compositions cited earlier are more idiomatic in meantone tuning, at least according to the author's taste.

Silbermann's temperament may be set up by ear with only a little more difficulty than meantone tuning. The procedure is the same as for meantone tuning (Ch. IX, Sec. 5), except that each fifth, or fourth, is tempered slightly less so as to produce the correct beat frequencies on the major thirds. It is better to check the thirds in the octave below middle C, since in the higher octave, the beats are a bit too fast to be counted accurately. Table 80 gives beat frequencies of perfect fifths, perfect fourths, and major thirds within the two-octave range starting an octave below middle C.

During the sixteenth, seventeenth, and eighteenth centuries, theorists proposed a variety of different temperaments based on a perfect fifth that is made smaller by a fractional part of a syntonic comma. All these are recognizable diatonic tunings that fall within the range of acceptability. Table 81 gives data for several of these tunings, and the numbers provide a useful illustration of many of the principles developed in this chapter.

TABLE 80
BEATS IN SILBERMANN'S TUNING

interval	beats per sec.	per min.	interval	beats per sec.	per min.	interval	beats per sec.	per min.
CG	−.82	−49	CF	1.09	66	CE	2.74	164
C#G#	−.86	−52	C#F#	1.15	69			
DA	−.92	−55	DG	1.23	74	DF#	3.07	184
			D#G#	1.29	77			
EbBb	−.98	−59	EbAb	1.31	78	EbG	3.27	196
EB	−1.03	−62	EA	1.37	82	EG#	3.44	206
FC	−1.09	−66	FBb	1.46	88	FA	3.66	220
F#C#	−1.15	−69	F#B	1.54	92			
GD	−1.23	−74	GC	1.64	98	GB	4.10	246
G#D#	−1.29	−77	G#C#	1.72	103			
AbEb	−1.31	−78				AbC	4.36	262
AE	−1.37	−82	AD	1.84	110	AC#	4.59	276
BbF	−1.46	−88	BbEb	1.95	117	BbD	4.89	293
BF#	−1.54	−92	BE	2.06	123	BD#	5.15	309
middle CG	−1.64	−98	CF	2.19	131	CE	5.48	329
C#G#	−1.72	−103	C#F#	2.30	138			
DA	−1.84	−110	DG	2.45	147	DF#	6.14	368
			D#G#	2.58	155			
EbBb	−1.95	−117	EbAb	2.61	157	EbG	6.53	392
EB	−2.06	−123	EA	2.75	165	EG#	6.87	412
FC	−2.19	−131	FBb	2.92	175	FA	7.32	439
F#C#	−2.30	−138	F#B	3.08	185			
GD	−2.45	−147	GC	3.28	197	GB	8.20	492
G#D#	−2.58	−155	G#C#	3.45	207			
AbEb	−2.61	−157				AbC	8.73	524
AE	−2.75	−165	AD	3.67	220	AC#	9.19	551
BbF	−2.92	−175	BbEb	3.91	234	BbD	9.78	587
BF#	−3.08	−185	BE	4.11	247	BD#	10.29	617

TABLE 81

amount of tempering	R	perfect fifth	major third
$\frac{1}{3}\overline{k}$	1.503722	694.786	379.145
$\frac{3}{10}\overline{k}$	1.559433	695.503	382.012
$\frac{2}{7}\overline{k}$	1.584319	695.810	383.241
$\frac{5}{18}\overline{k}$	1.598421	695.981	383.924
$\frac{1}{4}\overline{k}$	1.649393	696.578	386.314
$\frac{2}{9}\overline{k}$	1.703033	697.176	388.703
$\frac{3}{14}\overline{k}$	1.718879	697.347	389.386
$\frac{1}{5}\overline{k}$	1.748011	697.654	390.615
$\frac{1}{6}\overline{k}$	1.819204	698.371	393.482
$\frac{1}{7}\overline{k}$	1.873015	698.883	395.531
$\frac{1}{8}\overline{k}$	1.915118	699.267	397.067
$\frac{1}{9}\overline{k}$	1.948959	699.565	398.262
$\frac{1}{10}\overline{k}$	1.976752	699.804	399.217

XI   Equal Tunings and Closed Circles of Fifths

Introduction.   In this chapter, we investigate a special class of recognizable diatonic tunings—those in which the perfect fifths ultimately form a closed circle. In Section 1 it is shown that this property depends solely on whether R and v are rational numbers. In Section 2 we demonstrate that R and the ratio of the perfect fifth are incommensurable, and consequently irrational numbers are associated with all recognizable diatonic tunings in some respect. In Section 3 we show that if the notes forming any closed circle of intervals are reproduced in all registers by octave transpositions, the result is an equal tuning. The demonstration requires an understanding of the elementary properties of congruences and residues as set forth in Chapter III, Sec. 1, which the reader should review before continuing. Section 4 gives one method for assigning any note, given its name, to its proper position relative to C in an equal tuning formed by a closed circle of recognizable perfect fifths. It is also shown that such tunings always contain notes that are enharmonic. In Section 5 we prove the fundamentally important circle of fifths theorem, which provides another method for locating notes within an equal tuning when R is rational. The theorem is illustrated with the special familiar tuning where $R = 2$, resulting in an equal tuning of twelve notes. In Section 6 we present a detailed analysis of 12-note equal tuning, comparing its diatonic behavior with that of Pythagorean tuning, meantone tuning, and Silbermann's tuning. It is also shown that certain familiar aspects of chromatic harmony are associated exclusively with the tuning where $R = 2$. The applicability of 12-note equal tuning to the existing repertoire is also explored, and the conclusion is reached that this tuning may be satisfactorily—if imperfectly—applied to all polyphonic music written up to the present time. In Section 7 we give a procedure for putting a piano in 12-note equal tuning within the required very close tolerance. Section 8 presents a detailed investigation of the recognizable diatonic tunings where $R = \frac{3}{2}$ and $R = 3$, resulting in equal tunings of nineteen and seventeen notes, respectively. While both examples further illustrate the application of the circle of fifths theorem, the former is especially important, for $R = \frac{3}{2}$

is within the acceptable range as described in Chapter X, Secs. 1 and 4. It is also shown that every rational R generates a unique set of enharmonic equivalents, and consequently chromatic harmony exhibits a different behavior for every particular rational R. This is very different from the diatonic aspect, which conforms to the same structural interconnections as those found in Pythagorean tuning and all other diatonic tunings where $R > 1$ (Theorems 25 and 26; Ch. X, Sec. 2). In Section 9 we show which equal tunings contain recognizable diatonic scales and which do not, and Section 10 describes the special properties of certain equal tunings in which there are several separate circles of fifths.

1. Necessary and sufficient conditions for a particular extended diatonic tuning eventually to produce a closed circle of fifths.

We recall first that extension along the line of fifths of either Pythagorean tuning or meantone tuning, however far in either direction from the original seven notes, always produces notes not previously encountered (Ch. IV, Sec. 1, and Ch. IX, Sec. 1). It should also be noted that for meantone tuning, $12v = 12(\bar{v} - \frac{1}{4}\bar{k}) < 7a$; and for Pythagorean tuning, $12\bar{v} > 7a$. The actual values are $7a = 8400$ cents, $12(\bar{v} - \frac{1}{4}\bar{k}) = 8358.941$ cents, and $12\bar{v} = 8423.460$ cents (see also Ch. IX, Sec. 2). Clearly at some point between $v = \bar{v} - \frac{1}{4}\bar{k}$ and $v = \bar{v}$, we must have $12v - 7a = 0$, or $12v = 7a$. This expression depicts a closed circle of twelve perfect fifths; consequently any two pitches separated by twelve positions on the line of fifths differ by seven octaves, and hence are in fact the same note (Ch. I, Sec. 2). Therefore an extended diatonic tuning in which $12v = 7a$ produces a finite number of notes—in this case, twelve. The term "closed circle" is in contradistinction to the term "broken circle" in which one interval differs from all the others (Ch. III, Sec. 4).

It should be emphasized at this point that there is no reason whatever to assume that twelve is the only number of perfect fifths within the range of recognizability (Ch. X, Sec. 2) that may produce a closed circle; and it is equally without logical foundation to assume that any number of recognizable perfect fifths can be made to form a closed circle. Exactly what is true in this regard is not intuitively obvious, and will be the subject of a later discussion (Sec. 9 of this chapter).

In order to provide for the possibility—soon to be shown a fact—that a circle of recognizable perfect fifths may close at some point other than after the twelfth fifth, we consider the general case $mv = na$, where $a = 1200$, m and n are positive integers, and v lies within the range $\frac{4}{7}a < v < \frac{3}{5}a$. The necessary and sufficient conditions for the existence of the numbers m and n may be expressed in several ways, each having its own special conveniences. The subject is best approached by consideration of three separate theorems.

THEOREM 30. *A particular extended diatonic tuning produces a closed circle of fifths if and only if the size of the generating interval is a rational number.* From $mv = na$, we have at once $v = \dfrac{n}{m} a = 1200 \dfrac{n}{m} (m \neq 0)$. Now if the integers m and n exist, then v is rational, and conversely; and if m and n do not exist, then v is irrational by definition, and conversely.

THEOREM 31. *If a particular extended diatonic tuning produces a closed circle of fifths, then the size of every interval within the tuning is given by a rational number; and if the size of any one interval within the tuning (excluding octave multiples) is given by a rational number, then the tuning produces a closed circle of fifths.* Every interval within the tuning is of the form $iv + na = iv + 1200n$ where i and n are integers or zero (Ch. VIII, Sec. 2; Ch. X, Sec. 2). Now if v is rational, so is $iv + 1200n$, and conversely, irrespective of the actual values of the integers i and n.

It follows directly from Theorems 30 and 31 that if a given extended diatonic tuning does not produce a closed circle of fifths, then the size of the generating interval v—and consequently every interval within the tuning (except octave multiples)—is given by an irrational number.

Especially important, and having extensive practical application is the following:

THEOREM 32. *A necessary and sufficient condition for a particular extended diatonic tuning ultimately to produce a closed circle of fifths is that R should be a rational number.* (R is the ratio of the size of the major second to the size of the minor second, as defined in Ch. X, Sec. 4.) We begin by demonstrating the necessity of the condition. Let the circle of fifths be closed; then by Theorem 30, v is rational. But by definition, $R = \dfrac{2v - 1200}{3600 - 5v}$, and this number is rational for any v except $v = 720$ (causing the denominator to vanish). To demonstrate the sufficiency of the condition, let R be rational. Now we have $v = (1200)\left(\dfrac{3R + 1}{5R + 2}\right)$ (Ch. X, Sec. 5); and since this number is rational for any rational R ($R \neq -\frac{2}{5}$), the result follows directly from Theorem 30.

From Theorem 32, it follows that if a given diatonic tuning does not produce a closed circle of fifths, then R is irrational, and conversely. For example, since neither Pythagorean tuning nor meantone tuning produces a closed circle of fifths, the corresponding values for R (Ch. X, Sec. 4) are both irrational numbers. As another illustration, assume $R = 2$. Then

$$v = (1200)\left[\frac{(3)(2) + 1}{(5)(2) + 2}\right] = 700 \text{ cents, a rational number.}$$

It must not be assumed that the closing of the circle of fifths depends on the rationality of the number expressing the ratio of the size of any two intervals within the tuning. For example, a major third is equal to $2w$ throughout the range of recognizability (Table 75; Ch. X, Sec. 3), and hence a major second is exactly one half of a major third. In other words, $\frac{\text{int (4)}}{\text{int (2)}} = 2$, and this is true for all recognizable diatonic tunings.

It should also be observed that the inequalities defining v over the range of recognizability do not enter into the proofs of Theorems 30, 31, and 32; hence these theorems are true for the unrecognizable tunings as well as for all the others, using the definitions in terms of R derived in Chapter X, Sec. 5.

2. Diatonic tunings and irrational numbers. The theorems proved in the previous section may be used to throw additional light on the existence of rational and irrational numbers within diatonic tunings. We begin by restating Theorem 30 in terms of the ratio of the generating interval rather than its size:

THEOREM 33. *A particular diatonic tuning produces a closed circle of fifths if and only if the ratio of the generating interval is of the form $2^{\frac{n}{m}}$ where m and n are integers, $m \neq 0$, and $\frac{n}{m} \neq$ an integer.* Let the ratio of the perfect fifth be r; then if $v = \frac{n}{m} a$ (Theorem 30), we have at once $r = 2^{\frac{n}{m}}$ (Theorem 4; Ch. I, Sec. 5). As before, the stipulation that $\frac{n}{m} \neq$ an integer excludes the possibility that the generating interval might be an octave multiple.

THEOREM 34. *If a particular extended diatonic tuning ultimately produces a closed circle of fifths, the ratio of every interval in the tuning is an integral root of an integral power of* 2. If v is the size and r is the ratio of the generating interval, the size of every interval within the tuning is given by $iv + ha$ where h and i are integers. The ratio of $iv + ha$ is $r^i 2^h$; and if there exists a closed circle of fifths, we have also $r = 2^{\frac{n}{m}}$ (Theorem 33) and

$r^i = 2^{\frac{in}{m}}$. Hence under these conditions, $r^i 2^h = 2^{\frac{in}{m}} 2^h = 2^{\frac{in}{m}+h} = 2^{\frac{in+hm}{m}} = \sqrt[m]{2^{in+hm}}$. Since $in + hm$ is an integer, the result follows.

THEOREM 35. *If the ratio of any interval (excluding octave multiples) within a diatonic tuning is a rational number, then the tuning does not produce a closed circle of fifths.* In the preceding demonstration, we saw that if there exists a closed circle of fifths, then all the ratios are of the form $2^{\frac{in}{m}} 2^h$. In order to determine which of these ratios are rational or irrational, we observe first that in the expression $2^{\frac{in}{m}} 2^h$, 2^h is an integer, and so we need consider only $2^{\frac{in}{m}}$. Now let $2^{\frac{in}{m}} = x$; by Theorem 3 (Ch. I, Sec. 4), x is either an irrational number or an integer. Next assume x to be an integer; then $2^{in} = x^m$. By the unique prime factorization theorem (Theorem 1; Ch. I, Sec. 4), x must then be a power of 2, and $m|in$.[1] Under these conditions, the ratio $2^{\frac{in}{m}} 2^h$ represents an octave multiple, and hence all ratios other than octave multiples are irrational numbers. Therefore if $2^{\frac{in}{m}} 2^h$ is rational, the tuning does not produce a closed circle of fifths.

Example: During the discussion of Silbermann's tuning, in which $v = \bar{v} - \frac{1}{6}\bar{k}$ (Ch. X, Sec. 6), it was shown that $12v - 7a$ is a descending diaschisma. Since the ratio of this interval is $\frac{2025}{2048}$ (Ch. VI, Sec. 2)—a rational number—it follows that Silbermann's tuning does not produce a closed circle of fifths.

A combination of Theorems 32 and 35 yields the following important result:

THEOREM 36. *If the ratio of any interval (excluding octave multiples) within a diatonic tuning is a rational number, then R is irrational; and if R is rational, then the ratios of all intervals, excepting octave multiples, are irrational numbers.* In particular, Theorem 36 shows that r and R are incommensurable. From this, we see that in any diatonic tuning, at least one intuitively comprehensible element must be measured by an irrational number.

Theorem 36 does not mean, however, that R and r cannot both be irrational, and we may show that Silbermann's tuning is an example. We have just seen that this tuning does not yield a closed circle of fifths, and hence, by Theorem 32, R is irrational. We have also $r = \left(\frac{3}{2}\right)\left(\frac{80}{81}\right)^{1/6} = \frac{1}{2}\left[\frac{(729)(80)}{81}\right]^{1/6} = \frac{\sqrt[6]{720}}{2}$. Since $\sqrt[6]{720}$ is not an integer (the actual value is

---

[1] See Ch. I, note 5.

$\sqrt[6]{720} = 2.993795$), it is irrational (Theorem 3; Ch. I, Sec. 4), and so is $\dfrac{\sqrt[6]{720}}{2}$.

3. The equal tuning theorem. The concept of an equal tuning arises quite naturally in conjunction with the theory of diatonic tunings. We have already encountered the division of an octave into five and seven equal parts as the special, unrecognizable versions of the diatonic scale at the end points of the range of recognizability (Ch. X, Sec. 2). More generally, an m-note equal tuning is one in which all the adjacent intervals are equal to $\dfrac{a}{m}$, so that the pitches in ascending order within any one octave are higher than the initial pitch by $0, \dfrac{1}{m}a, \dfrac{2}{m}a, \dfrac{3}{m}a \ldots \dfrac{m-1}{m}a$. It is understood as usual that all such pitches are reproduced in all registers by octave transpositions. It follows at once that the ratios of each higher pitch within one octave to any fixed reference pitch are given by the numbers $1, 2^{\frac{1}{m}}, 2^{\frac{2}{m}}, 2^{\frac{3}{m}} \ldots 2^{\frac{m-1}{m}}$ (Theorem 4; Ch. I, Sec. 5). This, in combination with Theorem 34, strongly suggests that there is a connection between an equal tuning and a closed circle of fifths. The exact nature of this connection is one of the basic principles of music theory, and will henceforth be referred to as the *equal tuning theorem*.

Phrased in the most readily comprehensible musical terms, the equal tuning theorem states that if all the pitches forming any closed circle of intervals are reproduced in all registers by octave transpositions, the result is an equal tuning. However, the nature of the demonstration suggests that we can prove rather more than this, and accordingly we frame the theorem formally as follows:

THEOREM 37.   *Let there be an interval v forming a closed circle in such a manner that the sum of m v's is equal to the sum of n octaves (m and n positive integers). This array will have the following properties: (1) A necessary and sufficient condition for the number of notes generated to be equal to the number of intervals in the circle is that m and n should be coprime; and (2) If all the pitches forming the circle are reproduced in all registers by octave transpositions, and if $(m,n) = 1$, the result is an equal tuning of m notes.*[2]

[2] See Ch. I, note 6.

The transposition by octaves of all pitches into all registers makes it necessary only to examine the sizes of the adjacent intervals within one particular octave. To effect this, we adopt a procedure analagous to that employed in the generation of the diatonic scale from a broken circle of fifths. This requires the following two operations—all pitches forming the circle are transposed up or down some integral number (not excluding zero) of octaves in such a manner that the greatest interval formed by any two of the new pitches is less than one octave; the pitches so obtained are then rearranged in ascending order.

The distances of each pitch in the circle from the initial pitch are given by the numbers $0, v, 2v, 3v, \ldots$ and it will be convenient to denote this by iv where i takes successive integral values starting with zero. Then from $mv = na$, we have $v = \dfrac{n}{m} a$, and $iv = \dfrac{in}{m} a$. To effect the first operation, we may choose the initial pitch as a fixed reference point, this being the most convenient, and transpose all the other pitches down some number of octaves (if necessary) so that each new pitch is higher than the initial pitch by less than one octave. That is, if $\dfrac{in}{m} a > a$, we rearrange $\dfrac{in}{m} a$ in the form $\left(k + \dfrac{j}{m}\right) a$, where k is a positive integer chosen in such a manner that $0 \leqslant \dfrac{j}{m} < 1$. The expression $\left(k + \dfrac{j}{m}\right) a$ depicts every pitch in the circle as higher than the initial pitch by k octaves plus the fractional part of an octave $\dfrac{j}{m} a$. Hence the distance of each transposed pitch from the initial pitch is $\dfrac{j}{m} a$. Now from $\dfrac{in}{m} a = \left(k + \dfrac{j}{m}\right) a$, we have $\dfrac{in}{m} = k + \dfrac{j}{m}$, and $\dfrac{in - j}{m} = k$. In this last expression, we are interested in the behavior of j, but k is unimportant, since the number of octaves by which the pitches are transposed is immaterial. Thus since k is an integer, it is only necessary that $m \mid in - j$, or that

$$in \equiv j \pmod{m}$$

Since $0 \leqslant \dfrac{j}{m} < 1$, we have $0 \leqslant j < m$, or $0 \leqslant j \leqslant m - 1$, i.e., we select the j that is the least residue. The equal tuning theorem as framed is essentially a statement in musical terms of the known properties of this congruence relation as described in Theorem 11 (Ch. III, Sec. 1). A necessary and sufficient condition for the circle to contain m different notes is that $\dfrac{j}{m} a$, and therefore j, should assume m different values as i goes from zero to $m - 1$, and a necessary and sufficient condition for this to occur is that $(m, n) = 1$. This proves the first part of the theorem.

Now if $(m, n) = 1$, rearrangement of the m transposed pitches in ascending order simply requires arrangement of the numbers $\dfrac{j}{m} a$ in ascending order, this order being $0, \dfrac{1}{m} a, \dfrac{2}{m} a, \dfrac{3}{m} a \ldots \dfrac{m-1}{m} a$, and this is an equal tuning of m notes as defined. This proves the second part of the theorem.

It should be noted that the inequalities defining v do not enter into the proof, and hence the theorem is true for any size of generating interval whatever, without any further restriction except the one already described, viz., that v should be a rational number (Theorem 30; Sec. 1 of this chapter).

This form of the equal tuning theorem is adequate for most of the applications that follow, since we may usually assume that $(m, n) = 1$. If $(m, n) > 1$, the situation is rather more complicated, and so we defer this discussion to the time when it will be needed (Sec. 10 of this chapter). Of course, the stipulation that $(m, n) = 1$ does not in any way limit the number of values that v may assume.

Example: Let $12v = 7a$, this equation depicting a closed circle of twelve generating intervals. Now $v = \frac{7}{12}a$, and $(7, 12) = 1$. The distances of each pitch in the circle from any fixed reference pitch are $0, \frac{7}{12}a, \frac{14}{12}a, \frac{21}{12}a, \frac{28}{12}a, \frac{35}{12}a, \frac{42}{12}a, \frac{49}{12}a, \frac{56}{12}a, \frac{63}{12}a, \frac{70}{12}a, \frac{77}{12}a$. The corresponding distances after octave transpositions are $0, \frac{7}{12}a, \frac{2}{12}a, \frac{9}{12}a, \frac{4}{12}a, \frac{11}{12}a, \frac{6}{12}a, \frac{1}{12}a, \frac{8}{12}a, \frac{3}{12}a, \frac{10}{12}a, \frac{5}{12}a$. In this arrangement, it will be observed that the numerators are the twelve integers from 0 through 11. The distances from the initial pitch after arrangement in increasing order are $0, \frac{1}{12}a, \frac{2}{12}a, \frac{3}{12}a \ldots \frac{11}{12}a$, and this is an equal tuning of twelve notes.

4. Representation of certain equal tunings by the conventional musical notation.

If an interval v forms a closed circle as described in Theorem 37, and consequently generates an equal tuning, and if the size of v falls within the range of recognizability $\frac{4}{7}a < v < \frac{3}{5}a$ (Ch. X, Sec. 2), then the equal tuning must contain recognizable diatonic scales. Clearly any equal tuning that can be shown to contain at least one recognizable diatonic scale must contain the same number of scales as notes in the tuning. In addition, all the diatonic scales will have the same tuning, save for differences in register. Under these conditions, an equal tuning may be depicted by the conventional musical notation. We now show how the congruence relation developed in the previous section may be used to assign any note, given its conventional name, to its proper position within the equal tuning, relative to a fixed reference point.

To this end, we use the arrangement of notes developed during the discussion of Pythagorean tuning (Ch. IV, Sec. 1), and used again during the discussion of meantone tuning (Ch. IX, Sec. 1), where all the notes are envisioned as lying along the line of fifths, with the following number correspondences:

notes   ... -4 -3 -2 -1 0 1 2 3 4 5 6 7 8 9 10 ...
names   ... D♭ A♭ E♭ B♭ F C G D A E B F♯ C♯ G♯ D♯ ...

Let the initial pitch be F; then the distances of each pitch from F on the circle of fifths are $0, v, 2v, 3v \ldots$. In other words, pitch i is higher than F by the amount iv. But if v is a perfect fifth within the range of recognizability $\frac{4}{7}a < v < \frac{3}{5}a$, then the numbers i ($i \geqslant 0$) actually give the name of each note, and hence each pitch, according to the correspondences of the above diagram.

Example: C♯ is note 8; hence C♯ is higher than F on the circle of fifths by the amount $8v$.

Now let $v = \dfrac{n}{m}\, a$, $(m, n) = 1$. By the equal tuning theorem, this will generate an equal tuning of m notes. The distance of note i from note 0 within one octave is given by $\dfrac{j}{m}\, a$, where $in \equiv j \pmod{m}$ and $0 \leqslant j \leqslant m - 1$. If we think of the notes of the resulting equal tuning as the following distances up from note 0, and observe their positions relative to note 0,

$$\text{notes} \qquad 0 \quad \frac{1}{m}a \quad \frac{2}{m}a \quad \frac{3}{m}a \ \ldots \ \frac{m-1}{m}a$$

$$\text{positions} \quad 0 \quad 1 \quad 2 \quad 3 \quad \ldots \quad m-1$$

it is at once apparent that the numbers j give the positions occupied by notes i in the equal tuning relative to note 0, when i is positive.

Examples: Let $v = \frac{7}{12}a = 700$ cents, a value within the range of recognizability. Since $(7, 12) = 1$, this interval will generate an equal tuning of twelve notes in which note i will be in position j where $7i \equiv j \pmod{12}$, and $0 \leqslant j \leqslant 11$. We may calculate j given any positive i by the method described in Chapter III, Sec. 1, viz., we divide $7i$ by 12, obtaining a quotient which is immaterial, and a remainder which is the desired least residue. If F is in position 0, in what position is F$\sharp$? F$\sharp$ is note 7, hence $i = 7$; when 49 is divided by 12, the remainder is 1, and hence F$\sharp$ is in position 1. In what position is D? Here $i = 3$, and when 21 is divided by 12, the remainder is 9. In what position is C$\sharp$? Here $i = 8$, and when 56 is divided by 12, the remainder is 8.

It may easily be shown that the same process is valid for a negative i. The numbers $0, -v, -2v, -3v \ldots$ depict the circle of fifths as proceeding downward from the fixed reference point. If v is a perfect fifth within the range of recognizability and note 0 is the reference point, then the notes encountered are successively notes $0, -1, -2, -3, \ldots$ corresponding to F, B$\flat$, E$\flat$, A$\flat \ldots$. The argument of the previous section may be extended to include this situation. Whenever $\dfrac{in}{m} a \ (= iv) < 0$, as will always be the case when i is negative, we rearrange $\dfrac{in}{m} a$ into the form $\left(k + \dfrac{j}{m} \right) a$, where k is a negative integer chosen so that $0 \leqslant \dfrac{j}{m} < 1$. If the pitch lower than the initial pitch is transposed up k octaves, the resulting pitch is higher than the initial pitch by the fractional part of an octave $\dfrac{j}{m} a$ as before. The rest of the argument proceeds unchanged.

When i is negative, we may calculate j once again by simple division if we first transform the congruence by adding $-im$ to the left-hand side (Theorem 10; Ch. III, Sec. 1), and we have

$$(n - m)i \equiv j \,(\mathrm{mod}\ m)$$

If v is within the range of recognizability, then $\dfrac{4}{7} a < \dfrac{n}{m} a < \dfrac{3}{5} a$ and $\dfrac{n}{m} < \dfrac{3}{5}$; hence $m > n$, and $(n - m)i$ is positive.

In the general case, the number i may be calculated from the name of the note according to the following correspondences, which serve as definitions within the range of recognizability:

F	C	G	D	A	E	B	$\sharp$	$\flat$
0	+1	+2	+3	+4	+5	+6	+7	−7

This further extends the concept of the equal tuning theorem by actually locating every note relative to F within the equal tuning in all cases where the generating interval v is a perfect fifth within the range of recognizability.

Examples: If $v = \frac{7}{12}a$, and note F is in position 0 of the resulting 12-note equal tuning, in what position is G♭? From the diagram of correspondences above, G♭ is note $+2 - 7 = -5$, and so we use the transformed version of the congruence. Since $n = 7$ and $m = 12$, this is $-5i \equiv j$ (mod 12), and so $(-5)(-5) \equiv j$ (mod 12). When 25 is divided by 12, the remainder is 1, hence G♭ is in position 1. In what position is E♭♭? E♭♭ is note $+5 - 7 - 7 = -9$, and when 45 is divided by 12, the remainder is 9. In what position is D♭? D♭ is note $+3 - 7 = -4$, and when 20 is divided by 12, the remainder is 8. The reader should make a careful comparison between these examples and the previous three of this section.

Since we are concerned now specifically with the situation in which v is a perfect fifth within the range of recognizability, it should be remembered that under these conditions, intervals (-11) through (11) maintain the same interconnected organization and distributional patterns as those associated with Pythagorean tuning (Theorems 25–28; Ch. X, Sec. 2). Hence, even when the circle of fifths is closed, we may use all the techniques developed during the discussion of Pythagorean tuning to calculate various aspects of intervals expressed as int (i) when $-11 \leqslant i \leqslant 11$. As an illustration, we may use the congruence $in \equiv j$ (mod m) to find the size of int (i), given that $v = \frac{n}{m} a$, $\frac{4}{7}a < v < \frac{3}{5}a$, and $(m, n) = 1$. Since note i is higher than note 0 by int (i) (Theorem 7; Ch. II, Sec. 3), the size of int (i) is simply the distance in cents from note 0 to note i, and this is $\frac{j}{m} a$ where $in \equiv j$ (mod m), $0 \leqslant j \leqslant m - 1$.

Example: If $v = \frac{7}{12}a$, how large is int (4)? Since $i = 4$, we have $28 \equiv j$ (mod 12), hence $j = 4$, and the size is $(\frac{4}{12})(1200) = 400$ cents.

If the interval's name is given, we may determine i by the method of Chapter III, Secs. 3–6 and Chapter IV, Sec. 3. The names of intervals (-11) through (11) will be found in Tables 8, 11, and 12.

Example: If $v = \frac{7}{12}a$, how large is an augmented second? From Table 11, an augmented second is int (9), and so $63 \equiv j$(mod 12), $j = 3$, and the size is $(\frac{3}{12})(1200) = 300$ cents.

Example: By how many cents is E♭♭ higher than C♭? Since the interval between note x and note y is int $(y - x)$ (Theorem 6; Ch. II, Sec. 3), we find i from the expression (E♭♭) − (C♭) = $(5 - 7 - 7) - (1 - 7) = -3$.

Next, using the transformed version of the congruence, we have $15 \equiv j$ (mod 12), $j = 3$, and so the distance is $(\frac{3}{12})(1200) = 300$ cents.

We now come upon a feature exhibited only by extended diatonic tunings that produce a closed circle of fifths:

THEOREM 38. *In any extended recognizable diatonic tuning in which $mv = na$ (m and n positive integers), any two notes whose numbers differ by a multiple of m, i.e., which are congruent* (mod m), *are in fact the same.* By Theorem 10 (Ch. III, Sec. 1), if $in \equiv j$ (mod m) and $0 \leqslant j \leqslant m - 1$, then also $(i + km)n \equiv j$ (mod m) for any integer k. Hence if note i is in position j, the same is true for note $i + km$, and the result follows.

We may find another symbolic demonstration of this phenomenon from the expression $mv = na$ by replacing v by int (1) and na by int (0) to obtain m int (1) = int (0); it then follows at once that int (m) = int (0) (Ch. II, Sec. 3). Furthermore, since int (i) is always construed as being less than one octave, the value of int (0) in this case is zero. Hence under the conditions of Theorem 38, int (m) vanishes. The particular application of this general principle to the case where $m = 12$ and $n = 7$ explains the phenomenon— so familiar to trained musicians and so baffling to beginners—of distinctions within the notation (such as, for example, A♭ and G♯) which do not exist in 12-note equal tuning.

Examples: In earlier examples of this section, we found that F♯ and G♭ both occupy position 1 in 12-note equal tuning. Is F♯ $\equiv$ G♭ (mod 12)? Yes, because we find that (F♯) $-$ (G♭) $= (7) - (2 - 7) = 12$. Also both D and E♭♭ were found to occupy position 9. Is D $\equiv$ E♭♭ (mod 12)? Yes, because (D) $-$ (E♭♭) $= (3) - (5 - 7 - 7) = 12$. Again, C♯ and D♭ are both in position 8, and (C♯) $-$ (D♭) $= (1 + 7) - (3 - 7) = 12$.

Since it is customary to describe recognizable diatonic tunings relative to C rather than F, it is desirable to make a slight modification of the relation $in \equiv j$ (mod m) to accommodate this convention. We wish only that note 1, rather than note 0, should occupy position 0, and this is immediately accomplished by replacing i by $i - 1$ in the congruence. For convenience, we summarize the entire operation as follows:

If $v = \dfrac{n}{m} a$, $\frac{4}{7}a < v < \frac{3}{5}a$, and $(m, n) = 1$, and if C is in position 0 of the resulting m-note equal tuning, then note i is in position j where $n(i - 1) \equiv j$ (mod m) or $(n - m)(i - 1) \equiv j$ (mod m), and $0 \leqslant j \leqslant m - 1$.

Examples: If $v = \frac{7}{12}a$, and C is in position 0 of the resulting 12-note equal tuning, in what position is C♯? We have $(7)(1 + 7 - 1) \equiv j$ (mod 12), $49 \equiv j$ (mod 12), and $j = 1$. In what position is D? We have

$(7)(3 - 1) \equiv j \pmod{12}$, $14 \equiv j \pmod{12}$, and $j = 2$. In what position is E♭? In this case, $(-5)(5 - 7 - 1) \equiv j \pmod{12}$, $15 \equiv j \pmod{12}$, and $j = 3$.

The reader should become thoroughly familiar with the principle by working out other examples within the standard tuning where $v = \frac{7}{12}a$. It will soon be found that certain common musical assumptions are valid only in this particular situation, and that surprises are to be expected when n and m take values other than 7 and 12, respectively.

5. The circle of fifths theorem. The principles demonstrated in the previous section take on a much more comprehensible and pretty aspect if we express the generating interval in terms of R, R being the ratio of the size of the major second to the size of the minor second (Ch. X, Sec. 4). It will be recalled (Theorem 32; Sec. 1 of this chapter) that a necessary and sufficient condition for a particular extended diatonic tuning ultimately to produce a closed circle of fifths is that R should be a rational number. Now if R is rational, we may postulate the existence of two integers W and H, such that $R = \dfrac{W}{H}$. The letters W and H have been chosen to represent these integers because of a close connection between w and W, and between h and H (w and h are defined in Ch. X, Sec. 3), which will be revealed later in this section. It may be observed right away that since the expression for the range of recognizability in terms of R is simply $R > 1$ (Ch. X, Sec. 4), we may assume that both W and H are positive, and we have also $\dfrac{W}{H} > 1$, and hence $W > H$. We thus have finally

$$0 < H < W$$

This expression for the range of recognizability is usually more readily applicable to practical situations than $\frac{4}{7}a < v < \frac{3}{5}a$.

We next recall that the expression for a perfect fifth in terms of R is $v = \dfrac{3R + 1}{5R + 2} a$ (Ch. X, Sec. 5). Upon substituting $R = \dfrac{W}{H}$, we find that

$$v = \frac{3\dfrac{W}{H} + 1}{5\dfrac{W}{H} + 2} a$$

$$= \frac{3W + H}{5W + 2H} a$$

Now under any conditions where $(5W + 2H, 3W + H) = 1$, the equal tuning theorem is applicable. Such conditions are provided for in the following important lemma:

THEOREM 39.   *A necessary and sufficient condition for* $(5W + 2H,$ $3W + H) = 1$ *is* $(W, H) = 1$. To demonstrate the necessity of the condition, we show that if $(5W + 2H, 3W + H) = 1$, the assumption that $(W, H) = d$ where $d > 1$ is untenable. Now let $(5W + 2H, 3W + H) = 1$, and assume that there exists an integer d, such that $d\,|\,W$ and $d\,|\,H$, and $d > 1$. If $d\,|\,W$ and $d\,|\,H$, then $d\,|\,pW$ and $d\,|\,qH$ for any integers p and q; and also $d\,|\,pW + qH$. Hence if $d\,|\,W$ and $d\,|\,H$, then $d\,|\,5W + 2H$ and $d\,|\,3W + H$, contradicting the hypothesis that $(5W + 2H, 3W + H) = 1$.

To demonstrate the sufficiency of the condition, we show that if $(W, H) = 1$, the assumption that there exists an integer $d\,(d > 1)$ such that $d\,|\,5W + 2H$ and $d\,|\,3W + H$ is untenable. For if $d\,|\,5W + 2H$ and $d\,|\,3W + H$, then also $d\,|\,[2(3W + H) - (5W + 2H)]$, or $d\,|\,W$. But if $d\,|\,W$, then also $d\,|\,3W$; and since $d\,|\,3W + H$, we have also $d\,|\,H$, contradicting the hypothesis that $(W, H) = 1$, and hence the number d cannot exist.

A statement of this result in combination with the equal tuning theorem forms the larger part of the circle of fifths theorem—the most fundamentally important principle linking recognizable diatonic tunings and equal tunings.

THEOREM 40.   *Let there be a diatonic scale in which* $R = \dfrac{W}{H}$, *W and H are integers,* $0 < H < W$, *and* $(W, H) = 1$. *Under these conditions, this recognizable diatonic scale is actually part of an equal tuning of* $5W + 2H$ *notes, containing* $5W + 2H$ *distinct diatonic scales, each having the same tuning save for differences in register. The size of the perfect fifth is* $\dfrac{3W + H}{5W + 2H}$ *a, and* $5W + 2H$ *of these fifths form a closed circle. It is also true that* $\mathrm{int}\,(5W + 2H)$ *vanishes.* This follows directly from Theorems 38 and 39 if we set $m = 5W + 2H$ and $n = 3W + H$.

Example: If $R = 2$, we have $W = 2$ and $H = 1$; this recognizable diatonic scale is actually part of an equal tuning of $(5)(2) + (2)(1) = 12$ notes, containing twelve distinct diatonic scales, each having the same tuning save for differences in register. The size of the perfect fifth is $\dfrac{(3)(2) + 1}{(5)(2) + (2)(1)}\,a = \frac{7}{12}a$, and twelve of these fifths form a closed circle. In addition, $\mathrm{int}\,(12)$ vanishes.

Of course, this is thoroughly familiar to trained musicians. But it is not generally appreciated that the tuning where $R = 2$ is only one particular case of a general family of tunings; nor is it usually realized that other particular cases may be part of an equal tuning where the number of notes is greater than 12, but not a multiple of 12. In Section 8 of this chapter, we shall make a detailed investigation of the diatonic tunings in which $R = \frac{3}{2}$ and $R = 3$.

The size of intervals and the position of notes within the equal tuning may be found by the methods of the preceding section if we set $m = 5W + 2H$ and $n = 3W + H$. However, the same may be done directly in terms of W and H, and this method is easier to remember and apply in practical situations. To find the size of an interval in terms of W and H, we first determine the connection between w and W, and between h and H, referred to earlier in this section, and we begin by recalling the definations of w and h (Ch. X, Sec. 3):

$$w = 2v - a$$

$$h = 3a - 5v$$

We next set $v = \dfrac{3W + H}{5W + 2H}\, a$ in these expressions to obtain

$$w = \frac{2(3W + H)}{5W + 2H}\, a - a$$

$$= \frac{2(3W + H) - (5W + 2H)}{5W + 2H}\, a$$

$$= \frac{W}{5W + 2H}\, a$$

$$h = 3a - \frac{5(3W + H)}{5W + 2H}\, a$$

$$= \frac{3(5W + 2H) - 5(3W + H)}{5W + 2H}\, a$$

$$= \frac{H}{5W + 2H}\, a$$

If we rearrange these expressions for w and h to read

$$w = W\left(\frac{a}{5W + 2H}\right)$$

$$h = H\left(\frac{a}{5W + 2H}\right)$$

it is immediately apparent that for any p or q,

$$pw + qh = (pW + qH)\left(\frac{a}{5W + 2H}\right)$$

By this formula, the size of any interval may be written down immediately in terms of W and H if the interval is first expressed in terms of the major second and minor second. In Chapter X, Sec. 3, we showed how to express an interval as $pw + qh$ from either the interval's name, or its expression as int (i). This material is collected together in Table 75.

Examples: If $R = 2$, how large is a major third? A major third is equal to $2w = \dfrac{2W}{5W + 2H}\,a$. Setting $W = 2$, $H = 1$, and $a = 1200$, the result is $(\frac{4}{12})(1200) = 400$ cents. How large is a diminished seventh? A diminished seventh is equal to $3w + 3h = \dfrac{3W + 3H}{5W + 2H}\,a = (\frac{9}{12})(1200) = 900$ cents. How large is a major sixth? A major sixth is equal to $4w + h = \dfrac{4W + H}{5W + 2H}\,a = (\frac{9}{12})(1200) = 900$ cents.

The ratio of the interval $pw + qh$ may also be expressed directly in terms of W and H. Since its size is $\dfrac{pW + qH}{5W + 2H}\,a$, it follows that the ratio is $2\exp\dfrac{pW + qH}{5W + 2H}$ (Theorem 4; Ch. I, Sec. 5).[3]

To assign the notes C, D, E, F, G, A, and B to their proper positions within the equal tuning, and to express these numbers in terms of W and H, we recall that the distances of each of the above notes from C are as given in Table 77 (Ch. X, Sec. 5). If we replace $pw + qh$ in these expressions

[3] See Ch. X, note 9.

by $(pW + qH)\left(\dfrac{a}{5W + 2H}\right)$, we have the following number correspondences, if it is understood that in each case, $pW + qH$ is the coefficient of
$\dfrac{a}{5W + 2H}$:

note	C	D	E	F	G	A	B
number	0	W	$2W$	$2W + H$	$3W + H$	$4W + H$	$5W + H$

FIGURE 21

We next observe that the size of every adjacent interval within the equal
tuning is $\dfrac{a}{5W + 2H}$. Therefore the coefficient of $\dfrac{a}{5W + 2H}$, which is the
integer $pW + qH$, gives the number of these adjacent intervals between
C and the note associated with the number $pW + qH$. This is the same
as saying that the number $pW + qH$ gives the position of the note within
the equal tuning relative to C; so that if C is in position 0, then D is in
position W, E is in position $2W$, F is in position $2W + H$, G is in position
$3W + H$, A is in position $4W + H$, and B is in position $5W + H$. Thus
the number of adjacent intervals separating the successive notes of a diatonic scale will make the sequence W, W, H, W, W, W, H. This visualization is often helpful in practical situations.

Example: If $R = 2$ so that $W = 2$ and $H = 1$, then the notes are in the
following positions of the 12-note equal tuning:

position	0	2	4	5	7	9	11
notes	C	D	E	F	G	A	B

The tuning may be somewhat more conveniently visualized by the following diagram:

positions	0	1	2	3	4	5	6	7	8	9	10	11	12
notes	·	·	·	·	·	·	·	·	·	·	·	·	·
names	C		D		E	F		G		A		B	C

It will be observed that the number of positions separating the successive
notes of the above scale make the sequence 2, 2, 1, 2, 2, 2, 1.

The effect of a sharp or a flat follows from the fact that a sharp raises
a note by $w - h$, and a flat lowers a note by the same amount (Ch. X,
Sec. 3). Since $w - h = (W - H)\left(\dfrac{a}{5W + 2H}\right)$, this means that a sharp raises

a note and a flat lowers a note by $W - H$ of the adjacent intervals within the equal tuning. In other words, a sharp moves a note $W - H$ positions to the right, and a flat moves a note $W - H$ positions to the left. Hence if note x is in position $pW + qH$, then x sharp is in position $pW + qH + (W - H)$, and x flat is in position $pW + qH - (W - H)$.

The foregoing principles may be considered as part of the circle of fifths theorem, which may now be supplemented as follows:

If $R = \dfrac{W}{H}$, $0 < H < W$, and $(W, H) = 1$, then the notes are in the following positions of the resulting equal tuning of $5W + 2H$ notes:

notes	C	D	E	F	G	A	B
positions	0	W	$2W$	$2W + H$	$3W + H$	$4W + H$	$5W + H$

In addition, each sharp adds $W - H$, and each flat subtracts $W - H$.

Example: If $R = 2$ so that $W = 2$ and $H = 1$, then $W - H = 1$; hence a sharp moves a note to the right by one position ($\frac{1}{12}a$), and a flat moves a note to the left by one position. Thus the sharps are placed as follows:

positions	0	1	2	3	4	5	6	7	8	9	10	11	12
notes	·	·	·	·	·	·	·	·	·	·	·	·	·
names	B♯	C♯		D♯		E♯	F♯		G♯		A♯		B♯

In the case of the flats, we have

positions	0	1	2	3	4	5	6	7	8	9	10	11	12
notes	·	·	·	·	·	·	·	·	·	·	·	·	·
names		D♭		E♭	F♭		G♭		A♭		B♭	C♭	

The three diagrams showing positions, notes, and names, produce the following combination:

positions	0	1	2	3	4	5	6	7	8	9	10	11	12
notes	·	·	·	·	·	·	·	·	·	·	·	·	·
names	C	C♯	D	D♯	E	F	F♯	G	G♯	A	A♯	B	C
	B♯	D♭		E♭	F♭	E♯	G♭		A♭		B♭	C♭	B♯

FIGURE 22

We thus arrive theoretically at the arrangement of notes that every musician is obliged to commit to memory, but usually without a true understanding of the general principles behind it.

6. Diatonic and chromatic intervals in 12-note equal tuning. We may readily compare the diatonic scales contained by 12-note equal tuning ($R = 2$) with meantone tuning ($R = 1.649393$), Silbermann's tuning ($R = 1.819204$), and Pythagorean tuning ($R = 2.260017$), making use of the nearly linear relation between R and v within the acceptable range (Ch. X, Sec. 4). It is thus immediately apparent that the tuning where $R = 2$ is close to the upper limit of the range of acceptability ($1.5 \leqslant R \leqslant 2.2$), and hence has more nearly the character of Pythagorean tuning than meantone tuning. In addition, 2 is very nearly the mean between the values for R in Silbermann's tuning and Pythagorean tuning, and so the tuning where $R = 2$ may be expected to exhibit characteristics roughly midway between these two tunings.

More specifically, the perfect fifth of 700 cents is nearly pure, being too small by only 1.955 cents (a pure fifth contains 701.955 cents). Its ratio is $2 \exp \frac{7}{12} = 1.498307$ (Ch. X, Sec. 5), and the beat frequency produced by middle CG is $264[(2)(1.498307) - 3] = -.894$ per second (Ch. I, Sec. 3). This slow beat is virtually undetectable on the piano owing to the relatively rapid decay in intensity after the strings are struck. On the organ, the same fifth produces a slow wavering effect which is distinctly noticeable when the interval is sustained. If the sound comes from spread-out sources, such as two sections of violins, the slight impurity cannot be heard at all. In practical situations, the fifths of 12-note equal tuning are not disturbing, although it must be conceded that the slow beat, if audible, does not contribute anything desirable from a subjective musical standpoint.

The major third is somewhat more troublesome. This interval of 400 cents departs from the pure value (386.314 cents) by 13.686 cents; its ratio is $2 \exp \frac{4}{12} = \sqrt[3]{2} = 1.259921$, and the beat frequency produced by middle CE is $264[(4)(1.259921) - 5] = 10.477$ per second. This rapid beat, if audible, imparts a shivering quality to the third that is distinctly unmusical, even if less so than what is associated with Pythagorean major thirds (Ch. III, Sec. 7).

Much the same is true in the case of the major sixth. This interval contains 900 cents—larger than the pure version (ratio $\frac{5}{3}$, size 884.359 cents) by 15.641 cents. Its ratio is $2 \exp \frac{9}{12} = \sqrt[4]{8} = 1.681793$, and middle CA beats at $264[(3)(1.681793) - 5] = 11.980$ per second.

In the case of the triads, the impure thirds and sixths have a substantial effect on the tone, no matter what the instrumental medium. Even in situations where the distribution and timbre mask the beats entirely, a 12-note equal major triad is noticeably more shrill than the meantone version, and

TABLE 82

	perfect fifth		major third		major sixth	
	size in cents	beats per second middle CG	size in cents	beats per second middle CE	size in cents	beats per second middle CA
meantone $R = 1.649393$	696.578	−2.456	386.314	0.000	889.735	4.106
Silbermann $R = 1.819204$	698.371	−1.638	393.482	5.477	895.112	8.224
12-note equal $R = 2.000000$	700.000	−.894	400.000	10.477	900.000	11.980
Pythagorean $R = 2.260017$	701.955	0.000	407.820	16.500	905.865	16.500

the same is only a little less true of a minor triad. Fortunately both major and minor triads are far better than the discordant Pythagorean triads.

Table 82 compares data associated with the perfect fifth, major third, and major sixth in the four tunings thus far analyzed in detail. It is a useful coincidence that the values for R make nearly an arithmetic progression if we take the rounder numbers 1.6, 1.8, 2.0, and 2.2. We also observe that the perfect fifth gains an average of 1.8 cents with each successive increase in R; in the case of the major third, the average increase is 7.2 cents, and for the major sixth, 5.4 cents. This serves to illustrate the nearly linear relation between R and v, and shows how a given increase in int (1) (a perfect fifth) brings about a threefold increase in int (3) (a major sixth), and a fourfold increase in int (4) (a major third), as described in Chapter X, Sec. 1.

The major scale where $R = 2$ is perfectly acceptable, and many contemporary musicians prefer its rather small minor second (100 cents—larger than a Pythagorean limma by only 9.775 cents) to the larger version of meantone tuning (117.108 cents).

Obviously a major second is twice the size of a minor second only when $R = 2$, and hence the terms "whole step" and "half step" for these intervals are correct in the strictest sense only in 12-note equal tuning. It is also true that the term "chromatic semitone" for $w - h$ also implies $R = 2$, for then we have $w - h = \frac{1}{2}w$, $2w - 2h = w$, and $w = 2h$.

The 12-note equal chromatic scale has a special character, for unlike the other temperaments, it is simply the 12-note equal division itself; in other words, a chromatic semitone ($w - h$) is the same size as a minor sec-

TABLE 83

ENHARMONIC EQUIVALENTS IN 12-NOTE EQUAL TUNING

expressed as int (i)	in terms of w and h	names
int (11) = int (−1)	$3w - h = 2w + h$	augmented third and perfect fourth
int (10) = int (−2)	$5w = 4w + 2h$	augmented sixth and minor seventh
int (9) = int (−3)	$2w - h = w + h$	augmented second and minor third
int (8) = int (−4)	$4w = 3w + 2h$	augmented fifth and minor sixth
int (7) = int (−5)	$w - h = h$	chromatic semitone and minor second
int (6) = int (−6)	$3w = 2w + 2h$	augmented fourth and diminished fifth
int (5) = int (−7)	$5w + h = 4w + 3h$	major seventh and diminished octave
int (4) = int (−8)	$2w = w + 2h$	major third and diminished fourth
int (3) = int (−9)	$4w + h = 3w + 3h$	major sixth and diminished seventh
int (2) = int (−10)	$w = 2h$	major second and diminished third
int (1) = int (−11)	$3w + h = 2w + 3h$	perfect fifth and diminished sixth

ond (h). This is a direct consequence of the fact that $R = \dfrac{w}{h} = 2$, for then we have $w = 2h$, and $w - h = h$. Such intervals are said to be *enharmonically equivalent*.

We may systematically discover other enharmonic equivalents within 12-note equal tuning. Since int (12) vanishes in this tuning (Sec. 5 of this chapter), we have int (i) − int ($i - 12$) = int (12) = 0 (Ch. II, Sec. 3), and hence int (i) = int ($i - 12$). Other enharmonic equivalents are found by assigning all integral values from 1 through 11 to i in this last equation. The names of intervals (−11) through (11) will be found in Table 75 (Ch. X, Sec. 3).

Example: We have int (10) = int (−2); hence an augmented sixth and a minor seventh are enharmonic equivalents. Table 75 also gives expressions in terms of w and h for intervals (−11) through (11); in the present case, we have $5w = 4w + 2h$, and from this, we have at once $w = 2h$, and $\dfrac{w}{h} = R = 2$.

Table 83 lists the common enharmonic equivalents found in 12-note equal tuning. In every case, the linear equations in terms of w and h reduce directly to $\dfrac{w}{h} = 2$, showing that these intervals are equivalent only in the tuning where $R = 2$.

Practicing musicians hardly need Table 83, for they have committed the results to memory early in their training. However, the techniques illustrated will be useful in discovering the unfamiliar enharmonic equivalents associated with the tunings in which R is a rational number different from 2.

Since every chromatic interval ($i \geqslant 7$, $i \leqslant -7$) is equivalent to a diatonic interval ($-6 \leqslant i \leqslant 6$) when $R = 2$, the chromatic intervals are not excessively discordant, and may be used satisfactorily in a wide variety of situations. This is quite different from meantone tuning, where the augmented fifth, augmented second, and augmented third, along with their inversions, are so discordant as to have only very limited use. On the other hand, the meantone augmented sixth is perhaps a bit too smooth, given the conventional treatment of this interval as a dissonance (Ch. IX, Sec. 2).

As we have seen, the diatonic intervals of 12-note equal tuning are very close to the Pythagorean versions. It is significant that polyphonic music written during the Pythagorean period (roughly 1200–1400) does not use chromatic intervals as simultaneous combinations, nor do extended chromatic scales occur in individual parts; hence music written in this idiom is hardly compromised in any perceptible way when played in 12-note equal tuning. This is especially true if the sound is produced by spread-out sources, such as an unaccompanied chorus. The work of Machaut, analyzed earlier with respect to just tuning (Ch. VII, Sec. 1), is a case in point.

The appropriateness of 12-note equal tuning for music written during the meantone period (roughly 1550–1650) is rather more open to question. In this repertoire, the most frequently used harmonic units are triads, and as we have noted, these are noticeably more discordant in 12-note equal tuning. But scale passages in individual parts are common in both instrumental and choral works, and this raises the question of one's preference for the larger minor second of meantone tuning (117.108 cents) or the smaller one of 100 cents. In the author's opinion, the greater portion of the meantone repertoire, with its infrequent use of chromatic intervals and dominant seventh chords, is not unduly distorted when played in 12-note equal tuning, although the different expressive character of the two tunings is quite perceptible. If the di Lasso fragment (discussed earlier in Ch. VII, Sec. 2; Ch. IX, Sec. 6; and Ch. X, Sec. 6) is played slowly, first in 12-note equal tuning and then in meantone tuning, the more consonant meantone triads contrast quite noticeably with their 12-note counterparts.

If the example is played more rapidly, the difference in character between the scales becomes more significant, and that between the triads less so.

The difference between the two tunings is much more noticeable in the case of the small but important chromatic meantone repertoire. We have already touched upon this subject during the discussion of meantone tuning (Ch. IX, Sec. 6) and Silbermann's tuning (Ch. X, Sec. 6). It should be noted here that the dissonances that occur in meantone compositions are hardly any rougher than the triads when both are played in 12-note equal tuning. This feature of the tuning, along with its equal chromatic scale, imparts to chromatic compositions a uniformity of sound that is not disagreeable, although very sensibly different from the pleasantly sharp contrasts associated with meantone tuning. If Silbermann's tuning is less suited to chromatic meantone compositions than meantone tuning itself, then so much the more is true of 12-note equal tuning.

Clearly keyboard compositions making free use of harmonies that are wolves in meantone tuning are better suited to 12-note equal tuning. In the case of the extensive keyboard literature written during the first half of the eighteenth century, there is a choice to be made between 12-note equal tuning and mixed tunings such as Werckmeister's (Ch. IX, Sec. 7). These latter tunings have the practical advantage of being relatively easy to set up by ear. But Werckmeister's tuning, as we have seen, does not give a satisfactory tuning for D♭ major, and is not suited to styles making frequent use of the more remote triads. In the case of ensemble music combining stringed instruments with a keyboard instrument, 12-note equal is the recommended tuning, owing to the impracticality of making distinctions between tempered and pure fifths on both fretted and unfretted stringed instruments. Mixed tunings are not satisfactory on a modern piano, owing to that instrument's extreme sensitivity to impure fourths and fifths.[4]

For musical styles characterized by frequent modulations into remote keys, or containing a preponderance of dissonant harmonies, 12-note equal is the preferred temperament, because of its uniform tuning of all keys and relatively smooth versions of dissonant harmonies. The fragment of the Franck symphony, discussed earlier with reference to just tuning (Ch. VII, Sec. 4), is a representative example. Of the various harmonies on the seventeen quarters in this excerpt, eleven are dissonant and six are triads;

---

[4] See Ch. VIII, Sec. 1, where this is discussed with respect to meantone tuning.

in addition, there is a modulation from D minor into F♯ minor. Of course, the preference for 12-note equal tuning in this case has nothing whatever to do with the tone or practical limitations of keyboard instruments.

In sum, of all the tunings discussed in detail thus far, only 12-note equal may be satisfactorily—if imperfectly—applied to all polyphonic music written up to the present time. The other temperaments are limited to particular historical periods, and just tuning, as we have seen, is inappropriate for any of the existing repertoire (Ch. VII, Sec. 5).

7. Recommended procedure for putting a piano in 12-note equal tuning. Although it is possible to set up meantone tuning, Silbermann's tuning, and Werckmeister's tuning by counting beats on perfect fifths and fourths within the octave starting at middle C, this is not practical in the present case. In 12-note equal tuning, middle CG beats at under one per second (Table 82), and the rapid decay in tone makes it impossible to count the slow beats with sufficient accuracy. A better process involves counting beats from 4.9 per second to 7.3 per second produced by major thirds and major sixths whose pitches lie within the range

while using perfect fifths and fourths as checkpoints. Table 84 gives practical data for the intervals used to set up the tuning, based on both middle C = 264 Hz (A = 443.993 Hz), and middle C = 261.626 Hz (A = 440 Hz). The higher tuning is not advised, for the increased tension puts an undue strain on the plate and pin block. As can be seen, the differences in beat frequencies are insignificant, amounting to no more than $\frac{1}{10}$ beat per second. Beat frequencies are given within the register referred to above. It should also be noted that all the major thirds and major sixths are slightly larger than pure. Before starting, the two outer strings of each unison should be muted with a felt strip and the temperament then set, using the middle strings only. The unisons should be tuned next, then the higher and lower octaves should be set against pitches already tuned. The discussion that follows does not take into account either the accepted practice of tuning the top octave progressively sharp, or the possibility that harmonics producing the beats may be slightly out of tune, either by accident or by design.

First, using a fork or any other standard, set up major sixth CA so that its beat frequency is 5.9 per second. Next tune F against A, making

TABLE 84

BEATS IN 12-NOTE EQUAL TUNING

middle C = 264 A = 443.993		middle C = 261.626 A = 440	
interval	beats per second	interval	beats per second
BD♯	4.9	BD♯	4.9
CE	5.2	CE	5.2
D♭F	5.5	D♭F	5.5
BG♯	5.7	BG♯	5.6
DF♯	5.9	DF♯	5.8
CA	6.0	CA	5.9
E♭G	6.2	E♭G	6.2
D♭B♭	6.3	D♭B♭	6.3
EG♯	6.6	EG♯	6.5
FA	7.0	FA	6.9
F♯A♯	7.4	F♯A♯	7.3

FA beat at 6.9 per second, and then tune E against C, making CE beat at 5.2 per second. These subtle differences must be very accurately established by playing first CE, CA, and then FA, while listening for a slight increase in beat frequency. The first checkpoints are perfect fourths EA and CF; the impurity of these intervals should be virtually undetectable. Beginners tend to exaggerate the slight differences in beat frequencies, with the result that EA and CF are noticeably impure. If either fourth produces an audible beat, or takes on a nasal quality, the process should be started over.

Once, C, E, F, and A have been accurately tuned, set G♯ against E, making EG♯ beat at 6.5 per second. The progression of beat frequencies produced by CA, EG♯, FA should be virtually a uniform increase. Next tune B against G♯, making BG♯ beat at 5.6 per second. The progression of beat frequencies on CE, BG♯, CA should increase ever so slightly, and perfect fourth BE should now exhibit a barely detectable impurity. Next tune D♯ (E♭) against B, making BD♯ beat at 4.9 per second—slightly slower than CE. Perfect fourth D♯G♯ should be nearly pure and have the same quality as EA. Next tune G against E♭ (D♯), making E♭G beat at 6.2 per second, and check CA, E♭G, EG♯ for a uniform increase in beat frequencies.

At this point, a more critical test of the accuracy of the tuning should be made by trying perfect fifth CG. If there has been any tendency to exaggerate the tiny differences in beat frequencies produced by the thirds and sixths thus far used to establish the tuning, fifth CG will be noticeably too small. If this is the case, the source of the trouble may be tracked down by playing in succession BD♯, CE, BG♯, CA, E♭G, EG♯, FA. None of these intervals should beat more slowly than the one just preceding, and FA should beat at well under twice the rate of BD♯.

Next tune D♭ (C♯) against F, establishing the correct beat frequency of 5.5 per second by listening to the progression CE, D♭F, BG♯. Perfect fifth C♯G♯ is a critical check that should be made at this point in conjunction with perfect fourth C♯F♯. Next tune B♭ against D♭, listening to CA, D♭B♭, EG♯, and making D♭B♭ beat at 6.3 per second. Critical checkpoints for B♭ are perfect fifth E♭B♭ and perfect fourth FB♭. Next tune F♯ against A♯ (B♭), making F♯A♯ beat at 7.3 per second and comparing it with FA. The critical test for F♯ is perfect fifth BF♯ in conjunction with perfect fourth C♯F♯. Finally, tune D against F♯, making DF♯ beat at 5.8 per second. The most critical checkpoints are now DG and DA, both of which should be practically free of any noticeable impurities.

In general, the most critical fourths and fifths are those which result from a relatively greater number of thirds and sixths, since the tuning of each third and sixth is one separate operation. The least critical are fourths BE, CF, C♯F♯, D♯G♯, EA, and FB♭, each resulting from only two operations. Next come fifths CG, C♯G♯, and DA, resulting from five operations, followed by fifths BF♯ and E♭B♭, resulting from eight operations. Most critical of all is fourth DG, resulting from eleven operations. From this, it may be seen that the degree of accuracy of the tuning is gradually revealed as more notes are tuned. After all twelve notes are set up, further refinements may be possible upon playing all the major thirds and sixths in order of increasing beat frequency (see Table 84), and making slight adjustments as needed. It is by no means easy to get the tuning within the required tolerance, and beginners should be prepared to endure some rather frustrating experiences, at least on the first few tries.

It is helpful at first to check the accuracy of the tuning with a frequency counter; but after some practice, this becomes unnecessary. Table 85 gives frequencies in the octave above and including middle C for the standard A = 440 Hz. Similar data for middle C = 264 Hz will be found in Table 94 (Ch. XII, Sec. 3).

TABLE 85

note	frequency	note	frequency
middle C	261.626	F♯	369.994
C♯	277.183	G	391.995
D	293.665	G♯	415.305
E♭	311.127	A	440.000
E	329.628	B♭	466.164
F	349.228	B	493.883

8. Application of the conventional musical notation to the diatonic tunings where $R = \frac{3}{2}$ and $R = 3$. We are now in a position to use the known properties of the conventional musical notation in conjunction with the circle of fifths theorem to analyze and describe those diatonic tunings where R is a rational number other than 2. The particular case where $R = \frac{3}{2}$ is of especial interest, since this value produces a tuning that is not only recognizable, but acceptable for styles in which harmonies are largely confined to triads—even if at the lowest permissible limit for R (Ch. X, Sec. 4). Before formally applying the circle of fifths theorem, it should be observed that much can be said about the tuning simply from the value 1.5 for R, without actually calculating the relevant numbers. Since the relation between R and v is very nearly linear within the acceptable range (Ch. X, Sec. 4), the fact that 1.5 is a smaller value for R than in meantone tuning (meantone $R = 1.649393$) means that the perfect fifth will be slightly smaller than the meantone fifth, and therefore will beat somewhat faster. The major third will also be smaller than in meantone tuning, and hence will be smaller than the pure value. In addition, the major second will be smaller and the minor second will be larger than the same intervals in meantone tuning; consequently the leading tone will seem very flat to an ear habituated to 12-note equal tuning.

We now apply the circle of fifths theorem, setting $W = 3$ and $H = 2$, and noting that $(3, 2) = 1$. Thus the diatonic tuning where $R = \frac{3}{2}$ is actually part of an equal tuning of $5W + 2H = (5)(3) + (2)(2) = 19$ notes, containing nineteen distinct diatonic scales, each having the same tuning save for differences in register. The size of the perfect fifth is $\dfrac{3W + H}{5W + 2H} \, a =$

$\dfrac{(3)(3)+2}{(5)(3)+(2)(2)} a = \tfrac{11}{19}a = 694.737$ cents, slightly smaller than the mean-

tone value (696.578 cents), as expected. Its ratio is $2 \exp \tfrac{11}{19} = 1.493759$, and middle CG beats at $264[(2)(1.493759) - 3] = -3.295$ per second (Ch. I, Sec. 3), as compared with -2.456 for the meantone version. A major

third ($2w$) contains $\dfrac{2W}{5W + 2H} a = \tfrac{6}{19}a = 378.947$ cents, compared with

the meantone (pure) value of 386.314 cents. Its ratio is $2 \exp \tfrac{6}{19} = 1.244693$, and middle CE beats at $264[(4)(1.244693) - 5] = -5.605$ per

second. A minor third ($w + h$) contains $\dfrac{W + H}{5W + 2H} a = \tfrac{5}{19}a = 315.789$

cents, and is very nearly pure, the pure interval containing 315.641 cents.[5] Its ratio is $2 \exp \tfrac{5}{19} = 1.200103$. The subjective character of a major triad where $R = \tfrac{3}{2}$ is only slightly less smooth than the meantone version, but considerably smoother than the 12-note equal version; but even when taken out of context, its third seems distinctly flat. In the case of the scale,

we find that the major second contains $\dfrac{W}{5W + 2H} a = \tfrac{3}{19}a = 189.474$ cents,

and the minor second contains $\dfrac{H}{5W + 2H} a = \tfrac{2}{19}a = 126.316$ cents—a

value that most contemporary musicians find rather uncomfortably large.[6]

We next use the number correspondences of Figure 21 (Sec. 5 of this chapter), setting $W = 3$ and $H = 2$; thus the notes C, D, E, F, G, A, and B occupy respectively, positions 0, 3, 6, 8, 11, 14, and 17 of the 19-note equal tuning. The tuning is best visualized in a manner analogous to that employed earlier where $R = 2$:

```
positions 0  1  2  3  4  5  6  7  8  9  10 11 12 13 14 15 16 17 18 19
notes     ·  ·  ·  ·  ·  ·  ·  ·  ·  ·  ·  ·  ·  ·  ·  ·  ·  ·  ·  ·
names     C        D        E     F        G        A        B  C
```

All that was determined previously regarding the relative sizes of the perfect fifth, major and minor thirds, and major and minor seconds, may be observed directly from the above representation.

The operation of the sharp and the flat follows from the number $W - H = 1$, i.e., a sharp moves a note one position to the right, and a flat moves a note one position to the left. The sharps are thus placed as follows:

---

[5] The tuning in which the minor third is pure has been described in Ch. X, Sec. 2. In this case, $R = 1.503722$. The two tunings should be carefully compared.

[6] More complete numerical data will be found in Table 92 (Ch. XII, Sec. 3).

positions	0	1	2	3	4	5	6	7	8	9	10	11	12	13	14	15	16	17	18	19
notes	·	·	·	·	·	·	·	·	·	·	·	·	·	·	·	·	·	·	·	·
names		C♯		D♯		E♯	F♯		G♯			A♯			B♯					

The flats are placed as follows:

positions	0	1	2	3	4	5	6	7	8	9	10	11	12	13	14	15	16	17	18	19
notes	·	·	·	·	·	·	·	·	·	·	·	·	·	·	·	·	·	·	·	·
names			D♭		E♭	F♭		G♭			A♭			B♭		C♭				

A combination of the three preceding diagrams assigns every note along the line of fifths from F♭ to B♯ to its proper position within the 19-note equal tuning, as shown below:

positions	0	1	2	3	4	5	6	7	8	9	10	11	12	13	14	15	16	17	18	19
notes	·	·	·	·	·	·	·	·	·	·	·	·	·	·	·	·	·	·	·	·
names	C	C♯	D♭	D	D♯	E♭	E	E♯	F	F♯	G♭	G	G♯	A♭	A	A♯	B♭	B	B♯	C
								F♭											C♭	

FIGURE 23

The reader should make a careful study of Figure 23, comparing it with the similar diagram associated with $R = 2$ (Figure 22; Sec. 5 of this chapter). In the author's experience, most trained musicians are quite surprised by this application of the conventional notation to 19-note equal tuning, partly because 12 and 19 seem to be different sorts of numbers (12 is composite and 19 is prime), and partly because of the combination of the familiar and the unfamiliar regarding the notation. We first observe that notes with different names that musicians are accustomed to regarding as the same (G♯ and A♭, for example) are distinct in this tuning. Moreover, we note that position 7 is occupied by both E♯ and F♭. By the circle of fifths theorem, int (19) vanishes, hence E♯F♭ should be a multiple of int (19). Now E♯ is note $5 + 7 = 12$, and F♭ is note $0 - 7 = -7$ (Sec. 4 of this chapter), and the interval between them is int $(12 + 7) =$ int (19) (Theorem 6; Ch. II, Sec. 3). This is another way of saying that E♯ ≡ F♭ (mod 19), and it will also be found that B♯ ≡ C♭ (mod 19).

More light may be thrown on these enharmonic intervals if we use the method of Section 4 of this chapter to locate E♯, F♭, B♯, and C♭ relative to C. We have $v = \frac{11}{19}a$, and hence when C is in position 0 of the resulting 19-note equal tuning, note i is in position j where $11(i - 1) \equiv j$ (mod 19), or $(-8)(i - 1) \equiv j$ (mod 19), $0 \leqslant j \leqslant 18$. We use the former version when $i - 1$ is positive and the latter version when $i - 1$ is negative.

Examples: E♯ is note 12, and hence occupies position j where $(11)(11) \equiv j$ (mod 19). When 121 is divided by 19, the remainder is 7, and this is

TABLE 86

ENHARMONIC EQUIVALENTS IN 19-NOTE EQUAL TUNING

expressed as int (i)	in terms of w and h	names
int (11) = int (-8)	$3w - h = w + 2h$	augmented third and diminished fourth
int (10) = int (-9)	$5w = 3w + 3h$	augmented sixth and diminished seventh
int (9) = int (-10)	$2w - h = 2h$	augmented second and diminished third
int (8) = int (-11)	$4w = 2w + 3h$	augmented fifth and diminished sixth

the position relative to C. F♭ is note -7, and occupies position j where $(-8)(-8) \equiv j \pmod{19}$. When 64 is divided by 19, the remainder is once again 7. In the case of B♯ (note $6 + 7 = 13$), we have $(11)(12) \equiv j \pmod{19}$, and $j = 18$; and for C♭ (note $1 - 7 = -6$), $(-8)(-7) \equiv j \pmod{19}$, and again $j = 18$.

We may discover intervals that are enharmonic equivalents by using the technique employed during the discussion of 12-note equal tuning (Sec. 6 of this chapter). In the present case, we have int (i) − int $(i - 19)$ = int $(19) = 0$, and hence int (i) = int $(i - 19)$.

Example: We have int (10) = int (-9), hence an augmented sixth and a diminished seventh are enharmonic equivalents—a different situation from what was found in 12-note equal tuning. The size of an augmented sixth or diminished seventh is $5w = 3w + 3h = \frac{15}{19}a = 947.368$ cents, a value nearly midway between the sizes of these two intervals when $R = 2$ (1000 and 900 cents, respectively).

Table 86 lists the 19-note enharmonic equivalents for int (i) where $-11 \leqslant i \leqslant 11$. In every case, the linear equations in terms of w and h reduce directly to $\dfrac{w}{h} = \dfrac{3}{2}$, showing that these intervals are equivalent only in the tuning where $R = \frac{3}{2}$. It is also of interest to note that the size of an augmented third or diminished fourth is $\frac{7}{19}a = 442.105$ cents— larger than a Pythagorean major third (407.820 cents) by 34.285 cents, and a tuning that seems exceedingly discordant, even for chromatic dissonant intervals.

Regarding the familiar aspects of the notation, all major keys are notated as usual, with the five major seconds equal to $\frac{3}{19}a$, and the two minor seconds equal to $\frac{2}{19}a$, the major and minor seconds being distributed w, w, h, w, w, w, h. This insures that the structural interconnections among diatonic intervals in any key will be the same as in Pythagorean tuning and meantone tuning (Theorems 25 and 26; Ch. X, Sec. 2).

Example: In the key of E♭ major, the notes of the scale are E♭, F, G, A♭, B♭, C, D, E♭ (formal means for obtaining this result may be found in Ch. IV, Sec. 6). According to Figure 23, these notes occupy positions 5, 8, 11, 13, 16, 19 ≡ 0, 3, 5; the positions separating these notes in this order are respectively, 3, 3, 2, 3, 3, 3, 2, corresponding to the usual distribution of major and minor seconds, and the same as in C major.

Example: In the key of D♯ major, the notes of the scale are D♯, E♯, F✗, G♯, A♯, B♯, C✗, D♯. Now F✗ and C✗ will be one position to the right of F♯ and C♯, respectively, viz., in positions 10 and 2. Also in positions 10 and 2 are G♭ and D♭, respectively, and it may be easily verified that F✗ ≡ G♭ (mod 19), and that C✗ ≡ D♭ (mod 19). The notes of the D♯ major scale are thus in positions 4, 7, 10, 12, 15, 18, 21 ≡ 2, 4; again the positions separating these notes in this order are 3, 3, 2, 3, 3, 3, 2.

Since the behavior of major scales and diatonic harmony is the same in both 19-note equal and meantone tuning, it follows that polyphonic compositions whose harmonies are largely triads may be played without undue distortion in both tunings. But 19-note equal triads are less consonant than meantone triads, and the large minor second of 19-note equal tuning causes scale passages to take on a special, expressive character that seems somewhat out of style, at least to the author's taste. It is highly doubtful that 19-note equal tuning is better suited to any portion of the diatonic repertoire than meantone tuning or 12-note equal tuning.

When $R = \frac{3}{2}$, the 12-note chromatic scale as defined in Chapter IX, Sec. 3, has a very peculiar character, since a minor second ($\frac{2}{19}a$) is exactly twice the size of a chromatic semitone ($\frac{1}{19}a$). When these two intervals differ to such an extent, their asymmetric succession in a chromatic scale produces an alien effect that makes 19-note equal tuning ill-suited to music in which chromatic scales occur frequently in individual parts. The fragments of works by Franck, Scheidt, and Hassler cited earlier (Ch. VII, Sec. 4, and Ch. IX, Sec. 6) are representative examples.

We may easily show that a minor second is twice a chromatic semitone only if $R = \frac{3}{2}$, for from $h = 2(w - h)$, we have at once $3h = 2w$, and

$$\frac{w}{h} = R = \frac{3}{2}.$$

By now, the reader should suspect that chromatic harmony in 19-note equal tuning involves special relations that cannot be expected to conform

TABLE 87

interval	size in cents	ratio
perfect fifth	705.882	1.503407
major third	423.529	1.277162
minor third	282.353	1.177147
major second	211.765	1.130116
minor second	70.588	1.041616

to established musical habits. This point will be amplified later (Ch. XII, Sec. 7).

It is interesting to apply the same analytical techniques to the diatonic tuning in which $R = 3$. It can be seen at once, however, since R is greater than the Pythagorean value (2.260017), that this tuning is recognizable but not acceptable, owing to its very large major thirds. Upon setting $W = 3$ and $H = 1$, we find the number of notes in the equal tuning to be $(5)(3) + (2)(1) = 17$. The size of the perfect fifth is $3w + h = \frac{10}{17}a$, the major third is $2w = \frac{6}{17}a$, the minor third is $w + h = \frac{4}{17}a$, the major second is $w = \frac{3}{17}a$, and the minor second is $h = \frac{1}{17}a$. Other figures are collected in Table 87.[7] Perfect fifth middle CG is more nearly pure than a meantone fifth and produces beats at $264 [(2)(1.503407) - 3] = 1.799$ per second, and the major third, as anticipated, is larger than Pythagorean. A major triad is discordant to virtually the same degree as the wolves of meantone tuning (Ch. IX, Sec. 4).

Using the circle of fifths theorem, setting $W = 3$ and $H = 1$, we find that notes C, D, E, F, G, A, and B are in positions 0, 3, 6, 7, 10, 13, and 16, respectively, of the 17-note equal tuning. Since $W - H = 2$, a sharp moves a note two positions to the right, and a flat moves a note two positions to the left. Placement of all notes from F♭ through B♯ on the line of fifths is shown below:

```
positions  0  1   2  3  4   5  6 7  8   9 10  11 12 13 14  15 16 17
notes      .  .   .  .  .   .  . .  .   . .   .  .  .  .   .  .  .
names     {C Db  C# D  Eb  D# E F  Gb F# G  Ab G# A  Bb  A# B  C
          { B#         Fb     E#                      Cb
```

The reader is invited to verify that B♯ ≡ D♭, D♯ ≡ F♭, E♯ ≡ G♭, and A♯ ≡ C♭, all (mod 17).

[7] More complete numerical data will be found in Table 96 (Ch. XII, Sec. 3).

TABLE 88

ENHARMONIC EQUIVALENTS IN 17-NOTE EQUAL TUNING

expressed as int (i)	in terms of w and h	names
int (11) = int (-6)	$3w - h = 2w + 2h$	augmented third and diminished fifth
int (10) = int (-7)	$5w = 4w + 3h$	augmented sixth and diminished octave
int (9) = int (-8)	$2w - h = w + 2h$	augmented second and diminished fourth
int (8) = int (-9)	$4w = 3w + 3h$	augmented fifth and diminished seventh
int (7) = int (-10)	$w - h = 2h$	chromatic semitone and diminished third
int (6) = int (-11)	$3w = 2w + 3h$	augmented fourth and diminished sixth

It will be found that the notes of all major scales are separated, each from the next, by the following number of positions: 3, 3, 1, 3, 3, 3, 1. The small minor second makes the leading tone seem very high, and subjectively the entire scale sounds out of tune, every note except the fourth degree being sharp (Ch. X, Sec. 1).

The chromatic scale is also very awkward, owing to the fact that the chromatic semitone is twice the size of the minor second. This relation holds only if $R = 3$, for then we have $w - h = 2h$, $w = 3h$, and $\dfrac{w}{h} = R = 3$.

In order to discover which intervals are enharmonic equivalents, we use the equation int (i) = int $(i - 17)$; the results are given in Table 88.

It is increasingly apparent that every different rational value for R generates a unique set of chromatic relations which are not evident to a musician habituated to thinking in terms of 12-note equal tuning.

Of especial interest is the different arrangement of two notes separated by twelve positions on the line of fifths when $R = \frac{3}{2}$ and $R = 3$, such as A♭ and G♯. In the former tuning, we note that the succession G, G♯, A♭, A is ascending; but in the latter tuning, the corresponding ascending arrangement is G, A♭, G♯, A. In Pythagorean tuning, the interval A♭G♯ is equal to $12v - 7a$, which is positive (Ch. IV, Sec. 5); but in meantone tuning, this quantity is negative (Ch. IX, Sec. 2). Clearly G, A♭, G♯, A is ascending if $12v - 7a > 0$, or $\frac{7}{12}a < v < \frac{3}{5}a$; and if $12v - 7a < 0$, or $\frac{4}{7}a < v < \frac{7}{12}a$, then the ascending arrangement is G, G♯, A♭, A. It is more convenient to express these conditions in terms of R, and we have

$$12v - 7a = 12(3w + h) - 7(5w + 2h)$$
$$= w - 2h$$

Hence G, A♭, G♯, A is ascending when $w - 2h > 0$, or when $R > 2$; and if $1 < R < 2$, the ascending arrangement is G, G♯, A♭, A. Only if $R = 2$ do A♭ and G♯ coincide, and the same holds for any pair of notes separated by twelve positions on the line of fifths.

9. Equal tunings that do not contain recognizable diatonic scales. In order for any array of notes to contain recognizable diatonic scales, it is both necessary and sufficient that the array should contain seven adjacent intervals that are the same size, and are perfect fifths within the range of recognizability (Ch. X, Sec. 2). Now any equal tuning that contains one interval of a particular size must contain as many of these intervals as notes in the tuning. Hence a necessary and sufficient condition for a given equal tuning to contain recognizable diatonic scales is that the equal tuning should contain at least one interval that is a perfect fifth within the range of recognizability $\frac{4}{7}a < v < \frac{3}{5}a$, or $685.714 < v < 720.000$ cents. As we have seen, the equal tunings of twelve, seventeen, and nineteen notes meet this condition. But we may easily show that there exist equal tunings of more than nineteen notes that do not contain recognizable diatonic scales.

Example: In 23-note equal tuning, $\frac{13}{23}a = 678.261$ cents which is too small, and $\frac{14}{23}a = 730.435$ cents which is too large. Hence 23-note equal tuning does not include a generating interval within the range of recognizability, and consequently contains no recognizable diatonic scales. The interesting question of which equal tunings contain recognizable diatonic scales and which do not is answered by the following theorem:

THEOREM 41.   *The equal tunings that contain recognizable diatonic scales are those of* 12, 17, 19, 22, 24, 26, 27, 29, 31, 32, 33, *and* 34 *notes, and all those of* 36 *or more notes.* We first take up the question of the tunings of 36 or more notes. The endpoints of the open inequalities defining the range of recognizability are $\frac{4}{7}a$ and $\frac{3}{5}a$; hence the width of the range is the interval formed by the endpoints, which is $\frac{3}{5}a - \frac{4}{7}a = \frac{1}{35}a$. Therefore any equal tuning containing an interval smaller than $\frac{1}{35}a$, i.e., any equal tuning of 36 or more notes, must also contain an interval lying between $\frac{4}{7}a$ and $\frac{3}{5}a$. Hence any equal tuning of 36 or more notes must contain recognizable diatonic scales. The rest of the theorem may be proved by applying the test described at the beginning of this section to all the equal tunings of fewer than 36 notes. However, there are other techniques which are applicable, and which aid in the musical understanding of the interrelated principles involved.

Since the number of notes in a diatonic scale is seven, it is obvious that no equal tuning of fewer than seven notes contains recognizable diatonic scales, and we have already seen that 7-note equal tuning itself is not a recognizable diatonic scale (Ch. X, Sec. 2). By the equal tuning theorem (Sec. 3 of this chapter), if a given equal tuning contains an interval equal to $\frac{4}{7}a$, the number of notes must be seven, or a multiple of seven. But if the smallest interval in the tuning is greater than $\frac{1}{35}a$, then the smallest interval greater than $\frac{4}{7}a$ is also greater than $\frac{3}{5}a$. This shows directly that if the number of notes in an equal tuning is divisible by 7 and less than 36, the equal tuning does not contain recognizable diatonic scales. Similarly if a given equal tuning contains an interval equal to $\frac{3}{5}a$, the number of notes must be a multiple of 5. But if the smallest interval in the tuning is greater than $\frac{1}{35}a$, then the greatest interval less than $\frac{3}{5}a$ is also less than $\frac{4}{7}a$. Hence an equal tuning of fewer than 36 notes where the number of notes is divisible by 5 does not contain recognizable diatonic scales. We have shown that the equal tunings of 5, 7, 10, 14, 15, 20, 21, 25, 28, 30, and 35 notes do not contain recognizable diatonic scales.

But the most powerful and easily applied test involves the number R. Since R is rational for any diatonic tuning that is part of an equal tuning (Theorem 32; Sec. 1 of this chapter), we may postulate the existence of the integers W and H where $R = \dfrac{W}{H}$. Now the range of recognizability expressed in terms of W and H is $0 < H < W$ (Sec. 5 of this chapter), and by the circle of fifths theorem, if $(W, H) = 1$, the number of notes generated will be $5W + 2H$. This suggests that if the number of notes in an equal tuning may be expressed as $5W + 2H$ where $0 < H < W$ and $(W, H) = 1$, then the equal tuning contains recognizable diatonic scales. The condition as stated is sufficient, but not necessary. For if we take particular values for W and H that meet the above conditions, and then multiply W and H by an integer K, so that $(KW, KH) = K$, the value of R is unchanged, since $R = \dfrac{KW}{KH} = \dfrac{W}{H}$, and the number of notes generated is again $5W + 2H$. But it is obviously true that if an equal tuning of $5W + 2H$ notes contains recognizable diatonic scales, so does a tuning of $K(5W + 2H)$ notes for any integer K. Hence if $R = \dfrac{KW}{KH}$ and $(W, H) = 1$, it is true that an equal tuning of $5KW + 2KH$ notes contains recognizable diatonic scales. The stipulation that K may take all positive integral values means that an equal tuning of any multiple of $5W + 2H$ notes contains recognizable diatonic scales. In other words, if R is any improper fraction, an equal tuning in which the number of notes is five times the numerator plus two times the denominator contains recognizable diatonic scales, whether or not the fraction defining R is in its lowest terms. Therefore a necessary and sufficient condition for a given equal tuning to contain recognizable diatonic scales is that the number of notes must be expressible as $5W + 2H$ where W and H are integers such that $0 < H < W$.

It is at once apparent from the condition $0 < H < W$ that the least possible values for W and H are $W = 2$ and $H = 1$. Under these conditions, $5W + 2H = 12$, and therefore no equal tuning of fewer than twelve notes contains recognizable diatonic scales. Other values of $5W + 2H$ for an integral R $(H = 1)$ are as follows:

$R = \dfrac{W}{H}$	number of notes $5W + 2H$
2	12
3	17
4	22
5	27
6	32

It is unnecessary to carry the investigation any further, since any value for W greater than 6 yields a number of notes greater than 36.

If R is an improper fraction whose denominator is 2, we have the following correspondences:

$R = \dfrac{W}{H}$	number of notes $5W + 2H$
$\frac{3}{2}$	19
$\frac{4}{2}$	24
$\frac{5}{2}$	29
$\frac{6}{2}$	34

Again any value for W greater than 6 yields a number of notes greater than 36. The only other values for W and H satisfying $0 < H < W$ and for which $5W + 2H < 36$ are the following:

$$R = \frac{W}{H} \qquad \begin{array}{c} \text{number of notes} \\ 5W + 2H \end{array}$$

$R = \dfrac{W}{H}$	number of notes $5W + 2H$
$\frac{4}{3}$	26
$\frac{5}{3}$	31
$\frac{5}{4}$	33

A combination of these results completes the proof of the theorem.

Sometimes the theorem may be more readily applied if stated in the following equivalent form:

THEOREM 42. *Equal tunings of at least* 12 *notes which do not contain recognizable diatonic scales are those of* 13, 14, 15, 16, 18, 20, 21, 23, 25, 28, 30, *and* 35 *notes.*

It is interesting to observe that the only numbers in this list that are not divisible by 5 or 7 are 13, 16, 18, and 23.

10. Behavior of the circle of fifths when R is a fraction not in its lowest terms. This follows directly from the properties of the congruence $kx \equiv a \pmod{m}$, $0 \leqslant a \leqslant m - 1$, where $(k, m) > 1$. Accordingly, we first investigate this general abstraction, and then apply it to the subject in question. This discussion supplements the one in Chapter III, Sec. 1.

THEOREM 43. *If $kx \equiv a \pmod{m}$, $0 \leqslant a \leqslant m - 1$, and $(k, m) = d$, then as x goes from 0 to $m - 1$, the residues are all the multiples of d that are less than m in some order, this order occurring d times.* Let $kx \equiv a \pmod{m}$, $0 \leqslant a \leqslant m - 1$, and assume that $(k, m) = d$; it follows then that $\left(\dfrac{k}{d}, \dfrac{m}{d} \right) = 1$.

We next define a number a_1 by the congruence $\dfrac{k}{d} x \equiv a_1 \left(\bmod \dfrac{m}{d} \right)$, where

$0 \leqslant a_1 \leqslant \dfrac{m}{d} - 1$. By definition, $\dfrac{\dfrac{k}{d} x - a_1}{\dfrac{m}{d}}$ is an integer, and this integer is

also equal to $\dfrac{kx - da_1}{m}$; hence $kx \equiv da_1 \pmod{m}$. Since $0 \leqslant a_1 \leqslant \dfrac{m}{d} - 1$,

we may write $0 \leqslant a_1 < \dfrac{m}{d}$, or $0 \leqslant da_1 < m$, and finally $0 \leqslant da_1 \leqslant m - 1$.

But by hypothesis, $kx \equiv a \pmod{m}$ and $0 \leqslant a \leqslant m - 1$; hence $a = da_1$.
Thus if $kx \equiv a \pmod{m}$, $0 \leqslant a \leqslant m - 1$, and $(k, m) = d$, then the least

residue for a given x is da_1 where $\dfrac{k}{d}x \equiv a_1\left(\bmod \dfrac{m}{d}\right)$, $0 \leqslant a_1 \leqslant \dfrac{m}{d} - 1$. In this last congruence, as x takes successively the integral values from 0 to $\dfrac{m}{d} - 1$, a total of $\dfrac{m}{d}$ numbers, the residues are the integers from 0 through $\dfrac{m}{d} - 1$ in some order, each integer occurring once (Theorem 11; Ch. III, Sec. 1). Now if x continues to increase in the same manner, the same order of residues will recur over and over. Hence if x assumes in succession all integral values from 0 to $m - 1$ (a total of m numbers), then the sequence of residues (a total of $\dfrac{m}{d}$ numbers) will occur exactly d times; and since $a = da_1$, the result follows.

Example: Let $6x \equiv a \pmod{15}$. Here $d = 3$, and so a_1 is defined by $2x \equiv a_1 \pmod{5}$. As x goes from 0 to 4, the least residues are as follows:

$$x = 0, 1, 2, 3, 4$$

$$a_1 = 0, 2, 4, 1, 3$$

Therefore if $6x \equiv a \pmod{15}$, and x goes from 0 to 14, the residues will be 0, 6, 12, 3, 9, this order occurring three times:

$$x = 0, 1, \ 2, \ 3, 4, 5, 6, \ 7, \ 8, 9, 10, 11, 12, 13, 14$$

$$a = 0, 6, 12, 3, 9, 0, 6, 12, 3, 9, \ 0, \ \ 6, \ 12, \ 3, \ \ 9$$

This may be verified in the usual manner by long division, viz., we divide $6x$ by 15, obtaining a quotient which is immaterial, and a remainder which is the least residue.

To apply these principles to a recognizable diatonic tuning where $\dfrac{W}{H}$ is not in its lowest terms, we use the method of Section 4 of this chapter, which places note i in position j of the m-note equal tuning where $n(i - 1) \equiv j \pmod{m}$, $n = 3W + H$, $m = 5W + 2H$, and j is the least residue. As we have already seen, if $(W, H) = 1$, then $(3W + H, 5W + 2H) = 1$, and conversely (Theorem 39; Sec. 5 of this chapter); hence if $(W, H) = d$, then $(3W + H, 5W + 2H) = d$, or $(n, m) = d$. It is now true that note i is in position j of the equal tuning of $5W + 2H$ notes where $n(i - 1) \equiv$

$j \pmod{m}$, $0 \leqslant j \leqslant m - 1$, and $(n, m) = d$. Now as i takes successive integral values, j will assume all values that are multiples of d and less than m. Hence the circle of fifths will include only those notes which are in positions that are multiples of d, a total of $\dfrac{m}{d}$ or $\dfrac{5W + 2H}{d}$ notes, and all multiples of $\mathrm{int}\left(\dfrac{5W + 2H}{d}\right)$ will vanish.

Example: Consider an equal tuning of <u>twenty-four notes</u>. Since $24 =$ $(5)(4) + (2)(2)$ and $0 < 2 < 4$, this tuning contains recognizable diatonic scales. But $(4, 2) = 2$; hence the circle of fifths containing C will include only $\frac{24}{2} = 12$ notes, all in positions within the 24-note equal tuning that are even numbers. It should be noted that in this familiar "quarter-tone" tuning, the notes that are in odd-numbered positions are not included among those that are named in the conventional manner. However, the notes in the odd-numbered positions, being higher than those in the even-numbered positions by $\frac{1}{24}a$, must also form a circle of twelve equal perfect fifths.

More generally, if $(W, H) = d$ so that the number of notes in the circle of fifths is $\dfrac{5W + 2H}{d}$, then there are d separate circles of fifths, and any two notes that are within one of the circles are in positions that are congruent $\pmod{d}$. However, only those notes which are in positions that are multiples of d will be named in the conventional manner. Thus an equal tuning of $5W + 2H$ notes $(0 < H < W)$ in which $(W, H) > 1$ is only partially amenable to the conventional notation, and requires the introduction of a new symbol which raises or lowers each note within the circle that includes C by one adjacent interval—that is $\dfrac{a}{5W + 2H}$.

Example: In the case of an equal tuning of <u>fifty-one notes</u>, we find that $51 = (5)(9) + (2)(3)$, so that $W = 9$, $H = 3$, and $(W, H) = 3$. Since $\dfrac{W}{H} = 3$, the diatonic scale contained by this equal tuning is exactly the same as the second example described in Section 8 of this chapter. However, in the case of fifty-one notes, there are three separate circles of fifths, each containing seventeen fifths. The one containing C generates notes that are in positions 0, 3, 6, 9, 12, 15, 18, 21, 24, 27, 30, 33, 36, 39, 42, 45, and 48. If all these notes are transposed up by $\frac{1}{51}a$, the resulting notes in positions 1, 4, 7, 10, 13, 16, 19, 22, 25, 28, 31, 34, 37, 40, 43, 46, and 49 may also be arranged to form a circle of seventeen perfect fifths, and the same is true for the notes in positions 2, 5, 8, 11, 14, 17, 20, 23, 26, 29, 32, 35, 38, 41, 44, 47, and 50. Finally we note that if $(W, H) = d$, then $\left(\dfrac{W}{d}, \dfrac{H}{d}\right) = 1$. By

the circle of fifths theorem, the perfect fifth is equal to $\dfrac{3\dfrac{W}{d} + \dfrac{H}{d}}{5\dfrac{W}{d} + 2\dfrac{H}{d}} a =$

$\dfrac{3W + H}{5W + 2H} a$. Therefore the size of the perfect fifth is $\dfrac{3W + H}{5W + 2H} a$, whether or

not $(W, H) = 1$. It also follows that $W = \dfrac{W}{5W + 2H} a$ and $h = \dfrac{H}{5W + 2H} a$,

so that the method of the circle of fifths theorem for locating C, D, E, F, G, A, and B within the equal tuning, and for determining the effect of the sharp and flat, is still valid when $(W, H) > 1$.

XII   The Diatonic Equal
Tunings

Introduction. The subject of this final chapter is the distribution and behavior of certain equal tunings that contain diatonic scales or approximations to just tuning. The discussion makes extensive use of the circle of fifths theorem (Theorem 40; Ch. IX, Sec. 5), with which the reader should be thoroughly familiar.

Section 1 shows how all the diatonic equal tunings may be regarded as temperaments, and Section 2 describes the behavior of the principal commas of just tuning (syntonic comma, Pythagorean comma, schisma, diaschisma, and diesis) within the various temperaments with respect to R. Before studying Section 2, the reader will find it helpful to review Chapter VI, Sec. 2. For reference, Section 3 gives more detailed numerical data for the tunings discussed in Section 1. Section 4 explores the distribution of acceptable diatonic scales within the equal tunings of more than 35 notes, and gives the preferred method for locating notes in the unrecognizable diatonic tunings—those for which $R \leqslant 1$. Section 5 shows how to find a series of equal tunings that are successively closer approximations to a given diatonic tuning where R is irrational, using Pythagorean tuning, meantone tuning, and Silbermann's tuning as examples. Section 6 explores the properties of certain equal tunings that contain approximations to just tuning, and shows that the principal defect of true just tuning is present in every case—sometimes in an exaggerated manner. The discussion is based to a great extent on the properties of true just tuning as set forth in Chapter V, Secs. 1–3, which the reader should review; Chapter V, Sec. 4 and Chapter VI, Secs. 1–4 are also helpful. Section 7 shows that certain progressions involving enharmonic equivalents may exist in only one particular diatonic equal tuning, and that others behave differently for every different value of R.

1. The diatonic equal tunings regarded as temperaments.   From now on, we refer to any equal tuning that contains recognizable diatonic scales as *a diatonic equal tuning.* The recognizable perfect fifth contained by any diatonic equal tuning may be expressed in terms of the first two basic intervals (octave and pure perfect fifth) in a most revealing and interesting way. To this end, we begin with the representation of the recognizable perfect fifth as a fractional part of an octave (Ch. XI, Sec. 1), and transform it as follows:[1]

$$v = \frac{n}{m}\, a$$

$$= \bar{v} - \bar{v} + \frac{n}{m}\, a$$

$$= \bar{v} - \left(\bar{v} - \frac{n}{m}\, a\right)$$

$$= \bar{v} - \frac{1}{m}\,(m\bar{v} - na)$$

This shows that the recognizable perfect fifth contained by any diatonic equal tuning departs from the pure version by the amount $-\frac{1}{m}(m\bar{v} - na)$.

Example: Let $R = 2$, so that $n = 7$ and $m = 12$ (Ch. XI, Sec. 5). The size of the perfect fifth is then $\bar{v} - \frac{1}{12}(12\bar{v} - 7a)$. As we have seen, the quantity $12\bar{v} - 7a$ is the Pythagorean comma $\bar{p}$, and is equal to 23.460 cents (Ch. IV, Sec. 5). This perfect fifth is thus less than the pure version (701.955 cents) by one twelfth of 23.460, or 1.955 cents, and contains 700.000 cents. Hence 12-note equal tuning, which contains the version of the diatonic scale where $R = 2$, is actually a temperament in the sense of Chapter VIII, Sec. 1, since the Pythagorean comma is distributed in twelve equal parts uniformly over the twelve fifths.

The expression $v = \bar{v} - \frac{1}{m}(m\bar{v} - na)$ extends the concept of temperament to all diatonic equal tunings since in every case, the quantity $m\bar{v} - na$ is distributed in m equal parts uniformly over the m perfect fifths. Thus in every diatonic equal tuning, the quantity $m\bar{v} - na$ plays a role analo-

---

[1] The reader will recall that v denotes any perfect fifth that generates a recognizable diatonic scale, and that $\bar{v}$ is reserved for the pure version, i.e., $\bar{v} = \log \frac{3}{2}$, and $\frac{4}{7}a < v < \frac{3}{5}a$. A similar distinction is made between t and $\bar{t}$, k and $\bar{k}$, p and $\bar{p}$, s and $\bar{s}$, and d and $\bar{d}$. See also Ch. I, Sec. 5; Ch. III, note 7; Ch. IV, note 5; and Ch. VI, note 2.

gous to that of the Pythagorean comma in the tuning where $R = 2$. We further note that if v is smaller than pure, $m\bar{v} - na$ is positive; and if v is larger than pure, $m\bar{v} - na$ is negative. Since an increase in v corresponds to an increase in R and vice versa throughout the range of recognizability (Ch. X, Sec. 4), this may be restated as follows: If R is a rational fraction greater than the Pythagorean value of 2.260017, then $m\bar{v} - na$ is negative; and if R is a rational fraction less than the Pythagorean value, then $m\bar{v} - na$ is positive.

Example: Let $R = \frac{3}{2}$, so that $n = 11$ and $m = 19$ (Ch. XI, Sec. 8). Since $\frac{3}{2}$ is less than 2.260017, we expect that $19\bar{v} - 11a$ will be positive, and this is the case, its value being 137.145 cents. Each tempered fifth will be smaller than pure by $\frac{1}{19}$ of this amount, or 7.218 cents, and is equal to $701.955 - 7.218 = 694.737$ cents, and this is the same as $\frac{11}{19}a$.

Example: Let $R = 3$, so that $n = 10$ and $m = 17$. In this case, R is greater than 2.260017, hence $m\bar{v} - na$ will be negative, its actual value being $17\bar{v} - 10a = -66.765$ cents. The perfect fifth thus exceeds the pure value by $\frac{1}{17}$ of this, or 3.927 cents, and is equal to 705.882 cents, or $\frac{10}{17}a$.

It is useful at this point to make a compilation of similar data for all the recognizable diatonic scales contained by the diatonic equal tunings of fewer than 36 notes; results are collected in Table 89. We have not included those equal tunings of 24 and 34 notes, since they contain only recognizable diatonic scales that are exact duplicates of the scales contained by equal tunings of 12 and 17 notes, respectively (Ch. XI, Sec. 10). The tunings are listed in order of increasing values for R and v.

Table 89 illustrates many of the principles associated with diatonic tunings. For example, since all the expressions for R are in their lowest terms, we should expect the same to be true for $\dfrac{n}{m}$ (Theorem 39; Ch. XI, Sec. 5), and this is the case. It may also be noted that $m\bar{v} - na$ is positive in all cases where $R \leqslant 2$, and negative where $R \geqslant 2.5$; furthermore, the amount of tempering is least where R is near the Pythagorean value of 2.260017. It should be observed that the equal tunings of 12 and 29 notes contain very close approximations to a pure fifth, the ratios being $2 \exp \frac{7}{12} = 1.498307$ and $2 \exp \frac{17}{29} = 1.501294$, respectively (Theorem 4; Ch. I, Sec. 5; see also Ch. X, note 9). Beat frequencies produced by middle CG are $264[(2)(1.498307) - 3] = -.893$ Hz and $264[(2)(1.501294) - 3] = .683$ Hz, respectively. We observe that the perfect fifth is only a little larger than $\frac{4}{7}a$ (685.714 cents) when $R = 1.25$, and only a little smaller than $\frac{3}{5}a$ (720 cents) when $R = 6$. We also note

TABLE 89

R	$\dfrac{W}{H}$	m	$\dfrac{n}{m}$	$m\bar{v} - na$	$-\dfrac{m\bar{v} - na}{m}$	perfect fifth	major third
1.250	$\frac{5}{4}$	33	$\frac{19}{33}$	364.515	−11.046	690.909	363.636
1.333	$\frac{4}{3}$	26	$\frac{15}{26}$	250.830	−9.647	692.308	369.231
1.500	$\frac{3}{2}$	19	$\frac{11}{19}$	137.145	−7.218	694.737	378.947
1.667	$\frac{5}{3}$	31	$\frac{18}{31}$	160.605	−5.181	696.774	387.097
2.000	$\frac{2}{1}$	12	$\frac{7}{12}$	23.460	−1.955	700.000	400.000
2.500	$\frac{5}{2}$	29	$\frac{17}{29}$	−43.305	1.493	703.448	413.793
3.000	$\frac{3}{1}$	17	$\frac{10}{17}$	−66.765	3.927	705.882	423.529
4.000	$\frac{4}{1}$	22	$\frac{13}{22}$	−156.990	7.136	709.091	436.364
5.000	$\frac{5}{1}$	27	$\frac{16}{27}$	−247.215	9.156	711.111	444.444
6.000	$\frac{6}{1}$	32	$\frac{19}{32}$	−337.440	10.545	712.500	450.000

that the largest perfect fifth ($\frac{19}{32}a$) exceeds the smallest ($\frac{19}{33}a$) by $\frac{19}{1056}a$, and that the largest major third ($\frac{12}{32}a$) exceeds the smallest ($\frac{10}{33}a$) by $\frac{19}{264}a$. This latter amount is exactly four times the former, again showing how a given increase in the perfect fifth results in a fourfold increase in the major third (Ch. X, Sec. 1; see also Ch. XI, Sec. 6).

If we recall that the value for R in meantone tuning is 1.649393 (Ch. X, Sec. 4)—a number only a little smaller than $\frac{5}{3}(= 1.666667)$—this will explain the close approximation to a pure major third contained by the equal tuning of 31 notes. The difference is only $387.097 - 386.314 = .783$ cents, and beats produced by middle CE are at $264[(4)(2 \exp \frac{10}{31}) - 5] = 264[(4)(1.250566) - 5] = .597$ per second. The 31-note equal perfect fifth is larger than a meantone fifth by only $696.774 - 696.578 = .196$ cents, and thus 31-note equal tuning is an extremely close approximation to extended meantone tuning. Consequently any work for which meantone tuning is appropriate may be played with virtually the identical effect in 31-note equal tuning, including the radical chromatic works of Gesualdo, Hassler, Frescobaldi, and Scheidt examined during the discussion of meantone tuning (Ch. IX, Sec. 6).

But perhaps most significant, among the ten different diatonic tunings contained by equal tunings of fewer than 36 notes, only three are within the acceptable range (Ch. X, Sec. 4)—those contained by the equal tunings

of 12, 19, and 31 notes. It begins to appear that equal tunings that contain acceptable diatonic scales are more sparsely distributed than might
have been hoped.

**2. Representation of certain of the commas of just tuning in the diatonic
equal tunings.** We first recall that the schisma, diaschisma, and diesis
have simple expressions in terms of the syntonic and Pythagorean commas, viz., (Ch. VI, Sec. 2)[2]

$$\text{schisma} \qquad s = p - k$$

$$\text{diaschisma} \quad k - s = 2k - p$$

$$\text{diesis} \qquad d = 3k - p$$

The behavior of k is given by the following:

THEOREM 44. *The syntonic comma vanishes in all recognizable diatonic
tunings.* This property follows directly from the statement—valid throughout the range of recognizability—"int (4) is a major third" (Ch. III, Sec.
6, and Theorem 25; Ch. X, Sec. 2); for then we have $4v - 2a = t$, and
$4v - 2a - t = k = 0$.

Examples: Let $R = \frac{3}{2}$; *then* $v = \frac{11}{19}a$, $t = \frac{6}{19}a$ (Ch. XI. Sec. 8), and

$$4v - 2a - t = \frac{(4)(11) - (2)(19) - 6}{19} a = \frac{44 - 38 - 6}{19} a = 0. \quad \text{Let} \quad R = 3;$$

then $v = \frac{10}{17}a$, $t = \frac{6}{17}a$, and $4v - 2a - t = \frac{(4)(10) - (2)(17) - 6}{17} a =$

$$\frac{40 - 34 - 6}{17} a = 0.$$

An especially important consequence of Theorem 44 is that the conventional notation and nomenclature of notes and intervals fail to reveal
the presence of the syntonic comma. This explains the phenomenon described in Chapter I, Sec. 7 (see also Ch. V, Secs. 2 and 3).

In the case of the other commas cited above, we have:

THEOREM 45. *If $R > 2$, the Pythagorean comma and schisma are equal
and ascending, while the diaschisma and diesis are equal to the other two
commas, but descending; if $R < 2$, the situation is reversed.* We first note
that $p = 12v - 7a = 12(3w + h) - 7(5w + 2h) = w - 2h$; and since $k = 0$

---

[2] See note 1, *supra*.

and $s = p - k$, we have also $s = w - 2h$. In addition, if $k = 0$ we have $d = 3k - p = -p = 2h - w$, and $k - s = -s = 2h - w$. Now if $R = \dfrac{w}{h} > 2$, then $w > 2h$, and $w - 2h > 0$; and if $R < 2$, then $w < 2h$ and $w - 2h < 0$.

Now recalling that if R is rational, i.e., if $R = \dfrac{W}{H}$ where W and H are integers, we have $w = \dfrac{W}{5W + 2H}\, a$ and $h = \dfrac{H}{5W + 2H}\, a$ (Ch. XI, Sec. 5), and so the Pythagorean comma and schisma are equal to $\dfrac{W - 2H}{5W + 2H}\, a$, while the diaschisma and diesis are equal to $\dfrac{2H - W}{5W + 2H}\, a$.

Examples: If $R = 3$ $(W = 3, H = 1)$, the Pythagorean comma and schisma are equal to $\frac{1}{17}a$, while the diaschisma and diesis are equal to $-\frac{1}{17}a$. If $R = \frac{3}{2}$ $(W = 3, H = 2)$, the former two commas are equal to $-\frac{1}{19}a$, and the latter two are equal to $\frac{1}{19}a$.

It is also instructive to illustrate Theorem 45 by using the expressions $p = 12v - 7a$, $s = 8v + t - 5a$, $k - s = 3a - 4v - 2t$, and $d = a - 3t$ (Ch. VI, Sec. 2).

Examples: Let $R = 3$, then

$$12v - 7a = \frac{(12)(10) - (7)(17)}{17}\, a = \frac{120 - 119}{17}\, a = \tfrac{1}{17}\, a$$

$$8v + t - 5a = \frac{(8)(10) + 6 - (5)(17)}{17}\, a = \frac{80 + 6 - 85}{17}\, a = \tfrac{1}{17} a$$

$$3a - 4v - 2t = \frac{(3)(17) - (4)(10) - (2)(6)}{17}\, a = \frac{51 - 40 - 12}{17}\, a = -\tfrac{1}{17} a$$

$$a - 3t = \frac{17 - (3)(6)}{17}\, a = \frac{17 - 18}{17}\, a = -\tfrac{1}{17} a$$

Let $R = \frac{3}{2}$, then

$$12v - 7a = \frac{(12)(11) - (7)(19)}{19}\, a = \frac{132 - 133}{19}\, a = -\tfrac{1}{19} a$$

$$8v + t - 5a = \frac{(8)(11) + 6 - (5)(19)}{19}\, a = \frac{88 + 6 - 95}{19}\, a = -\tfrac{1}{19} a$$

$$3a - 4v - 2t = \frac{(3)(19) - (4)(11) - (2)(6)}{19} a = \frac{57 - 44 - 12}{19} a = \tfrac{1}{19}a$$

$$a - 3t = \frac{19 - (3)(6)}{19}a = \frac{19 - 18}{19}a = \tfrac{1}{19}a$$

An important corollary is the following:

THEOREM 46. *The syntonic comma, Pythagorean comma, schisma, diaschisma, and diesis all vanish only in the diatonic tuning where $w = 2h$, i.e., in 12-note equal tuning.* This follows directly from Theorem 44 and 45.

Theorems 44, 45, and 46 throw further light on the question regarding the relative proximity of two notes separated by twelve positions on the line of fifths, such as A♭ and G♯ (see also Ch. IV, Secs. 4 and 5; Ch. VI, Sec. 2; Ch. IX, Sec. 2; and Ch. X, Sec. 6).

Other commas formed by the first three basic intervals may vanish in a particular recognizable diatonic tuning where R is different from 2. For example, consider the comma $a - 5\bar{v} + 6\bar{t} = 8.107$ cents, ratio $\frac{15625}{15552}$ (Ch. VI, Sec. 5). In 12-note equal tuning, this comma is equal to $\dfrac{12 - (5)(7) + (6)(4)}{12} a = \dfrac{12 - 35 + 24}{12} a = \tfrac{1}{12}a = 100$ cents—a greatly enlarged version. If it is to vanish, we must have $a - 5v + 6t = (5w + 2h) - 5(3w + h) + 6(2w) = 0$, or $2w - 3h = 0$, $2w = 3h$, and $\dfrac{w}{h} = R = \tfrac{3}{2}$. Since this relation is linear, the comma $a - 5v + 6t$ vanishes only in the diatonic tuning where $R = \tfrac{3}{2}$, i.e., in 19-note equal tuning. In a later discussion (Sec. 7 of this chapter), we shall show how this property generates a unique chromatic progression which connects two triads whose roots differ by a perfect fifth.

3. Numerical data pertaining to the diatonic equal tunings of fewer than 36 notes.

In this section, we collect together more comprehensive numerical data for the diatonic equal tunings containing relatively few notes. For each recognizable tuning, we show the placement of all notes along the line of fifths from F♭♭ to B𝄪 (35 notes in all) in their proper positions in the resulting equal tuning. The reader will find it a useful exercise to verify these diagrams, using either the circle of fifths theorem (Theorem 40; Ch. XI, Sec. 5) or the method of Chapter XI, Sec. 4.

TABLE 90

$$\frac{w}{h} = \frac{5}{4}, \text{ NUMBER OF NOTES} = 33$$

		notes			positions	cents up from C	ratio with C	frequency
♭♭	♭	♮	♯	✕				
		C			0	0.000	1.000000	264.000
			C♯		1	36.364	1.021227	269.604
				C✕	2	72.727	1.042904	275.327
D♭♭					3	109.091	1.065041	281.171
	D♭				4	145.455	1.087648	287.139
		D			5	181.818	1.110735	293.234
			D♯		6	218.182	1.134313	299.459
				D✕	7	254.545	1.158390	305.815
E♭♭					8	290.909	1.182979	312.306
	E♭				9	327.273	1.208089	318.936
		E			10	363.636	1.233733	325.706
			E♯		11	400.000	1.259921	332.619
F♭♭				E✕	12	436.364	1.286665	339.680
	F♭				13	472.727	1.313976	346.890
		F			14	509.091	1.341868	354.253
			F♯		15	545.455	1.370351	361.773
				F✕	16	581.818	1.399439	369.452
G♭♭					17	618.182	1.429144	377.294
	G♭				18	654.545	1.459480	385.303
		G			19	690.909	1.490460	393.481
			G♯		20	727.273	1.522097	401.834
				G✕	21	763.636	1.554406	410.363
A♭♭					22	800.000	1.587401	419.074
	A♭				23	836.364	1.621096	427.969
		A			24	872.727	1.655507	437.054
			A♯		25	909.091	1.690647	446.331
				A✕	26	945.455	1.726534	455.805
B♭♭					27	981.818	1.763183	465.480
	B♭				28	1018.182	1.800609	475.361
		B			29	1054.545	1.838830	485.451
			B♯		30	1090.909	1.877862	495.756
C♭♭				B✕	31	1127.273	1.917722	506.279
	C♭				32	1163.636	1.958429	517.025
		C			33	1200.000	2.000000	528.000

Frequencies are given with reference to a middle C of 264 Hz, which is the recommended standard for all theoretical work. If a different middle C is preferred, its frequency should be multiplied by all the numbers in the ratio columns.

TABLE 91

$$\frac{w}{h} = \frac{4}{3}, \text{ NUMBER OF NOTES} = 26$$

notes					positions	cents up from C	ratio with C	frequency
♭♭	♭	♮	♯	✗				
		C			0	0.000	1.000000	264.000
			C♯		1	46.154	1.027018	271.133
D♭♭				C✗	2	92.308	1.054766	278.458
	D♭				3	138.462	1.083264	285.982
		D			4	184.615	1.112531	293.708
			D♯		5	230.769	1.142590	301.644
E♭♭				D✗	6	276.923	1.173460	309.794
	E♭				7	323.077	1.205165	318.164
		E			8	369.231	1.237726	326.760
F♭♭			E♯		9	415.385	1.271167	335.588
	F♭			E✗	10	461.538	1.305512	344.655
		F			11	507.692	1.340784	353.967
			F♯		12	553.846	1.377009	363.530
G♭♭				F✗	13	600.000	1.414214	373.352
	G♭				14	646.154	1.452423	383.440
		G			15	692.308	1.491664	393.799
			G♯		16	738.462	1.531966	404.439
A♭♭				G✗	17	784.615	1.573357	415.366
	A♭				18	830.769	1.615866	426.589
		A			19	876.923	1.659524	438.114
			A♯		20	923.077	1.704361	449.951
B♭♭				A✗	21	969.231	1.750409	462.108
	B♭				22	1015.385	1.797702	474.593
		B			23	1061.538	1.846272	487.416
C♭♭			B♯		24	1107.692	1.896155	500.585
	C♭			B✗	25	1153.846	1.947385	514.110
		C			26	1200.000	2.000000	528.000

TABLE 92

$$\frac{w}{h} = \frac{3}{2}, \text{ NUMBER OF NOTES } = 19$$

notes					positions	cents up from C	ratio with C	frequency
♭♭	♭	♮	♯	✖				
		C		B✖	0	0.000	1.000000	264.000
D♭♭			C♯		1	63.158	1.037155	273.809
	D♭			C✖	2	126.316	1.075691	283.982
		D			3	189.474	1.115658	294.534
E♭♭			D♯		4	252.632	1.157110	305.477
	E♭			D✖	5	315.789	1.200103	316.827
F♭♭		E			6	378.947	1.244693	328.599
	F♭		E♯		7	442.105	1.290939	340.808
		F		E✖	8	505.263	1.338904	353.471
G♭♭			F♯		9	568.421	1.388651	366.604
	G♭			F✖	10	631.579	1.440247	380.225
		G			11	694.737	1.493759	394.352
A♭♭			G♯		12	757.895	1.549260	409.005
	A♭			G✖	13	821.053	1.606822	424.201
		A			14	884.211	1.666524	439.962
B♭♭			A♯		15	947.368	1.728444	456.309
	B♭			A✖	16	1010.526	1.792664	473.263
C♭♭		B			17	1073.684	1.859271	490.847
	C♭		B♯		18	1136.842	1.928352	509.085
		C		B✖	19	1200.000	2.000000	528.000

TABLE 93

$$\frac{w}{h} = \frac{5}{3}, \text{ NUMBER OF NOTES} = 31$$

		notes			positions	cents up from C	ratio with C	frequency
♭♭	♭	♮	♯	✕				
		C			0	0.000	1.000000	264.000
D♭♭				B✕	1	38.710	1.022611	269.969
			C♯		2	77.419	1.045734	276.074
	D♭				3	116.129	1.069380	282.316
				C✕	4	154.839	1.093560	288.700
		D			5	193.548	1.118287	295.228
E♭♭					6	232.258	1.143573	301.903
			D♯		7	270.968	1.169431	308.730
	E♭				8	309.677	1.195873	315.711
F♭♭				D✕	9	348.387	1.222914	322.849
		E			10	387.097	1.250566	330.149
	F♭				11	425.806	1.278843	337.614
			E♯		12	464.516	1.307759	345.248
		F			13	503.226	1.337329	353.055
G♭♭				E✕	14	541.935	1.367568	361.038
			F♯		15	580.645	1.398491	369.202
	G♭				16	619.355	1.430113	377.550
				F✕	17	658.065	1.462450	386.087
		G			18	696.774	1.495518	394.817
A♭♭					19	735.484	1.529334	403.744
			G♯		20	774.194	1.563914	412.873
	A♭				21	812.903	1.599276	422.209
				G✕	22	851.613	1.635438	431.756
		A			23	890.323	1.672418	441.518
B♭♭					24	929.032	1.710234	451.502
			A♯		25	967.742	1.748905	461.711
	B♭				26	1006.452	1.788450	472.151
C♭♭				A✕	27	1045.161	1.828889	482.827
		B			28	1083.871	1.870243	493.744
	C♭				29	1122.581	1.912532	504.908
			B♯		30	1161.290	1.955777	516.325
		C			31	1200.000	2.000000	528.000

TABLE 94

$$\frac{w}{h} = 2, \text{ NUMBER OF NOTES} = 12$$

notes					positions	cents up from C	ratio with C	frequency
bb	b	$\natural$	$\sharp$	✖				
Dbb		C	B$\sharp$		0	0.000	1.000000	264.000
	Db		C$\sharp$	B✖	1	100.000	1.059463	279.698
Ebb		D		C✖	2	200.000	1.122462	296.330
Fbb	Eb		D$\sharp$		3	300.000	1.189207	313.951
	Fb	E		D✖	4	400.000	1.259921	332.619
Gbb		F	E$\sharp$		5	500.000	1.334840	352.398
	Gb		F$\sharp$	E✖	6	600.000	1.414214	373.352
Abb		G		F✖	7	700.000	1.498307	395.553
	Ab		G$\sharp$		8	800.000	1.587401	419.074
Bbb		A		G✖	9	900.000	1.681793	443.993
Cbb	Bb		A$\sharp$		10	1000.000	1.781797	470.395
	Cb	B		A✖	11	1100.000	1.887749	498.366
Dbb		C	B$\sharp$		12	1200.000	2.000000	528.000

TABLE 95

$$\frac{w}{h} = \frac{5}{2}, \text{ NUMBER OF NOTES} = 29$$

bb	b	♮	#	✗	positions	cents up from C	ratio with C	frequency
		C			0	0.000	1.000000	264.000
			B#		1	41.379	1.024190	270.386
	Db				2	82.759	1.048964	276.927
			C#		3	124.138	1.074338	283.625
Ebb				B✗	4	165.517	1.100326	290.486
		D			5	206.897	1.126942	297.513
Fbb				C✗	6	248.276	1.154203	304.710
	Eb				7	289.655	1.182122	312.080
			D#		8	331.034	1.210717	319.629
	Fb				9	372.414	1.240004	327.361
		E			10	413.793	1.269999	335.280
Gbb				D✗	11	455.172	1.300720	343.390
		F			12	496.552	1.332184	351.697
			E#		13	537.931	1.364409	360.204
	Gb				14	579.310	1.397413	368.917
			F#		15	620.690	1.431216	377.841
Abb				E✗	16	662.069	1.465836	386.981
		G			17	703.448	1.501294	396.342
				F✗	18	744.828	1.537610	405.929
	Ab				19	786.207	1.574804	415.748
			G#		20	827.586	1.612898	425.805
Bbb					21	868.966	1.651913	436.105
		A			22	910.345	1.691872	446.654
Cbb				G✗	23	951.724	1.732798	457.459
	Bb				24	993.103	1.774714	468.524
			A#		25	1034.483	1.817643	479.858
	Cb				26	1075.862	1.861611	491.465
		B			27	1117.241	1.906643	503.354
Dbb				A✗	28	1158.621	1.952764	515.530
		C			29	1200.000	2.000000	528.000

TABLE 96

$$\frac{w}{h} = 3, \text{ NUMBER OF NOTES} = 17$$

| | | notes | | | | cents up | ratio | |
bb	b	♮	#	✗	positions	from C	with C	frequency
		C		A✗	0	0.000	1.000000	264.000
	Db		B#		1	70.588	1.041616	274.987
Ebb			C#		2	141.176	1.084964	286.430
Fbb		D		B✗	3	211.765	1.130116	298.351
	Eb			C✗	4	282.353	1.177147	310.767
	Fb		D#		5	352.941	1.226135	323.700
Gbb		E			6	423.529	1.277162	337.171
		F		D	7	494.118	1.330312	351.202
	Gb		E#		8	564.706	1.385674	365.818
Abb			F#		9	635.294	1.443341	381.042
		G		E✗	10	705.882	1.503407	396.899
	Ab			F✗	11	776.471	1.565972	413.417
Bbb			G#		12	847.059	1.631142	430.621
Cbb		A			13	917.647	1.699024	448.542
	Bb			G✗	14	988.235	1.769730	467.209
	Cb		A#		15	1058.824	1.843379	486.652
Dbb		B			16	1129.412	1.920093	506.905
		C		A✗	17	1200.000	2.000000	528.000

TABLE 97

$$\frac{w}{h} = 4, \text{ NUMBER OF NOTES} = 22$$

notes					positions	cents up from C	ratio with C	frequency
♭♭	♭	♮	♯	✗				
		C			0	0.000	1.000000	264.000
	D♭			A✗	1	54.545	1.032008	272.450
E♭♭			B♯		2	109.091	1.065041	281.171
F♭♭			C♯		3	163.636	1.099131	290.171
		D			4	218.182	1.134313	299.459
	E♭			B✗	5	272.727	1.170620	309.044
	F♭			C✗	6	327.273	1.208089	318.936
G♭♭			D♯		7	381.818	1.246758	329.144
		E			8	436.364	1.286665	339.680
		F			9	490.909	1.327849	350.552
	G♭			D✗	10	545.455	1.370351	361.773
A♭♭			E♯		11	600.000	1.414214	373.352
			F♯		12	654.545	1.459480	385.303
		G			13	709.091	1.506196	397.636
	A♭			E✗	14	763.636	1.554406	410.363
B♭♭				F✗	15	818.182	1.604160	423.498
C♭♭			G♯		16	872.727	1.655507	437.054
		A			17	927.273	1.708496	451.043
	B♭				18	981.818	1.763183	465.480
	C♭			G✗	19	1036.364	1.819619	480.379
D♭♭			A♯		20	1090.909	1.877862	495.756
		B			21	1145.455	1.937969	511.624
		C			22	1200.000	2.000000	528.000

Table 98

$$\frac{w}{h} = 5, \text{ NUMBER OF NOTES} = 27$$

notes					positions	cents up from C	ratio with C	frequency
♭♭	♭	♮	♯	✖				
		C			0	0.000	1.000000	264.000
	D♭				1	44.444	1.026004	270.865
E♭♭				A✖	2	88.889	1.052685	277.909
F♭♭			B♯		3	133.333	1.080060	285.136
			C♯		4	177.778	1.108146	292.551
		D			5	222.222	1.136963	300.158
	E♭				6	266.667	1.166529	307.964
	F♭			B✖	7	311.111	1.196864	315.972
G♭♭				C✖	8	355.556	1.227988	324.189
			D♯		9	400.000	1.259921	332.619
		E			10	444.444	1.292685.	341.269
		F			11	488.889	1.326300	350.143
	G♭				12	533.333	1.360790	359.249
A♭♭				D✖	13	577.778	1.396177	368.591
			E♯		14	622.222	1.432483	378.176
			F♯		15	666.667	1.469734	388.010
		G			16	711.111	1.507954	398.100
	A♭				17	755.556	1.547168	408.452
B♭♭				E✖	18	800.000	1.587401	419.074
C♭♭				F✖	19	844.444	1.628681	429.972
			G♯		20	888.889	1.671034	441.153
		A			21	933.333	1.714488	452.625.
	B♭				22	977.778	1.759072	464.395
	C♭				23	1022.222	1.804816	476.471
D♭♭				G✖	24	1066.667	1.851749	488.862
			A♯		25	1111.111	1.899903	501.574
		B			26	1155.556	1.949309	514.618
		C			27	1200.000	2.000000	528.000

TABLE 99

$$\frac{w}{h} = 6, \text{ NUMBER OF NOTES} = 32$$

notes								
♭♭	♭	♮	♯	✗	positions	cents up from C	ratio with C	frequency
		C			0	0.000	1.000000	264.000
	D♭				1	37.500	1.021897	269.781
E♭♭					2	75.000	1.044274	275.688
F♭♭				A✗	3	112.500	1.067140	281.725
			B♯		4	150.000	1.090508	287.894
			C♯		5	187.500	1.114387	294.198
		D			6	225.000	1.138789	300.640
	E♭				7	262.500	1.163725	307.223
	F♭				8	300.000	1.189207	313.951
G♭♭				B✗	9	337.500	1.215247	320.825
				C✗	10	375.000	1.241858	327.850
			D♯		11	412.500	1.269051	335.029
		E			12	450.000	1.296840	342.366
		F			13	487.500	1.325237	349.862
	G♭				14	525.000	1.354256	357.523
A♭♭					15	562.500	1.383910	365.352
				D✗	16	600.000	1.414214	373.352
			E♯		17	637.500	1.445181	381.528
			F♯		18	675.000	1.476826	389.882
		G			19	712.500	1.509164	398.419
	A♭				20	750.000	1.542211	407.144
B♭♭					21	787.500	1.575981	416.059
C♭♭				E✗	22	825.000	1.610490	425.169
				F✗	23	862.500	1.645755	434.479
			G♯		24	900.000	1.681793	443.993
		A			25	937.500	1.718619	453.715
	B♭				26	975.000	1.756252	463.651
	C♭				27	1012.500	1.794709	473.803
D♭♭					28	1050.000	1.834008	484.178
				G✗	29	1087.500	1.874168	494.780
			A♯		30	1125.000	1.915207	505.615
		B			31	1162.500	1.957144	516.686
		C			32	1200.000	2.000000	528.000

4. Distribution of various versions of recognizable and unrecognizable diatonic scales within the equal tunings. As we have seen, the only equal tunings of less than 36 notes that contain diatonic scales within the acceptable range (Ch. X, Sec. 4) are those of 12, 19, 24, and 31 notes. It is of considerable interest to examine equal tunings of more than 36 notes in order to determine which ones contain scales where $1.5 \leqslant R \leqslant 2.2$. Results are given in Table 100, the upper limit being arbitrarily selected at 75 notes.

An inspection of the values of R associated with each diatonic equal tuning reveals that only those tunings marked with one or two asterisks contain scales within the range $1.5 \leqslant R \leqslant 2.2$. If these results are combined with those of the previous section, we find that of all the equal tunings of 75 notes or less, only those of 12, 19, 24, 31, 36, 38, 43, 48, 50, 55, 57, 60, 62, 65, 67, 69, 72, and 74 notes contain diatonic scales that are acceptable as defined. Furthermore, some of these duplicate others—for $R = 2$, the number of notes is either 12, 24, 36, 48, 60, or 72; for $R = \frac{3}{2}$, the number of notes is either 19, 38, or 57; and for $R = \frac{5}{3}$, the number of notes is either 31 or 62 (Ch. XI, Secs. 9 and 10). Thus only ten different acceptable diatonic tunings are contained by equal tunings of 75 notes or less—those associated with 12, 19, 31, 43, 50, 55, 65, 67, 69, and 74 notes. These are identified by two asterisks in Table 100. As anticipated, the distribution of equal tunings containing acceptable diatonic scales among those having relatively few notes is rather sparse.

It may be noted that in many cases, a given equal tuning contains two different recognizable diatonic tunings. For example, in the case of 47 notes, we have $47 = (5)(7) + (2)(6)$, and $47 = (5)(9) + (2)(1)$; hence 47-note equal tuning contains two different recognizable diatonic tunings—one in which $R = \frac{7}{6}$, and another in which $R = 9$. If the condition for containing a recognizable diatonic scale is that the equal tuning should contain an interval between $\frac{4}{7}a$ and $\frac{3}{5}a$ (Ch. XI, Sec. 9), then the condition for containing two different recognizable diatonic scales is that the equal tuning should contain two such intervals. If we apply the line of reasoning used to prove Theorem 41 (Ch. XI, Sec. 9), it follows that any equal tuning of more than 70 notes must contain at least two different diatonic tunings. More generally, if an equal tuning contains more than $35n$ notes, it must contain at least n different tunings of recognizable diatonic scales. Hence as the number of notes in an equal tuning increases, the number of different tunings of recognizable diatonic scales contained by the equal tuning also increases, with a corresponding gradual and irregular increase in the frequency of distribution of acceptable diatonic scales.

If we take the acceptable limits for R to be $1.5 \leqslant R \leqslant 2.2$, and recall that when $R = \frac{3}{2}$, $v = \frac{11}{19}a$, and when $R = \frac{11}{5}$, $v = \frac{38}{65}a$ (Table 100), we see that the range of acceptability in terms of v is $\frac{11}{19}a \leqslant v \leqslant \frac{38}{65}a$. Now the extent of this range is $\frac{38}{65}a - \frac{11}{19}a = \frac{7}{1235}a = 6.802$ cents, and hence any equal tuning containing an interval smaller than 6.802 cents—any equal tuning of 177 or more notes—must contain at least one recognizable diatonic tuning that is also acceptable. If we investigate individual equal tunings of less than 177 notes, we find that the equal tuning having the largest number of notes that does not contain acceptable diatonic scales as defined is the one of 159 notes—if $v = \frac{92}{159}a$, then $R = \frac{25}{17} = 1.470588$; and if $v = \frac{93}{159}a$, then $R = \frac{27}{12} = 2.250000$.

We may now prove another interesting theorem, again using a technique similar to that used to prove Theorem 41:

THEOREM 47.   *Any diatonic equal tuning must contain at least one recognizable diatonic scale in which* $\frac{7}{6} \leqslant R \leqslant 9$. An inspection of Tables 89 (Sec. 1 of this chapter) and 100 shows that the theorem is true for all the diatonic equal tunings of 47 notes or less. In the case of 47 notes, if $R = \frac{7}{6}$, then $v = \frac{27}{47}a$; and if $R = 9$, then $v = \frac{28}{47}a$. Since an increase in v produces an increase in R throughout the range of recognizability (Ch. X, Sec. 4), it follows that if $\frac{27}{47}a \leqslant v \leqslant \frac{28}{47}a$, then $\frac{7}{6} \leqslant R \leqslant 9$. Now any equal tuning containing an interval smaller than $\frac{1}{47}a$, i.e., any equal tuning of more than 47 notes, must contain at least one interval lying between $\frac{27}{47}a$ and $\frac{28}{47}a$, generating at least one diatonic scale in which R lies between $\frac{7}{6}$ and 9, and this completes the proof.

If $R = \frac{7}{6}$, the chromatic semitone is $\frac{1}{47}a$; and if $R = 9$, the minor second is $\frac{1}{47}a$. In either case, the amount $\frac{1}{47}a = 25.532$ cents is sufficiently great that one can distinguish, say, C from C♯, or B from C. Hence every diatonic equal tuning contains at least one diatonic scale that is "recognizable" in the strictest psychological sense of the word, and the most discordant of all the diatonic equal tunings is the one of 47 notes. Of course, the actual threshold of recognizability in terms of R can only be determined by a carefully controlled experiment.[3]

Of great interest is the question of how readily a subject can learn to identify common chord progressions or melodies when played in one of

---

[3] The reader will find it useful to review Ch. X, Sec. 2 at this point.

TABLE 100

number of notes 5W + 2H	3W + H	W	H	$R = \dfrac{W}{H}$	perfect fifth $\dfrac{3W + H}{5W + 2H}a$	major third $\dfrac{2W}{5W + 2H}a$
*36	21	6	3	2.000	700.000	400.000
37	22	7	1	7.000	713.514	454.054
*38	22	6	4	1.500	694.737	378.947
39	23	7	2	3.500	707.692	430.769
40	23	6	5	1.200	690.000	360.000
41	24	7	3	2.333	702.439	409.756
42	25	8	1	8.000	714.286	457.143
**43	25	7	4	1.750	697.674	390.698
44	26	8	2	4.000	709.091	436.364
45	26	7	5	1.400	693.333	373.333
46	27	8	3	2.667	704.348	417.391
47	27	7	6	1.167	689.362	357.447
47	28	9	1	9.000	714.894	459.574
*48	28	8	4	2.000	700.000	400.000
49	29	9	2	4.500	710.204	440.816
**50	29	8	5	1.600	696.000	384.000
51	30	9	3	3.000	705.882	423.529
52	30	8	6	1.333	692.308	369.231
52	31	10	1	10.000	715.385	461.538
53	31	9	4	2.250	701.887	407.547
54	31	8	7	1.143	688.889	355.556
54	32	10	2	5.000	711.111	444.444
**55	32	9	5	1.800	698.182	392.727
56	33	10	3	3.333	707.143	428.571
*57	33	9	6	1.500	694.737	378.947
57	34	11	1	11.000	715.789	463.158
58	34	10	4	2.500	703.448	413.793
59	34	9	7	1.286	691.525	366.102
59	35	11	2	5.500	711.864	447.458
*60	35	10	5	2.000	700.000	400.000
61	35	9	8	1.125	688.525	354.098
61	36	11	3	3.667	708.197	432.787
*62	36	10	6	1.667	696.774	387.097
62	37	12	1	12.000	716.129	464.516
63	37	11	4	2.750	704.762	419.048
64	37	10	7	1.429	693.750	375.000
64	38	12	2	6.000	712.500	450.000
**65	38	11	5	2.200	701.538	406.154
66	38	10	8	1.250	690.909	363.636
66	39	12	3	4.000	709.091	436.364
**67	39	11	6	1.833	698.507	394.030
67	40	13	1	13.000	716.418	465.672

(*continued*)

TABLE 100 (*Continued*)

number of notes $5W + 2H$	$3W + H$	W	H	$R = \dfrac{W}{H}$	perfect fifth $\dfrac{3W + H}{5W + 2H}\,a$	major third $\dfrac{2W}{5W + 2H}\,a$
68	39	10	9	1.111	688.235	352.941
68	40	12	4	3.000	705.882	423.529
**69	40	11	7	1.571	695.652	382.609
69	41	13	2	6.500	713.043	452.174
70	41	12	5	2.400	702.857	411.429
71	41	11	8	1.375	692.958	371.831
71	42	13	3	4.333	709.859	439.437
*72	42	12	6	2.000	700.000	400.000
72	43	14	1	14.000	716.667	466.667
73	42	11	9	1.222	690.411	361.644
73	43	13	4	3.250	706.849	427.397
**74	43	12	7	1.714	697.297	389.189
74	44	14	2	7.000	713.514	454.054
75	43	11	10	1.100	688.000	352.000
75	44	13	5	2.600	704.000	416.000

TABLE 101

C	D	E	F	G	A	B	C
0	$\frac{7}{29}a$	$\frac{14}{29}a$	$\frac{11}{29}a$	$\frac{18}{29}a$	$\frac{25}{29}a$	$\frac{32}{29}a$	$\frac{29}{29}a$

the unrecognizable tunings. It must be remembered, however, that the relative sizes of intervals (1) through (11) are maintained only within the range of recognizability (Theorem 27; Ch. X, Sec. 2). We have already seen how int (12) exhibits a jump discontinuity where $v = \frac{7}{12}a$ (Ch. IX, Sec. 2), and it may also be observed that int (7) (a chromatic semitone) and int (-5) (a minor second) are similarly discontinuous where $v = \frac{4}{7}a$ and $v = \frac{3}{5}a$, respectively (see also Theorem 28; Ch. X, Sec. 2). If it is desired to explore the behavior of diatonic scales and chords outside the range of recognizability in such a manner that there is a smooth and uniform transition from recognizable to unrecognizable, it is better to use the representation of intervals and notes in terms of R, derived in Chapter X, Sec. 5 (see Tables 76 and 78), for $\dfrac{pR + q}{5R + 2}$ is continuous for every integral p and q at all points except when $R = -\frac{2}{5}$, causing the denominator to vanish.

TABLE 102

C	D	E	F	G	A	B	C
0	$\frac{2}{16}a$	$\frac{4}{16}a$	$\frac{7}{16}a$	$\frac{9}{16}a$	$\frac{11}{16}a$	$\frac{13}{16}a$	$\frac{16}{16}a$

It should also be noted that the proof of the circle of fifths theorem (Theorem 40; Ch. XI, Sec. 5) does not depend in any way on the value of R, and hence is true for all values. Therefore any rational R ($R \neq -\frac{2}{5}$) produces a closed circle of generating intervals, and this in turn produces an equal tuning in which notes and accidentals may be assigned their proper positions by the expressions of Figure 21 (Ch. XI, Sec. 5).

Example: Let $R = -\frac{7}{3}$. We have either $W = 7$ and $H = -3$, or $W = -7$ and $H = 3$, both giving the same result. According to Theorem 40, the notes make the intervals with middle C that are shown in Table 101. It will be observed that minor seconds EF and BC are each equal to $-\frac{3}{29}a$, and that this is also the case for C♯D. It should also be noted that each perfect fifth is equal to $\frac{18}{29}a = 744.828$ cents—larger than $\frac{3}{5}a$.

Example: Let $R = \frac{2}{3}$. We then have the arrangement shown in Table 102. In this case, a chromatic semitone is equal to $-\frac{1}{16}a$, and a perfect fifth is equal to $\frac{9}{16}a = 675$ cents—less than $\frac{4}{7}a$. The reader will find it a useful exercise to make a graph of the two scales above. The diagrams will have the same appearance as the unrecognizable configurations of Figures 18 and 19 (Ch. X, Sec. 2).

Scales associated with certain values of R are sometimes not only ridiculously unrecognizable, but may take on an amusing aspect, especially if they result in equal tunings of only a very few notes, say, fewer than five. The reader will find it both instructive and entertaining to investigate those scales where $R = -\frac{2}{3}$, $R = -1$, $R = 0$, and $R = -\frac{1}{2}$.

5. Equal tunings that are successively closer approximations to Pythagorean tuning, meantone tuning, and Silbermann's tuning. In some applications, it may be useful to find a series of equal tunings that are successively closer approximations to a particular diatonic tuning where R is irrational. To this end, we need to derive a sequence of rational fractions which approach R as a limit. A convenient means of doing this is afforded by the theory of simple continued fractions; although the complete theory is too long to be presented here, the reader should consult Chrystal's

Algebra, which presents a readable account of what is needed for purposes of music theory.[4] We consider those fractions of the form

$$a_1 + \cfrac{1}{a_2 + \cfrac{1}{a_3 + \cfrac{1}{a_4 + \cfrac{1}{a_5 + \cfrac{1}{a_6 + \cdots}}}}}$$

where a_1, a_2, etc. are positive integers. The number a_n is called the *n*th *partial quotient,* and that portion of the continued fraction that includes only the first *n* partial quotients is called the *n*th *convergent.* Thus the first convergent is a_1, the second convergent is $a_1 + \dfrac{1}{a_2}$, the third convergent is $a_1 + \cfrac{1}{a_2 + \cfrac{1}{a_3}}$, and so on. It may be shown that every convergent is a closer approximation to the true value of the continued fraction than any convergent previously obtained,[5] and it is this feature that is useful for purposes of music theory.

It is an elementary matter to convert any decimal to a continued fraction, and if the decimal represents a rational number, the process will eventually terminate. If, however, the decimal represents an irrational number, the process will continue indefinitely.[6] The method for converting a decimal to a continued fraction consists of finding the values for positive integers $a_1, a_2, a_3 \ldots$ corresponding to the given decimal. It will be convenient to denote the value of the given decimal, and hence the continued fraction, by x_1, and we next define x_2, x_3, etc. as follows:

$$x_2 = a_2 + \cfrac{1}{a_3 + \cfrac{1}{a_4 + \cfrac{1}{a_5 + \cdots}}} \qquad\qquad x_3 = a_3 + \cfrac{1}{a_4 + \cfrac{1}{a_5 + \cfrac{1}{a_6 + \cdots}}}$$

---

[4] G. Chrystal, *Algebra,* (2nd ed.; London: A. and C. Black, 1926), vol. 2, 423–452.
[5] Ibid. 437.
[6] Ibid. 424–428.

If we now choose a_1 so that a_1 is the greatest integer less than x_1, we have

$x_1 = a_1 + \dfrac{1}{x_2}$, and $x_2 > 1$. Since x_2 is itself a continued fraction greater

than unity, we may apply the identical process to obtain $x_2 = a_2 + \dfrac{1}{x_3}$,

where a_2 is the greatest integer less than x_2, insuring that $x_3 > 1$. We

now have $x_1 = a_1 + \dfrac{1}{a_2 + \dfrac{1}{x_3}}$. Clearly the process may be similarly con-

tinued, and we find next that

$$x_1 = a_1 + \cfrac{1}{a_2 + \cfrac{1}{a_3 + \cfrac{1}{x_4}}}$$

where a_3 is the greatest integer less than x_3, insuring that $x_4 > 1$. By now, it is apparent that the partial quotients may be computed in order by a recurrence relation that connects x_{n+1} with x_n, viz., x_{n+1} is the reciprocal of the decimal portion of x_n. Also, each partial quotient a_n is the integral portion of x_n, and therefore

$$x_{n+1} = \frac{1}{x_n - a_n}$$

Example: Let $x_1 = 2.260017$, the Pythagorean value for R. We then

have at once $a_1 = 2$, and $x_2 = \dfrac{1}{.260017} = 3.845906$.[7] From this, we find

that $a_2 = 3$, and $x_3 = \dfrac{1}{.845906} = 1.182164$. More of the calculation is

shown in Table 103. For reasons soon to be apparent, it is of little use to carry the expansion any further. We have found that the Pythagorean

---

[7] The recurrence relation that generates the numbers x_{n+1} is unstable, i.e., there is an accumulating rounding error which quickly overwhelms the numbers wanted. If the expansion is continued beyond what is shown in Table 103, the seventh partial quotient will be incorrect if we start with the value $R = 2.260017$, since the fraction will converge to this number, and not the true value of R. Further convergents may be correctly calculated if a sufficiently accurate value for R is used. The value of R to 25 decimals is 2.2600167526708245359312761.

TABLE 103

$x_1 =$	$2.260017,$	$a_1 = 2$
$x_2 = \dfrac{1}{.260017} =$	$3.845906,$	$a_2 = 3$
$x_3 = \dfrac{1}{.845906} =$	$1.182164,$	$a_3 = 1$
$x_4 = \dfrac{1}{.182164} =$	$5.489547,$	$a_4 = 5$
$x_5 = \dfrac{1}{.489547} =$	$2.042704,$	$a_5 = 2$
$x_6 = \dfrac{1}{.042704} =$	$23.416790,$	$a_6 = 23$
$x_7 = \dfrac{1}{.416790} =$	2.399291	

value for R is equal to

$$2 + \cfrac{1}{3 + \cfrac{1}{1 + \cfrac{1}{5 + \cfrac{1}{2 + \cfrac{1}{23 + \cfrac{1}{2.399291}}}}}}$$

The first three convergents to this continued fraction are 2, $2 + \frac{1}{3} = \frac{7}{3}$, and $2 + \cfrac{1}{3 + \cfrac{1}{1}} = 2 + \frac{1}{4} = \frac{9}{4}$. Successive convergents may be computed similarly, although the process becomes laborious. However, the nth convergent may also be calculated by a recurrence relation involving the two preceding convergents and the nth partial quotient: if the nth convergent is $\dfrac{p_n}{q_n}$, we have generally[8]

$$\frac{p_n}{q_n} = \frac{a_n p_{n-1} + p_{n-2}}{a_n q_{n-1} + q_{n-2}}$$

[8] Chrystal, *Algebra*, vol. 2, 432.

TABLE 104

nth partial quotient	computation	nth convergent
$a_1 = 2$		$\dfrac{2}{1} = 2.000000$
$a_2 = 3$		$\dfrac{7}{3} = 2.333333$
$a_3 = 1$	$\dfrac{(1)(7) + 2}{(1)(3) + 1} =$	$\dfrac{9}{4} = 2.250000$
$a_4 = 5$	$\dfrac{(5)(9) + 7}{(5)(4) + 3} =$	$\dfrac{52}{23} = 2.260870$
$a_5 = 2$	$\dfrac{(2)(52) + 9}{(2)(23) + 4} =$	$\dfrac{113}{50} = 2.260000$
$a_6 = 23$	$\dfrac{(23)(113) + 52}{(23)(50) + 23} = \dfrac{2651}{1173} = 2.260017$	

Using this formula, we may calculate more convergents to the same continued fraction; results are shown in Table 104. In the case of the sixth convergent, the approximation is so close that more decimal places are needed to reveal the true situation; to eight significant figures, the values are $\frac{2651}{1173} = 2.2600171$, and $R = 2.2600168$.

The decimal values of the convergents suggest that the nature of the convergence is oscillatory, and it is generally true that the convergents of an odd order are all less, and those of an even order are all greater than the true value of the continued fraction.[9]

By another theorem from the theory of continued fractions, every convergent to any simple continued fraction is a fraction in its lowest terms;[10] and this is most convenient as regards music theory, for it makes possible the application of the simpler form of the circle of fifths theorem (Theorem 40; Ch. XI, Sec. 5) to each fractional approximation to R. If each fractional approximation to R is equal to $\dfrac{W}{H}$, the diatonic tuning associated with R is part of an equal tuning of $5W + 2H$ notes; and if

[9] Ibid. 437–439.
[10] Ibid. 435.

TABLE 105

$R = \dfrac{W}{H}$		$\frac{2}{1}$	$\frac{7}{3}$	$\frac{9}{4}$	$\frac{52}{23}$	$\frac{113}{50}$	$\frac{2651}{1173}$
number of notes $= 5W + 2H$		12	41	53	306	665	15601

TABLE 106

$R = \dfrac{W}{H}$	$v = \dfrac{3W + H}{5W + 2H}\, a$	$2 \exp \dfrac{3W + H}{5W + 2H}$
$\frac{2}{1}$	$\frac{7}{12}a = 700.000$	1.498307
$\frac{7}{3}$	$\frac{24}{41}a = 702.439$	1.500419
$\frac{9}{4}$	$\frac{31}{53}a = 701.887$	1.499941
$\frac{52}{23}$	$\frac{179}{306}a = 701.961$	1.500005
$\frac{113}{50}$	$\frac{389}{665}a = 701.955$	1.500000

$(W, H) = 1$, $5W + 2H$ is the least number of equally tuned notes that contains the tuning in question (Ch. XI, Sec. 10). The number of notes produced by each fractional approximation to R is shown in Table 105. The impracticality of equal tunings containing many thousands of notes is obvious.

Since each of the above tunings is successively nearer to Pythagorean tuning, we should expect them to produce a series of perfect fifths whose ratios converge in an oscillatory manner to $\frac{3}{2}$. Recalling that the ratio of each perfect fifth is $2 \exp \dfrac{3W + H}{5W + 2H}$ and the size is $\dfrac{3W + H}{5W + 2H}\, a$ (Ch. XI, Sec. 5), we have the results shown in Table 106. In the case of 665 notes, the approximation is so close that more decimal places are needed to reveal the true situation, and we have $2 \exp \frac{389}{665} = 1.499999902$.

In general, a convergent whose associated partial quotient immediately precedes a much larger partial quotient is a correspondingly closer approximation to the value of the continued fraction.[11] The fifth convergent of Table 104 is an illustration of the principle. It may also be shown that a particular convergent to a continued fraction is a closer approximation

[11] Ibid. 438.

TABLE 107

$R = \dfrac{W}{H}$	$\dfrac{2W}{5W + 2H}\, a$	$2 \exp \dfrac{2W}{5W + 2H}$
$\frac{2}{1}$	$\frac{4}{12}a = 400.000$	1.259921
$\frac{7}{3}$	$\frac{14}{41}a = 409.756$	1.267041
$\frac{9}{4}$	$\frac{18}{53}a = 407.547$	1.265426
$\frac{52}{23}$	$\frac{104}{306}a = 407.843$	1.265642
$\frac{113}{50}$	$\frac{226}{665}a = 407.820$	1.265625

to the continued fraction's true value than any fraction whose numerator and denominator are less than those of the convergent.[12] Hence there is, for example, no fraction whose numerator is less than 113, or whose denominator is less than 50, that is closer to 2.260017 than $\frac{113}{50}$. Consequently there is no equal tuning of fewer than 665 notes that contains a closer approximation to a pure perfect fifth than $\frac{389}{665}a$. From this, it appears that equal tunings that furnish successively closer approximations to a pure perfect fifth are very sparsely distributed.

By the circle of fifths theorem, the size of a major third is $\dfrac{2W}{5W + 2H}\, a$, and its ratio is $2 \exp \dfrac{2W}{5W + 2H}$. If we substitute the values for W and H associated with the six different fractional values for R (Table 104) in the above expressions, the numbers obtained will converge in an oscillatory manner to the size and ratio of a Pythagorean major third (407.820 cents and $\frac{81}{64} = 1.265625$, respectively); the actual sizes and ratios are shown in Table 107.

We next recall that in meantone tuning, the major thirds are pure; hence if we find a series of equal tunings that are successively closer approximations to meantone tuning, their major thirds will become successively more nearly pure. To this end, we convert the meantone value for R ($= 1.649393$) to a continued fraction,[13] first finding the values of the partial quotients as shown in Table 108. Thus the meantone value for R

[12] Ibid. 445.
[13] The numbers given correspond to a more accurate value for R than 1.649393. The value to 25 decimals is 1.6493927971805120809349852.

TABLE 108

$$x_1 = \quad\quad = 1.649393, \quad a_1 = 1$$

$$x_2 = \frac{1}{.649393} = 1.539900, \quad a_2 = 1$$

$$x_3 = \frac{1}{.539900} = 1.852195, \quad a_3 = 1$$

$$x_4 = \frac{1}{.852195} = 1.173441, \quad a_4 = 1$$

$$x_5 = \frac{1}{.173441} = 5.765657, \quad a_5 = 5$$

$$x_6 = \frac{1}{.765657} = 1.306069, \quad a_6 = 1$$

$$x_7 = \frac{1}{.306069} = 3.267240, \quad a_7 = 3$$

$$x_8 = \frac{1}{.267240} = 3.741949$$

is equal to

$$1 + \cfrac{1}{1 + \cfrac{1}{1 + \cfrac{1}{1 + \cfrac{1}{5 + \cfrac{1}{1 + \cfrac{1}{3 + \cfrac{1}{3.741949}}}}}}}$$

The first two convergents are 1 and $\frac{1}{2}$, and after this, the others may be computed by the recurrence relation $\dfrac{p_n}{q_n} = \dfrac{a_n p_{n-1} + p_{n-2}}{a_n q_{n-1} + q_{n-2}}$. The convergents are shown in Table 109.

The number of notes in each resulting equal tuning is given in Table 110.

It is interesting to note that the fourth convergent $\frac{5}{3}$ immediately precedes a relatively large partial quotient ($a_4 = 1$, $a_5 = 5$), and this explains

TABLE 109

nth partial quotient	computation	nth convergent
$a_1 = 1$		$\dfrac{1}{1} = 1.000000$
$a_2 = 1$		$\dfrac{2}{1} = 2.000000$
$a_3 = 1$	$\dfrac{(1)(2)+1}{(1)(1)+1} =$	$\dfrac{3}{2} = 1.500000$
$a_4 = 1$	$\dfrac{(1)(3)+2}{(1)(2)+1} =$	$\dfrac{5}{3} = 1.666667$
$a_5 = 5$	$\dfrac{(5)(5)+3}{(5)(3)+2} =$	$\dfrac{28}{17} = 1.647059$
$a_6 = 1$	$\dfrac{(1)(28)+5}{(1)(17)+3} =$	$\dfrac{33}{20} = 1.650000$
$a_7 = 3$	$\dfrac{(3)(33)+28}{(3)(20)+17} =$	$\dfrac{127}{77} = 1.649351$

TABLE 110

$R = \dfrac{W}{H}$	$\frac{1}{1}$	$\frac{2}{1}$	$\frac{3}{2}$	$\frac{5}{3}$	$\frac{28}{17}$	$\frac{33}{20}$	$\frac{127}{77}$
number of notes $= 5W + 2H$	7	12	19	31	174	205	789

further why 31-note equal tuning contains a recognizable diatonic scale that is an unexpectedly close approximation to meantone tuning (see also Sec. 1 of this chapter.)

The anticipated behavior of the major thirds is illustrated in Table 111.

In the case of the perfect fifths, the ratios converge in an oscillatory manner to $\sqrt[4]{5} = 1.495349$, and the sizes converge to 696.578, which is the size of a meantone fifth (Ch. VIII, Sec. 1), as illustrated in Table 112.

The reader should now have no difficulty in applying the same techniques to Silbermann's tuning (analyzed in detail in Ch. X, Sec. 6). Recalling that in this case, $R = 1.819204,$[14] we develop the following continued

[14] The value to 25 decimals is 1.8192036189183493521363123.

TABLE 111

$R = \dfrac{W}{H}$	$t = \dfrac{2W}{5W + 2H}\,a$	$2\exp\dfrac{2W}{5W + 2H}$
$\frac{1}{1}$	$\frac{2}{7}a = 342.857$	1.219014
$\frac{2}{1}$	$\frac{4}{12}a = 400.000$	1.259921
$\frac{3}{2}$	$\frac{6}{19}a = 378.947$	1.244693
$\frac{5}{3}$	$\frac{10}{31}a = 387.097$	1.250566
$\frac{28}{17}$	$\frac{56}{174}a = 386.207$	1.249923
$\frac{33}{20}$	$\frac{66}{205}a = 386.341$	1.250020
$\frac{127}{77}$	$\frac{254}{789}a = 386.312$	1.249999

TABLE 112

$R = \dfrac{W}{H}$	$v = \dfrac{3W + H}{5W + 2H}\,a$	$2\exp\dfrac{3W + H}{5W + 2H}$
$\frac{1}{1}$	$\frac{4}{7}a = 685.714$	1.485994
$\frac{2}{1}$	$\frac{7}{12}a = 700.000$	1.498307
$\frac{3}{2}$	$\frac{11}{19}a = 694.737$	1.493759
$\frac{5}{3}$	$\frac{18}{31}a = 696.774$	1.495518
$\frac{28}{17}$	$\frac{101}{174}a = 696.552$	1.495326
$\frac{33}{20}$	$\frac{119}{205}a = 696.585$	1.495355
$\frac{127}{77}$	$\frac{458}{789}a = 696.578$	1.495348

fraction (details are left to the reader as an exercise):

$$1 + \cfrac{1}{1 + \cfrac{1}{4 + \cfrac{1}{1 + \cfrac{1}{1 + \cfrac{1}{7 + \cfrac{1}{1.842703}}}}}}$$

The first six convergents to this fraction are $\frac{1}{1}$, $\frac{2}{1}$, $\frac{9}{5}$, $\frac{11}{6}$, $\frac{20}{11}$, and $\frac{151}{83}$, and the equal tunings associated with these values for R are those of 7, 12, 55, 67, 122, and 921 notes. The sizes and ratios of the perfect fifths and major

TABLE 113

$R = \dfrac{W}{H}$	$\dfrac{3W+H}{5W+2H}a$	$2\exp\dfrac{3W+H}{5W+2H}$	$\dfrac{2W}{5W+2H}a$	$2\exp\dfrac{2W}{5W+2H}$
$\frac{1}{1}$	$\frac{4}{7}a = 685.714$	1.485994	$\frac{2}{7}a = 342.857$	1.219014
$\frac{2}{1}$	$\frac{7}{12}a = 700.000$	1.498307	$\frac{4}{12}a = 400.000$	1.259921
$\frac{9}{5}$	$\frac{32}{55}a = 698.182$	1.496734	$\frac{18}{55}a = 392.727$	1.254639
$\frac{11}{6}$	$\frac{39}{67}a = 698.507$	1.497016	$\frac{22}{67}a = 394.030$	1.255584
$\frac{20}{11}$	$\frac{71}{122}a = 698.361$	1.496889	$\frac{40}{122}a = 393.443$	1.255158
$\frac{151}{83}$	$\frac{536}{921}a = 698.371$	1.496898	$\frac{302}{921}a = 393.485$	1.255189

thirds are given in Table 113. These numbers should be compared with the values for Silbermann's perfect fifth and major third; the fifth and third contain 698.371 and 393.482 cents, respectively, and the ratios are 1.496898 and 1.255187.

Equal tunings of less than 75 notes which appear in the three expansions so far investigated are those of 7, 12, 19, 31, 41, 53, 55, and 67 notes—an interesting list when compared with the list obtained in Section 4 of this chapter.

Although the mathematical aspects of the subject are intriguing, the author cannot escape the conviction that they are of little interest musically. Nothing further is revealed about diatonic equal tunings of fewer than 75 notes that has not been already suggested by other considerations, nor do the continued fractions lead to more nearly perfect temperaments. However, the very close approximations to Pythagorean or meantone tuning contained by certain equal tunings of many notes may be practically useful if limitations in computer programs or other electronic devices permit the use of equal tunings only.

6. Equal tunings that contain approximations to just tuning. We recall first the just tuning of a C major scale as described in Chapter V, Sec. 1, where the seven diatonic notes are arranged so that the three primary triads are tuned purely. This is the tuning $C_0D_0E_{-1}F_0G_0A_{-1}B_{-1}C_0$, where C_0, D_0, F_0, and G_0 are the same as in Pythagorean tuning, and E_{-1}, A_{-1}, and B_{-1} are lower than their Pythagorean counterparts E_0, A_0, and B_0 by a syntonic comma, thereby making C_0E_{-1}, F_0A_{-1}, and G_0B_{-1} pure major thirds. Clearly any equal tuning that approximates just tuning must contain a nearly pure major third as well as a nearly pure perfect fifth, and we call such tunings *nearly just equal tunings*. In order to discover whether a given equal tuning is nearly just, the most straightforward approach is simply to determine which intervals contained by the equal tuning are nearest to 701.955 cents and 386.314 cents; if these are not within a certain range of tolerance, there is little point in carrying the investigation further. Table 114 gives relevant data for all equal tunings of 12 through 75 notes.

TABLE 114

number of notes	each adjacent interval	closest perfect fifth	departure from pure	closest major third	departure from pure
12	100.000	$\frac{7}{12}a = 700.000$	−1.955	$\frac{4}{12}a = 400.000$	13.686
13	92.308	$\frac{8}{13}a = 738.462$	36.507	$\frac{4}{13}a = 369.231$	−17.083
14	85.714	$\frac{8}{14}a = 685.714$	−16.241	$\frac{5}{14}a = 428.571$	42.258
15	80.000	$\frac{9}{15}a = 720.000$	18.045	$\frac{5}{15}a = 400.000$	13.686
16	75.000	$\frac{9}{16}a = 675.000$	−26.955	$\frac{5}{16}a = 375.000$	−11.314
17	70.588	$\frac{10}{17}a = 705.882$	3.927	$\frac{5}{17}a = 352.941$	−33.373
18	66.667	$\frac{11}{18}a = 733.333$	31.378	$\frac{6}{18}a = 400.000$	13.686
19	63.158	$\frac{11}{19}a = 694.737$	−7.218	$\frac{6}{19}a = 378.947$	−7.366
20	60.000	$\frac{12}{20}a = 720.000$	18.045	$\frac{6}{20}a = 360.000$	−26.314
21	57.143	$\frac{12}{21}a = 685.714$	−16.241	$\frac{7}{21}a = 400.000$	13.686
22	54.545	$\frac{13}{22}a = 709.091$	7.136	$\frac{7}{22}a = 381.818$	−4.496
23	52.174	$\frac{13}{23}a = 678.261$	−23.694	$\frac{7}{23}a = 365.217$	−21.096
24	50.000	$\frac{14}{24}a = 700.000$	−1.955	$\frac{8}{24}a = 400.000$	13.686
25	48.000	$\frac{15}{25}a = 720.000$	18.045	$\frac{8}{25}a = 384.000$	−2.314
26	46.154	$\frac{15}{26}a = 692.308$	−9.647	$\frac{8}{26}a = 369.231$	−17.083
27	44.444	$\frac{16}{27}a = 711.111$	9.156	$\frac{9}{27}a = 400.000$	13.686
28	42.857	$\frac{16}{28}a = 685.714$	−16.241	$\frac{9}{28}a = 385.714$	−.599
29	41.379	$\frac{17}{29}a = 703.448$	1.493	$\frac{9}{29}a = 372.414$	−13.900
30	40.000	$\frac{18}{30}a = 720.000$	18.045	$\frac{10}{30}a = 400.000$	13.686
31	38.710	$\frac{18}{31}a = 696.774$	−5.181	$\frac{10}{31}a = 387.097$	.783
32	37.500	$\frac{19}{32}a = 712.500$	10.545	$\frac{10}{32}a = 375.000$	−11.314
33	36.364	$\frac{19}{33}a = 690.909$	−11.046	$\frac{11}{33}a = 400.000$	13.686
34	35.294	$\frac{20}{34}a = 705.882$	3.927	$\frac{11}{34}a = 388.235$	1.922
35	34.286	$\frac{20}{35}a = 685.714$	−16.241	$\frac{11}{35}a = 377.143$	−9.171
36	33.333	$\frac{21}{36}a = 700.000$	−1.955	$\frac{12}{36}a = 400.000$	13.686
37	32.432	$\frac{22}{37}a = 713.514$	11.559	$\frac{12}{37}a = 389.189$	2.875
38	31.579	$\frac{22}{38}a = 694.737$	−7.218	$\frac{12}{38}a = 378.947$	−7.366
39	30.769	$\frac{23}{39}a = 707.692$	5.737	$\frac{13}{39}a = 400.000$	13.686

(*continued*)

TABLE 114   (*Continued*)

number of notes	each adjacent interval	closest perfect fifth	departure from pure	closest major third	departure from pure
40	30.000	$\frac{23}{40}a = 690.000$	-11.955	$\frac{13}{40}a = 390.000$	3.686
41	29.268	$\frac{24}{41}a = 702.439$	.484	$\frac{13}{41}a = 380.488$	-5.826
42	28.571	$\frac{25}{42}a = 714.286$	12.331	$\frac{14}{42}a = 400.000$	13.686
43	27.907	$\frac{25}{43}a = 697.674$	-4.281	$\frac{14}{43}a = 390.698$	4.384
44	27.273	$\frac{26}{44}a = 709.091$	7.136	$\frac{14}{44}a = 381.818$	-4.496
45	26.667	$\frac{26}{45}a = 693.333$	-8.622	$\frac{14}{45}a = 373.333$	-12.980
46	26.087	$\frac{27}{46}a = 704.348$	2.393	$\frac{15}{46}a = 391.304$	4.991
47	25.532	$\frac{27}{47}a = 689.362$	-12.593	$\frac{15}{47}a = 382.979$	-3.335
48	25.000	$\frac{28}{48}a = 700.000$	-1.955	$\frac{15}{48}a = 375.000$	-11.314
49	24.490	$\frac{29}{49}a = 710.204$	8.249	$\frac{16}{49}a = 391.837$	5.523
50	24.000	$\frac{29}{50}a = 696.000$	-5.955	$\frac{16}{50}a = 384.000$	-2.314
51	23.529	$\frac{30}{51}a = 705.882$	3.927	$\frac{16}{51}a = 376.471$	-9.843
52	23.077	$\frac{30}{52}a = 692.308$	-9.647	$\frac{17}{52}a = 392.308$	5.994
53	22.642	$\frac{31}{53}a = 701.887$	$-.068$	$\frac{17}{53}a = 384.906$	-1.408
54	22.222	$\frac{32}{54}a = 711.111$	9.156	$\frac{17}{54}a = 377.778$	-8.536
55	21.818	$\frac{32}{55}a = 698.182$	-3.773	$\frac{18}{55}a = 392.727$	6.414
56	21.429	$\frac{33}{56}a = 707.143$	5.188	$\frac{18}{56}a = 385.714$	$-.599$
57	21.053	$\frac{33}{57}a = 694.737$	-7.218	$\frac{18}{57}a = 378.947$	-7.366
58	20.690	$\frac{34}{58}a = 703.448$	1.493	$\frac{19}{58}a = 393.103$	6.790
59	20.339	$\frac{35}{59}a = 711.864$	9.909	$\frac{19}{59}a = 386.441$	.127
60	20.000	$\frac{36}{60}a = 700.000$	-1.955	$\frac{19}{60}a = 380.000$	-6.314
61	19.672	$\frac{36}{61}a = 708.197$	6.242	$\frac{20}{61}a = 393.443$	7.129
62	19.355	$\frac{36}{62}a = 696.774$	-5.181	$\frac{20}{62}a = 387.097$	.783
63	19.048	$\frac{37}{63}a = 704.762$	2.807	$\frac{20}{63}a = 380.952$	-5.361
64	18.750	$\frac{37}{64}a = 693.750$	-8.205	$\frac{21}{64}a = 393.750$	7.436
65	18.462	$\frac{38}{65}a = 701.538$	$-.417$	$\frac{21}{65}a = 387.692$	1.379
66	18.182	$\frac{39}{66}a = 709.091$	7.136	$\frac{21}{66}a = 381.818$	-4.496
67	17.910	$\frac{39}{67}a = 698.507$	-3.448	$\frac{22}{67}a = 394.030$	7.716
68	17.647	$\frac{40}{68}a = 705.882$	3.927	$\frac{22}{68}a = 388.235$	1.922
69	17.391	$\frac{40}{69}a = 695.652$	-6.303	$\frac{22}{69}a = 382.609$	-3.705
70	17.143	$\frac{41}{70}a = 702.857$	.902	$\frac{23}{70}a = 394.286$	7.972
71	16.901	$\frac{42}{71}a = 709.859$	7.904	$\frac{23}{71}a = 388.732$	2.419
72	16.667	$\frac{42}{72}a = 700.000$	-1.955	$\frac{23}{72}a = 383.333$	-2.980
73	16.438	$\frac{43}{73}a = 706.849$	4.894	$\frac{24}{73}a = 394.521$	8.207
74	16.216	$\frac{43}{74}a = 697.297$	-4.658	$\frac{24}{74}a = 389.189$	2.875
75	16.000	$\frac{44}{75}a = 704.000$	2.045	$\frac{24}{75}a = 384.000$	-2.314

If a close approximation is wanted, it is suggested that perfect fifth middle CG should beat no faster than once per second, and that the beat frequency of the less sensitive major third middle CE should be no faster than three per second. In round numbers, this means a departure from pure of no more than two cents in the case of the perfect fifth, and four cents in the case of the major third. Regarding the fifth, the tunings to consider are those of 12, 24, 29, 36, 41, 48, 53, 58, 60, 65, 70, and 72 notes; for the third, the corresponding tunings are those of 25, 28, 31, 34, 37, 40, 50, 53, 56, 59, 62, 65, 68, 69, 71, 72, 74, and 75 notes. It will be observed that the only tunings to appear on both lists are those of 53, 65, and 72 notes.

Further insights into the nearly just behavior of 53-note equal tuning may be obtained by regarding a pure major third as a Pythagorean major third reduced by a syntonic comma. Since a syntonic comma contains 21.506 cents, we can find a close approximation, say, within 2 cents, to this interval in any equal tuning that contains an interval lying between 19.506 cents and 23.506 cents. The tunings having the least number of notes that contain an interval within this range are those of 51 to 61 notes, and hence any equal tuning of 51 to 61 notes that contains a close approximation to Pythagorean tuning—and consequently to a pure perfect fifth—must also contain a close approximation to just tuning. Since 53-note equal tuning is known to contain a very close approximation to Pythagorean tuning (Sec. 5 of this chapter), it must also be a nearly just equal tuning. Now in any nearly just equal tuning, as in true just tuning, we must have $t = 4v - 2a - k$ (Ch. III, Sec. 7).[15] In the present case, $v = \frac{31}{53}a$ as before, and $k = \frac{1}{53}a$; consequently $t = \dfrac{(4)(31) - (2)(53) - 1}{53} a =$

$\dfrac{124 - 106 - 1}{53} a = \frac{17}{53}a = 384.906$ cents, in agreement with Table 114.

We may assign the notes of the approximate Pythagorean tuning to their proper positions within 53-note equal tuning by recalling that in this diatonic equal tuning, $R = \frac{9}{4}$ (Sec. 5 of this chapter), and then using the circle of fifths theorem (Theorem 40; Ch. XI, Sec. 5). The results are as follows:

positions	0	9	18	22	31	40	49	53
notes	C_0	D_0	E_0	F_0	G_0	A_0	B_0	C_0

---

[15] See note 1, supra.

In the nearly just tuning, E_{-1}, A_{-1}, and B_{-1} will be lower than their Pythagorean counterparts by $k = \frac{1}{53}a$, i.e., in position 17, 39, and 48, respectively, and thus we have:

positions 0   9   17   22   31   39   48   53
notes C_0 D_0 E_{-1} F_0 G_0 A_{-1} B_{-1} C_0

From this, it may be seen at once that major tones C_0D_0, F_0G_0, and $A_{-1}B_{-1}$ are all equal to $\frac{9}{53}a = 203.774$ cents; minor tones D_0E_{-1} and G_0A_{-1} are equal to $\frac{8}{53}a = 181.132$ cents, and diatonic semitones $E_{-1}F_0$ and $B_{-1}C_0$ are equal to $\frac{5}{53}a = 113.208$ cents. The corresponding intervals in true just tuning are $\log \frac{9}{8} = 203.910$ cents, $\log \frac{10}{9} = 182.404$ cents, and $\log \frac{16}{15} = 111.731$ cents, respectively.

What was determined in Chapter V, Sec. 2 regarding the relative sizes of the diatonic just intervals is essentially retained in the representation of these intervals in the nearly just equal tuning of 53 notes. In particular, minor thirds $E_{-1}G_0$, $A_{-1}C_0$, and $B_{-1}D_0$ are equal to $\frac{14}{53}a = 316.981$ cents—very near to the pure value of 315.614 cents. However, D_0F_0 is more nearly Pythagorean than pure, being equal to $\frac{13}{53}a = 294.340$ cents, and perfect fifth D_0A_{-1} is a close approximation to the discordant fifth $\bar{v} - \bar{k}$, and is equal to $\frac{30}{53}a = 679.245$ cents. Hence as before, the second-degree triad requires rectification which may be achieved by using D_{-1} as its root, rather than D_0 (Ch. V, Sec. 3). In 53-note equal tuning, D_{-1} is lower than D_0 by $k = \frac{1}{53}a$, and hence occupies position 8. Since D_{-1} is needed as the root of the second-degree triad and D_0 serves as the fifth of the fifth-degree triad, any progression from II to V in which D appears in the same part must bring D_{-1} and D_0 side by side in order to avoid a modulation downward by $\frac{1}{53}a = 22.642$ cents. To illustrate, we consider once again the progression I-VI-II-V-I, as illustrated in Figure 6 (Ch. V, Sec. 3). Using the principles stated regarding D_{-1} and D_0, we give the notes forming the four triads and their positions in 53-note equal tuning in Table 115. If D_{-1} is retained as the fifth of the fifth-degree triad, and if all other notes common to two successive triads are similarly treated, the tuning is as given in

TABLE 115

triads	G_0	31	A_{-1}	39	A_{-1}	39	B_{-1}	48	C_0	53
	E_{-1}	17	E_{-1}	17	F_0	22	G_0	31	G_0	31
	C_0	0	C_0	0	D_{-1}	8	D_0	9	E_{-1}	17
degrees	I		VI		II		V		I	

TABLE 116

triads	G_0	31	A_{-1}	39	A_{-1}	39	B_{-2}	47	C_{-1}	52
	E_{-1}	17	E_{-1}	17	F_0	22	G_{-1}	30	G_{-1}	30
	C_0	0	C_0	0	D_{-1}	8	D_{-1}	8	E_{-2}	16
degrees	I		VI		II		V		I	

Table 116. In this arrangement, the progression modulates downward by $\frac{1}{53}a$, and if repeated over and over, the pitch drops by this amount with each repetition. This produces the same confounding, disagreeable effect as that associated with true just tuning.

The fragment of the di Lasso motet *Ave regina coelorum*, analyzed earlier during the discussion of just tuning (Ch. VII, Sec. 2), may be played in 53-note equal tuning with virtually the identical effect. Other notes needed beside those of C major are E_0 and A_0 (positions 18 and 40); also F_{-1} (the best 53-note representation of $F_{-\bar{z}}$) and G_{-1}, lower than F_0 and G_0 by $k = \frac{1}{53}a$ and thus in positions 21 and 30. In addition, we must have $F\sharp_{-1}$ and $G\sharp_{-2}$, higher than D_0 and E_{-1} by a nearly pure major third of $\frac{17}{53}a$, and hence in positions 26 and 34; and finally $B\flat_{+1}$, higher than G_0 by a nearly pure minor third of $\frac{14}{53}a$, and thus in position 45. To recapitulate, the fifteen notes needed are in the following positions relative to C:

positions	0	8	9	17	18	21	22	26
notes	C_0	D_{-1}	D_0	E_{-1}	E_0	F_{-1}	F_0	$F\sharp_{-1}$

positions	30	31	34	39	40	45	48
notes	G_{-1}	G_0	$G\sharp_{-2}$	A_{-1}	A_0	$B\flat_{+1}$	B_{-1}

More data concerning the representation of just intervals within 53-note equal tuning will be found in Table 117. The size of each interval may be obtained from its representation in terms of a, $\bar{v}$, and $\bar{t}$ by replacing a by $\frac{53}{53}a$, $\bar{v}$ by $\frac{31}{53}a$, and $\bar{t}$ by $\frac{17}{53}a$.[16]

Examples: A major chroma $(3\bar{v} + \bar{t} - 2a)$ is equal to

$$\frac{(3)(31) + 17 - (2)(53)}{53} a = \frac{93 + 17 - 106}{53} a = \frac{4}{53}a = 90.566 \text{ cents.}$$

[16] The most important just intervals are collected together in Table 44 (Ch. VI, Sec. 8). References in Table 44 will direct the reader to a more complete description of how the interval arises, and this always includes the interval's representation in terms of a, $\bar{v}$, and $\bar{t}$.

TABLE 117

REPRESENTATION OF JUST INTERVALS IN 53-NOTE EQUAL
TUNING

interval	size in cents	departure from just
perfect fifth	$\frac{31}{53}a = 701.887$	$-.068$
perfect fourth	$\frac{22}{53}a = 498.113$	$.068$
Pythagorean major third	$\frac{18}{53}a = 407.547$	$-.273$
pure major third	$\frac{17}{53}a = 384.906$	-1.408
schismatic major third	$\frac{17}{53}a = 384.906$	$.546$
pure minor third	$\frac{14}{53}a = 316.981$	1.340
Pythagorean minor third	$\frac{13}{53}a = 294.340$	$.205$
major tone	$\frac{9}{53}a = 203.774$	$-.136$
minor tone	$\frac{8}{53}a = 181.132$	-1.272
maximum semitone	$\frac{6}{53}a = 135.849$	2.611
apotome	$\frac{5}{53}a = 113.208$	$-.477$
diatonic semitone	$\frac{5}{53}a = 113.208$	1.476
major chroma	$\frac{4}{53}a = 90.566$	-1.613
limma	$\frac{4}{53}a = 90.566$	$.341$
minor chroma	$\frac{3}{53}a = 67.925$	-2.748
diesis	$\frac{2}{53}a = 45.283$	4.224
Pythagorean comma	$\frac{1}{53}a = 22.642$	$-.819$
syntonic comma	$\frac{1}{53}a = 22.642$	1.135
diaschisma	$\frac{1}{53}a = 22.642$	3.089
schisma	$\frac{0}{53}a = 0.000$	-1.954

A diaschisma $(3a - 4\bar{v} - 2\bar{\imath})$ is equal to

$$\frac{(3)(53) - (4)(31) - (2)(17)}{53}\, a = \frac{159 - 124 - 34}{53}\, a = \frac{1}{53}\, a = 22.642 \text{ cents.}$$

We observe further that $\frac{17}{53}a$ is nearer the value of a schismatic major third than a pure major third, and that the schisma itself vanishes. These elements combine to give the nearly just configuration of 53-note equal tuning virtually the identical character and behavior associated with the "schismatic tuning" that may be selected from the notes of extended Pythagorean tuning (Ch. VI, Sec. 3).

In the case of 65 notes, we recall that this is the diatonic equal tuning where $R = \frac{11}{5}$ (Table 100; Sec. 4 of this chapter); applying the circle of

TABLE 118

REPRESENTATION OF JUST INTERVALS IN 65-NOTE EQUAL
TUNING

interval	size in cents	departure from just
perfect fifth	$\frac{38}{65}a = 701.538$	$-.417$
perfect fourth	$\frac{27}{65}a = 498.462$	$.417$
Pythagorean major third	$\frac{22}{65}a = 406.154$	-1.666
pure major third	$\frac{21}{65}a = 387.692$	1.379
schismatic major third	$\frac{21}{65}a = 387.692$	3.332
pure minor third	$\frac{17}{65}a = 313.846$	-1.795
Pythagorean minor third	$\frac{16}{65}a = 295.385$	1.250
major tone	$\frac{11}{65}a = 203.077$	$-.833$
minor tone	$\frac{10}{65}a = 184.615$	2.212
maximum semitone	$\frac{7}{65}a = 129.231$	-4.007
apotome	$\frac{6}{65}a = 110.769$	-2.916
diatonic semitone	$\frac{6}{65}a = 110.769$	$-.962$
major chroma	$\frac{5}{65}a = \ \ 92.308$	$.129$
limma	$\frac{5}{65}a = \ \ 92.308$	2.083
minor chroma	$\frac{4}{65}a = \ \ 73.846$	3.174
diesis	$\frac{2}{65}a = \ \ 36.923$	-4.136
Pythagorean comma	$\frac{1}{65}a = \ \ 18.462$	-4.998
syntonic comma	$\frac{1}{65}a = \ \ 18.642$	-3.045
diaschisma	$\frac{1}{65}a = \ \ 18.642$	-1.091
schisma	$\frac{0}{65}a = \ \ \ 0.000$	-1.954

fifths theorem (Theorem 40; Ch. XI, Sec. 5), we have $v = \frac{38}{65}a = 701.538$ cents—smaller than pure by .417 cents. A Pythagorean major third is represented by $\frac{22}{65}a = 406.154$ cents, and a pure major third by $\frac{21}{65}a = 387.692$ cents—greater than the true version by 1.379 cents. Thus a syntonic comma is represented by $\frac{1}{65}a = 18.462$ cents and the major tone, minor tone, and diatonic semitone are equal to $\frac{11}{65}a$, $\frac{10}{65}a$, and $\frac{6}{65}a$, respectively. The schisma vanishes in this tuning also, and hence the equal tunings of 65 and 53 notes exhibit practically the same behavior when construed as nearly just tunings, the principal difference being that the approximation is slightly rougher in the case of 65 notes. More comprehensive numerical data are given in Table 118.

Clearly there is a limit to the accuracy of any nearly just equal tuning in which the schisma vanishes. If a closer approximation is wanted, there must be a discrete representation of the schisma, so that the distinction between a pure major third t and a schismatic major third $t - s$ will be present. However, since a schisma contains only 1.954 cents, such a tuning would have to contain in the neighborhood of 600 notes. We may find a tuning of this nature by consideration of an unusual combination of co-incidental circumstances. It will first be observed that a syntonic comma is very nearly eleven times the size of a schisma, the actual ratio between the sizes of the two being $\dfrac{\log \frac{81}{80}}{\log \frac{32805}{32768}} = 11.007862$. Hence any equal tuning that contains a close approximation to a schisma must also contain a close approximation to a syntonic comma, by virtue of the relation $\bar{k} \cong 11\bar{s}$. The equal tuning of about 600 notes that contains the closest approximation to a schisma is the one whose number of notes is the nearest integer to $\dfrac{1200}{1.954}$, or 614 notes. What is wanted is an equal tuning of nearly 614 notes that contains a very close approximation to a pure perfect fifth. It will be recalled that the equal tuning of 306 notes contains such an interval, viz., $\frac{179}{306}a = 701.961$ cents, ratio $2 \exp \frac{179}{306} = 1.500005$ (Sec. 5 of this chapter). Since $(2)(306) = 612$—a number very close to 614—it appears that the equal tuning of 612 notes has the desired property if we take $v = \frac{179}{306}a = \frac{358}{612}a$, $s = \frac{1}{612}a = 1.961$ cents, and $k = \frac{11}{612}a = 21.569$ cents. A Pythagorean major third will be equal to $\dfrac{(4)(358) - (2)(612)}{612} a = \dfrac{1432 - 1224}{612} a = \frac{208}{612}a = 407.843$ cents, and a pure major third will be less than that by k, i.e., $\dfrac{208 - 11}{612} a = \frac{197}{612}a = 386.275$ cents, ratio $2 \exp \frac{197}{612} = 1.249972$. Further numerical data will be found in Table 119.

If the just intervals are compared with their 612-note equal tuning counterparts, it will be seen that the greatest departure occurs in the case of the diesis, which is .118 cents too large. All the other intervals depart from their true just values by less than one tenth of a cent.

The scale resulting from a particular approximation to just tuning may be described by a method much like that used to describe a particular diatonic equal tuning. To this end, let the number of adjacent intervals adding to a major tone, minor tone, and diatonic semitone be M, N, and

TABLE 119

REPRESENTATION OF JUST INTERVALS IN 612-NOTE
EQUAL TUNING

interval	size in cents	departure from just
perfect fifth	$\frac{358}{612}a = 701.961$	.006
perfect fourth	$\frac{254}{612}a = 498.039$	−.006
Pythagorean major third	$\frac{208}{612}a = 407.843$	.023
pure major third	$\frac{197}{612}a = 386.275$	−.039
schismatic major third	$\frac{196}{612}a = 384.314$	−.046
pure minor third	$\frac{161}{612}a = 315.686$	.045
Pythagorean minor third	$\frac{150}{612}a = 294.118$	−.017
major tone	$\frac{104}{612}a = 203.922$	.012
minor tone	$\frac{93}{612}a = 182.353$	−.051
maximum semitone	$\frac{68}{612}a = 133.333$	.096
apotome	$\frac{58}{612}a = 113.725$	.040
diatonic semitone	$\frac{57}{612}a = 111.765$	.033
major chroma	$\frac{47}{612}a = 92.157$	−.022
limma	$\frac{46}{612}a = 90.196$	−.029
minor chroma	$\frac{36}{612}a = 70.588$	−.084
diesis	$\frac{21}{612}a = 41.176$	.118
Pythagorean comma	$\frac{12}{612}a = 23.529$	.069
syntonic comma	$\frac{11}{612}a = 21.569$	.062
diaschisma	$\frac{10}{612}a = 19.608$	.055
schisma	$\frac{1}{612}a = 1.961$	.007

S, respectively. The notes of the nearly just scale will be separated, each
from the next, by the following number of adjacent intervals:

notes	C_0	D_0	E_{-1}	F_0	G_0	A_{-1}	B_{-1}	C_0
adjacent intervals	M	N	S	M	N	M	S	

The octave thus consists of $3M + 2N + 2S$ notes; a perfect fifth is repre-
sented by $\dfrac{2M + N + S}{3M + 2N + 2S}\, a$, and a major third by $\dfrac{M + N}{3M + 2N + 2S}\, a$.

In the case of the equal tuning of 612 notes (just analyzed), we find
that $M:N:S = 104:93:57$, and more particularly that $\frac{104}{93} = 1.118280$,

$\frac{93}{57} = 1.631579$, and $\frac{104}{57} = 1.824561$. We may get further insights into the accuracy of this nearly just equal tuning by comparing these numbers with the corresponding values for true just tuning, and we have $\dfrac{\log \frac{9}{8}}{\log \frac{10}{9}} = $ 1.117905, $\dfrac{\log \frac{10}{9}}{\log \frac{16}{15}} = 1.632521$, and $\dfrac{\log \frac{9}{8}}{\log \frac{16}{15}}$ 1.825004.

For the nearly just equal tuning of 53 notes, $M:N:S = 9:8:5$, and in the case of 65 notes, we find that $M:N:S = 11:10:6$. This suggests a means of discovering equal tunings that are rougher approximations to just tuning using fewer than 53 notes. If the relative sizes of major tones, minor tones, and diatonic semitones are to be preserved, we must have $0 < S < N < M$, and the least integers satisfying these inequalities are $S = 1$, $N = 2$, and $M = 3$. Under these conditions the number of notes is equal to $(3)(3) + (2)(2) + (2)(1) = 15$; and we have also $v = \dfrac{(2)(3) + 2 + 1}{15} a = $ $\frac{9}{15}a = 720.000$ cents—too large by 18.045 cents—and $t = \dfrac{3 + 2}{15} a = \frac{5}{15}a = $ 400.000 cents—too large by 13.686 cents. These departures from the pure versions are sufficiently great that 15-note equal tuning cannot realistically be denominated "nearly just."

If $M:N:S = 4:2:1$, then $v = \frac{11}{18}a = 733.333$ cents and $t = \frac{6}{18}a = 400.000$ cents; and if $M:N:S = 4:3:1$, then $v = \frac{12}{20}a = 720.000$ cents and $t = \frac{7}{20}a = $ 420.000 cents. Thus the equal tunings of 18 and 20 notes are even less "nearly just" than the one of 15 notes.

If $M:N:S = 4:3:2$, a much more interesting situation results. We find that $v = \frac{13}{22}a = 709.091$ cents—larger than pure by 7.136 cents—and $t = \frac{7}{22}a = 381.818$ cents—smaller than pure by 4.496 cents. If these intervals are compared with their 19-note counterparts (Ch. XI, Sec. 8), it will be noted that the perfect fifths are impure to virtually the same degree (the 19-note fifth is smaller than pure by 7.218 cents), while the 22-note major third is slightly better (the 19-note version is smaller than pure by 7.366 cents). However, the 22-note minor third of $\frac{6}{22}a = 327.273$ cents is larger than pure by 11.631 cents, whereas the 19-note version is virtually pure (the departure is only .148 cents). Subjectively, a 22-note major triad is considerably less consonant than a 19-note triad, but noticeably better than a 12-note triad. Since 22 is not an impractically large number of notes, the nearly just behavior of this tuning merits a closer scrutiny.

In order to discover the character of the major scale, we first note that the major tone, minor tone, and diatonic semitone are represented by $\frac{4}{22}a$, $\frac{3}{22}a$, and $\frac{2}{22}a$, respectively, and thus the notes of the nearly just C major scale occupy the following positions relative to C_0:

positions	0	4	7	9	13	16	20	22
notes	C_0	D_0	E_{-1}	F_0	G_0	A_{-1}	B_{-1}	C_0

FIGURE 24

Subjectively, this scale sounds badly out of tune—in particular, E_{-1}, A_{-1}, and B_{-1} seem very flat. Especially disturbing are the melodic successions C_0-D_0-E_{-1} and F_0-G_0-A_{-1}, making E_{-1} and A_{-1} seem all the more flat.

As in true just tuning, fifth D_0A_{-1} is out of tune, being equal to $\frac{12}{22}a = 654.545$ cents—smaller than pure by 47.410 cents—and greatly exaggerating an already undesirable situation. This may be rectified as before by using D_{-1} as the root of the triad on II; but in the present case, $D_{-1}D_0$ is represented by $\frac{1}{22}a = 54.545$ cents—more than twice the size of a syntonic comma in true just tuning (21.506 cents). In consequence, the distortion of the progression I-VI-II-V-I as arranged in Figure 6 (Ch. V, Sec. 3), bringing D_{-1} and D_0 side by side in the superior part, in truly grotesque and totally unacceptable—at least to the author's ears. In addition, the representations of the schismatic major third, maximum semitone, apotome, and Pythagorean comma are so inaccurate that these intervals are distorted beyond recognition. More numerical data pertaining to this tuning will be found in Table 120.

The di Lasso fragment, as notated in Chapter VII, Sec. 2, may be played in 22-note equal tuning by using the correspondences of Figure 24 and the following diagram; the correspondences are found by the method used during the discussion of 53-note equal tuning:

positions	3	8	11	12	14	17	19
notes	D_{-1}	E_0	$F\sharp_{-1}$	G_{-1}	$G\sharp_{-2}$	A_0	$B\flat_{+1}$

In the present case, F_0 is a far better representation of $F_{-\bar{z}}$ than F_{-1} (position 8), for the latter coincides with E_0.

But both the scales and triads are noticeably out of tune, especially the scales, and the modulation up by an enlarged syntonic comma at bar 8 is especially jarring. If true just tuning is unsuited to any portion of the

TABLE 120

REPRESENTATION OF JUST INTERVALS IN 22-NOTE
EQUAL TUNING

interval	size in cents	departure from just
perfect fifth	$\frac{13}{22}a = 709.091$	7.136
perfect fourth	$\frac{9}{22}a = 490.909$	-7.136
Pythagorean major third	$\frac{8}{22}a = 436.364$	28.544
pure major third	$\frac{7}{22}a = 381.818$	-4.496
schismatic major third	$\frac{6}{22}a = 327.273$	-57.087
pure minor third	$\frac{6}{22}a = 327.273$	11.631
Pythagorean minor third	$\frac{5}{22}a = 272.727$	-21.408
major tone	$\frac{4}{22}a = 218.182$	14.272
minor tone	$\frac{3}{22}a = 163.636$	-18.767
maximum semitone	$\frac{3}{22}a = 163.636$	30.399
apotome	$\frac{3}{22}a = 163.636$	49.951
diatonic semitone	$\frac{2}{22}a = 109.091$	-2.640
major chroma	$\frac{2}{22}a = 109.091$	16.912
limma	$\frac{1}{22}a = 54.545$	-35.680
minor chroma	$\frac{1}{22}a = 54.545$	-16.127
diesis	$\frac{1}{22}a = 54.545$	13.487
Pythagorean comma	$\frac{2}{22}a = 109.091$	85.631
syntonic comma	$\frac{1}{22}a = 54.545$	33.039
diaschisma	$\frac{0}{22}a = 0.000$	-19.553
schisma	$\frac{1}{22}a = 54.545$	52.592

existing polyphonic repertoire (Ch. VII, Sec 5), then so much the more is true of 22-note equal tuning, since it is disturbingly out of tune when construed as a nearly just tuning, and unacceptable when arranged as the diatonic equal tuning in which $R = 4$ (Ch. X, Sec. 4, and Ch. XI, Sec. 9).

We might also observe that the equal tuning of 34 notes contains a closer approximation to just tuning if we take $v = \frac{20}{34}a = 705.882$ cents—larger than pure by 3.927 cents—and $t = \frac{11}{34}a = 388.235$ cents—larger than pure by 1.922 cents. A major tone is equal to $2v - a = \dfrac{(2)(20) - 34}{34} a =$

$\frac{6}{34}a$, a minor tone is $a + t - 2v = \dfrac{34 + 11 - (2)(20)}{34} a = \frac{5}{34}a$, and a dia-

TABLE 121

REPRESENTATION OF JUST INTERVALS IN 34-NOTE
EQUAL TUNING

interval	size in cents	departure from just
perfect fifth	$\frac{20}{34}a = 705.882$	3.927
perfect fourth	$\frac{14}{34}a = 494.118$	−3.927
Pythagorean major third	$\frac{12}{34}a = 423.529$	15.709
pure major third	$\frac{11}{34}a = 388.235$	1.922
schismatic major third	$\frac{10}{34}a = 352.941$	−31.419
pure minor third	$\frac{9}{34}a = 317.647$	2.006
Pythagorean minor third	$\frac{8}{34}a = 282.353$	−11.782
major tone	$\frac{6}{34}a = 211.765$	7.855
minor tone	$\frac{5}{34}a = 176.471$	−5.933
maximum semitone	$\frac{4}{34}a = 141.176$	7.939
apotome	$\frac{4}{34}a = 141.176$	27.491
diatonic semitone	$\frac{3}{34}a = 105.882$	−5.849
major chroma	$\frac{3}{34}a = 105.882$	13.704
limma	$\frac{2}{34}a = 70.588$	−19.637
minor chroma	$\frac{2}{34}a = 70.588$	−.084
diesis	$\frac{1}{34}a = 35.294$	−5.765
Pythagorean comma	$\frac{2}{34}a = 70.588$	47.128
syntonic comma	$\frac{1}{34}a = 35.294$	13.788
diaschisma	$\frac{0}{34}a = 0.000$	−19.553
schisma	$\frac{1}{34}a = 35.294$	33.340

tonic semitone is $a - v - t = \dfrac{34 - 20 - 11}{34}\, a = \frac{3}{34}a$, and we thus have

$M:N:S = 6:5:3$. This tuning is an improvement over the one of 22 notes, but still quite inaccurate. A syntonic comma is represented by $\frac{1}{34}a = 35.294$ cents, too large by 13.788 cents, and once again, the schismatic major third, maximum semitone, apotome, and Pythagorean comma appear in excessively distorted versions. More comprehensive numerical data will be found in Table 121.

It should be clear that for a major scale to have the essential character of just tuning, it must make the distinction between a major tone and a

minor tone, and this is another way of stating that in all such arrangements, $k > 0$. Hence the acceptable diatonic equal tunings (Sec. 4 of this
chapter) cannot be regarded as nearly just equal tunings, since in all these
cases, $k = 0$. In view of this, it is clear that the presence of a close approximation to a major triad within a given equal tuning is not a sufficient
indicator that the tuning is applicable to the existing polyphonic repertoire. In particular, if v is slightly larger than pure, then $4v - 2a$ is larger
than Pythagorean, and hence unacceptably discordant, and if this is rectified by taking a t smaller than $4v - 2a$, then $4v - 2a - t = k > 0$, resulting in the discontinuity involving D_{-1} and D_0 in the progression II-V.
Consequently any tuning in which v is larger than pure is unsuited to the
existing repertoire, even though it may contain an acceptably consonant
triad. The equal tunings of 22 and 34 notes are illustrations of the principle.

It must be concluded that at the present time, the nearly just equal
tunings of 22, 34, 53, 65, and 612 notes are of little more than theoretical
interest, and that this will remain so until a repertoire is composed for
these tunings specifically.

7. Enharmonic modulations and modulating sequences. An *enharmonic
modulation* is one that makes use of the enharmonic equivalence of two
particular intervals, and is thus associated exclusively with equal tunings
(Ch. XI, Secs. 5, 6, and 8). As a familiar example, an augmented sixth and
a minor seventh are equivalent in 12-note equal tuning, and thus it is possible to effect a modulation by construing the same harmony as a dominant
seventh in one key and an augmented sixth chord in another, as illustrated
below:

In this modulation from C major to B major, GBDF is the dominant
seventh in the former key, and its equivalent GBDE♯ is the German sixth
in the latter.

TABLE 122

G 11	F♯ 9	F♯ 9	E♯ 7
E 6	E♭ 5	D♯ 4 ≡ 23	C𝄪 2 ≡ 21
C 0 ≡ 19	C 0 ≡ 19	B♯ 18	A♯ 15
	A♭ 13	G𝄪 13	

As we have seen (Ch. XI, Sec. 8), the different enharmonic equivalents associated with each different diatonic equal tuning can be expected to generate a unique set of chromatic relations, although the diatonic behavior remains the same in every case (Theorems 25 and 26; Ch. X, Sec. 2). In order to explore briefly the special chromatic relations associated with a different diatonic equal tuning, we first recall that in the acceptable tuning where $R = \frac{3}{2}$ (giving a closed circle of nineteen fifths), an augmented sixth and a diminished seventh are enharmonic equivalents, as are their inversions, viz., a diminished third and an augmented second (Table 86; Ch. XI, Sec. 8). The former are equal to $\frac{15}{19}a = 947.368$ cents, and the latter are equal to $\frac{4}{19}a = 252.632$ cents. Now imagine starting with a C major triad and moving directly to German sixth chord A♭CE♭F♯. Next, making use of the enharmonic equivalence A♭ ≡ G𝄪 (mod 19), we may construe the two outer notes as diminished seventh G𝄪F♯. If this interval is now treated as the major third and minor ninth of a dominant whose root is E♯, its normal resolution is to an A♯ triad, and this provides a unique means of modulating downward by a diminished third, or $\frac{4}{19}a$. The notes needed are shown in Table 122, along with their respective positions in 19-note equal tuning. It is interesting to note that two of the parts each descend a diminished second of $\frac{1}{19}a = 63.158$ cents—E♭ to D♯, and C to B♯, respectively.

When we recall that a perfect fourth is equal to $\frac{8}{19}a$, it is apparent that if this modulation is repeated starting at A♯ major, the next triad will be lower than the initial C major triad by $\frac{8}{19}a$, and consequently will be enharmonically equivalent to G major. Since A♯ ≡ B♭♭ (mod 19), the most convenient way to notate the continuation is to write the roots of the three triads as C, A♯ ≡ B♭♭, G, in positions 0 ≡ 19, 15, and 11, respectively, illustrating the equivalence of diminished third A♯C and augmented second GA♯. The second modulation (from B♭♭ to G) is an exact transposition of the first down by an augmented second of $\frac{4}{19}a$. This establishes a unique chromatic connection between a triad and its dominant, as illustrated below:

Subjectively, the arrival of the first G major triad is an agreeable surprise that is quite striking, but very strange indeed—at least to a conventionally trained musician. The progression cannot be realistically approximated in 12-note equal tuning—or in any other different diatonic equal tuning for that matter, for the equation int $(19) = 0$ holds only if $R = \frac{3}{2}$.

We may discover another intriguing progression in 19-note equal tuning that provides a unique chromatic link between a tonic and its subdominant. We found earlier (Sec. 2 of this chapter) that the comma $a - 5v + 6t$ vanishes when $R = \frac{3}{2}$, and hence in 19-note equal tuning we have $a + v = 6(v - t)$; i.e., the sum of six minor thirds equals an octave plus a perfect fifth. Thus if we start with a C major triad, then move to an A major triad and next to F♯ major, then continue similarly, always making the roots descend a minor third, the root of the seventh triad will be F. The successive roots are C, A, F♯, D♯ ≡ E♭♭, C♭, A♭, and F, as illustrated below:

This progression differs from the preceding in that it is not confined to one particular diatonic tuning; however, for every different value of R, it will be found that the progression ends in a different key. For example, let $R = 2$; then $a - 5v + 6t = \frac{1}{12}a = 100$ cents (Sec. 2 of this chapter), and thus the final triad will be higher than the initial triad by 100 cents, making the progression end in C♯:

As another example, let $R = 3$ so that $v = \frac{10}{17}a$ and $t = \frac{6}{17}a$ (Ch. XI, Sec. 8); now $a - 5v + 6t = \dfrac{17 - (5)(10) + (6)(6)}{17}\, a = \dfrac{17 - 50 + 36}{17}\, a = \frac{3}{17}a = 211.765$ cents, and now the progression will end in D. Recalling that when $R = 3$, we have D♯ ≡ F♭, F𝄪 ≡ A♭, and A♯ ≡ C♭, all (mod 17), and thus the notation is as follows:

The reader should make a careful study of the last three examples, even though a true musical comprehension of what happens when $R = \frac{3}{2}$, or $R = 3$, probably goes beyond the capability of human imagination without some means of actually hearing the progressions.

We now return to the concept of a passage that modulates from one key to another and is then played again, but beginning in the new key and modulating by the same means to yet another key. We call such a re-peating pattern a *modulating sequence*, and it is clear that each repetition is an exact transposition of any other. More particularly, the initial tonics in any two successive repetitions are distant by the same interval, and this interval is called the *interval of transposition*.

We may now show that under certain familiar conditions, a modulating sequence will eventually return to its initial key. Let the interval of trans-position be int (i); if the modulating sequence returns to its initial key after x repetitions, we must have x int $(i) = $ int (0). This equation depicts a closed circle of intervals, which in turn generates an equal tuning

(Theorem 37; Ch. XI, Sec. 3). Now applying Theorem 32 (Ch. XI, Sec. 1), we see that a necessary and sufficient condition for a given modulating sequence eventually to return to its initial key is that R should be a rational number. Since R is irrational in Pythagorean tuning, meantone tuning, and Silbermann's tuning (Ch. XI, Secs. 1 and 2), no modulating sequence in these tunings, whatever its nature, can ever return to its initial key after any number of transposed repetitions.

In the case of a diatonic equal tuning, it is interesting to determine the number of keys traversed by a given modulating sequence before the sequence returns to its initial key. The behavior of modulating sequences within the familiar 12-note equal tuning indicates that there are several possibilities.

Example: Consider the sequence where the tonic in the old key is construed as the Neapolitan in the new key, viz.,

FIGURE 25

In 12-note equal tuning, each tonic is lower than the preceding by $\frac{1}{12}a$, and hence the sequence will eventually traverse all twelve keys.

Example: Consider the sequence in which the sixth degree in the old key becomes the minor subdominant in the new key:

FIGURE 26

In this case, the sequence traverses only the three keys of C, E, and G♯ ≡ A♭ (mod 12).

The general question may be answered by making use of the known properties of elementary congruences. The following discussion closely parallels the method used to prove the equal tuning theorem (Theorem 37; Ch. XI, Sec. 3).

Recalling that every interval within any equal tuning may be expressed as a fractional part of an octave, we next assume that the interval of transposition is $\frac{j}{m}a$, where j and m are integers, and m is the total number of notes. If we choose any note of the m-note equal tuning as a fixed reference point, making this the tonic of the initial pattern, the tonics of each successive repetition are higher than the initial tonic by $\frac{j}{m}a, \frac{2j}{m}a, \frac{3j}{m}a \ldots$ or more generally by $\frac{xj}{m}a$, where $x = 1, 2, 3. \ldots$ In order to determine the number of tonics, and thereby the number of keys traversed by the modulating sequence, we make octave transpositions in such a manner that all the tonic notes lie within one octave, then determine the position within the equal tuning occupied by each tonic note. Hence if $\frac{xj}{m}a > a$, we write $\frac{xj}{m}a = \frac{y}{m}a + ka$, where k is chosen so that $0 \leqslant y \leqslant m - 1$. Then $\frac{xj - y}{m} = k$, or $xj \equiv y \pmod{m}$. Thus the xth tonic is in position y of the m-note equal tuning where $xj \equiv y \pmod{m}$, and $0 \leqslant y \leqslant m - 1$. Now applying Theorem 11 (Ch. III, Sec. 1), we see that the condition that y should take all integral values from zero through $m - 1$ is that $(j, m) = 1$, or that $\frac{j}{m}$ should be in its lowest terms.[17] Thus if the interval of transposition is $\frac{j}{m}a$ and $(j, m) = 1$, the modulating sequence will traverse all keys within the tuning before returning to the initial tonic. From this, it follows directly that if the number of notes in a diatonic equal tuning is prime, then every modulating sequence, whatever its nature, will exhibit this property. The acceptable diatonic equal tunings of 19, 31, and 43 notes are illustrations.

Example: In 19-note equal tuning where $R = \frac{3}{2}$, the sequence of Figure 26 will traverse all nineteen keys before returning to the initial tonic. In this case, the interval of transposition is up a major third, or $\frac{6}{19}a$.

---

[17] See Ch. I, note 6.

Since B♯ ≡ C♭, F✗ ≡ G♭, C✗ ≡ D♭, and E♯ ≡ F♭ all (mod 19), the succession of nineteen tonics, along with their positions within the equal tuning, is shown below. The positions are the least residues y in the congruence $6x \equiv y \pmod{19}$ as x takes all integral values from zero through 19.

positions	0	6	12	18	5	11	17	4	10	16
tonic	C	E	G♯	B♯ ≡ C♭	E♭	G	B	D♯	F✗ ≡ G♭	B♭

positions	3	9	15	2	8	14	1	7	13	0
tonics	D	F♯	A♯	C✗ ≡ D♭	F	A	C♯	E♯ ≡ F♭	A♭	C

Example: In 19-note equal tuning, the sequence of Figure 25 must also traverse all nineteen keys. The interval of transposition is down a minor second, or $-\frac{2}{19}a$, and positions occupied by the tonics are thus y in the congruence $-2x \equiv y \pmod{19}$ as x goes from zero through 19. The residues may be more conveniently calculated if we add $19x$ to the left-hand side (Theorem 10; Ch. III, Sec. 1), so the congruence becomes $17x \equiv y \pmod{19}$. Thus the succession of nineteen tonics and positions relative to C within 19-note equal tuning are as follows:

positions	0	17	15	13	11	9	7	5	3	1
tonics	C	B	A♯ ≡ B♭♭	A♭	G	F♯	E♯ ≡ F♭	E♭	D	C♯

positions	18	16	14	12	10	8	6	4	2	0
tonics	B♯ ≡ C♭	B♭	A	G♯	F✗ ≡ G♭	F	E	D♯	C✗ ≡ D♭	C

The reader will find it helpful to study the two preceding diagrams while referring to Figure 23 (Ch. XI, Sec. 8).

If $\dfrac{j}{m}$ is not in its lowest terms, the situation is clarified by Theorem 43 (Ch. XI, Sec. 10). In musical terms, this means that if $(j, m) = d$ where $d > 1$, then the sequence will traverse only $\dfrac{m}{d}$ keys; and if one of the tonics is C (position 0), then all the others are in positions that are multiples of d. More generally, if the sequence does not traverse the key of C, then any two of the tonics are in positions that are congruent (mod d).

Example: In the sequence of Figure 26, the interval of transposition is up a major third, which in 12-note equal tuning is equal to $\frac{4}{12}a$. But $(4, 12) = 4$, and hence the sequence traverses only $\frac{12}{4} = 3$ keys. If C is one of the tonics, the others are in positions 4 (E) and 8 (G♯ ≡ A♭). If one of the tonics is in position 1 (C♯ ≡ D♭), the others are in positions 5 (F) and 9 (A). The other two possibilities place the tonics in positions 2, 6, and 10

$(D, F\sharp \equiv G\flat, B\flat)$, and 3, 7, 11 $(E\flat, G, B \equiv C\flat)$. In each case, any two of the tonics are in positions that are congruent (mod 4).

An important musical consequence of Theorem 43 is that if a modulating sequence within a diatonic equal tuning of m notes traverses fewer than m keys, then the number of keys traversed must be a factor of m. Thus in 12-note equal tuning, we may construct modulating sequences that traverse two, three, four, or six keys, but not five keys.[18] On the other hand, if $R = \frac{8}{5}$, resulting in an equal tuning of 50 notes (Sec. 4 of this chapter), we may find modulating sequences that traverse 2, 5, 10, 25, or all 50 keys.

Example: Consider once again the sequence of Figure 25 in which the interval of trasposition is down a minor second; if $R = \frac{8}{5}$, this amounts to $-\frac{5}{50}a$. But $(5, 50) = 5$, and hence the sequence will traverse $\frac{50}{5} = 10$ keys. If the initial key is C, the others are as follows:

positions	0	45	40	35	30	25
tonics	C	B	A$\sharp$	G$\boldsymbol{\times}$	F$\sharp\sharp\sharp$	E$\sharp\sharp\sharp$ $\equiv$ A$\flat\flat\flat\flat$

positions	20	15	10	5	0
tonics	G$\flat\flat\flat$	F$\flat\flat$	E$\flat\flat$	D$\flat$	C

The reader should verify that E$\sharp\sharp\sharp$ $\equiv$ A$\flat\flat\flat\flat$ (mod 50), using the method employed in Chapter XI, Secs. 4 and 8.

Example: Let the sequence of Figure 26 be played in the tuning where $R = \frac{4}{3}$, i.e., in the diatonic equal tuning of 26 notes (Ch. XI, Sec. 9, and Sec. 1 of this chapter). In this tuning, a major third is equal to $\frac{8}{26}a$; but $(8, 26) = 2$, and so the sequence will traverse $\frac{26}{2} = 13$ keys. Since we have D$\boldsymbol{\times}$ $\equiv$ E$\flat\flat$ and C$\boldsymbol{\times}$ $\equiv$ D$\flat\flat$ (mod 26), the tonics and their positions are as follows:

positions	0	8	16	24	6	14	22
tonics	C	E	G$\sharp$	B$\sharp$	D$\boldsymbol{\times}$ $\equiv$ E$\flat\flat$	G$\flat$	B$\flat$

positions	4	12	20	2	10	18	0
tonics	D	F$\sharp$	A$\sharp$	C$\boldsymbol{\times}$ $\equiv$ D$\flat\flat$	F$\flat$	A$\flat$	C

---

[18] Examples of such sequences may be found in the standard repertoire. For a sequence traversing two keys, see A. Scriabin, Piano Sonata No. 3 in F$\sharp$ minor, Op. 23 (1898), fourth movement, bars 95–99 (B$\flat$ minor, E minor, B$\flat$ minor). For a sequence traversing three keys, see F. Schubert, Piano Sonata No. 10 in A major, D. 959 (1828), first movement, bars 82–91 (E major, C major, A$\flat$ major, E major). For a sequence traversing four keys, see P. I. Tchaikovsky, Symphony No. 6 in B minor, Op. 74 (1893), first movement, bars 30–37 (B minor, D minor, F minor, G$\sharp$ minor, B minor).

The positions are the least residues y in the congruence $8x \equiv y \pmod{26}$ as x takes successive integral values starting with zero. The reader will find it helpful at this point to refer to Table 91 (Sec. 3 of this chapter).

The examples of this section show how each diatonic equal tuning generates its own particular set of chromatic relations, while at the same time maintaining the structural patterns and interconnections associated with all recognizable diatonic scales (Theorems 25, 26 and 27; Ch. X, Sec. 2). At present, there is no generally known repertoire that makes use of any of the special chromatic relations found in the diatonic equal tunings except those associated with the standard one of 12 notes. The musical use to which the other diatonic equal tunings might be put thus remains a matter of speculation.

At this point, our discussion, which up to now has been a description of how things are, must close; speculations about how things might be are better the subject of another book. The recent development of electronic musical devices that can be accurately put in a variety of tunings will surely invite theorists and composers to explore and use this expanded resource; but at this juncture, one can only guess what styles might emerge. For example, what musical use might be made of the special chromatic relations found only in 19-note equal tuning or in 31-note equal tuning? What tonal idiom might be associated with the nearly just configuration of 22-note equal tuning, given the special restriction associated with the progression II-V? What unfamiliar but categorically recognizable modal configurations might be discovered in the non-diatonic equal tunings? The contributions of several new generations to music history will be needed before these questions can be satisfactorily answered.

Index

LIBRARY OF CONGRESS CATALOGING IN PUBLICATION DATA

Blackwood, Easley.
    The structure of recognizable diatonic tunings.

    Includes index.
    1. Musical temperament.   2. Tuning.   3. Musical intervals and scales.
    4. Music—Acoustics and physics.   I. Title.
ML3809.B49   1985   781'.22   85-42972
ISBN 0-691-09129-3